Guns, Grenades, and Grunts

APPROACHES TO DIGITAL GAME STUDIES

Volume 2

Guns, Grenades, and Grunts

First-Person Shooter Games

**EDITED BY
GERALD A. VOORHEES,
JOSH CALL, AND KATIE
WHITLOCK**

continuum

Continuum International Publishing Group

A Bloomsbury Company

80 Maiden Lane, New York, NY 10038

The Tower Building, 11 York Road, London SE1 7NX

www.continuumbooks.com

Library of Congress Cataloging-in-Publication Data

A catalog record for this book is available from the Library of Congress

ISBN: HB: 978-1-4411-4224-5
PB: 978-1-4411-9353-7

Typeset by Fakenham Prepress Solutions, Fakenham, Norfolk NR21 8NN
Printed and bound in the United States of America

Contents

PART TWO Campaign 131

PART THREE Multiplayer 249

Introduction— Things That Go Boom: From Guns to Griefing

Gerald Voorhees, Josh Call, and Katie Whitlock

Shotgun? Check. Armor? Check. Plenty of rounds? Check. Blue key? No? Well, you'll have to wander around until you find it then. We know this scenario well. We're armed to the teeth, carrying seven different guns (one of which is always a shotgun). We have a metric ton of ammunition, and for once we're not riddled with bullet holes, bite marks, plasma burns, and a veritable cornucopia of other unpleasant injuries (no tele-fragging just yet!). We have slowly, painstakingly, obliterated every single armed menace possessed of the grave misfortune to cross our path. We have thoroughly redefined the idea of collateral damage, and completely disregarded all rhetoric of proportional response. And now we are at the end of it all, staring down the gun-sights of success, fame, glory, and an epic stomping of whatever monstrosity orchestrated all this madness to begin with (because we certainly didn't start things). But here we are… held up because we can't unlock the door. Thus goes a day in the life of the FPS player.

If the above description seems a bit extreme, almost silly, then it's well placed. As a game genre the history of the FPS is written in an excess that has gradually tempered over time. In each of the examples above we could imagine a multitude of titles that employ those conventions and experiences as a function of the gameplay. Readers will, we hope, forgive us the "Blue key" reference to *DOOM* (id Software 1993), which seemed to particularly delight in forcing players to continuously re-navigate level maps hunting the one key that stands between the player and progress. The early FPS genre of the late 1980s and early 1990s was built on a formula, both ludic and mechanistic. It was a recipe for success invented largely on the back of id Software's now legendary *DOOM*. From those formulaic and humble beginnings, the contemporary FPS game has evolved.

And it has evolved in numerous, divergent directions, some of which have converged in interesting configurations. Now, you are just as likely to find yourself running and gunning your way across a historical battlefield or a contemporary Middle-Eastern city as you are a space station or Martian research facility. You are almost as likely to find yourself tactically considering how to move without breaking cover, with the aid of a helper's suppressive fire, to assault a fortified position. Perhaps one of those weapons you're carrying is a crossbow or a M1 Garand or a plasma rifle. Or, maybe, in a small nod to realism, you're limited to two weapons. Don't worry, you'll still have access to a shotgun. Are you wearing a uniform? Are you cybernetically augmented? Can you conjure supernatural powers? How you answer these questions speaks to what path you've followed in the evolution of the FPS.

Delimiting the FPS

No doubt due in part to its thematic and ludic diversity, the genre is arguably the most popular at the moment. And given the centrality of guns and combat, it is one of the most frequently discussed genres. Policy advocates and social crusaders discourse endlessly about the FPS. And academics have given FPS games more attention than any other single game genre.

Despite all of the scholarship concerning FPS games, as yet no one has endeavored to do more than crudely sketch the contours of the genre. As if it were a commonplace, the FPS is typically described in a sentence or two. Even Aki Järvinen's (2002) short essay/game review of *Halo: Combat Evolved* (Bungie 2001), "Anatomy of the FPS," does little to help familiarize readers with the morphology of the genre. After a brief discussion of the status of genre in game studies, Järvinen claims that *Halo* "does everything a little bit better than its predecessors … hitting the FPS genre with a 'new high'." Järvinen goes on to discuss *Halo*'s cutscenes, movement, sound, destructible environments and control scheme, but neither claims that this set of elements sufficiently defines the genre nor attempts to explain in what configurations sound or controller layouts are representative of the FPS as a genre. And while one might assume Galloway's (2006) "Origins of the First-Person Shooter" would have something to say about the essential qualities characteristic of the genre, that assumption is incorrect; Galloway is concerned almost entirely with the visual spectacle of the FPS. The same might be said of Morris's (2002) "First-Person Shooters – A Game Apparatus." However, borrowing the construct of the apparatus from film theory, Morris is less concerned with the FPS as a game genre constituted by specific formal structures as she is with describing the "intersecting processes involved in audience interaction with a media form" (81). This flippant treatment of the genre is not uncommon, however, of scholarly treatments of the FPS.

The few detailed considerations of the FPS we have tend to focus on one or another quality of the genre at the expense of the composite image. In order to further theorize immersion, for instance, Grimshaw, Charlton, and Jagger (2011) consider narrative, spatial, visual, and auditory elements of the FPS, but only insofar as they organize the player's attention and contribute to immersion. Grimshaw and Schott (2008) examine the "acoustic ecology" of FPS games in an effort to map how sound is imbricated in the play experience. More attention has been paid, however, to the visual and aesthetic character of the FPS. While Lahati (2003) and Morris (2002) attend to the importance of the FPS's representation of three-dimensional space, Slocombe (2005) and Jones (2008) theorize the relationship between the first-person perspective and player immersion in the gameworld, and Morris (2002) and Rehak (2003) consider how the first-person perspective impacts player identification with player-characters. Of course, while this research does enable interested scholars to reflect on the properties characteristic of the FPS and will, in the pages that follow, be put to this very use, it does not identify the constitutive elements of the genre.

What, then, are the essential components of an FPS? In what follows, we identify the distinctive features constitutive of the FPS, the elements that players, developers, designers, critics, and scholars expect in an FPS. We arrive at this conclusion aided by the foresight of others who have ventured to define the FPS, but in so doing note the same problem mentioned above: the FPS is a taken-for-granted form. Game reviews praise or blame one title or another for giving or failing to give fans of the genre everything they have come to expect of an FPS without enumerating what those expectations are; interviews in gaming magazines and on *Gamastura* speculate about the future of the FPS without pausing to consider its present; and players make lists of the top ten FPS games to debate the merits of different titles without any criteria for comparison. Given these circumstances, we turn to the few definitions that can be found in contemporary games scholarship, terse or topical as they are.

In an essay on the enactment of war in digital games, Nieborg (2006) offers the following definition to frame a discussion of *America's Army* (US Army 2002) and *Counter-Strike* (Valve 2000): "In FPS games the player navigates through a virtual world from a first person perspective and interacts in single- or multiplayer combat sequences with multiple enemies by using a range of weaponry in order to complete an objective" (108). Nieborg's definition lays a number of characteristics on the table, particularly: navigation through a virtual world, indicating that the FPS involves the player controlling movement within a digital space; first-person perspective, which speaks to the player's view of the gameworld from the point of view of the player character; single- or multiplayer game modes enabling the player to compete against the machine or other players, alone or with the cooperation of other players; and a range of weaponry, identifying the crucial resources of an FPS and affirming the centrality of conflict to gameplay. Indeed, the rough taxonomy here outlines what might arguably be the cornerstone assumptions of what, according to player expectation, is required of an FPS game. Often described as a "run and gun" experience, the FPS has a history rooted in a kind of "one-person army."

This rhetoric of survival and resource management is echoed in other scholarship. Focusing on the mechanics of FPS gameplay, King and Krzywinska (2006) write:

> … key hooks found across the genre include action hooks such as navigation of the player-character through space, shooting at enemies and taking cover. These are combined with resource hooks, principally monitoring of ammunition, health and the supply of weapons and other necessary equipment, and with tactical and strategic hooks – how to combine shooting with taking cover or which weapon to use to maximum effect in certain circumstances. (23–4)

The central focus here is on the player as active agent, and between the navigation, shooting, and dodging bullets, there is a great deal of action to keep players in a twitchy state of excitement. But King and Krzywinska also point to the contemplative side of the FPS; managing resources and thinking through strategies for minimizing risk, maximizing cover and, in short, out-maneuvering enemies highlights the often-overlooked cerebral side of the genre.

While this particular combination of conventions is germane to the genre, it is important to consider that these elements, as such, are not unique to FPS games. The FPS shares several core ludic and mechanistic features of other games: resource management, pattern recognition, directional awareness, perceptual and narrative hooks—the list goes on. Mäyrä notes that FPS games share many similarities with maze games like *Pac Man* (Namco 1980) in which the player must traverse labyrinths filled with obstacles, platform games that require players to climb or teleport from one floor to another to collect items and power-ups, and adventure games in which items must be discovered and collected to open doors and solve puzzles (104–5). We could just as readily add real-time strategy games, given the frequent need to manage time and limited resources to overcome an enemy. Attending to other elements of the FPS, Morris (2002) identifies the typical narrative structure: "… you find yourself, usually unintentionally, in a strange, hostile place, unarmed and vulnerable … You must explore the place to find weapons and other useful items, moving through the many game arenas or levels on some form of quest. In the process you must fight and/or avoid many enemies and monsters" (82–3). While each of these conventions is arguably a function of nearly every imaginable FPS title, we might also see them as narrative conventions of, say, *The Legend of Zelda* (Nintendo 1986) or *Super Mario Bros.* (Nintendo 1985). If, indeed, its narrative conventions and mechanics are not unique to the genre, how do we define the FPS?

We maintain that the FPS, as a genre, is defined by its combination of ludic structures rather than its thematic milieu or intended purpose (Voorhees, Call, and Whitlock 2011). FPSs can be further distinguished by theme, e.g. historical, science-fiction, military, and survival-horror, and even purpose, considering the entertainment orientation of *Quake* (id Software 1996) in comparison to the propaganda function of *America's Army* or *Under Ash* (Dar al-Fikr 2001). Still, the FPS is not defined by the necessity of any particular milieu or message. The player's navigation of space, the primacy of obstacles overcome by the act of shooting, and the first-person perspective are the essential components constitutive of the FPS.

However, an important question both frames and gives significance to the discussion that follows. A question that needs to be taken up when considering the FPS as a genre is whether it deserves the moniker or is, in fact, a subgenre or specific type of *shooter* game. A ludic genre is defined by the rules that structure play, but what rules can be considered to substantively structure play?

If the ludic constitution of a core mechanic, "the essential play activity that players perform again and again in a game" (Salen and Zimmerman 2004, 316), is *the* means of distinguishing genres, then there is some cause to prioritizing shooting over movement and think of the FPS as a type of shooter rather than as a genre in its own right. After all, movement is a near-ubiquitous element of a broad swath of games. But, considered in this general light, it is ill-defined; movement in *Counter-Strike* is quite different from movement in *Tomb Raider* (Core Designs 1996), *Super Mario Bros.*, or *Command & Conquer* (Westwood 1995). Indeed, *Duck Hunt* (Nintendo 1984) is rarely described as an FPS though the only action the player takes is shooting at ducks (or the laughing dog, for the more malicious) from the point of view of the hypothetical hunter.

In fact, it would be difficult to attain unanimous consent for the idea that shooting is *the* core mechanic of an FPS. After all, Mäyrä (2008), Fullerton (2004), and King and Krzywinska (2006) list movement, and more specifically player-guided navigation through a three-dimensional space, before shooting in their discussion of FPS mechanics. Contrasting the FPS with third-person shooting games such as *Tomb Raider* and first-person puzzle games such as *Myst* (Cyan 1993), Morris (2002) emphasizes navigation. She writes, "FPS games create a 3D-rendered environment on the computer [sic] screen that is seen by players from a first-person point of view as they 'move around' the 3D world …" (85). Perhaps, then, the FPS is defined by both shooting and moving in that the "first-person" label implies a relationship to a represented three-dimensional space.

This provisional answer, however, only begs a more difficult question: do the formal, aesthetic properties governing the player's visual perception of the gamespace structure play? But, in the spirit of inquiry we are compelled to ask. So, is the first-person perspective constitutive of the play that emerges from those games we tend to, as yet uncritically, call first-person shooters? Does this way of looking impact the core mechanic, the essential play activity, and thus constitute a ludic structure? Or, is it at most a way of distinguishing a subgenre of shooter?

Having already staked a claim to the navigation of space as a key component of the FPS, we affirm that the shooter genre is an inadequate container for the FPS. Following Salen and Zimmerman's (2004) continued discussion of core mechanics, we argue that the first-person perspective is more than a point of view on play, it is an act. Furthermore, it is an act integral to FPS gameplay. Salen and Zimmerman write:

> Designing the activity of play means creating the system that includes the game's sensory output to the player and the player's ability to make input, as well as guiding the internal cognitive and psychological processes by which a player makes decisions. The core mechanic is not limited to just one component of this experiential process, but exists as an activity that permeates all three. (317)

To wit, if we understand a core mechanic as the fundamental activity of gameplay encompassing both the player's perception of the game and his or her psychic and physical response, then the first-person perspective is fundamental. The first-person form of vision is an inseparable element of the player's ability to navigate the gamespace and shoot at enemies. It functions so in at least two ways, by facilitating the mutually reinforcing processes of immersion and identification.

If we imagine the idea of identification as an appropriation of an object outside of the "self," an "other" that re-invests the object with subjective value and meaning (a kind of narcissistic/emotional connection), then we have a beginning point for understanding how this process intervenes in play. The game's player-character, or avatar, serves as the portal through which players are allowed access to the game and the means by which the player's presence in the game is represented. Thus the avatar becomes, by extension, the active agent of the player by proxy. The very etymology of the word "avatar" from its Sanskrit origin means "to cross over," and is suggestive of the transubstantial movement of deities. Read in this light, the player is imagined as "crossing over" and sharing substance with the avatar through the interface of the games controls. Indeed, channeling Ted Friedman's early theorizations of cyborg subjectivity, Slocombe (2006) understands the identification that takes place in an FPS as a symbiotic relationship in which the line between the player's consciousness and that of the machine is difficult to distinguish. However Slocombe does hone in one moment where this line is brought into relief: when the first-person perspective shifts to third-person at the moment of avatar death. It is in this moment that the interrelationship between player and PC is driven home; the human *spirit* that once animated the avatar's *sprite* is torn from the digital realm and cast back out into real life.

The avatar's function as a kind of "shared self" is not only part of the aesthetic logic that drives FPS design regarding how little of the avatar we see, but its ludic logic as well. There are rarely identifying features in FPS avatars that distinguish race (or, in some cases, gender). Master Chief is always masked and fully armored, so we have no clues to identify him beyond our own assumptions. While other characters are identified through the game's narrative context, the lack of reinforcement of those markers allows for a kind of re-identification through gameplay. Players may know that Gordon Freeman is a Caucasian man with glasses and a beard, but that is rarely (if ever) revealed in the gameplay itself. Players of the *Metroid* series are often surprised as the ex-army bounty hunter Samus Aran breaks gender stereotypes and is revealed as a female only in the end of the first game of the series. Indeed, many FPS games afford little view of the avatar beyond the perceptual appearance of the hands and whatever weapon they hold. As Galloway (2006) and McMahan (2002) have noted, the gun is an integral element of the FPS display. These visual and ludic conventions lead players to assume a certain kind of experience with the FPS genre.

We might better grasp that experience through one set of concept-metaphors used to explain how identification occurs. Informed by Lacanian psychoanalysis, Rehak (2003) argues that the tension between player and PC is the most crucial conflict in an FPS. Rehak's analysis could be generalized across any number of games in which the player interacts with the gameworld by means of an avatar if not for the special relationship enabled by the first-person perspective. According to a Lacanian approach, looking is vital to the imbrication of player and player-character because it mediates the mirror stage, the process in which the subject misapprehends his or herself and dons the misrecognized identity. In the case of the FPS, the player's will is enacted by the avatar and through the conflation of *mimesis* for consubstantiality the avatar, like a suit of armor, is donned by the player. In this manner, the game is experienced both as the player and the avatar. The boundaries between the "I" of the player and the "I" of the player-character lose definition, such that the gameworld and the real world interface at the location of the avatar.

Imagined as a counterpart to identification, immersion suggests the degree to which players see their avatar self as inseparable from the game's environment and context. Jones (2008) discusses the HUD (heads-up display), which provides a continuous feed of data to the player, in comparison to helper NPCs commonly found in digital role-playing games. He argues that as a device that facilitates story-telling and gameplay, the HUD facilitates the player's immersion in the gameworld, especially in contrast to "traditional displays" that interfere with the "suspension of disbelief" (75). While a common feature of digital role-playing games, the HUD was a prominent extension of the early FPS genre. Early examples of the genre like *DOOM, Wolfenstein 3D* (id Software 1989) and *Blake Stone: Aliens of Gold* (JAM Productions 1993) emphasized the necessity of the HUD as a means to track engagement with specific data or game hooks. Ammunition, health, keys, and armor levels tended to be common features of the HUD. They manifested in easily visible ways the mechanistic information players needed for successful navigation of the game.

More recent examples in the genre have focused on a scaling-back of the HUD, removing all but the most necessary of features in order to reflect a more seamless continuity between player and game. McMahan (2003) musters VR literature to make the case for FPS games as immersive experiences *par excellence*. She argues that, with the first-person perspective, they provide a "transparent" game interface that allows the player to feel a heightened sense of presence (71). Coming games look to take advantage of the growing interest in motion control to tighten the connection between the body of the player to the actions of the avatar, further altering the HUD to a level of seamless integration. The reduction in presence of the HUD serves to facilitate this sense of presence by reducing the visibility of the mechanistic data and increasing the visibility of the gameworld. Not unlike the tensions associated with *cinéma vérité*, the presence of the camera, or viewing portal (in this case made consubstantial with the avatar) should be as grounded in the "real" as much as possible. Galloway (2006) places the origins of the FPS in the cinematic "subjective shot." Read this way, the "real" represents as little mediation as possible between the player and the avatar, and the avatar and the world.

This level of representational work is not uncomplicated. Lahati (2003) discusses the pioneering use of 3D in FPS games as integral to fostering a high degree of immersion. He describes their import in terms of creating an "... impression of a limitless game space with choice of direction in movement ..." and also giving life to the objects populating that space by allowing them to emerge from off-screen, acting and reacting before they are even seen (160–1). This has become an expectation of the genre that necessarily links game design with hardware evolution. By now, players, fans, and scholars are likely familiar with the rhetoric of "Crysis benchmarking," a process by which games are compared based on their ability to push high polygon counts and render complex graphical data with ease (most recently relying on the game *Crysis* [Crytek Frankfurt 2007] as a point of comparison). This has been a part of the genre since *DOOM* and *Wolfenstein 3D*. Similarly, the FPS genre has relied on gameplay that is seamless, as opposed to the more traditional forms of turn-based role-playing games or strategy games. After all, if you're being shot at, the appropriate idea is to move and find cover, rather than politely waiting for your turn. As a result, FPS games require hardware capable of handling faster play, intuitive player reactions, and a control interface that makes such play possible. More recent examples of these spatial and temporal imperatives can be seen in games like Gearbox Studios' blockbuster *Borderlands* (2009), which invests considerable system and graphical resources in providing the illusion of limitless scope for movement, shooting, and player direction. The resulting product here is often described as a "sandbox game," allowing players a broader range of direction, engagement, and choice in controlling the pace of the game's narrative and interaction. This reliance on real-time play as opposed to turn-based mechanics generates a frenetic level of identification that moves beyond the simple sharing of visual perspective. After all, to play *Mirror's Edge* (DICE 2008) is in no way the same thing as to play *Eye of the Beholder* (Westwood Associates 1990) despite the shared viewpoint. The former moves at an increasingly frantic pace, imagining the body as malleable in the parkour-style gameplay, while the latter affords a level of complex meta-game management as players keep an internal checklist of resources, management, and outcomes. Extending this, we might recall Morris's (2002) work through Lacanian-inspired screen theory and link the first-person perspective to a greater sense of embodiment in the gameworld, heightening the player's sense of agency and "contributing to a more visceral game experience because of the sense of immersion created" (89). It is precisely this level of viscera and immersion that results from the real-time experience of first-person play.

In this regard, by facilitating heightened identification and immersion, the first-person perspective is certainly a ludic structure that governs the player's engagement with the game. The player's ability to navigate three-dimensional space and shoot enemies is enabled by the sense of presence players experience as their avatars.

Still, despite its importance to the genre, the first-person visual perspective is by no means universal, even within FPS games. Many rely on shifting perspectives as dictated by gameplay. The *Halo* franchise is a clear example of this. While the bulk of the gameplay operates from the protagonist's perspective, the numerous iterations of vehicle combat shift the player's view to a third-person perspective. This is a common enough practice in the genre such that *Far Cry* (Crytek 2004) and *Half-Life 2* (Valve 2004) are notable as exceptions. This is not to suggest that the first-person shooter is a misleading rhetorical classification. More to the point, the FPS is fluid; as a genre it contains contradictions and represents divergent paths designed to evoke distinct play experiences.

It is easy to find examples of games which push strict definitions. Take, for example, Bethesda's *Elder Scrolls* franchise. While clearly definable as a role-playing game for its ludic and mechanistic components (complex character generation, more involved narrative architecture, leveling mechanics, and skill systems), it nevertheless meets the existing criteria for an FPS game as well—unless, of course, one claims that the "shooting" mechanic is largely absent, having been replaced by melee combat and spell-casting. Still, this would lead a savvy player to ask what the functional difference might be between a sword in an *Elder Scrolls* game and the chainsaw from *DOOM* (or the energy sword from a *Halo* game).

Elder Scrolls, like the *Mass Effect* series, is also a good touchstone for another limit case of the FPS. In these games, the player configures the interface by choosing to either utilize a third-person perspective or first-person orientation. While in some situations there are advantages to using the third-person perspective, the choice is left purely to player preference, allowing the traditional RPG player the safety of the removal from the avatar while the FPS player remains locked in the familiar perspective. But moving out of the first-person perspective is not always a choice. Though few would call them anything but FPS games, *Tom Clancy's Rainbow Six: Vegas* (Ubisoft Montreal 2006) and *Brothers in Arms: Hell's Highway*

(Gearbox Software 2008) both switch to a third-person point of view when the player takes cover.

As we tour the borders of the FPS genre, we might also be compelled to consider the *Thief* franchise, which employs first-person gameplay while consistently reminding the player that combat is something to be avoided. The franchise is often described as an FPS where the "S" is not for shooting, but for "sneaking" or "stealth." Though the player-character does have a bow, its primary purpose is not to be used as a weapon but as tool for navigating hostile environments.

Clearly, in terms of naming and classifying games according to genre, there is more involved than simply saying "one of these things is like the other." These outliers from the pure ludic conventions indicated by the FPS moniker can be seen as healthy outgrowths of a thriving market for the genre that loves the deceptive simplicity of the form while still appreciating the occasional derivation. While exact fixity of classification may be both exhausting and impossible, the conversation that takes place in this introduction and subsequent chapters engages the very issues that meaningful discussion of the FPS genre requires. In the end, the language is sometimes imprecise and complicated. This does not absolve us of the need to engage it with diligence and complexity, but it does make it hard to locate starting points and even more difficult to suggest one single way of thinking about the coherent lines of argument that tie together the following chapters.

Mission Briefing

This book is organized in three sections: Tutorial, Campaign, and Multiplayer. These terms have specific denotations and, amongst gaming cultures, relatively fixed connotations in the context of specific genres. Our use of these terms is less literal than figurative (though most chapters that look at one or the other mode of play can be found within the respective heading). We intend, rather, for the Tutorial, Campaign, and Multiplayer sections to, respectively, take up issues that are germane to the genre as a whole, the psychic life of the player, and the social dimensions and dynamics of play. Of course, this is simply one set of conversations that stand in slightly starker relief than others, and certainly not the only conversations one can trace in this volume.

Tutorial

In games, and the FPS genre in particular, the tutorial is an opportunity for the player to get their bearings. Do you prefer a standard control scheme or inverted controls? Can you walk, run, jump, and crouch? Well you can now. Do you know how to shoot, aim, and reload? Learn fast, the enemy is just a mission briefing or a set of reinforced doors away. We see chapters in this Tutorial section helping readers get their bearings vis-à-vis the FPS genre. However, maybe you are a seasoned veteran and feel you can skip basic training. Particularly apropos this Tutorial and its use as an organizational tool for this volume, more recently FPS tutorials are seamlessly integrated into the stream of gameplay. The chapters in this section do important historical and meta-critical work framing the conversations that follow, but the reader would be doing him- or herself a disservice to treat them solely as forematter.

The first several chapters scrutinize formal characteristics of the FPS. Mark J. P. Wolf's chapter on the origin of the FPS looks closely at the history of the genre, tracing trajectories across computers, arcades, home consoles, and fairgrounds. An eye-opening reminder that computers are just one way to mediate games, Wolf identifies elements of the FPS in electro-mechanical carnival games from the early twentieth century and documents the adoption of additional elements of the genre as shooting games moved into virtual environments over the next fifty years. The game Wolf locates at the origin of the genre, Atari's *BattleZone* (1980) is no less troubling to taken-for-granted, presentist constructions of the FPS that assume games in the genre concern person-to-person combat. James Manning's chapter on the visual style of *Team Fortress 2* (Valve 2007) also draws attention to decisions made during the development of the game. By bringing the aesthetic theories underpinning animation and comic-strip art to bear, Manning argues convincingly that Valve's use of a cartoonish style instead of photorealistic graphics enables competitive FPS gameplay. Victor Navarro puts the FPS avatar under the microscope in his chapter investigating and delineating the "avatarness" of player-characters in various FPS games. In so doing, Navarro highlights how the choices made in the design and construction of FPS games have the potential to impact the player's relationship to the game. Focusing on the development and deployment of some of the constituent elements of FPS games, these first chapters provide a solid grounding in the ludic properties of the genre.

The last two chapters in this section consider the FPS as a cultural, political discourse. Gerald Voorhees' cultural history of the genre starts from the observation that FPS games garnered less controversy as they began to depict more realistic gun violence. By tracing parallel shifts in the narratives and themes of FPS games, Voorhees argues that the genre has become less controversial and more mainstream as it abandoned fantasy and adopted realism, incorporating advocacy for American militarism and foreign interventions aimed at securing American strategic interests. Toby Miller's chapter takes stock of the contemporary landscape of the FPS, looking at game technologies developed for commercial and military purposes, and scrutinizes the unmitigated celebration of American imperialism. He draws attention to the shameful triangle—the collusion between North American games research focused on professionalization, the game industry which is fraught with exploitative labor practices, and the American military. A poignant meta-analysis of the field, Miller calls upon critical scholars to attend to the exacerbation of material inequalities by the state and capital that are enabled by games and by game studies. No less a primer on the FPS, these chapters survey the genre and bring to the fore the biases of the media form.

Campaign

Most FPS games offer a single-player mode, often called a campaign, which features a series of missions or scenarios for individual players to challenge themselves. More recently, players can engage these missions cooperatively in the *Halo*, *Army of Two* (EA Montreal 2008) and *Left 4 Dead* (Turtle Rock Studios and Valve 2008) series, but in the main the campaign is a solitary experience that challenges the player to think and act for his- or herself. The chapters in this section are reminiscent of the individual experience of the FPS campaign to the extent that they focus on the psychic life of the FPS player. Who are you? What are you supposed to do? What are you going to become? How do you know? These are not only the questions players need to answer in order to orient themselves to the campaign, they are the questions we need to ask in order to understand how players relate to FPS games. The chapters in this section address the FPS as a means to know oneself and construct identity.

The first three chapters start from the player-character, or avatar, and interrogate how this vehicle for the player's involvement impacts the formation and maintenance of a sense of self. Josh Call explores the convention of the FPS avatar through the lens of cyborg theory. He argues that the player-avatar dynamic is a direct function of the hybrid construction that drives cyborg ontology. Call's analysis of FPS game mechanics demonstrates how they support this construction by reinforcing bodily rhetorics that privilege a synthesis of the biological and mechanical. By focusing on both the mechanics and visual perception of movement in the *BioShock* series, Gwyneth Peaty's chapter engages the avatar as cyborg from another angle. Peaty articulates public and scientific discourses of genetic engineering to the rampant gene-splicing players undertake in order to overcome the obstacles in Rapture and argues that *BioShock* (2K Boston 2007) allows players to engage with the cultural anxieties surrounding genetic engineering through gameplay. In order to come to terms with the sense of power and agency players experience, Dan Pinchbeck's close readings of the Ukrainian-produced *S.T.A.L.K.E.R.* (GSC Game World 2007) and *Metro 2033* (4A Games 2010) series considers avatars in terms of their inter-relationships with the gameworlds they inhabit. Starting from the adaptation of the games from novels, Pinchbeck tracks the negation of the power of the environment that accompanies the translation of diegetic worlds into gameworlds. In so doing, he highlights the constraints of the medium of the game and its bias to privilege the player-character as active agent. By centering the FPS avatar, these chapters bringing into relief different ways that it functions as a focal point for players to understand their selves.

The last two chapters in this section take different tacks to inter-rogate the construction and maintenance of identity in the FPS. Alan

Meades looks at transgressive play, practices that (often) violate the rules of the game and norms of player communities, enacted by hackers and the players that exploit hacks. Meades unearths both resistance to the norms of play and adherence to the norms of the more encompassing technoculture and hegemonic masculinity that valorize achievement and success at all cost. In this regard, he calls attention to patterns of play that perform a powerful identity. Daniel Ashton and James Newman do similar work in their chapter analyzing game walkthroughs. Rethinking the bounds of gameplay, Ashton and Newman approach game walkthroughs as sites where games are engaged by players, and call attention to the ways that players use them as platforms for managing their identities and performing their expertise. These chapters demonstrate that FPS games can have a significant role to play in the configuration of identity even when the avatar is not foregrounded.

Multiplayer

Since *DOOM*, the first widely popular FPS, multiplayer gaming has been a mainstay of the genre. Over the years multiplayer matches played on LANs, linked consoles, and over the internet have taken a plethora of different forms. While certain games allow free-for-all and asymmetrical matches pitting a single player against a group of opponents, the most common multiplayer games put teams of players against one another. And whether the game is objective-based scenario such as capture the flag or king of the hill, or a competition for the most kills, these matches share a social dimension. Like the chapters in this section, they force players to figure out what it means to play well with others, to re-examine the wisdom of patterns of activity that make sense in a single-player environment, and question the implications, for good or ill, of sharing a playspace with other people. At their core, these chapters consider the social and cultural impact of the FPS.

The first two chapters in this section are concerned with the entailments of communication practices specific to multiplayer FPS gameplay. Nick Taylor's ethnographic account of the communicative norms of competitive FPS players reveals play practices that emerge only in the context of a well-disciplined team. In multiplayer matches and the social spectacles of e-sports, Taylor's chapter argues that distinct forms of communication germane to competitive FPS gaming are constitutive of this community and the type of play as properly professional. Evan Snider, Tim Lockridge, and Dan Lawson approach multiplayer communication from a different angle, rethinking the practices of griefing as rhetorical tactics that trouble the ideological work of FPS games. As Snider, Lockridge, and Lawson argue, griefing is not possible absent the social dimension of FPS multiplayer, but it frequently acts to subvert and inhibit the masculinist and militaristic social norms. Though seemingly at odds, the first two chapters in this section explore the dynamics of multiplayer FPS communication.

The last four chapters in this section (and the volume) reflect on the FPS as means of understanding historical, cultural, and political processes. Stephanie Fisher considers the historical FPS as a site where game-based learning occurs and examines the ways in which WWII is represented in mainstream titles. Fisher's chapter takes to task the great majority of FPS games that overwhelmingly deploy a 'best possible story' version of history that obfuscates the contingency of historical events. Ultimately, Fisher argues that FPS games have the capacity, though they may lack the courage or creativity, to model for players just how precarious history is. Chris Moore's chapter theorizes invigoration as the affective process through which players are invested in structures of play articulated to political implications in the real world. While Moore concentrates on the affective attachments that permeate multiplayer gameplay, his piece offers insights on the FPS's capacity to mobilize subjects by means of embodied rhetorics. Taking up the body from a feminist critical perspective, Aaron Duncan and Jessy Ohl examine the indy FPS *Hey Baby*, which was developed and released with the aim of spurring discourse about sexual harassment. Duncan and Ohl argue that by only allowing the player to resist harassment through violent retaliation, *Hey Baby* ultimately encourages players to enact feminized performances of hegemonic masculinity that threaten to undermine the messages the game hopes to help disseminate. Timothy Welsh's chapter offers an antidote to the logic that conceives of the Columbine effect as the ultimate trajectory of the FPS. Welsh argues that instead of desensitizing players to gun violence and dematerializing the deaths of soldiers, FPS games actually portray the player's targets as human subjects, and therefore contain the possibility of unsettling the militarism that cuts across the genre. Though they center different spheres of activity, the chapters in this final part of the book consider the FPS as a truly multiplayer experience that involves a multitude of players, some of whom are situated in and others outside of gamespaces.

As a whole, the chapters in this volume have much to say concerning the state of the FPS and its importance as a mediated cultural form. It is our hope that readers without their own agendas will find the organization of this volume appealing and, building upon the tutorial, engage the psychic and social implications and relations of the FPS in turn. Of course, others will pick and choose, and still others will see different conversations coming together as they connect the topics, methods, and objects of inquiry in various chapters. That is expected, and welcomed. This volume is, ultimately, an open world for the reader to explore. Just don't forget to pick up the shotgun before you get into the thick of things.

References

Fullerton, Tracy. 2004. *Game Design Workshop: Designing, Prototyping and Playtesting Games*. Lawrence, KA: Elsevier.

Galloway, Alexander R. 2006. "Origins of the First Person Shooter." In *Gaming: Essays on Algorithmic Culture*, 39–69. Minneapolis, MN: University of Minnesota Press.

Grimshaw, Mark, Charlton, John P., and Jagger, Richard. 2011. "First-Person Shooters: Immersion and Attention." *Eludamos* 5.1: (29–44).

Grimshaw, Mark and Schott, Gareth. 2008. "A Conceptual Framework for the Analysis of First-Person Shooter Audio and its Potential Use for Game Engines." *International Journal of Computer Game Technology* 2008 (7). doi:10.1155/2008/720280.

Järvinen, Aki. 2002. "Halo and the Anatomy of the FPS." *Game Studies* 2(1). http://www.gamestudies.org/0102/jarvinen/

Jones, Steven E. 2008. *The Meaning of Video Games: Gaming and Textual Strategies*. NYC: Routledge.

King, Geoff and Krzywinska, Tanya. 2006. *Tomb Raiders & Space Invaders: Videogame Forms & Contexts*. NYC: I.B. Taurus.

Lahati, Martti. 2003. "As We Become Machines: Corporealized Metaphors in Video Games." In *The Video Game Theory Reader*, edited by Mark J. P. Wolf and Bernard Perron, 157–70. NYC: Routledge.

Mäyrä, Frans. 2008. *An Introduction to Game Studies: Games in Culture.* Los Angeles: Sage.

McMahan, Alison. 2003. "Immersion, Engagement, and Presence: A Method for Analyzing 3-D G." In *The Video Game Theory Reader,* edited by Mark J. P. Wolf and Bernard Perron, 67–86. NYC: Routledge.

Morris, Sue. 2002. "First-Person Shooters – A Game Apparatus." In *ScreenPlay: cinema/videogames/interfaces,* edited by Geoff King and Tanya Krzywinska, 81–97. NYC: Wallflower.

Nieborg, David B. 2006. "First Person Paradoxes – The Logic of War in Computer Games." In *Game, Set and Match II: On Computer Games, Advanced Geometries and Digital Technologies,* edited by Kas Oosterhuis and Lukas Feireiss, 107–15. Rotterdam: Episode.

Rehak, Bob. 2003. "Playing at Being: Psychoanalysis and the Avatar." In *The Video Game Theory Reader,* edited by Mark J. P. Wolf and Bernard Perron, 103–28. NYC: Routledge.

Salen, Katie and Zimmerman, Eric. 2004. *Rules of Play: Game Design Fundamentals.* Cambridge, MA: MIT Press.

Slocombe, Will. 2006. "A 'Majestic' Reflexivity: Machine-Gods and the Creation of the Playing Subject in *Deus Ex* and *Deus Ex: Invisible War.*" In *Digital Gameplay: Essays on the Nexus of Game and Gamer,* edited by Nate Garrelts, 36–51. Jefferson, NC: MacFarland & Co.

Voorhees, Gerald, Call, Josh, and Whitlock, Katie. 2012. "Series Introduction – Genre and Disciplinarity in the Study of Games." In *Dungeons, Dragons and Digital Denizens: Digital Role-playing Games,* edited by Gerald Voorhees, Josh Call, and Katie Whitlock, 1–10. NYC: Continuum Books.

Games

2K Boston. 2007. *BioShock* [Mac OS X, Microsoft Windows, PlayStation 3, Xbox 360]. 2K Games.

4A Games. 2010. *Metro 2033* [Microsoft Windows, Xbox360]. THQ.

Atari. 1980. *BattleZone* [arcade]. Atari.

Core Designs. 1996. *Tomb Raider* [DOS, Microsoft Windows, PlayStation, Sega Saturn]. Eidos Interactive.

Crytek. 2004. *Far Cry* [Microsoft Windows]. Ubisoft.

Crytek Frankfurt. 2007. *Crysis* [Microsoft Windows]. Electronic Arts.

Cyan. 1993. *Myst* [Mac OS]. Bröderbund.

DICE. 2008. *Mirror's Edge* [iOS, Microsoft Windows, PlayStation 3, Xbox 360]. Electronic Arts.

EA Montreal. 2008. *Army of Two* [PlayStation 3, Xbox 360]. Electronic Arts.

Gearbox Software. 2008. *Brothers in Arms: Hell's Highway* [Microsoft Windows, PlayStation 3, Xbox 360]. Ubisoft.

GSC Game World. 2007. *S.T.A.L.K.E.R.: Shadow of Chernobyl* [Microsoft Windows]. THQ.

id Software. 1989. *Wolfenstein 3D* [DOS]. Apogee.

—1993. *DOOM* [DOS]. id Software.

JAM Productions. 1993. *Blake Stone: Aliens of Gold* [DOS]. Apogee.

Namco. 1980. *Pac Man* [arcade]. Namco.

Nintendo. 1984. *Duck* Hunt [Nintendo Entertainment System]. Nintendo.

—1985. *Super Mario Bros.* [Nintendo Entertainment System]. Nintendo.

—1986. *The Legend of Zelda* [Nintendo Entertainment System]. Nintendo.

Turtle Rock Studios and Valve. 2008. *Left 4 Dead* [MAC OS X, Microsoft Windows, Xbox 360]. Valve.

Ubisoft Montreal. 2006. *Tom Clancy's Rainbow Six: Vegas* [Microsoft Windows, PlayStation 3, Xbox 360]. Ubisoft.

US Army. 2002. *America's Army* [Microsoft Windows, Xbox, Xbox 360]. U.S. Army.

Valve. 2000. *Counter-Strike* [Microsoft Windows]. Valve.

—2004. *Half-Life 2* [Microsoft Windows]. Valve.

—2007. *Team Fortress 2* [Microsoft Windows, PlayStation 3, Xbox 360]. Valve.

Westwood. 1995. *Command & Conquer* [DOS, MAC OS, Microsoft Windows]. Virgin Interactive.

Westwood Associates. 1990. *Eye of the Beholder* [DOS]. Strategic Simulations Inc.

PART ONE

Tutorial

1

BattleZone and the Origins of First-Person Shooting Games

Mark J. P. Wolf

Atari's arcade game *BattleZone* (Atari 1980) was not the first shooting game, nor the first to have a first-person perspective, nor even the first to combine the two. But the game does represent the coalescence of the first-person shooter (FPS) genre (or subgenre of the shooting game genre, since not all shooting games are from a first-person perspective), as it brought together all the necessary elements now recognized as being essential to the first-person shooter as it is typically defined today. *BattleZone* combined them into a single game that was commercially available in wide release to the general public, and, as such, became a milestone and turning point in the history of the FPS. The influences, precursors, and development of the elements found in *BattleZone* occurred over more than a century, so it is to these that we must first turn our attention, as we examine how shooting became a game, how shooting games became virtual, and finally how they arrived at the form taken in *BattleZone*.

Shooting Becomes a Game

If the idea of shooting projectiles developed to allow one to do damage at a distance without putting one's self into harm's way, that is, within reach of whatever was being shot at, it makes sense to assume that increasing one's accuracy would be a good thing. Shooting practice would be the result, and if two or more individuals practiced shooting, it seems natural that it would turn into a competition, and finally, into a kind of game.

Shooting competitions have probably existed for as long as projectile weapons have been around, and were no doubt the inspiration for shooting galleries on carnival fairgrounds from the late 1890s onward, which we might consider the very first first-person shooting games. As a fairground attraction with less dangerous guns, shooting galleries allowed carnival patrons to try their hand at shooting even if they would normally never handle real guns. This reduced possibility of danger helped to enhance the game-like nature of competitive shooting, allowing more concentration on its more playful aspects. Shooting galleries, however, still required safety measures and operators who tended the games, and it would be some time before technology had advanced sufficiently such that these could be eliminated.

Meanwhile, other outdoor games were adapted into indoor versions. For example, croquet was turned into billiards, and during the late 1700s in France the pool table used for billiards was narrowed and posts were added, becoming the game Bagatelle. Players would use cues to send balls up the table and ricochet them off pegs and into holes. During the 1800s, Bagatelle games became smaller, and eventually table-top versions were made. French soldiers brought Bagatelle to America during the Revolutionary War, and the tables became popular in the United States. In 1869, British inventor Montague Redgrave started producing Bagatelle tables in Ohio, but he replaced the pool cues with plungers and glassed over the Bagatelle table, making the game more self-contained. After further innovation and redesign, Bagatelle became known as pinball, which went on to even greater success during the twentieth century, during which time such features as backlights, bumpers, and flippers were added, and the game was electrified.

As pinball began to find success, other fairground games were adapted into electromechanical games, and among them were shooting gallery games. The Mechanical Trading Co. produced the coin-operated *Automatic Shooting Range* in 1895, and the Automatic Sports Company of London, England, produced several coin-operated shooting games for the arcade into the 1920s. Automatic Sports' coin-operated games took place in glass-enclosed cases atop fanciful pedestals designed to bring the games up to the right height for standing players. Electromechanical games further sanitized and automated shooting galleries through the use of easily resettable targets, reusable ammunition, a mounted gun, and an enclosed space that contained all the elements of the game apart from the controls of the gun. Everything stayed within the game cabinet, and targets and guns were automatically reset, so no operator was required, allowing players to play unattended and greater profits to be made. Shooting games became less like shooting with real guns; gone was the noise and recoil of a real gun, and the field of action was miniaturized to only a few feet across, making timing far less important since the short distances eliminated the need to anticipate the movements of targets and compensate one's aim as a result (although some games did attempt to simulate these things, like Chicago Coin's *Pistol* (1947), which advertised "Realistic Recoil and Report Action" on its flyer; and some games also used mirrors within their cabinets to increase the shooting distance). From a design point of view, this meant that moving targets and other elements of difficulty became more important, since the use of distant targets was no longer possible. Overall, however, encased coin-operated games abstracted shooting games to an even greater degree than had fairground shooting galleries, and skills needed for the games no longer translated into the skills needed for the use of real weaponry.

Electromechanical games were the dominant coin-operated arcade games from the late 1930s to the early 1970s, and shooting games released during this time included such games as A. B. T. Manufacturing Corporation's *Challenger* (1939), Chicago Coin's *Pistol*

(1947), Genco's *Sky Gunner* (1953), Midway's *Trophy Gun* (1964), and Chicago Coin's *Super Circus Rifle Gallery* (1969) and *Sharp Shooter* (1971). Although today the abilities of electromechanical games seem very limited when compared with possibilities that video games offer, by the time arcade video games appeared in 1971, electromechanical games had become quite advanced, even to the point of offering competitive machine-controlled players. Midway's *Wild Kingdom* (1971), for example, had "Jungle Charlie" who competed against the player; according to pinball and game collector Clay F. Harrell,

> Midway's *Wild Kingdom* is a very challenging gun game because the player is shooting against "Jungle Charlie", a 3" high moving mechanical marksman on the game's playfield. Unlike say *Haunted House* where the player can take their time and shoot as slow as they want, *Wild Kingdom* forces the player to shoot fast. After the first shot is taken, the player is shooting against Jungle Charlie (the first shot is a 'warm up' shot and the player can take as long as they want for the first shot). If the player takes too long to shoot, Jungle Charlie shoots the animal instead causing the animal to retreat, and Jungle Charlie *never* misses. To slow Jungle Charlie, the player can fire his gun – Jungle Charlie can not shoot if the player is shooting (and likewise the player can not shot [sic] if Jungle Charlie is shooting). Each game gets 25 shots, with Jungle Charlie shooting out of the 25 shots. If the player is slow he may only get the first shot, and Jungle Charlie will use the other 24 shots! Jungle Charlie's movement speed can be adjusted. If he's adjusted too fast the game is nearly impossible to shoot as Jungle Charlie is too quick. At 3000 points the game automatically speeds up Jungle Charlie too. (Pinrepair.com 2011b)

Although early video games represented a technological novelty, they could not provide some of the kinds of play experiences that electromechanical games could. Eventually, video games improved and surpassed electromechanical games, ending their dominance in the arcade, and video games offered additional benefits for arcade operators as well, especially when it came to repairs.

Whereas electromechanical arcade games did not need constant supervision from a human attendant the way that carnival games did, they still needed frequent maintenance due to their many moving parts and occasional breakdowns. Video games, with far few moving parts (usually only the controllers), were less likely to break down and more reliable, and technologically they were much less idiosyncratic in their design; all used a monitor for their imagery instead of plastic or metal models that had to be painted, assembled, and tested. After *PONG* (Atari 1972) proved that arcade video games could be successful, it was natural that games would begin the transition from electromechanical contraptions to virtual on-screen versions of the same activities. But shooting games had already begun the process of becoming virtual as early as the 1920s.

Shooting Games Become Virtual

The first element of shooting games to become virtual was ammunition. So long as actual physical projectiles of some kind flew through the air between the player's gun and the target, the field of action between the two had to be encased for safety reasons, as well as to recycle the ammunition and keep it from leaving the system. By using a light beam instead of a physical projectile, guns could once again be used in the open air just as in carnival shooting galleries; all that was needed was a way to sense when the beam of light struck its target.

William Gent used an electrical light gun in his *Electric Rifle* game of the 1920s (Pinrepair 2011c), and in 1936 the jukebox manufacturer Seeburg Corporation used the newly invented phototube, a vacuum tube with a light sensor inside it, in a duck shooting arcade game called *Ray-O-Lite* (Pinrepair 2011a). Players held a full-sized rifle which shot a light beam at the moving targets, each of which contained a phototube inside it; when the phototube detected the light beam, the hit was registered and the score increased. The "Ray-O-Lite" technology went on to be used in other Seeburg games like *Shoot the Bear* (1947), and other companies began to use similar light gun-based technologies. Eventually light gun technology became available in a consumer product for home use; in 1970, Nintendo released Gunpei Yokoi's *Beam Gun* toy, a light gun that came with targets with photoelectric cells on them.

The Magnavox Odyssey was the first home video game system with a light gun peripheral (released in 1972, and based on Ralph Baer's prototype of 1968), and reversed the usual hardware configuration by putting the photoelectric cell inside the gun barrel, where it would detect the light of the target on the television screen (though it would also register hits if pointed at a light bulb or any light source). Four Odyssey games used the light gun (*Prehistoric Safari* [1972], *Shooting Gallery* [1972], *Dogfight* [1972], and *Shootout* [1972]), in which the player fired at on-screen targets. The Odyssey's shooting games represented a further advancement of the first-person shooting game into the virtual realm, as both their ammunition and their targets were now virtual.

Virtual shooting found its natural home in the video game, and video games had involved shooting from their very beginning. The first patent for an interactive electronic game, United States patent #2,455,992, "Cathode-Ray Tube Amusement Device," was filed by Thomas T. Goldsmith, Jr. and Estle Ray Mann on January 25, 1947 and issued on December 14, 1948 (it did not involve a video signal, however, and could therefore arguably be denied the status of a "video" game). The description of the proposed device's content describes a scenario with shooting going on:

In carrying out the invention a cathode-ray tube is used upon the face of which the trace of the ray or electron beam can be seen. One or more targets, such as pictures of airplanes, for example, are placed upon the face of the tube and controls are available to the player so that he can manipulate the trace or position of the beam which is automatically caused to move across the face of the tube. This movement of the beam may be periodic and its repetition rate may be varied. Its path is preferably caused to depart from a straight line so as to require an increased amount of skill and care for success in playing the game.

The game can be made more spectacular, and the interest therein both from the player's and the observer's standpoint can be increased, by making a visible explosion of the cathode-ray beam take place when the target is hit. (United States Patent 2,455,992)

Some of the earliest video games, such as the mainframe game *Spacewar!* (1962) and commercial games based on it like *Galaxy Game* (1971) and *Computer Space* (1971), also involved shooting. In these games, the weaponry, the ammunition, and the targets were all virtual; but as these games featured shooting from a third-person perspective, they provided a much different kind of shooting experience than first-person shooting games. The third-person perspective required the control of an on-screen avatar, and its top-down or side view was less immersive than a first-person perspective. But a first-person perspective required z-axis depth and a three-dimensional game-space, something that electromechanical games, with their physical game-spaces, could not help providing, but which video games would struggle to simulate during the 1970s.

Video games and First-Person Perspective

Actual shooting, and shooting games involving a hand-held gun of some sort, naturally make use of the first-person perspective of the player's own vision, since shooting depends greatly on the player's ability to aim while assessing the three-dimensional position of targets, whether they are moving or static. This close connection between shooting and perspective is apparent in the sharp divide that we find between first-person and third-person shooting games; no other genre of video game finds itself so divided according to player point-of-view. For example, racing games are available from both first-person and third-person perspectives, but we do not speak of "first-person racers" as often as we do "first-person shooters" (a Google search performed on April 8, 2011, found 17,100,000 results for "first-person shooter" but only 4,420 results for "first-person racer"; a ratio of more than 3868 to 1).

As video games, shooting games had to wait until the mid-1970s for first-person perspective. The Odyssey's four shooting games had flat graphics, and were little more than the back wall of a shooting gallery, and although it might be argued that the use of the light gun made the games first-person perspective shooting games, such an argument would broaden the sense of the term to the point where the usual distinctions made between perspectives would be lost.

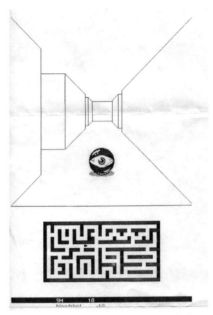

Figure 1.1 *Maze War* (Colley 1974) was one of the earliest shooting games to feature a first-person perspective.

One would be able to argue that *Pac-Man* (Namco 1980) had a first-person perspective of someone hovering over the maze and looking down at the figures moving within it; the term "first-person" would come to encompass all third-person points of view as well as the usual meaning of subjective, optical viewpoints located at characters' positions. (It is interesting to note how this problem does not occur in media involving lens-based imaging, like photography, film, and television; every view shown in these media is either from a character's point of view or at the very least a point of view that has a distinct position in the three-dimensional space of the image's diegesis; but the two-dimensional worlds of video games are seen from views from a standpoint outside of their worlds.)

The first two shooting games to use a first-person perspective were both mainframe games; *Maze War* (Colley 1974) on the Imlac PDS-1 (see Figure 1.1), and *Spasim* (Bowery 1974), which was short for *space simulator*, on the PLATO system. Mainframe games had more processing power and speed than arcade games or home video games of the day, and were the incubators where many genres of video games were born, including the FPS. Both *Maze War* and *Spasim* depicted movement through a three-dimensional space, and including the shooting of enemy figures when they were on-screen and positioned in the player's view. In *Spasim*, movement advanced in jumps from one position to another, with time needed in between to render the next view, as opposed to movement and shooting that occurred in real time. In *Maze War*, movement in a straight line down hallways was relatively smooth, but turning was done in 90-degree increments, resulting in potentially confusing graphics as the vanishing point stays the same during 90-degree turns while everything else changes abruptly.

Maze War and *Spasim* were both networked multiplayer games, allowing players to shoot at each other. Thus, unlike almost all shooting games that had gone before them, competitive shooting no longer meant only a competition to see who could hit the most targets or who had the most accurate shooting, but rather who could shoot the other player's avatar first; thus did shooting games go from friendly competition to kill-or-be-killed deathmatches, a move that would set the stage and tone for most of the FPSs that followed. *Maze War* also contained "robots" that would automatically shoot you if they were in line with you down a hallway, so even in a single-player game, danger could lurk just around the corner.

But if danger was just around the corner, it could be avoided. Although *Maze War* allowed players to switch between the first-person point of view and an overhead map of the maze (making it also the first game to incorporate both points of view and allow a player to choose between them), the map only showed the player's location in the maze, and not those of the other players. Because it was so easy to turn a corner and suddenly be surprised and shot at, an additional feature allowed the player to peek around a corner without being seen, momentarily disconnecting the first-person view from the player's actual location ("The Maze War 30 Year Retrospective at the DigiBarn", Digibarn Computer Museum website), a feature prefiguring the separation of point-of-view from movement.

Another new twist introduced in *Maze War* was the possibility of getting shot at and killed from behind, without ever even seeing your attacker. Instead of the fixed and unchanging point of view found in a shooting gallery, *Maze War* required you to change your view as well as keep watch on the space all around you. Unlike all other video games up to this point, one did not merely watch the game's world from some point outside it, but rather from within the world, and there was a sense of off-screen space surrounding the player and events that were occurring unseen in those spaces.

Both *Maze War* and *Spasim* used vector graphics to display their views (raster versions of *Maze War* appeared later). Since lines of perspective extending to a vanishing point are almost always diagonal lines, vector graphics had an advantage over early raster graphics in creating a first-person perspective. Raster graphics could only roughly approximate diagonal lines, by linking blocks corner to corner diagonally, or spacing them apart like the pylons in Atari's *Night Driver* (1976). Vector graphics, drawn on the screen one line at a time in any direction, could produce a stronger sense of lines converging at a vanishing point. Vector graphics came to the arcade with Cinematronics's release of *Space Wars* (1977), and another of the company's games, *Speed Freak* (1978) featured the first real-time rendered three-dimensional computer animation in an arcade video game, an explosion of car parts when the player crashed.

Yet although they both represented advances in the genre, what *Maze War* and *Spasim* lacked was the kind of aiming and shooting that players enjoyed in third-person perspective shooting games. In both games, shooting was done with a keystroke, and aiming was limited to facing in the right direction, due to the limitations of the positioning of the player's point-of-view, like the 90-degree incremental turns in *Maze War*.

The following year, another multiplayer shooting game on PLATO advanced the genre a step further. John Edo Haefeli's tank simulator *Panther* (1975) was even more complex, with an entire screen listing the game's features and their keyboard shortcuts. The tank and its turret could be turned independently of each other, there were gross, coarse, and fine adjustments for turret positioning, the player's view could be zoomed in and out, and the controls allowed the player to determine the distance to targets, fire shells, deploy mines, and move ammunition and fuel from one player's tank to another. Whereas *Maze War* allowed the player to switch between a first-person view and an overhead map of the game's space, *Panther* had an overhead view of the tank (showing the direction that the tank and its gun turret was facing) that appeared in the corner of the first-person view, splitting the player's attention between the two different views. The game also had hidden line removal, and simulated the physics of shooting along a trajectory, accounting for source and target speeds, and even the curvature of the earth. Two years later, an updated version of *Panther* with better graphics, known as *Panzer* (1977), was produced by Northwestern University along with the US Army Armor School at Fort Knox. (For other takes on militarism in FPS games, see the essays by Voorhees, Miller, and Moore in this volume.)

The games on PLATO were far more advanced than the simpler and more streamlined games of the arcade, and, as networked games, sometimes slower in their operation as well. They were operated entirely by keyboard, and could take time to learn, due to all their features and commands. That *PONG* (1972) was so much more successful than *Computer Space* (Nutting Associates 1971) demonstrated that simplified controls were needed to reach a mass audience at the arcade, where shorter game times meant more money and steep learning curves were bad for business. While *Panther* enjoyed a following of technology-savvy users on mainframe computers, it would take another first-person tank game to break through to the mass commercial market of the arcades: *BattleZone* (1980).

The Arrival of BattleZone

Atari's *BattleZone* was a three-dimensional vector graphics game and the first arcade video game to feature a computationally true three-dimensional environment. Its green vector graphics depicted a barren landscape with cubical and pyramidal obstacles and mountains on the horizon (including an erupting volcano), and enemy tanks (and a UFO) that came at the player's tank from any direction on the plane, forcing the player to watch the radar scope that revealed enemy positions within a short radius. Above the action were red vector graphics (the screen used a color overlay) displaying the score, high score, tanks remaining, and the radar scope. Released the same year as *Pac-Man* (1980) and *Defender* (Williams 1980), *BattleZone* joined the ranks of the most popular arcade video games to appear during the Golden Age of the arcade.

Because *BattleZone* is both a tank game and a vector graphics game, it is often compared to *Panther*, which is assumed to be its inspiration. But apart from the tank theme and vector graphics, the games differ in many ways, and a more likely candidate for *BattleZone*'s inspiration can be found in an earlier tank arcade game from Atari; *Tank!* (1974), the groundbreaking and influential game which was the first arcade game to use read-only memory (ROM) and which inspired *Combat* (1977), the cartridge packaged with the Atari VCS 2600.

Unlike *Panther*, which used a computer keyboard, *BattleZone*'s controls were, like *Tank!*, a pair of joysticks and a fire button which allowed the player to move forward, move backward, right turn, left turn, and fire. Firing was done only in the direction the tank was facing, meaning you could not fire and run away at the same time (as you could in *Panther*); *BattleZone* was almost like a first-person version of *Tank!* since both tanks were operated in a similar fashion. Both games were also designed at Atari, as commercial arcade games. Finally, there is the admission from Ed Rotberg, the designer of *BattleZone*, that *Tank!* was more of an influence than *Panther*:

Actually it wasn't based on *Panther*. It may have inspired whoever originally suggested the idea at the brainstorming meeting where it was proposed, but I seriously doubt it. It was more a matter of the success of the original, top-down *Tank* game Atari did and the advent of the vector generator. There is only so much you can do with vectors, a tank concept, and somewhat limited processor power. While I did play on PLATO, I don't ever remember playing *Panther*, though I was aware of it. The design of *BattleZone* was primarily mine. (Ed Rotberg, e-mail to the author, April 12, 2011)

BattleZone combined shooting with a first-person shooting perspective, a three-dimensional environment, a mobile viewpoint, computer-controlled enemies, smooth movement in all directions,

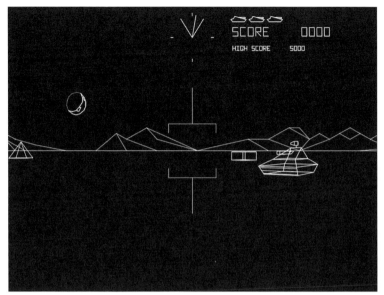

Figure 1.2 *BattleZone* (Atari 1980) was the first FPS to become available to a general public audience.

and simple controls with a shallow learning curve, and made them available to a mass audience as an arcade video game.

For many people, *BattleZone* was their first encounter with an FPS video game (and with interactive three-dimensional computer graphics, for that matter), and it is no wonder that it became one of the most popular and influential games of the 1980s. *BattleZone* was ported to other game systems, including the Atari 2600 in 1983, and Atarisoft released home computer versions of *BattleZone* for the Apple II, the Commodore 64, and MS-DOS in 1983, the Sinclair ZX Spectrum in 1984, the Atari ST in 1986, the Atari XE in 1987, the Nintendo Game Boy in 1996, and the PlayStation Portable in 2006. Updated versions of *BattleZone* include the four-player networked *BattleZone 2000* (1995) for the Atari Lynx, a 1996 Java version that can be played online, a 3D remake in 1998, Pandemic Studios's *BattleZone II: Combat Commander* (1999), a high-definition version for Xbox Live Arcade in 2008, and a download for Microsoft's Game Room service for the Xbox 360 in 2010. A host of *BattleZone* clones also appeared, for various consoles and computers, including Atari's own *Red Baron* (1980), which used the same hardware but depicted dogfights between biplanes instead of tanks. In 1981, a more advanced version of *BattleZone* known as the "Bradley Trainer" was also developed for the US military for tank training, but only two prototypes were ever produced.

Eventually the FPS would undergo other refinements, most notably in the relationship between *looking* and *aiming*. Just as the later, more advanced version of *Panther* allowed one to aim in a different direction than the direction of movement (a feature not found in *BattleZone*), later FPS games would make the direction of one's aim less dependent on the direction of one's view. Whereas in *BattleZone* the gunsight is always centered in the player's point of view, making "looking" and "aiming" the same thing, these games allowed the gunsight to be moved around freely within the player's point of view, limited only by the edges of the screen. Although earlier games, like Taito's *Interceptor* (1976) and Atari's *Missile Command* (1980), had gunsights that could move around the screen, the player's point-of-view itself was fixed and immovable. Such a feature could have been incorporated into *BattleZone*, but it would not have made sense due to the vehicular nature of the player's avatar, since the aiming of a tank is much less flexible than that of standing and aiming a pistol with one's own arm. During the mid to late 1990s, however, "free looking," also known as "mouselooking," would become a standard feature of the FPS.

Although *BattleZone* significantly shaped the development of the FPS, many of its features had already appeared in one form or another in earlier games, so it was the combination of these in a single game, and, most importantly, the game's availability to a wide audience, that was its main contribution to the genre. In this sense, *BattleZone* helped the FPS coalesce into a full-fledged subgenre of the shooting game genre (or, as some would have it, a genre all its own); and *BattleZone*'s iconic status as a video game and widespread popularity set a standard that helped make certain elements seem indispensable to the FPS, even if it was not the first game to introduce those elements. As such, *BattleZone* was both a milestone in the development of the FPS and one of the main games to promote it to the public, and it will always be remembered along with the great games of the video arcade game's Golden Age.

References

Digibarn Computer Museum. 2011. "The Maze War 30 Year
   Retrospective at the DigiBarn" http://www.digibarn.com/collections/
   games/xerox-maze-war/index.html#started.
Goldsmith, Thomas T. and Estle Ray Mann. 1948. "Cathode-Ray Tube
   Amusement Device." United States Patent 2,455,992, filed January
   25, 1947 and issued December 14, 1948.
International Arcade Museum. 2012. "Automatic Shooting Range."
   http://www.arcade-museum.com/game_detail.php?game_id=704.
Nintendoland.com. 2011. "Toys & Arcades – (1969–82)." http://
   nintendoland.com/History/Hist2.php.
Pinrepair.com. 2011a. "1936 Seeburg Ray-O-Lite." http://www.pinrepair.
   com/arcade/rayolit.htm.
—2011b. "Wild Kingdom." http://www.pinrepair.com/arcade/wildkin.htm.
—2011c. "William Gent Mfg Electric Rifle." http://www.pinrepair.com/
   arcade/gent.htm.

Games

A. B. T. Manufacturing Corp. *Challenger* [arcade]. A. B. T. Manufacturing
   Corp., 1939.
Atari. 1972. *PONG* [arcade]. Atari.
—1974. *Tank!* [arcade]. Atari.
—1976. *Night Driver* [arcade]. Atari.
—1977. *Combat* [Atari VCS 2600]. Atari.
—1980. *BattleZone* [arcade]. Atari.
—1980. *Missile Command* [arcade]. Atari.
—1980. *Red Baron* [arcade]. Atari.
—1995. *BattleZone 2000* [Atari Lynx]. Atari.
Bowery, Jim. 1974. *Spasim* [PLATO System]. Bowery.
Chicago Coin. 1947. *Pistol* [arcade]. Chicago Coin.
—1969. *Super Circus Rifle Gallery* [arcade]. Chicago Coin.
—1971. *Sharp Shooter* [arcade]. Chicago Coin.
Cinematronics. 1977. *Space Wars* [arcade]. Cinematronics.
—1978. *Speed Freak* [arcade]. Cinematronics.
Colley, Steve. 1974. *Maze War* [Imlac PDS-1]. Colley.
Genco. 1953. *Sky Gunner* [arcade]. Genco.
Haefeli, John Edo. 1975. *Panther* [PLATO System]. Haefeli.
—1977. *Panzer* [PLATO System]. Haefeli.
Maganvox. 1972. *Dogfight* [Magnavox Odyssey]. Magnavox.
—1972. *Prehistoric Safari* [Magnavox Odyssey]. Magnavox.

—1972. *Shooting Gallery* [Magnavox Odyssey]. Magnavox.

—1972. *Shootout* [Magnavox Odyssey]. Magnavox.

Mechanical Trading Co. 1895. *Automatic Shooting Range* [arcade]. Mechanical Trading Co.

Midway. 1964. *Trophy Gun* [arcade]. Midway.

—1971. *Wild Kingdom* [arcade]. Midway.

Namco. 1980. *Pac-Man* [arcade]. Midway.

Nutting Associates. 1971. *Computer Space* [arcade]. Nutting Associates.

Pandemic Studios. 1999. *BattleZone II: Combat Commander* [Microsoft Windows]. Activision.

Pitts, Bill and Hugh Tuck. 1971. *Galaxy Game* [DEC PDP-11/20]. Pitts and Tuck.

Russell, Steve, et al. 1962. *Spacewar!* [PDP-1]. Russell.

Seeburg Corporation. 1936. *Ray-O-Lite* [arcade]. Seeburg Corporation.

—1947. *Shoot the Bear* [arcade]. Seeburg Corporation.

Taito. 1976. *Interceptor* [arcade]. Taito.

William Gent. circa 1920s. *Electric Rifle* [arcade]. William Gent.

Williams. 1980. *Defender* [arcade]. Williams.

2

Call to Action, Invitation to Play: The Immediacy of the Caricature in *Team Fortress 2*

James Manning

T*eam Fortress 2* (hereafter TF2) was released by Valve as part of *The Orange Box* compilation in October 2007 for PC, Xbox 360 and later, Playstation 3. Arguably the third release of this multiplayer, team-based FPS following the *Quake* (id Software 1996) modification *Team Fortress* (1996) and Valve's own *Half-Life* (Valve 1998) mod *Team Fortress Classic* (1999). As such, many of the series' defining gameplay elements were already in place, including the character classes and team-oriented play dynamic (PlanetFortress n.d.). During its lengthy nine-year development, the designers of TF2 were able to focus on refining these core mechanics whilst experimenting with suitable visual styles in an attempt to serve two, self-identified aims—in terms of branding, to differentiate TF2 from other multi-player FPS games (Wicklund 2007) and, in terms of gameplay, to focus the players' attention towards achieving the goals of the game during the intensity of play (Diaz 2007). It is the latter which concerns us here.

The scope of this chapter is to focus on the visual information presented on-screen to the player during play. This is not to suggest the overall aesthetic appeal of TF2 is one based solely on a reading of the screen, rather it is how TF2 makes explicit use of the affordance of the screen that forms the basis of and delimits our discussion here. If, as Barry Atkins suggests, the "gamer's gaze" is one focused on the future possibilities of action, how such possibilities manifest in this way should be of paramount concern to the game developer; "[v]ideo games prioritize the participation of the player as he or she plays, and that player always apprehends the game as a matrix of future possibility. [... This] places the player at the center of experience as its principle creator, necessarily engaged in an imaginative act, and always oriented toward the future" (Atkins 2006, 137). In recent years, the increased computational power made available to game developers via modern gaming platforms has provided the game artist with a near-infinite number of visual possibilities to exploit and yet, for the majority of Western developers, the predominant choice seems to be in pursuit of a photo-realistic image (see, for example, Moore in this same volume). As explored later, such demands often place undue emphasis on the *appearance* of the image over and above its ability to enable play. It is under such conditions that the success of the image seems often to be determined more by its ability to provide for the player an approximation of a photographic image, rather than its ability to provide the visual cues necessary for the player to construct a coherent space within which to play. In contrast, by adopting a non-photorealistic visual style, TF2 avoids such double-scrutiny, enabling the design of the image to be driven by the demands of the game operating as a constant reinforcement as to the possibilities of play[1].

In recognition of their technical and artistic achievements, the rendering techniques developed by Valve have already been well documented, noting the illustrative style as heavily influenced by the commercial paintings of early to mid-twentieth century American illustrators J. C. Leyendecker, Dean Cornwell, and Norman Rockwell (Mitchell, Francke, and Eng 2007; Mitchell 2008). Such material provides keen insight from the perspective of the developers as does the developers' commentary available within the game and underpins the formation of the wider discussion here. As such, this chapter begins by tracing a particular history of animation practice through the comic strip and caricature. Returning to games, by separating the screen space into three distinct yet interrelated parts—the heads-up display, the contested space of the game environment, and the animated space of the player-characters—the proceeding sections provide an account as to how the non-photorealistic style adopted by TF2 exploits the visual economies and pictorial effects associated with animation practices in order to best serve the demands of a team-oriented, class-based, multiplayer FPS game.

Amplification Through Simplification

Art historian Ernst Gombrich, in his seminal study of the developments in representational art, recognizes the demands placed on artists to continually evolve their pictorial image-making techniques through what Gombrich refers to as "the gradual modification of the traditional schematic conventions of image making" (2002, xi). For Gombrich, this is a process of trial and error, of "lumbering advance and subsequent simplification"; a process most noticeable when considering the canon of work by a single artist where initial reliance on "heavy technique" is later replaced by "sublime simplification" (2002, 280). To give an example, Gombrich compares the gold braid detailing in two portraits by Dutch artist Rembrandt of twenty years apart: "he had to learn to build up the image of sparkling gold braid in all its detail before he could find out how much could be omitted for the beholder ready to meet him halfway" (2002, 280). Important here is the role the viewer plays in deciphering the visual information or, as is here, the affective qualities of the pictorial effects. The success of an image is one defined by both artist and viewer as, for Gombrich, it is the viewer's expectations that condition his or her perceptions and understanding of an image (2002, 210–11). The viewer interprets the singular brush-stroke as gold braid in

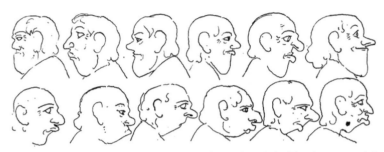

Figure 2.1 Extract from Rodolphe Töpffer's "Essai de Physiognomonie" (Schmid 1845).

Rembrandt's later simplification not because the brush-stroke would in isolation resemble the detailing itself; rather the brush-stroke within the context of the painting is enough of an indication to conjure up the idea of gold braiding sewn into a cloak draped over the shoulder of the man represented in the portrait. It is the context of the image that provides the means for the viewer to ascertain the function of the brush-strokes themselves.

Rembrandt's visual shorthand developed through a process of experimentation with pictorial effects, eliminating the unnecessary so that only the necessary remains. Gombrich provides an account of how such experimental tendencies enabled comic-strip inventor Rodolphe Töpffer to develop his image-making technique through systematic alteration of the arrangement of forms in his line or contour drawings (2002, 287–8). Töpffer's selective style suited the technological advancements in the printing press of the time and the graphical styles made accessible through the developments in lithographic reproduction (Gombrich 2002, 284). Similarly, art historian Edward Lucie-Smith suggests that all caricatures, including strip cartoons, can be categorized as having one thing in common— they were all designed for print; "[c]aricature is generally two things – popular and public – and it is print which enables it to be both" (1981, 13). Increased demands for the printed press and associated demands for the printed image shaped the very nature of the caricature both in terms of its subject-matter and associated graphical techniques (Lucie-Smith 1981, 14).

Comic-book artist Scott McCloud refers to this process as "amplification through simplification" in that "[w]hen we abstract an image through cartooning, we're not so much eliminating details as we are focusing on specific details" (McCloud 1994, 30, emphasis removed). Drawing from semiotics, McCloud defines a scale of "iconic abstraction" where the iconicity of the image (images that bear at least some resemblance to their referent) can be defined in *relative* terms to each other, with greater or lesser degrees of abstraction (1994, 46). In a similar vein, recognizing the opposing tendencies in animation and live-action production practices, Maureen Furniss conceives of a "mimesis/abstraction continuum" upon which all "motion picture production" can be mapped:

> In constructing this continuum, it is probably best to use more neutral terms than 'animation' or 'live-action' to constitute the ends of the spectrum. Although the terms 'mimesis' and 'abstraction' are not ideal, they are useful in suggesting opposing tendencies under which animation and live-action imagery can be juxtaposed. The term 'mimesis' represents a desire to reproduce natural reality (more like live-action work) while the term 'abstraction' describes the use of pure form – a suggestion of a concept rather than an attempt to explicate it in real life terms (more like animation). (Furniss 1998, 5)

Parallels can be drawn between Furniss's "suggestion of concept" and McCloud's notion of "iconic abstraction" in that both have a tendency to oppose the desire to reproduce the appearance of reality. Crucially, early developments in animated form borrowed much from the physical humor and visual pun associated with the comic strip and the vaudevillian performances of the time (Wells 1998, 17–20; 131–2). For the vaudevillian performer, the need to quickly establish with the audience a character with personality in terms of status and identity formed just as much an integral part of the vaudevillian routine as for, through its derivation, the seven-minute cartoon. Under such demands for immediacy and clarity, stereotype, caricature and its associated level of visual shorthand played a central role in the development of both form and content of the animated cartoon. As such, the graphic conventions and associated physical humor came to define the "golden era" of the cartoon from the 1920s to the 1950s; a style that, according to Paul

Wells, "prioritizes 'the visual,' illustrates the *exploitation* of the form, and determines the schemata which underpins an audience's *expectation* of the cartoon." (1998, 135, original emphasis). Such expectation is driven by both the visual qualities of the image and the kinetic sense of the movements depicted. John Halas and Roger Manvell consider the role of the animator as not one driven by mimesis or a tendency to, as Furniss suggests, "reproduce natural reality" (1998, 5), but rather to exploit both the aesthetic principles of graphic distortion and the advantages gained by exaggerating the physical laws of motion:

> A cartoon's virtues lie in simplification, distortion and caricature. It distorts for its own purpose and affects both character and behavior. It observes the physical laws of nature only to defy them. It conforms wholly to naturalism at its peril, because it then invites comparison with something fit to be reproduced only by the live-action camera. As the animator draws away from naturalism the powers of his medium increase; there is nothing but the limits of his imagination and his technical resources to hold him back. (Halas and Manvell 1959, 68)

Furthermore, Halas and Manvell consider the technical and pragmatic reasons for animated cartoons to adopt a graphical, therefore selective, visual style. Less detailing minimized the potential to incur any unwanted deviations during the many processes (and therefore many hands) involved in production; "[e]xaggeration and associated simplification are therefore both aesthetically and functionally proper; they are vitally necessary to the medium" (1959, 64).

Here exaggeration, simplification, distortion, and caricature all form an integral part of the visual language of animation. Rather than attempt to reconcile the animated image with the kinesthetic sensibilities of live-action imagery, it is advantageous for the animator to establish the terms and conditions of their animated performances as plausible in their own, *graphical* terms. Paul Ward puts forward a similar consideration when discussing videogames, noting there is often a notable gap between the visual fidelity of the videogame image and the fidelity of the movement depicted. Ward suggests it is by adopting an animated or cartoonal visual style that such disconnect can often be avoided:

> [A]nimation can offer more compelling gameplay if certain rules (such as those of gravity and the solidity of objects) are obeyed up to a point even when characters are performing actions that seem unbelievable by real-world standards. A certain degree of 'plausibility' at one level helps to emphasize the pleasure of engaging in vicarious activities that go beyond the bounds of normal physical capability. [... T]he aim is not to achieve a zenith of naturalism, but a game in which movements and actions are plausible in their own terms. (Ward 2002, 126)

Games that attempt by computational means to provide for the player a photo-realistic image are in danger of having to maintain both the visual fidelity and kinetic sensibilities associated with live-action imagery—something cartoon animation explicitly avoids. In contrast, as we shall explore in more detail later, by appropriating the codes and conventions of cartoon animation, TF2 is able to avoid such discrepancy as the relationship between image and movement can be established in their own terms, or at least in terms of an animated cartoon. As such, the player's attention is much more likely to be concerned with achieving the objectives of the game rather than interrogating how photo-realistic or other the game appears to be.

Here we have traced a history of animation practice through the comic strip and the caricature, arriving at a potential benefit to games design. In order to support our analysis further, it will prove instructive to separate the screen into three distinct yet interrelated parts or layers of visual information. Taking each in turn will reveal how each element contributes to the overall visual design, one informed by the visual economies associated with animation and related practices, in an attempt to identify how such information has been designed to best serve the objectives of the game.

Screen Space

In multiplayer shooting games such as TF2, the player's attention is predominantly focused on assessing what the other players are doing through observing the other players' game characters. Understandably, therefore, the majority of the screen is dedicated to providing a view of the game environment populated by the other players' characters. As a first-person shooter, this viewpoint is drawn from the first-person perspective of the player's own character. As TF2 is a multiplayer, arena-based FPS, the structural form of the gamespace shares much in common with other arena-based shooters such as *Quake III Arena* (id Software 1999), *Unreal Tournament* (Epic Games 1999), and Valve's own *Half-Life* mod, *Counter-Strike* (Valve 2000). All these games share a common visual means of presenting the gamespace to the player—that of a monocular projection of the game environment from the perspective of the player's character. It is perhaps quite obvious why, in common parlance, this point-of-view is often referred to as a first-person 'camera', as Michael Nitsche suggests, "[b]y analogy, these viewpoints refer to the established domain of film cameras. In that way, ... the moving image infuses the virtual world with a perspective" (2008, 77). For a similar reading of the first-person perspective, see Welsh in this same volume. Filmic allusions aside, let us first consider an important aspect true to most FPS games—the on-screen information or heads-up display (HUD).

The point on the screen given most attention by the player is at its center. This is where the reticule resides, indicating the direction the wielded weapon is facing and, more importantly, is shooting. Around the edge of the screen, strategic information such as time remaining, state of objectives, health, ammo, in-game chat and a score-based feed (denoting certain achievements, successes/ failures, kill information etc.) are made readily available to the player at all times, arranged in such a way as to sit alongside the main focus of the player. The complimentary information contained in these read-outs raises player awareness of the dynamic conditions of play. However, not all on-screen artifacts have been rendered so unobtrusively, and deliberately so. The wielded weapon portrayed in the lower-right of the screen acts as a helpful visual indication of the current state of the weapon selected but also as a hindrance, as it occupies a large proportion of the screen. Although a stalwart for FPS games, the wielded weapon in TF2 serves as a complementary way for the designers to optimize the balance between character classes and weapons. For example, during reloading, the weapon object is animated in such a way as to occupy more of the screen space. As such, weapons of high damage (e.g. Scout's Scattergun or Soldier's Rocket Launcher) can be balanced in part by having lower ammo capacity or longer reload times, occupying more of the screen more frequently or for longer. Additional to the permanent elements surrounding the edge of the screen, more centrally placed information appears temporarily under certain play conditions. Pop-up boxes appear under the player's reticule when directed at a teammate denoting health remaining and player nametag, flames dance around the screen when your character is on fire, directional red damage indicators appear when hit from either the side or behind. These heads-up display artifacts, whilst obfuscating to a certain degree, keep the player constantly informed as to the unfolding of the gameplay, the centrality of their appearance denoting their priority.

Whereas it is possible to label the HUD as a mere distraction—antithetical to those who consider the first-person view in games as analogous to the point-of-view shot in film—instead we may

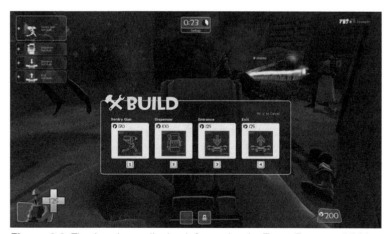

Figure 2.2 The heads-up display information in *Team Fortress 2* (Valve 2007).

consider the HUD as an appropriate and convenient means to convey certain information quickly. Lev Manovich adopts the term "image-interface" as a way to differentiate between computer images that provide an illusionistic image similar to that of cinema, and computer images that offer the user a means to interact with the computer via some kind of simulated control panel or Graphic User Interface (GUI) (2001, 16–17). Whereas cinematic form relies heavily upon generating the necessary depth cues on-screen in order to construct the illusion of three-dimensional space, a successful human-computer interface does not. Such consideration enables Manovich to place image-interfaces in opposition to the illusionistic tendencies inherent in film and are therefore less "a computer screen as window into illusionistic space" and more a "computer screen as flat control panel" (2001, 17). Where the HUD in TF2 has not been specifically designed to provide the same level of human-computer interaction as a GUI (as during gameplay there are no buttons to click or icons to drag), such comparison does draw attention to the efficient means by which it provides information for the player to act upon. Moreover, diagrammatic loadouts appearing on screen as prompts for the player to choose from the Engineer's building types or Spy's class disguises seem very much in keeping with the logic of GUI—less so the language of cinematic form.

The heads-up display information used in TF2 is an effective way to communicate strategic information quickly. However, as mentioned at the beginning of this section, the majority of the screen comprises of a perspectival rendering of the game environment. The next section addresses the screen as gamespace and by what means we conceive of the gamespace on-screen.

Gamespace/The Playing Field

According to Espen Aarseth, "[t]he defining element in computer games is spatiality. Computer games are essentially concerned with spatial representation and negotiation" (2001, 154). For Aarseth, gamespaces are allegories of real space in that they are "figurative comments on the ultimate impossibility of representing real space." (2001, 169). Furthermore, it is their status as allegory—as symbolic representation—that enables play. On the contrary, if they were real spaces—or at least indistinguishable from our experiences of the real—then they would not evoke the necessary ludic response in order to make them playable. As Aarseth suggests,

> [S]patial representation in computer games [is] a reductive operation leading to a representation of space that is not in itself spatial, but symbolic and rule-based. The nature of space is not revealed in this operation, and the resulting product, while fabricating a spatial representation, in fact uses the reductions as a means to achieve the object of gameplay, since the difference between the spatial representation and real space is what makes gameplay by automatic rules possible. In real space, there would be no automatic rules, only social rules and physical laws. (Aarseth 2001, 163)

Let us consider the miniature model landscapes or playing fields used in tabletop war-games. The symbolic function of a tabletop battlefield is two-fold: to serve the purpose of clearly denoting a surface with boundaries (e.g. the edges of the table), and to differentiate between the elements within the gamespace that are significant in terms of their impact on the rules of the game (e.g. the denotation of topological detailing such as forests, hills, rivers, buildings, etc.). It seems, under such conditions, the appearance of these demarcations need be no more real to life than distinct from each other. Whether the miniature forest comprises of numerous miniature trees or not should have no effect on the rules of the game. Such concerns are perhaps more for the model-maker than they are for the game-player[2]. Moreover, such inclusion of detail may well impede upon gameplay, as the physicality of each tree may interfere with the necessary repositioning of the playing pieces or miniature figures. As such, a cut-out piece of painted cardboard may suffice and perform just as well in that the edges of the forest are clearly defined and its surface as distinct from the table. Likewise, hills are less likely to be sculptural organic forms—a far more practical solution would be to stack a series of wooden flats together to form steps upon which the troops can remain standing.

In a similar way to the tabletop battlefield, virtual or computer gamespaces are symbolic and rule-based. However, unlike the tabletop, computer gamespaces comprise of nothing more than a set of geometric data processed via algebraic computation as rendered on-screen. In order to be conceived of as spatial information, the algorithms used during these calculations are based upon the mathematical concept of perspective—a conceptual spatial framework used to calculate the representation of three-dimensional space on a two-dimensional plane. Such a process, although generated by computational means, derives from the Western tradition of illusionistic image-making practices. As Manovich suggests, "the Cartesian coordinate system is built into computer graphics software and often into the hardware itself" (2001, 254). By adhering to such rules of perspectival projection, the images on-screen enable the player to conceive of the game space irrespective of its status as virtual or real. For Manovich, it is *perspective* that "establishes the precise and reciprocal relationship between objects and their signs" (2001, 167–8). For Aarseth, "[virtual spaces] and other such phenomena (e.g. computer games) are constituted of signs and are therefore already dependent on our bodily experience in, and of, real space to be 'hallucinated' as space" (2001, 162). Aarseth borrows the term "hallucinated" from William Gibson's definition of cyberspace; "[h] is 'space' is 'consensually hallucinated,' not real (a 'nonspace of the mind') but effective and dominant" (Aarseth 2001, 153). The perspectival information embedded in the image provides adequate means for the player to conceive of the image as a spatial representation and therefore conceived of as space.

Our conception of the gamespace is made possible by deference to a pervasive spatial framework and its associated modes of representation. The rendering algorithms used to generate the gamespace on the screen include projections in perspective that present a consistency irrespective of from where within the space they are viewed. In TF2, the function of the gamespace is to relay distance cues to the player in order for them to formulate future-oriented activity—the logic of the gamer's gaze. These perceptual cues are the means necessary for the player to locate their view, and hence locate their character, within the gamespace. Furthermore, they enable the player to discern the location of the other players, again feeding the future-orientation of play. In a similar way to the symbolic

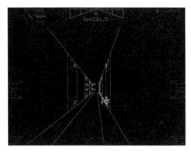 

Figures 2.3 & 2.4 Wireframe projections construct a sense of three-dimensional space (Atari 1983).

demarcations of a tabletop battlefield, the function of a virtual gamespace is not to appear real, but rather as a means to provide a consistent experience of a cogent space in which to do battle.

As with the vector displays used in the original arcade cabinets of *BattleZone* (Atari 1980) and *Star Wars* (Atari 1983), the success of the image is one less concerned with the *what* that is presented, rather the *how* it performs within the context of play. In both cases, the perspectival projection rendered to screen provides a visual means for the player to establish spatial relations between the objects within the gamespace. Returning to TF2 as we shall go on to discover, by choosing to render the game environment in an illustrative style derived from early twentieth-century American illustrators, the designers are able to further prioritize certain gameplay goals.

In TF2 the opposing teams are denoted by either the color red or blue. As many of the game modes center round the occupation of territory, being able to ascertain which direction you need to be travelling in is a significant part of the game. As such, the architectural elements and color palettes of each team's base have been specifically tailored to help orient the player—the red team has a more rustic design with warmer hues and angular geometry, while the blue team is much more industrial with cooler shades and orthogonal forms. Mutually beneficial environmental elements such as health and ammo pickups are indicated by increased levels of saturation and environmental hazards are signified by the color yellow. Such stylistic determinates are used throughout the environmental design

Figure 2.5 The distinctive visual style denoting the red team's base helps orient the player at all times (Valve 2007).

in order to emphasize the key features of the game. In keeping with the illustrative style, each texture map maintains a painterly quality taking reference from the background plates used in cel animation production, most notably the work of anime film director and animator Hayao Miyazaki (Mitchell, Francke, and Eng 2007). As Mitchell, Francke and Eng (2007) outline, "[n]ot only does this hand-painted source material create an illustrative [non-photorealistic] style in rendered images, but we have found that these abstract texture designs hold up under magnification better than textures created from photo reference due to their more intentional design and lack of photo artifacts."

Here we have a combination of a monocular projection depicting a painterly space taking on the appearance of a background plate used in cel animation production. As such, the environmental design contains similar visual traits to those found in animation. The next section explores this codification in relation to the player-characters where the visual and kinetic design further appropriates the language of animation. By tracing a history of animation practice through comic strip and the caricature, we can see how TF2 exploits the visual and kinetic qualities found in animation to best effect.

Animated Space/The Playing Pieces

As with many games, TF2 uses a combination of scripted (keyframe) and procedural (generated) animation techniques to bestow movement into the characters of the game. Whereas other games seek to blend the keyframed with the simulated in order to achieve a "zenith of naturalism" (Ward 2001, 126)—the use of NaturalMotion's Euphoria engine in *Grand Theft Auto IV* (Rockstar North 2008) can be considered a notable example of such a technique—TF2 instead appropriates the visual conventions and kinesthetic sensibilities of animated cartoons in order to create movements that are "plausible in their own terms" (Ward 2002, 126). Moreover, as I will go on to discuss, it is advantageous for the player of TF2 to be able to distinguish between movements that are simulated and movements that are animated.

Following the analogy of the tabletop battlefield, we can consider the player-characters and all their associated keyframed animation as separate from the gamespace in much the same way as the playing pieces are separate from the battlefield or tabletop. In order to be playable, the playing pieces need only be distinct from each other in terms of their associated rules—similar classes or troops can, for all functional purposes, look identical. By considering how the movements in-game are generated, two distinct layers of movement are apparent. First, continuing the tabletop analogy, the game characters are no more than playing pieces moved around the board in accordance with the rules of the game. However, as with most videogames, TF2 is a dynamic, run-time experience, so rather than being physically moved by hand, these playing pieces are repositioned in accordance with the run-time calculations performed by the game system as it processes the commands given via player input and the demands of the physics simulation. This is one level of game movement and it is here that the consequences of the game's simulation manifest.

Second, on the level of the keyframed animation, the game characters' movements are determined by scripted animation routines where each routine can be played out in full, in part, or blended with other routines to create hybrid performances[3]. Here the movements are limited to those routines already defined and stored in the animation data for each character or in combination. As the players move their characters around, suitable animation routines are called forth in order to signify their actions to other players. However, although the characters move in a convincing manner while under direct control of the players, when forced sideways by a nearby explosion and the physics engine takes over control, the characters are merely displaced in accordance to the physics calculation and do not perform a reaction in keeping with their characterization, failing to display the same qualities of movement as those defined in the scripted routines. The scripted animation may well offer up numerous permutations of action but not, as it seems, of re-action. Indeed, blast a rocket at the feet of a character who is momentarily stationary and watch as they get knocked back as though hit by considerable force yet, at the same time, fail to react as an animated character as they remain locked in their current state or pose. No direct player input, no animation routine called forth. On the level of keyframed animation, the player-characters do not react to the forces generated by the physics simulation other than being simply displaced as though, when not also under the duress of player input, they are nothing more than just painted figurines. As such, there is an obvious distinction between the movements performed as a consequence of player input—movement as written on the characters themselves—and the displacement performed by the physics simulation. Significantly, it is only when the player-character is killed that the physics engine takes over full control of the character's bodily movements as it either gibs or rag-dolls. In all cases, such clear distinctions between movement types enable the discerning player to gain tactical advantage over the other players while seeking the potential opportunities for future action.

The gamespace operates on the level of presenting the player with a visual representation of a 3D environment—a 3D environment that, through its status as representation, enables play. The player is able to ascertain vital spatial information by responding to the consistent set of visual cues as rendered on-screen. Furthermore, the gamespace is where the simulation takes place. It is here that the physics engine calculates the collisions between each object as a consequence of player-game interaction.

The animated space—the space of the player-characters—is

Figure 2.6 During the heat of battle, visual economies help focus the player's attention (Valve 2007).

distinct from the gamespace in both visual and procedural terms. The physics engine knows only of the collision boxes denoting the location of each player-character. As the physics engine responds to the dynamics of play, the position of each object is calculated in accordance with the rules of the game. For the player, however, each player-character acts as significantly more than just an object on a board. As each animation sequence denotes a particular player action, each sequence can be learnt in order to inform future activity. Assessing when characters are or will be doing what—for example, reloading or in the midst of a jump—coupled with knowing how long each animation routine takes, can seriously affect the outcome of each encounter. This in itself is not necessarily unique to TF2, however it is the means by which this information has been intentionally designed that significantly impacts on the player's ability to read such cues effectively.

As previously noted, the overall visual style of TF2 has been heavily influenced by early twentieth-century illustrators, most notably the distinctive style of Joseph Christian Leyendecker (Francke 2007). Studying in Paris, Leyendecker drew inspiration from the popular poster artists of the time, Henri de Toulouse-Lautrec and Alphonse Mucha (Cutler and Cutler 2008, 29). As such, "The Leyendecker Look" evolved into a bold, graphic style with distinct shapes, "strong iconic images, wide brushstrokes with Impressionistic influences" (Cutler and Cutler 2008, 243). Leyendecker's visual style became synonymous with the art of advertising during the commercial boom in America during the 1920s, and he was noted for his ability to convey a single idea in a simple manner through his idealized depictions of the human form (Cutler and Cutler 2008, 71–3). As already mentioned, in multiplayer games such as TF2, the player's attention is predominantly focused on assessing what the other players are doing. Furthermore, in a class-based encounter, it is essential that the player is able to quickly recognize the potential threat level associated with each player-character. As such, the designers of TF2 developed a "read hierarchy" as a means to prioritize what information the player needs to know about the other player-characters—friend or foe (red or blue), class type, and finally, which weapon is wielded (Diaz 2007). By appropriating the visual conventions identified in "The Leyendecker Look," each character remains identifiable through unique silhouette information, textured in such a way as to create high contrast around the chest area where the weapon is situated (Diaz 2007).

TF2 employs a unique combination of view-independent and view-dependent lighting techniques effectively creating a rim highlight around each player-character unique to each player's point-of-view (Mitchell, Francke, and Eng 2007). This not only emphasizes the character's shape in order for the player to quickly ascertain vital class and weapon information, but also acts as a reminder that the game characters are separate from the game environment. Such distinction is as apparent here as it is in 2D animations produced using cel animation techniques. Here the codes and conventions of animated cartoons enable the player to accept the visual distinction as appropriate to its stylistic reference. Further, it negates the need to blend movement types together in order to maintain a coherent and consistent game experience. More importantly, the savvy player can gain a considerable tactical advantage by familiarizing him- or herself with the apparent discrepancies in movement in order to ascertain the future possible actions of the other players.

Conclusion

The gamescreen is part of the means by which players form a dialogue with the game. The information that appears on the screen becomes an integral part of play. In multiplayer games like TF2, most of the content is generated by the other players. Therefore, players seeking future possibilities need to be able to discern the actions of others.

Gamespaces are allegorical: their status as representational (in that they are not real) enables play. The TF2 gamespace is coded as cartoon animation. Visual complexity is pared down through a process of iconic abstraction where less information equals less confusion equals less noise. The clarity and immediacy of the visual presentation combined with the deliberate separation of character from background, focuses the player's attention on the task in hand—assessing the potential actions of the other players through observing the movements of the other player-characters. It is advantageous for players to be able to distinguish between the movements generated by the physics simulation and the movements performed as a direct consequence of the other players' input. Often it is the ability of the players to react to these visual cues that determines the outcome of battle.

The screen as information-image, its status as intermediate between player and game, the stylistic qualities encoded therein and the associated logic of cartoon animation, all function towards best serving the future orientation of the gamer's gaze. In games like TF2, the immediacy of the caricature operates as a potent call to action, a substantial invitation to play.

Notes

1 Of course this assumes that the player is first seeking to engage *in* playing by the rules of the game rather than to define an alternative style of play *with* the game itself. See Snider et al. in this same volume for such an account.

2 It is recognized that part of the appeal of miniature gaming may be due to the opportunity for participants to act as both model-maker and game-player. The inherent physical nature of the game enables participants to fashion the appearance of the playing pieces in accordance with the demands of the game and/or historical evidence ("History of Wargaming" 2008).

3   Although discussing the technology used in an earlier, unreleased iteration of TF2, designer Robin Walker outlines the benefits of being able to blend together a number of keyframed animations in a process referred to as "Parametric Animation" (Yahoo! Games n.d.).

References

Aarseth, Espen. 2001. "Allegories of Space: The Question of Spatiality in Computer Games." In *CyberText Yearbook 2000*, edited by Markku Eskelinen and Raine Koskimaa, 152–71. http://cybertext.hum.jyu.fi/articles/129.pdf

Atkins, Barry. 2006. "What Are We Really Looking At? The Future-Orientation of Video Game Play." *Games and Culture* 1 (2): 127–40. doi: 10.1177/1555412006286687.

Cutler, Laurence S., and Judy Goffman Cutler. 2008. *J. C. Leyendecker: American Imagist*. New York: Abrams.

Diaz, Ariel. 2007. "Well Developer Commentary – Team Fortress Wiki." Transcript of developer's in-game commentary. http://wiki.teamfortress.com/wiki/Well_developer_commentary

Francke, Moby. 2007. "Hydro Developer Commentary – Team Fortress Wiki." Transcript of developer's in-game commentary. http://wiki.teamfortress.com/wiki/Hydro_developer_commentary

Furniss, Maureen. 1998. *Art in Motion: Animation Aesthetics*. Sydney: John Libbey.

Gombrich, E. H. 2002. *Art and Illusion: A Study in the Psychology of Pictorial Representation*. 6th ed. New York: Phaidon Press.

Halas, John, and Roger Manvell. 1959. *The Techniques of Film Animation*. London: Focal Press.

"History of Wargaming." 2008. Accessed 22 May 2011. http://www.hmgs.org/history.htm

Lucie-Smith, Edward. 1981. *The Art of Caricature*. London: Orbis Publishing.

Manovich, Lev. 2001. *The Language of New Media*. Cambridge, MA: MIT Press.

McCloud, Scott. 1994. *Understanding Comics: The Invisible Art*. New York: HarperPerennial.

Mitchell, Jason, Moby Francke, and Dhabih Eng. 2007. "Illustrative Rendering in Team Fortress 2." Paper presented at NPAR 2007:

5th International Symposium on Non-Photorealistic Animation and Rendering, San Diego, August 2007. http://www.valvesoftware.com/publications/2007/NPAR07_IllustrativeRenderingInTeamFortress2.pdf
——2008. "Stylization with a Purpose: The Illustrative World of Team Fortress 2." Slides presented at Game Developer's Conference, San Francisco, February 2008. http://www.valvesoftware.com/publications/2008/GDC2008_StylizationWithAPurpose_TF2.pdf
Nitsche, Michael. 2008. *Video Game Spaces: Image, Play, and Structure in 3D Worlds*. Cambridge, MA: MIT Press.
PlanetFortress. "The TFC Survival Guide: Introduction." Accessed 15 May 2011. http://www.planetfortress.com/tfc/guide/introduction.shtml
Töpffer, Rodolphe. 1845. *Essai de Physiognomonie*. Genève: Schmid.
Ward, Paul. 2002. "Videogames as Remediated Animation." In *Screenplay: Cinema/Videogames/Interfaces*, edited by Geoff King and Tanya Krzywinska, 122–35. London: Wallflower.
Wells, Paul. 1998. *Understanding Animation*. London: Routledge.
Wicklund, Andrea. 2007. "Hydro Developer Commentary – Team Fortress Wiki." Transcript of developer's in-game commentary. http://wiki.teamfortress.com/wiki/Hydro_developer_commentary
Yahoo! Games. "Team Fortress 2: Brotherhood of Arms." Accessed 10 May 2011. http://uk.videogames.games.yahoo.com/pc/previews/team-fortress-2--brotherhood-of-arms-d88b8f.html

Games

Atari, Inc. 1980. *BattleZone* [arcade]. Atari Corporation.
——1983. *Star Wars* [arcade]. Atari Corporation.
Epic Games.1999. *Unreal Tournament* [Microsoft Windows]. GT Interactiv.
id Software. 1996. *Quake* [Microsoft Windows]. GT Interactive.
——1999. *Quake III Arena* [Microsoft Windows]. Activision.
Rockstar North. 2008. *Grand Theft Auto IV* [Microsoft Windows, PlayStation 3, Xbox 360]. Take-Two Interactive.
Valve. 1998. *Half-Life* [Microsoft Windows]. Valve.
——2000. *Counter-Strike* [Microsoft Windows]. Valve.
——2007. *Team Fortress 2* [Microsoft Windows, PlayStation 3, Xbox 360]. Valve.

3

I Am a Gun: The Avatar and Avatarness in the FPS

Victor Navarro

Player *embodiment* is one of the most studied elements in game research. The player has a series of tools to interact with the game: they act as her embodiment within the gameworld and usually coincide with (but are not limited to) the *avatar*. A detailed definition of what the avatar is, its relation with the player, and its functions can be elaborated through existing literature. The avatar has a dual role as a set of mechanics and a protagonist character, thus providing *dual embodiment* that results in a relation of *identification*. In the first part of this chapter, I analyze the general nature of the avatar.

The study of the avatar may give the impression that embodiment is a binary state, either present or absent. I suggest that embodiment can be constructed via several design choices that can be of more or less importance: identification, then, would be not a binary state but a degree. For this I propose the term "*avatarness*" and present, in the second part of this chapter, a list of traits of the controllable object that can be used to describe its degree and type of avatarness. This allows me to take a closer look at the avatar in FPS. As a genre, FPS is defined by a visual point-of-view (first-person) and a main mechanic (shooting). The point-of-view affects embodiment in a specific manner that I examine in five key aspects: *navigation, interaction, self-perception, sensorial perception*, and *heads-up display* (hereafter *HUD*). The genre determines certain design choices and mechanics. Considering this, I propose a description of the *FPS avatar* and the possibilities of its avatarness.

The Avatar within the Game

A videogame is a set of rules, mechanics, goals, and penalties. Brian Sutton-Smith defines it as "an exercise of voluntary control systems in which there is an opposition between forces" (1971, 7). As technologically remediated games, videogames can have highly detailed *gameworlds* inhabited by objects that take part in that "opposition." These two layers are what Linderoth (2002) calls *system* and *guise*: the rule-based system of the game and the visible gameworld, narrative and characters overlaid on it, respectively. In an ideal design, they help and sustain each other. Narrative, for example, can provide information about the gameplay and the ruleset and act as a breathing space or a reward.

Guise is not binary but, as Jason Rhody explains, consists of the "degrees to which different genres of games use fictional *devices* as native elements of the game to enable the player's engagement in meaningful play" (2005, 3). Rhody calls this "game fiction."

In their paper "Heavy Hero or Digital Dummy," Burn and Schott equate this complementary duality with *offer* and *demand* structures: "The game is not only offering a narrative statement but telling the player to do something" (2005, 216). The avatar, then, is part of a complex structure that demands action from the player and offers her a fiction. Not just a regular part, but often a pivotal part of it; even, as in some FPS, when it cannot be seen.

Embodiment, Objects, and Subjects

The player needs to be given some kind of embodiment that can modify the gameworld. This can be a virtual body or just a set of means to interact with the game. In his text "The Myth of the Ergodic Videogame," James Newman (2002) affirms "the player encounters the game by relating to everything within the gameworld simultaneously." For Newman, controllable subjects are no more than a set of tools. While this can be a simplification, it is true that in a functional sense the player is embodied by the game *mechanics* (actions allowed and prearranged by the rules). In FPS, as I will explain later, the player is mainly embodied by the shooting mechanic and the point-of-view.

As Kristine Jörgensen says, "players tend to accept all features that aid them in understanding how to play the game" (2009, 1). Arranging these mechanics around a *controllable object* can be of help when presenting them to the player. These controllable objects can go from elements of the interface (the mouse cursor, for instance, in point-and-click adventures or strategy games) to highly detailed fictional characters. Here, I would like to make a distinction between objects and subjects:

- *Objects* are entities that inhabit the gameworld. They exist as part of its fiction and system. They feature at least attributes, and possibly abilities, that the player manages, modifies, or interacts with at some level. That is, an object has functional traits. Examples of objects would be abstract pieces in a puzzle, items, or power-ups.

- *Subjects* are objects with an extra fictional layer made of signs of intelligence, personality and will. This is what traditional narrative scholars call *characters*. As Rune Klevjer explains, a character is "a general category that applies equally to novels or films as well as to drama or computer games;" he describes it as "an independent subject, someone who can act [...] some sort of animated being with goals and intentions" (2006, 116). I prefer to use the term "subject" in videogames because a character can appear

Figure 3.1 Gabriel, the controllable subject in *Castlevania: Lords of Shadow* (Mercury Steam 2010)

separated from the system (for instance, in cutscenes) and have none of the object attributes. Subjects, then, have functional and fictional traits.

Controllable objects, according to Linderoth (2005), can act as *roles* for social interaction, *tools* for handling the game states, an extension of player agency and *props* for the presentation of self in the social arena surrounding the game. Some of these uses are often attributed to avatars, but by linking them to controllable objects (a more manageable concept) we are starting to overcome the binary model of what the avatar is and is not.

Embodiment, then, is the result of a complex design that allows the player to relate "to everything in the gameworld simultaneously" while providing her with markers in the form of controllable objects. As Jason Rhody affirms, "videogame play requires the negotiation of multiple synchronic points-of-view enabled through the use of cameras, avatars, interfaces, and vignettes" (1).

What is, then, the avatar, and where does it fit in this complex design?

Avatar and Dual Embodiment

The avatar, as we know it now, is a subject that embodies the player within both system and guise: not only does it feature functional and fictional traits, but also shares its fictional point-of-view and goals with the player.

Burn and Schott affirm that "the avatar is a two-part structure, partly designed in conventional narrative terms as a protagonist of popular narrative, and partly as a vehicle for interactive game-play" (abstract). The two sides of the videogame help each other also in the case of the avatar, as Burn and Schott add, "producing a sense of dynamic play and of involvement with a fictional character." (In this volume, Call writes about mechanics and how players can upgrade them by constructing their avatars; function and fiction are built in parallel in games like *Deus Ex*.)

Janet Murray (1997) compares game characters with Homeric heroes, in that they are formulaic vehicles for the poet to construct upon, the same way the player uses the avatar as a vehicle to affect the gameworld. This shows a strong identification that can be called *dual embodiment*: the avatar provides both functional and *fictional agency*.

What is this fictional agency? As Rune Klevjer (2006) sustains, for a subject to be an avatar it also has to establish the "framing" of the fictional world for the player. Klevjer uses the example of the paddle in *Breakout* (Atari 1976); it embodies the mechanics available to the player, but does not allow her to act as an agent of the narrative of the game. Klevjer writes:

> The avatar is not a cursor or a mere instrument, but gives the player a meaningful embodied presence and agency. [It] is not just significant because of what it can do, but because of what happens to it. […] Through the avatar, instrumental agency is replaced with fictional agency and fictional destiny; the player is incarnated as a fictional body-subject who belongs to and is exposed to the environment that it inhabits. (2006, 130)

Just being player-controlled does not turn a subject into an avatar: the controllable subject and the player have to share the same narrative point-of-view, that is, experience the events in the same way. The player and her avatar have to endure the same events together, have the same goals and abide by the same rules. If the fiction requires the avatar to act in some way, the game rules should require the player to act in the same way.

The avatar is the player's body within the system and the guise of the game. As Jörgensen explains, this body "must be a functional extension of the player into that gameworld both emotionally and by allowing the player direct action into it; and there must be a real-time and continuous relationship between the player and the avatar" (2009, 2).

Narrative point-of-view is not to be confused with camera or visual point-of-view. The first one would be comparable to the narrator in traditional narrative and it defines, among other things, where in the narrative is the player or what information do her and her avatar share. The second one is the visual solution chosen to show the action.

Bob Rehak investigates player-avatar relationships by combining the roles of camera (visual point-of-view), narrative, and avatar. He talks about the "intent" behind their use, which for him is "to produce a sense of diegetic embodiment" (2003, 110).

Laurie N. Taylor explains this diegetic embodiment: "I will define it here as diegetic immersion, where the player is immersed in the act of playing the videogame, and as intra-diegetic or situated immersion, where the player is immersed in playing the game and in the experience of the game space as a spatial and narrated space" (2002, 12). Fictional embodiment should provide this intra-diegetic engagement.

So, these are pretty strict requirements. By these standards, most of the controllable subjects in videogames would not be avatars. But here is where the notion of avatarness can be of help, since, as Rhody says, "the player's view of the screen, the avatar's role in a story, and the difference between third and first-person cameras each provide a unique and separate point-of-view into the game world" (2005, 2). There is not just one type of avatar; not all of them have to share the same traits and do it with the same prominence. Each controllable subject can have its own avatarness.

Avatarness

Some videogames, like *Metal Gear Solid 3: Snake Eater* (Konami CEJ/ Kojima Productions 2004), may change the narrative point-of-view during their vignettes (cutscenes, texts, dialogs …). *Castlevania: Lords of Shadow* (Mercury Steam 2010) features a narrator other than the main character, Gabriel, with whom she shares the narrative point-of-view. Other games, such as *Eternal Darkness* (Silicon Knights 2002), feature multiple controllable subjects. There are even games where the player controls more than one character at once, like *Kirby: Mass Attack* (HAL Laboratory 2011). According to the definition of avatar shown before, these controllable subjects would not be one. But are they?

The aforementioned subjects provide functional agency as well as some kind of fictional agency, even if it is not continuous or complete. James Newman (2002) talks about "online" and "offline" states of controllable subjects: when the player has control over them and when they act in an autonomous fashion, respectively. He links the online state with system and the offline with guise. While I do not agree completely (these two sides are complementary and inform each other continually), it shows that the relation between player and subject is a variable one, and that identification can be a stream rather than an absolute and constant bond.

Kristine Jörgensen conducted an experiment about player-subject relationship with several games from different genres: *Crysis* (Crytek 2007) (FPS), *Command and Conquer 3: Tiberium Wars* (EA 2007) (Real-Time Strategy), *Diablo 2* (Blizzard 2000) (Role Playing Game), and *The Sims* (Maxis 2000) (simulation/strategy). In all games, she says, "the player takes on a role. However, this is not to say that they take on the role of a character. A character needs characterization or a degree of personality, but a role is a social function and behavior associated with it" (2009, 7). She analyses the effect of not seeing the subject in *Crysis* and sharing the visual point-of-view with it (some respondents of the experiment easily assume its role but have problems when the subject shows characterization, as in when it speaks) or the use of a cursor as an intermediary between player and subject: "Two respondents compare *Diablo 2* to puppet theatre […] Positioning the mouse cursor as the main access point in the game implies a closer relationship between player and cursor than between player and figure." For her, then, "all player actions therefore are one step removed from gameworld."

In *Command and Conquer 3*, she notes, the game "addresses the players even though they have no avatar or representation in the gameworld." Steven Poole (2000) also writes about Real-Time Strategy games in "Trigger Happy," stating that "there is no continuous, real-time, emotional relationship between player and units." The Sims (the subjects in the homonym game), according to Jörgensen (2009, 6), "are even more autonomous" and have "clear intentions that they will pursuit [sic] even without the player's help." She explains that some players used the Sims as assets while other tried to create a virtual version of themselves and project narratives on them.

Some videogames have a main, controllable subject. Some of these, as in FPS, may be relatively invisible to the player. Some other games may present different controllable subjects with fictional traits. Others may have subjects and objects just as tools, and most of them will ask the player to assume a role. Certain elements of fiction (and thus different types of fictional agency) may be present, resulting in different degrees and types of identification. This is what I call avatarness.

I propose not a measurable scale with a mathematical formula, but a list of characteristics that constitute the dual embodiment offered to the player. I want to make clear that, while some controllable subjects may present a higher degree of avatarness than others, some may just make use of different devices and therefore offer a different kind of experience. Moreover, some types of avatarness may be expected from certain genres (as in non-talking subjects in FPS) but that does not mean that specific games in those genres cannot differ. The next characteristics, then, should be considered general guidelines to study each case separately. These are the eight main aspects of avatarness:

● *Controllable subjects.* The subject, or subjects, the player controls in a direct fashion. The ones she can control indirectly may add to the avatarness in some cases. Other games may put the player in control of a party, or make her swap controllable subjects mid-game, as in the aforementioned *Eternal Darkness* or *Metal Gear Solid 2: Sons of Liberty* (KCEJ 2001).

● *Method of control.* The techniques used to send inputs from the player to the controllable subject. Does she have direct control via a controller or a keyboard or does she have to give instructions using a mouse cursor, menus, or a set of verbs?

● *Addressing the player.* Videogames need to provide instructions to the player about the system. Some games do it indirectly by having some non-playable characters explain them to the controllable subject. Others address the player directly. Another option, as Jörgensen (2009, 6) explains with *Command and Conquer 3*, is to give the player a role within the game without using a subject. The RPG *Baten Kaitos* (tri-Crescendo 2003) has a controllable subject that speaks in a direct manner to the player, who is supposed to assume the role of a deity that guides it. In the experiment conducted

Figure 3.2 *Portal* (Valve 2007) uses a clever trick to show the subject using the main mechanic of the game.

by Jörgensen, "the respondents do not see the dual position of the player situated in the physical world while having the power to act within the gameworld as a paradox, but a necessary way of communication in games" (1). The way the game handles this communication may affect avatarness.

- *Visible bodily and facial features.* The type of visual depiction of the subject. In some games, like *Final Fantasy VII* (Square 1997), it can have more than one depending on the gaming space (cutscenes, general navigation, combats). Other games let the player take a closer look at the subject in interface elements such as menus. In FPS the subject is invisible to the player, and some games in the genre use audiovisual tricks to show it.

- *Control over the subject looks.* The controllable subject may have a fix design consistent throughout the whole game. It can change due to the use of modificators such as power-ups and items. It can as well be modified using aesthetic rewards with no functional purposes. Narrative in the game fiction may require this physical aspect to change. In some cases, the player may be given the choice to design her own controllable subject, as in *Mass Effect* (BioWare 2007). Character editors are a popular tool in games like *The Sims*, where some players try to create a virtual version of themselves.

- *Autonomy of the subject.* The capacity of the controllable subject to act on its own, be it simple idle animations (as in *Sonic the Hedgehog*) or complex behavior. In some cases, this is related to the online-offline states described by Newman, while in others, actions ordered by the player and autonomous actions may coincide (like in *Uncharted: Drake's Fortune*, [Naughty Dog 2007] where the controllable subject, Nate, speaks as the player plays). Expressive gestures (facial and bodily) are part of this autonomy, since the subject is portraying feelings and reactions without the player expressly ordering it.

- *Dialogue.* The ability of the subject to speak. *The Legend of Zelda* (Nintendo 1986–2011) games have the subject, Link, speak to other characters, but Link's sentences are always omitted. Most games let the subject speak for itself. Dialogue can become a mechanic when the player has a branching tree of responses to converse with other characters, as in *Mass Effect* or traditional graphic adventures like *The Secret of Monkey Island* (Lucasfilm Games 1992).

● *Interaction with other subjects.* A good way to show a character's traits is to make him interact with another one. The richer the interactions are, the stronger the feeling of intra-diegetic embodiment will be. The player will have a more intense sense of being in the gameworld and being able to interact with it if there are other subjects that respond to her actions in believable ways.

By analyzing and describing these aspects of any given game (and its controllable subject), a researcher will have a clearer idea of what kind of functional and fictional agency that game provides and can predict the level of identification the player will experience when playing it.

The First-Person Avatar

With this knowledge about the avatar and avatarness I can finally talk about controllable subject in first-person videogames. I will first analyze the main design aspects of the controllable subject in first-person perspective and their possible impact on avatarness: navigation, interaction, self-perception, sensorial perception, and HUD. Then, I will take into account the main characteristics of FPS to describe the avatarness possibilities in that genre.

As Rouse says, the chosen visual point-of-view will affect the genre possibilities of the game (1999, 9). However, they are not the same, and first-person view can be used in a wide array of genres such as shooters, adventures, or puzzles, e.g. *Portal* (Valve 2007). The nature of first-person view demands a controllable subject normally controlled directly by the player via a controller or a keyboard and a mouse (though certain adventures, such as *Myst* [Cyan 1993], combine point-and-click mechanics with this view) and not obligatorily visible to the player. These are the aspects of avatarness that show a closer link to the chosen perspective. But how are they linked?

Navigation

Navigation (that is, moving through the gameworld) could be considered the most basic and common game mechanic. Bernadette Flynn considers movement as "a defining feature of games" (2003, 1). In a sense, videogames are a spatial language: the gameworld has to be designed to reflect the virtual conflict, obstacles, rules, and goals of the game. Henry Jenkins talks about "narratively-impregnated *mise-en-scene*" (2002, 127). Lev Manovich (2002) says that space itself has become a media type. Flynn adds that games are based on "constructing an experience of shifting perspective and illusionism gained through the process of navigation" (2003, 2). By navigating, the player can explore and "read" the gameworld. Navigating requires a controllable object; as Flynn writes, "to experience geography of space requires a navigator" (2). The way the controllable object or subject allows navigation defines partially its avatarness.

The first videogames, like *PONG* (Atari 1972), used to show just a single screen with all the characters in it. Later videogames, like *Berzerk* (Stern Electronics 1980), added more screens, which the player could visit by moving to the screen's edges. This technique was called *flip-screen*. The next big leap was *scrolling* as seen, for example, in *Super Mario Bros.* (Nintendo 1985), a technique that moves the screen as the player navigates it. This permitted the creation of long, continuous areas that added uniformity to gameworlds. For the first time there was a sense of a "camera" moving alongside the player.

The first videogames to utilize three-dimensional engines were, at the same time, the first ones to use a first-person perspective: this seemed natural since controlling a camera within a 3D environment was a perfect way of navigating it. It also spared the developers the problems of dealing with a controllable character and a controllable camera simultaneously.

The first control schemes in *Catacomb 3D* (id 1991), *Wolfenstein 3D* (id 1989), and *DOOM* (id 1993) had what can be called *single navigation*: the player could navigate the environment by changing her position in it. In that sense, it was no different from 2D games. Later on, a second kind of movement was added: in games like *Hexen* (Raven Software 1995) the player could simultaneously change her position and her view. The distinction between where the player is and where the player is looking at creates what can be called *dual navigation*.

Subsequent 3D games separated the controllable subject from the controllable camera, like *Super Mario 64* (Nintendo 1996), although the latter will always be subordinate to the former. Dual navigation mimics the human movements of the body and the head (or eyes) but its nature is different in first- and third-person games: in the former, it is a single object that can perform those two movements; in the latter there are two discrete objects—controllable subject (where the player is) and camera (where the player is looking at). As Manovich puts it, "directing the virtual camera becomes as important as controlling the hero's actions" (2002, 84).

Figure 3.3 The subject is not visible in *Quake III Arena* (id Software 1999)

The dual navigation specific of first-person games (usually set to a keyboard and a mouse or to two different analog sticks in a controller) gives a great importance to the *aiming* (sub)mechanic: the eyes movement is usually matched to a crosshair at the center of the screen. This is specially favorable to the shooter genre. Though some parts of the avatar body can be seen in some first-person games, they are irrelevant to functional embodiment; in these games, a controllable camera functionally embodies the player.

Some scholars defend that the first-person view feels more natural to the player. Bob Bates writes: "There is a great sense of being 'in the world' as the player sees and hears along with his character. Third-person games [...] are less immersive but help the player build a stronger sense of identification with the character he is playing" (2001, 48). In the experiment conducted by Jörgensen, a respondent "describes navigation in *Crysis* as having close resemblance to the experience of moving around in the real world" (2009, 2). Jörgensen writes about the identification achieved by this: "[it] creates the feeling that the player becomes the avatar when playing the game." However, some information about the gameworld that the player expects to perceive naturally is lost in this view, as I will detail in some of the next points.

Interaction

The majority of mechanics of a videogame involve interacting with game objects, be they hostile, allied, or neutral. The use of first-person view influences the design of these interactions. Many videogames use enemies as the obstacles in the virtual conflict and provide the player with attack mechanics to beat them. Action (as *enemy-defeating*) is common in games. Though not all games using the first-person view are FPS, this perspective facilitates their design; since aiming is part of its navigation, the use of the *shooting* mechanic is easy to include.

Some action games using the first-person view include other enemy-defeating mechanics, such as punching or brawling. That is the case of *Zeno Clash* (Ace Team 2009) and *Condemned* (Monolith 2006). Unlike navigating or shooting, fighting does require a representation of a physical body, no matter the perspective; this way, functional embodiment is expanded, the system requires a more complex guise and thus forces a stronger avatarness.

The first-person view gives an intuitive sense of visual focus-of-attention. It allows the player to investigate every corner of the gameworld in detail, as in *Metroid Prime* (Retro Studios 2002), where the player has to aim and "scan" certain objects and parts of the gameworld to obtain information. The survival horror-adventure *Amnesia: The Dark Descent* (Frictional Games 2010) uses the first-person perspective for that effect, encouraging players to explore in depth.

Modern games tend to polarize interaction in two mechanics: attack and interact (*context-sensitive action*, not exclusive to but very common in first-person videogames). One single button serves to open doors, pick up objects, talk to subjects, or any non-hostile interaction. This can be seen, for instance, in *Half-Life* (Valve 1998). These context-sensitive actions can be ornamental and thus produce no valorized consequence (positive or negative), like Duke Nukem using the toilet in *Duke Nukem 3D* (3D Realms 1996) or Gordon Freeman using the vending machines in *Half-Life*. These actions are there to enrich the game fiction, make the gameworld more complex and add personality to the controllable subject (therefore adding avatarness to it).

The first-person perspective can also affect interaction with Non-Playable Characters (NPCs), forcing the player to face-to-face confrontations with enemies. For more about this, read Welsh in this volume.

Self-Perception

Videogames in third-person view need an object to establish the player's position and perform mechanics, but this is not mandatory in first-person games. Navigating and interacting in those games can be done with just a controllable camera and a crosshair. The player, however, will have a sense of presence within the gameworld and can reasonably expect some bodily representation. In *Wolfenstein 3D* or *DOOM* everything the player could see were guns or, at the very best, hands holding them. This, according to Taylor, did not qualify as bodily representation: "the hand is a visual aid as to what item the hand is holding, a targeting help, or is merely there" (2002, 28).

The first games to feature dual navigation (and thus freedom of aiming), like *Quake* (id Software1996), let the player look at the ground but did not feature any legs to represent the subject. The embodiment by just the camera was made more evident, diminishing the avatarness. It can be argued that the system of first-person view games does not need a body, but the guise does.

Mohler and Bülthoff write about the relation between subject and space and the convenience of a "virtual body," arguing that it "could provide a metric for scaling of absolute dimensions of space" and act "as a frame of reference" (2008, 1).

Almost every modern first-person videogame portrays the avatar body to some extent. Some use it to add physical characterization or personality traits. This, in principle, adds to the avatarness, but in Jörgensen's experience, subject autonomy can produce the opposite effect: "From Eric's experience [...] making the avatar break from this consistency by allowing it to talk without the player initiating it is a serious deviation from this" (2009, 3).

Mirror's Edge (DICE 2008), a first-person platformer, builds its gameplay on free-running and parkour-like movements and

Figure 3.4 Faith's body in *Mirror's Edge* (DICE 2008).

emphasizes the presence of the subject's (Faith) body to illustrate them. Running, jumping, crouching, sliding, or rolling will result in Faith's body appearing on screen. Her movements are shown unmistakably, which fortifies both functional and fictional embodiment. Ellison studies the subject in that game: "Faith's body is unusually visible for a videogame perspective character. […] The body is visible in a perspective that matches the player's proprioceptive map of their own body, reinforcing the illusion that Faith and they are one" (2010, 28).

Another example of the first-person self-perception helping the function and fiction of the game is *BioShock*, which Peaty explores in depth in this same volume.

Another way of showing physical features of the subject is through extra-diegetic interface elements, such as menus or the HUD. *DOOM* represents the latter, with a face in the center of the bottom of the screen that also mirrors the health status. Representations like this offer *visual cues* of gameplay elements such as the mentioned subject state (health, etc.), the use of modifiers (objects that alter the subject's attributes) or even abilities (as invisibility). Some other visual tricks can portray the subject within the diegetic reality of the gameworld, like the use of mirrors and other reflective surfaces.

Even if the subject is not shown in the controllable segments of the game, there are still vignettes (narrative spaces) where it can be seen. In a cutscene created with a traditional film-like aesthetic the subject will appear as any other character. The change of perspective, however, loses the first-person view and so this "self-perception" is missed.

Ignoring any of these ways of portraying the avatar's body can be beneficial for certain fictions; it can create an ethereal, ghostly point of view that establishes out-of-body states or spectral subjects like those in *Geist* (n-Space 2005) or *Mindjack* (Feelplus 2011).

The first person perspective, then, determines an altogether unique set of descriptions of the subject's bodily and facial features.

Sensorial Perception

In a first-person videogame, the player perceives the gameworld from the point-of-view of the subject, so the audiovisual depictions will be, to a certain degree, representations of that subject's senses. Although they do not need to be an exact match, it is hard to imagine a blind subject in a game with perfect visual depictions. The shared point-of-view seems to push developers to establish *shared sensorial perception*. However, as Jörgensen states, only two senses can be properly recreated: sight and hearing. Taste and smell can be described in audiovisual media, but they cannot be recreated and transferred. Sight and hearing can. Touch can be recreated, in a limited manner, with the use of *haptic* devices (controllers and other input systems that include vibrators and gyroscopes).

Jörgensen affirms that in her experiment, "due to the first-person perspective of *Crysis*, the players describe that they merge with the figure in the sense of sharing and taking over its perceptual properties" (2009, 3). For Taylor, on the contrary, some perceptions are lost in this view: "Perception often includes the ability to sense when another presence moves right behind or next to a person. In first-person games, this is lost" (2010, 29).

The most notable thing lost in this "sensorial translation" would be *peripheral vision*. Human sight covers a considerable arc up, down, and to the sides of the focus of attention; in first-person games sight is limited by the frame of the screen. Some games try to compensate this by having a wider view angle, although this can result in an unnatural perspective. Looking at the gameworld from a first-person perspective, hence, will always imply having to tilt the head (or, in game terms, aim) continually.

Even with the tunnel vision, the first-person perspective seems more capable of representing the perception of the controllable subject. Therefore, it can be used to improve fictional embodiment, especially if its senses differ from those of a regular human. Different senses can also change gameplay, as in *The Chronicles of Riddick* (Starbreeze/Tigon 2004), where the avatar can see in the dark, or *Alien versus Predator* (Rebellion 1999), where controlling a Predator allow the player to use the heat vision made famous by the homonymous films. This is a clear case of system and guise complementing each other.

The lack of sensorial information of the first-person view can be compensated in some ways (thus improving functionality and adding avatarness). One way to do it is with sound: the player can infer what is around her, in the area she is not looking at, by listening to the gameworld sounds. When studying perspective in *Mirror's Edge*, Ellison details how sound also creates a sense of self or a physical presence of the subject (2010, 28).

The next and also last design choice that I will list can also be of great importance when compensating this lack of sensorial information of the first-person view: the HUD.

HUD

Videogames have to communicate information about the ruleset and the game state to the player, and this is usually done via extra-diegetic interface elements such as menus or text boxes. Some information needs to be constantly visible, like health, time, ammunition, or location, so it is placed on-screen in an additional layer frequently known as HUD. Jörgensen, writing about *Crysis*, affirms that this HUD is also a method "for integrating the player perceptually into the gameworld." A respondent in her experiment seems to agree, suggesting that it is "an abstraction of something that indeed may be interpreted as real in the universe of the game" (2009, 3).

The perception limitations of first-person view might make the geography of the game difficult to read. Rhody writes about the HUD and location: "Alongside the camera and avatar, the use of radars and maps are fictive constructions that enable the game's creation of a sense of presence" (2005, 7).

The HUD, as extra-diegetic interface, has to share the screenspace with the diegetic view of the gameworld. As a result, according to Rodhy, "the point-of-view of a camera or character, and the point-of-view of a player to the material screen, are therefore synchronic and distinct" (4). But Jörgensen minimizes the impact of this distinctness in game fiction, stating that players accept it as a necessary aid (2009, 1). Nevertheless, there is a tendency in modern games to

Figure 3.5 The classical HUD in *Doom 2* (id 1994).

reduce the HUD elements or even hide them and deliver the information through other means (visual cues on the subject's look,
desaturated colors as the subject receives damage, and so on).

Other games, like *Dead Space* (Visceral Games 2008), incorporate the HUD into the gameworld diegetic reality: menus are
holograms the subject accesses and life and energy are bars in its
space suit. These diegetic HUDs can be used in first-person games
too. In the *Metroid Prime* series, Samus (the controllable subject)
sees the gameworld through her helmet and the information is
projected on it. It can be argued that diegetic HUD lays a bridge
between system and guise, and this can have a positive impact on
avatarness.

Avatarness and FPS

In this chapter, I have described the complementary dual nature of
videogames (system and guise), the role of objects and subjects, and
dual embodiment (functional and fictional). These are the basics of

the current, most widely accepted notion of avatar. Then, I proposed a slightly different approach: avatarness as a general quality that can differ in intensity but also in style. Different elements of game design will determine the relation between player and subject and the sense of identification that the former gets from playing.

Throughout the article I have been using the term "controllable object" (or "subject," if it has some degree of characterization), because I see it more fitting and descriptive than avatars. However, my point is that we should not be that strict with the term avatar and accept it, as players and designers seem to do, as a subject with a sufficient and valid enough avatarness, one that provides a sense of intra-diegetic engagement.

In the second part of this chapter, I have aimed to describe the five design elements that are more likely to affect the avatarness (and the eight points that make it) in first-person view videogames of all genres. FPS seems to be the more prominent genre using that perspective, and the very easy manner of aiming and interacting it provides are a clear explanation of this. As a genre, FPS are very simple to dissect: they are the sum of a particular view with a particular mechanic.

At the most raw level of design, FPS need just that: a first-person view that allows some sort of aiming and the shooting mechanic. In that sense, players are basically embodied by a controllable camera and a crosshair. The next key element in the construction of the FPS avatarness would be the weapon and/or the hands holding it; as Klevjer says, "the navigable point of view is controlled directly, and the visible objective avatar is mounted onto the frame of vision as a pair of hands or weapon" (2007, 152).

These are the mandatory parts of the controllable subject in FPS. At this point, the subject is virtually invisible, when not directly absent. The addition of an HUD fills a functional gap, making up for the missing perception of the perspective. From this point on, every other design element added to the subject will be either the response to an extra mechanic in the system or the construction of a more elaborated guise, leading to a stronger fictional embodiment. Visible bodily and facial features, control over the subject looks, traits of autonomy of the subject, dialogue and methods for interaction other than shooting can be added to the subject via certain design choices in interaction, self-perception, sensorial perception, and the HUD.

There are plenty of different types of controllable subjects in FPS, each one with its own kind and degree of avatarness. From the silent and visually defined Master Chief in *Halo* (Bungie, 2001) to the highly modifiable, anonymous warriors of *Quake III Arena* (id Software 1999) to the talkative and expressive Duke Nukem, the possibilities for their design seem as vast as in other, third-person genres.

At the end of the day, two things will end up defining the FPS subjects: the way the designers decide to deal with the need of urgency and the conventions of the genre, and the very basic core of a camera, a crosshair, and a gun on which the rest of that subject will rest upon. Giving the players a first-person view and a gun seems self-explanatory enough to make them assume a certain role and immerse themselves in the system and guise of FPS.

References

Bates, Bob. 2001. *Game Design: The Art and Business of Creating Games.* Rocklin, CA: Prima Tech.

Burn, Andrew, and Gareth Schott. 2004. "Heavy Hero or Digital Dummy: Multimodal Player-Avatar Relations in *Final Fantasy 7.*" *Visual Communication* 3 (2): 213–33.

Ellison, Fraser. 2010. "The Videogame as Prosthetic Imagination: Immersion in *Mirror's Edge.*" Thesis. RMIT University, School of Media and Communication.

Flynn, Bernadette. 2003. "Languages of Navigation within Computer Games." Paper presented at the 5th International Digital Arts and Culture Conference in Melbourne.

Jenkins, Henry. 2001. "Game Design as Narrative Architecture." In *First Person*, edited by Pat Harrington and Noah Wardrip-Fruin, 118–30. Cambridge: MIT Press.

Jørgensen, Kristine. 2009: "'I'm Overburdened!' An Empirical Study of the Player, the Avatar, and the Gameworld." *Proceedings from DiGRA 2009: Breaking New Ground: Innovation in Games, Play, Practice and Theory.* http://www.digra.org/dl/db/09287.20429.pdf

Klevjer, Rune. 2006. "What is the Avatar? Fiction and Embodiment in Avatar-Based Single Player Computer Games." PhD Diss. University of Bergen.

Linderoth, Jonas. 2002. "Making Sense of Computer Games:

Learning with new Artefacts." Paper presented at the International conference on Toys, Games and Media, London University, Institute of Education, August 2002.

—2005. "Animated Game Pieces. Avatars as Roles, Tools and Props." Paper presented at the Aesthetics of Play Conference, University of Bergen, Norway.

Manovich, Lev. 2002. *The Language of New Media*. Cambridge: MIT Press.

Mohler, Bett J. and Bülthoffm, Heinrich H. 2008. "A Full-Body Avatar Improves Distance Judgments in Virtual Environments." *Proceedings of the ACM/SIGGRAPH 2008 Symposium on Applied Perception for Graphics and Visualization.*

Murray, Janet. 1997. *Hamlet on the Holodeck: The Future of Narrative in Cyberspace*. Cambridge MA: MIT Press.

Newman, James. 2002. "The Myth of the Ergodic Videogame. Some Thoughts on Player-Character Relationships in Videogames." *Game Studies* 2 (1). http://gamestudies.org/0102/newman

Rehak, Bob. 2003. "Playing at Being: Psychoanalysis and the Avatar." In *The Video Game Theory Reader*, edited by Mark J. P. Wolf and Bernard Perron, 103–28. New York: Routledge.

Rhody, Jason. 2005. "Game Fiction: Playing the Interface in *Prince of Persia: The Sands of Time* and *Asheron's Call.*" *Proceedings of DiGRA 2005. Conference: Changing Views – Worlds in Play.*

Rouse, Richard III. 1999. "What's Your Perspective?" *Computer Graphics* 33(3): 9–12.

Poole, Steven. 2000. *Trigger Happy. The Inner Life of Video Games*. London: Fourth Estate.

Taylor, Laurie N. 2002. "Video Games: Perspective, Point-of-view, and Immersion." MA Thesis. University of Florida.

Games

2K Boston. 2007. *BioShock* [Mac OS X, Microsoft Windows, PlayStation 3, Xbox 360]. 2K Games.

3D Realms. 1996. *Duke Nukem 3D* [DOS]. GT Interactive Software.

Ace Team. 2009. *Zeno Clash* [Microsoft Windows, Xbox Live Arcade]. Valve.

Atari. 1972. *PONG* [arcade]. Atari.

BioWare. 2007. *Mass Effect* [Microsoft Windows, Xbox 360]. Electronic Arts.

Blizzard North. 2000. *Diablo 2* [Microsoft Windows]. Blizzard Entertainment.

Bungie. 2001. *Halo: Combat Evolved* [Xbox]. Microsoft Game Studios.

Crytek Frankfurt. 2007. *Crysis* [Microsoft Windows]. Electronic Arts.

Cyan. 1993. *Myst* [Mac OS]. Bröderbund.

DICE. 2008. *Mirror's Edge* [iOS, Microsoft Windows, PlayStation 3, Xbox 360. Electronic Arts.

EA Los Angeles. 2007. *Command and Conquer 3: Tiberium Wars* [Mac OS X, Microsoft Windows, Xbox 360]. Electronic Arts.

feelplus. 2011. *Mindjack* [Xbox 360, PlayStation 3]. Square Enix.

Frictional Games. 2010. *Amnesia: The Dark Descent* [Mac OS X, Microsoft Windows, Linux]. Frictional Games.

HAL Laboratory. 2011. *Kirby: Mass Attack* [Nintendo DS]. Nintendo.

id Software. 1989. *Wolfenstein 3D* [DOS]. Apogee.

—1991. *Catacomb 3D* [MS-DOS]. Softdisk.

—1993. *DOOM* [MS-DOS]. id Software.

—1994. *DOOM 2* [MS-DOS]. GT Interactive.

—1996. *Quake* [Microsoft Windows]. GT Interactive.

—1999. *Quake III Arena* [Microsoft Windows]. Activision.

Ion Storm. 2000. *Deus Ex* [Mac OS X, Microsoft Windows, PlayStation 2]. Eidos Interactive.

KCEJ. 2001. *Metal Gear Solid 2: Sons of Liberty* [PlayStation 2]. Konami.

Konami CEJ/Kojima Productions. 2004. *Metal Gear Solid 3: Snake Eater* [PlayStation 2]. Konami.

Lucasfilm Games. 1992. *The Secret of Monkey Island* [MS-DOS]. LucasArts.

Maxis. 2000. *The Sims* [Microsoft Windows]. Electronic Arts.

Mercury Steam, Kojima Productions. 2010. *Castlevania: Lords of Shadow* [Xbox 360, PlayStation 3]. Konami.

Monolith Productions. 2006. *Condemned: Criminal Origins* [Microsoft Windows, Xbox 360]. Sega.

Naughty Dog. 2007. *Uncharted: Drake's Fortune* [PlayStation 3]. Sony Computer Entertainment.

Nintendo. 1985. *Super Mario Bros.* [Nintendo Entertainment System]. Nintendo.

—1986. *The Legend of Zelda* [Nintendo Entertainment System]. Nintendo.

Nintendo EAD. 1996. *Super Mario 64* [Nintendo 64]. Nintendo.

N-Space. 2005. *Geist* [GameCube]. Nintendo.

Raven Software. 1995. *Hexen* [MS-DOS]. id Software.

Rebellion Developments. 1999. *Alien vs. Predator* [Mac OS X, Microsoft Windows]. Fox Interactive.

Retro Studios. 2002. *Metroid Prime* [GameCube]. Nintendo.

Silicon Knights. 2002. *Eternal Darkness* [GameCube]. Nintendo.

Square. 1997. *Final Fantasy VII* [PlayStation]. Square.

Starbreeze/Tigon. 2004. *The Chronicles of Riddick* [Xbox]. Vivendi Games.

Stern Electronics. 1980. *Berzerk* [arcade, Atari 2600, Atari 5200, GCE Vectrex]. Stern Electronics.

tri-Crescendo. 2003. *Baten Kaitos* [GameCube]. Namco.

Valve. 1998. *Half-Life* [Microsoft Windows]. Sierra Entertainment.

—2007. *Portal* [Microsoft Windows, Mac OS X, Xbox 360, PlayStation 3]. Valve.

Visceral Games. 2008. *Dead Space* [Microsoft Windows, Xbox 360, PlayStation 3]. Electronic Arts.

4

Monsters, Nazis, and Tangos: The Normalization of the First-Person Shooter

Gerald Voorhees

This chapter examines the militarization and corresponding normalization of the FPS. Once the targets of public vitriol when players ran around killing demons, zombies, and aliens, now that players are more typically tasked with killing other human beings FPS games are largely uncontroversial touchstones of contemporary popular culture. Though the cultural status of the FPS vis-à-vis its increasingly realistic depictions of violence seems counterintuitive, I show that public perceptions of FPS games improved as their themes became more militaristic and their narratives more directly supportive of American imperialism. In other words, the normalization of the genre is a result of its imbrication within a powerful regime of truth that articulates militarism, nationalism, and xenophobia to the FPS game form, rendering it an intelligible nodal point in the matrix of American life.

The following section outlines a Foucauldian theoretical lens that posits the newness of the media form as a threat to established ways of knowing, and its normalization as an effect of its incorporation into existing structures of power. This is followed by a brief examination of public controversy concerning digital games, paying particular attention to the place of the FPS in the public outcry over representations of violence in games. The final substantive section works to explicate the thematic and narrative development of the FPS in order to make evident the cultural work of a handful of seminal titles that constitute critical touchstones of the genre. Finally, this chapter concludes by considering the normalization of the FPS as a product of the increasing intelligibility of the genre, a lesson broadly applicable to scholars of new media forms and technologies.

The Unintelligible Threat

Public discourses decrying representations of violence in digital games (in general and FPS games in particular) can be seen as an iteration of a recurring problematic germane to new media and media forms. In this chapter, I explore controversy over FPS games as a reaction to their unintelligibility and track their transformation into intelligible statements in the discursive formations that govern American culture. To this end, this section sketches out Foucault's theorization of the discursive formation as it relates to intelligibility in order to clear a conceptual space where controversy over new media and media forms might be situated in this context.

While Foucault would later turn to genealogical methods in order to understand the political, economic, institutional, and material conditions that facilitate (or militate) the transition from one regime of truth to another, his early work is archaeological; it endeavors to describe the rules—the grammar, logic, and rhetoric—of the systems of thought, belief, and knowledge that he variously termed discursive formations or regimes of truth. As a method, archeology is invaluable to critical-cultural studies in that it enables scholars to map out the grid of intelligible statements (and positions) possible within a discursive formation during any one localized historical moment. Rejecting four typical means of identifying discursive "unities"— they are centered on a common object, share a style of expression, concern themselves with a relatively fixed set of concepts, and contain persistent themes—Foucault (1972) argues that the unity of a discursive formation lies

> [i]n the different possibilities that it opens of reanimating already existing themes, of arousing opposing strategies, of giving way to irreconcilable interests, of making it possible, with a particular set of concepts, to play different games[.] Rather than seeking the permanence of themes, images, and opinions through time, rather than retracing the dialectic of their conflicts in order to individualize groups of statements, could one not rather mark out the dispersion of the points of choice, and define prior to any option, to any thematic preference, a field of strategic possibilities? (36–7)

In other words, a discursive formation is the total assemblage of possible statements that might be made in the context of a specific domain of knowledge, ideology, or science. Most pertinent to the main argument of this chapter, this means that the discursive formation is not constituted by any internal element but rather by its boundaries, the frontiers determined by its "rules of formation" (38). It is in this context that discourse is either intelligible or unintelligible. For Foucault, verbal performance (spoken, written or otherwise mediated) that obeys the rules of formation is a "statement." The discursive formation constitutes the "associated field that turns a sentence or a series of signs into a statement, and which provides them with a particular context, a specific representative content" (98). Absent this context, the otherwise meaningful statement says nothing; it is unintelligible. That which disregards or exceeds the rules of formation becomes an impossible utterance lacking the capacity to mean within a given discursive formation.

It is my contention that digital games in general, and FPS games in particular, initially failed to register as intelligible performances within the discursive formations operating in American cultural life. In short, when FPS games were gory and fantastical shooting galleries, Americans simply did not know what to make of them. They were unintelligible, abject, and thus obscene (Butler 1993). As such, they troubled the grids of intelligibility where power/knowledge governs social order (Foucault 1990, 93). However, FPS games have been domesticated. They have been studied; scientific and moralistic discourses have examined them and, by doing so, enabled game developers to reimagine FPS games as popular entertainment that actively contributes to the militarism and exceptionalism pervasive in American culture.

This way of thinking about new media and media forms is not entirely novel; other (new) media researchers working from a variety of approaches have generated similar insights. Indeed, Lisa Gitelman and Geoffrey Pingree (2003), and separately Carolyn Marvin (1988), have done important work by first pointing out the obvious but oft-forgotten principle that all media are at some point "new", and second, examining the early years of various "old" media in order to draw attention to the social and cultural turmoil that accompanied their emergence. What they found is that concern about novel media forms is a historical constant, a phenomenon attributed to uncertainty regarding the potential of technologies that "embody the possibility that accustomed orders are in jeopardy" (Marvin 1988, 8). And while these studies point to concerns about how media technologies reconfigure communication processes, a similar set of issues arises regarding innovations in the communication norms that constitute genres. For instance, Springhall's (1998) work on moral panics examines public fears manifest in response to a variety of media forms: the penny dreadful, gangster film, horror comic, and rap music. Notably, it is not the book, the film, the comic, or the record—in other words, not the technology of the medium—but the genre and its conventional contents that Springhall identifies at the center of public condemnation.

Several scholars have looked at both new media and media forms and found similar phenomena. In addition to examining controversy about the internet as a medium, Lumby (1997) also demonstrates the potential for specific genres to trouble established sensibilities when she identifies a similar set of concerns pertaining to the increased popularity of the "reality TV" format. Perhaps the most illuminating analysis of panic discourse related to new media is Drotner's (1999) survey of the reception of popular fiction and film. Looking at the medium of film as well as popular fiction as a specific form of the book, Drotner traces public outcry to concerns about the management of identities and ideologies characteristic of modernity. More pointedly, Drotner argues that "The media uses of the young perspectivise with particular clarity contradictions that are intrinsic to modernity itself" (614). In this analysis, the very episteme that characterizes modernity is threatened by the prevalence of discourses unintelligible to those thoroughly subject to power but wholly intelligible to youths in the process of transforming their selves into subjects. As a whole, this body of work buttresses the notion that novel media and media forms are received as dubious, disruptive potentialities. The common thread identified and centered by this research is the fear of the unknown that permeates public response to the new.

Of course, digital games have not avoided panic discourses, and neither have scholarly treatments of digital games. In a review essay in which he examines some early research on children and gaming, Jenkins (1993) warns that American culture, and the academic researchers situated in it, risk treating digital games as carriers of an alien "x-logic." He maintains that games are often experienced in ways adults find alien but, in fact, encode many traditional ideologies. In another meta-critical moment, Miller (2006) notes that scholars tend to either celebrate or panic over digital games. He concedes that this is an understandable reaction as "...new communication and cultural technologies and genres offer forms of mastery that threaten, however peripherally, the established order. Each new one has brought with it concerns about supposedly unprecedented and unholy new risks..." (7). Miller ultimately argues for games criticism to "Follow the money, follow the labor" (9)—and in this volume Miller extends and supplements this set of critical imperatives—but along the way, points to panic as an important force shaping the current state of the field. Both Miller and Jenkins remind that academic discourses are entangled in cultural discourses, and must therefore be understood in the context of anxieties about the impact of digital games on society. More pertinent to this chapter, they call attention to how the efforts to reduce the uncertainty about and better know

digital games vacillate between trumpeting their supposed emancipatory potential and denouncing them as a threat to the ways that
people know themselves and their relationships to the world.

In this chapter, I hope continue to explore how FPS games
have been treated as an unintelligible threat and to do the work
called for by both Jenkins and Miller. On one register, I endeavor
to explain how the FPS, at different times, offers playgrounds
for imaginative experiences and entrenches established ways of
knowing. Moreover, though my focus is not the economics of game
development and publishing, one would be hard-pressed to divorce
the changing character of the FPS genre from the increasing
revenue associated with the mainstreaming of the media form. The
following section maps the changing character of the FPS from its
early, juvenile fantasies immensely popular among the niche culture
of computer gaming to its contemporary realism and commercial
console success.

Contesting the FPS

The first sustained public conversation about electronic games was
couched in terms of the harms to which they exposed American
youth, but, more accurately, it was about the potential threats – the
unknown qualities – of games that exceed the parameters of human
knowledge. In a 1982 episode of *PBS's McNeil-Lehrer Report*,
Long Island PTA president and anti-gaming activist Ronnie Lamm
asked: "We've taken away their guns and holsters and cowboys
and Indians, and we're now giving them a cartridge with the same
kind of violent themes. What is this doing to our young people?"
Armed with uncertainty, Lamm, who had in 1976 led protests
against Exidy's arcade pariah *Death Race*, was mobilizing against the
proliferation of arcades, which she and other parents charged were
corrupting American youth by serving as dens of disrepute: normal-
izing violence, glorifying crime, encouraging truancy, and contributing
to juvenile delinquency. On the same program, Paul Trachtman,
Science Advisor for Capital Children's Museum in Washington DC,
inarticulately defended videogames as playgrounds for "the world
that we're moving into," where players play for "cognitive highs...

to exercise a part of the mind that doesn't get much exercise." By resorting to poorly conceived metaphors, both Lamm and Trachman give striking testimony to the inability to really understand and explain the impact of digital games in American culture.

I argue that this transformation from scary new media form to normal media fun parallels thematic and narrative shifts toward realism. Thematically, FPS games moved from fantastic and futuristic milieus to more contemporary settings while, narratively, they abandoned the idea of the player as protagonist championing humanity in order to save the world and adopted the cause of ensuring America's continued access to strategic interests abroad. Critically, my understanding of realism is grounded in Galloway's (2006) distinction between "realisticness" and "social realism." Galloway acknowledges that photorealistic graphics and precise, accurate simulations of action have a strong claim to realism as "realisticness," especially given common usage and the professional and promotional nomenclatures of the game industry. Still, he argues that game studies would be better served examining realism as "social realism," the congruence of the social reality of the gamer with the experience of the game. This "fidelity of context," Galloway argues in his discussion of *America's Army*, may ring true with something beyond the player's individual, lived experience and resonate with and extend the political reality in which the player is located (83). By embracing this form of realism and incorporating themes and narratives that resonate profoundly with American culture, contemporary FPS games are readily intelligibile statements affirming militarism, imperialism, and expectionalism.

In order to more clearly delineate and explore these shifts, this chapter examines a number of FPS games produced in the two decades since the inception of the genre, focusing on the most influential, critically acclaimed, and widely popular titles: *DOOM*, *Duke Nukem 3D*, *Goldeneye 007*, *Medal of Honor*, *America's Army*, and *Call of Duty: Modern Warfare*. However, it first turns briefly to early controversy responding to representations of violence in digital games.

Before the FPS

Initially, public outcry over digital games was broadly aimed at violence and obscenity. 1976 saw the first organized protest against a digital game, *Death Race*, in which the player could earn points by running over pedestrians thinly disguised as "gremlins." The National Transportation Safety Board lent credence to these concerns by condemning *Death Race* as "morbid" (Gross 2011). While this protest generated publicity for *Death Race* and the arcade industry, it also helped convince developer and manufacturer Exidy to stop production of the game (Kirsch 2011). Games once again catapulted into public discourse in 1982 thanks to a pair of games released by the developer Mystique. The pornographic *Beat 'Em and Eat 'Em* was widely considered obscene, and the orientalist rape fantasy *Custer's Revenge* spurred the National Organization for Women and New York's American Indian Community House to work together to protest its racist, sexist depictions of a naked, erect Custer dodging arrows in order to mount and rape a naked, bound Native American woman (Kohler 2007).

New business models that emerged after the game industry crashed in 1984 allowed console-makers to control the content of games published by third-party developers and thus better control the public image of digital gaming. The resuscitated home console industry's strict licensing requirements forced third-party developers to self-censor. During this time, Nintendo dominated the American home console market with family-friendly titles played on the *Nintendo Entertainment System* (marketed in Japan as the *Family Computer*), most of which were developed in-house. Third-party developers were forbidden from distributing sexually explicit and sexually violent content like that featured in *Beat 'Em and Eat 'Em* and *Custer's Revenge*, but also prevented from representing the symbols of religious or ethnic groups and depicting the use of profanity, drugs, alcohol, and tobacco.

But renewed competition from Sega in the early 1990s also renewed the potential for controversy. Sega, having a large share of the Japanese home console (and arcade) market, made a hard push for American game-players by branding itself as the young, edgy console. Sega games featured adult themes, blood, and, most memorably, fatalities. A pair of third-party titles released for the Sega Genesis – *Night Trap* in 1992 and *Mortal Kombat* in 1993 – brought the public's attention back to digital games. In 1993, Senators Joe Lieberman and Herbert Kohl led the US Senate to convene a joint hearing of the Judiciary and Government Affairs Committees to admonish these games and pave the way for a proposed Video Game Rating Act, which was to have established a comprehensive ratings system. This legislation was withdrawn when the game industry returned to the Senate in 1994 to announce the establishment of self-regulation in the form of the Electronic Software Ratings Board (hereafter, ESRB).

Perhaps because it was released the day after the December 1993 Senate hearings ended, or possibly because it was distributed as shareware without any organized marketing or guaranteed revenue, *DOOM* (id 1993) escaped mention by Senators Lieberman and Kohl. However, *DOOM* would catalyze the controversy over digital games, spurring it to reorganize around the FPS.

Shooting Monsters

While id's 1992 *Castle Wolfenstein* has the best claim to it, *DOOM* is typically considered the origin of the FPS genre (though in this volume, Wolf locates that origin in Atari's *BattleZone*) and for several years FPS games were described as *DOOM* clones. It was also the first FPS to attract sustained public criticism. A science-fiction themed game set on Mars in the distant future, *DOOM's* plot revolves around a teleportation experiment gone wrong that opens a passage to hell. The player takes the role of the last surviving space marine and must fight off the raging hordes of hell in order to save every last human on Earth. Lesser enemies encountered early in the game include formerly human *zombiemen*, possessed *heavy weapon dudes*, beige humanoid *imps* covered in spikes, and *cacodemons*, floating red masses of eyes, teeth, and spikes. Later in the game, the play encounters massive *hell knights* with goat-like faces and the legs of a bull, as well as *arachnotrons*, pulpy brains with beady blue eyes that stomp around on mechanical legs. *DOOM* was a little grotesque and certainly immature (Kushner 2003); impaled bodies decorated the landscape and a well-aimed shotgun

Figure 4.1 The shotgun-wielding player confronts a *cacodemon* in *DOOM* (id 1993).

blast would tear monsters apart in a spray of blood. Still, while the game was gory, its violence was not only comical, it was directed against decidedly inhuman demons from hell.

Nevertheless, *DOOM* was criticized for its violence and gore, though often in the same breath as it was praised for its innovative business model and technological sophistication. *DOOM* attracted ire from proponents of media violence and even prompted the Washington State Senate to consider legislation that would prohibitively tax "virtual reality games" that create "an enhanced illusion of three-dimensional, real-time or near-real-time interactive reality through the use of software" (Washington Senate 1994, SBR 6174). When its 1994 sequel *Doom II* was the first game released with an M (for Mature) rating, pundits wondered if the ESRB's rating system was really a marketing scheme.

Duke Nukem 3D (3D Realms 1996), premised on a similarly fantastic story, also received a good amount of criticism. Picking up where the side-scrolling first and second iterations of the series left off, aliens have invaded Earth, turning Los Angeles police officers into pig-faced monsters and abducting women. Only Duke Nukem, the loud, brash, self-aggrandizing and often offensive stereotype of hyper-masculinity who is both protagonist and punchline, can stop them. As Duke, the player fights through alien-infested Los Angeles and a lunar base before returning to Earth to finish the fight against reptilian *assault troopers*, mutated *pig-cops* and terrifying *octobrains*, pulsating masses of grey matter floating amidst a mess of tentacles and claws. *Duke Nukem 3D* was criticized for its mix of violence and sexuality. Duke fights through some of the seedier streets of Los Angeles, traversing adult book stores, strip clubs, and peepshows filled with pin-up posters and scantily clad women who jiggle their chests when interacted with. Much like *Grand Theft Auto*, *Duke Nukem 3D* was accused of encouraging violence against women by rewarding player with points for "the murder of female prostitutes" (Grossman and DeGaetano 1999). However, in fact, while the player can kill the captive dancers, doing so is not rewarded (and the player does not score points ever) but punished with a surprise attack of alien forces.

FPS games went from notable to notorious when, six years after *DOOM's* initial release, the game became the center of the most intense anti-games rhetoric to date and public condemnation of videogames entered a new era focused on the FPS. This reorganization of the outrage against digital games began in 1997 when three students were murdered at Heath High School in Kentucky. Infamous anti-videogame litigator Jack Thompson filed suit against Miramax, makers of the movie *Basketball Diaries*, and against Austin, Texas-based id Software, the makers of *DOOM*, *Quake*, and *Castle Wolfenstein*. The complaint, filed on behalf of the victims' families, alleged that Miramax and id were integral links in a "causal chain" liable for the shooting. Though the lawsuit was ultimately dismissed, it brought the issue of videogame violence back into public consciousness and focused the spotlight squarely on FPS games.

Over the next two years, a score of children and teachers would fall victim to school shootings (and another two score would be injured in such attacks) in Arkansas, Tennessee, Pennsylvania, Oregon, Virginia, Georgia, New Mexico, and Oklahoma. The single most deadly incident, widely termed the Columbine Massacre, occurred

Figure 4.2 Wielding a shotgun, the player as Duke encounters an *octobrain* in *Duke Nukem 3D* (3D Realms 1996)

in April 1999 at Columbine High School in Littleton, Colorado. After two students murdered a dozen classmates and two teachers, it was soon discovered and widely reported that the killers played (and even modded) *DOOM*. Thompson made the talk-show circuit describing FPS games as murder simulators that teach children how to prepare for and enact these school shootings. Retired Army psychologist David Grossman became a go-to source for news programs speaking about how the US military uses FPS games to normalize killing. A new set of congressional hearings was convened in 2000 and a range of FPS games released in the last decade were brought to the table, chastised and rebuked by lawmakers and parent organizations alike, despite expert testimony that there was (and still is) no evidence of a causal relationship between games and violent crime. Public discourses concerning videogames and violence reorganized around the FPS, which were frequently cited over the next several years as various states and localities sought to regulate videogames, including the cities of Indianapolis and St. Louis, and the states of Illinois, Louisiana, Oklahoma, Minnesota, and Michigan.

But, even as these states endeavored to enact policy, the narrative and thematic entailments of the FPS had begun to change. *DOOM* and *Duke Nukem 3D* are typical of FPS games in the early to mid-1990s. Set in fantastic science-fiction milieus, they allowed players into crudely rendered worlds (by contemporary standards) populated by ridiculously outlandish foes.[1] Beating the game and saving the world from certain destruction were co-terminus. Several *DOOM* sequels followed suit, as well as id's follow-up *Quake* series, which pitted the player against inter-dimensional enemies; Bungie's *Marathon* series, in which the player fought to drive an alien invasion from a spaceship; and the *System Shock* series, wherein hostile cyborgs and aliens are the primary foes. One of the few FPS games from the early 1990s that required players to kill virtual humans, id's 1992 *Castle Wolfenstein 3D*, dehumanized the enemies in a different manner; the player fought Nazis early and later a cyborg-Hitler. FPS games still pit players against zombies, demons, and aliens, but the genre had already begun to seek new enemies in new places shortly after Duke saved the world.

Shooting People

Though still a mainstay of computer gaming, in the mid-1990s FPS games began moving to consoles. In addition to offering a larger market than personal computers, which were largely the domain of hobbyists and enthusiasts, the home console market also presented game developers and publishers with a decidedly younger audience (Lenhart, Jones, and Macgill 2008). In this regard, it is odd that the simultaneous migration of FPS games to consoles and targeting of human enemies did not provoke a strong public response, even during the uproar that followed Columbine. However, looking at the narrative and thematic bent of games from this era evidences their embrace of militarism and defense of American interests internationally.

Rare's *Goldeneye 007* (1997) for the *Nintendo64* was the first FPS that tasked players with killing enemies represented as human. The game follows the plot of the previous year's James Bond movie, *Goldeneye*, and tasks the player, as Bond, with stopping the Janus crime syndicate from bringing down the British economy and

Figure 4.3 One shot to the neck kills a Russian soldier in *Goldeneye 007* (Rare 1997).

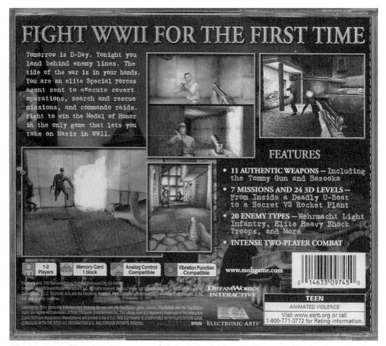

Figure 4.4 The back cover of *Medal of Honor* (DreamWorks Interactive 1999) orders the player to fight WWII.

thereby destabilizing the world economy. Along the way *terrorists*, *arctic commandos*, *Janus Special Forces*, and named henchmen and women, including *Baron Samedi* and *Xenia Onnatopp*, must be killed. And though *Goldeneye 007* does require the player to exercise stealth in many situations, this does not prevent killing of human enemies but only manages and defers it. In fact, combined with restrained depictions of blood that curtail splatters in favor of red spots on shirts, the mixture of stealth and killing produced an aura of restraint for the first game to allow players to target specific body parts and thus cripple enemies before executing them. Perhaps because of these choices concerning blood and stealth, *Goldeneye 007* avoided negative scrutiny.

Famed film director and producer Steven Spielberg would help continue to push FPS games with human opponents into the mainstream with *Medal of Honor* (DreamWorks Interactive 1999), released a year after his blockbuster movie, *Saving Private Ryan*, on Veterans Day. A historical game set in World War II, *Medal of Honor* puts protagonist Jimmy Patterson behind enemy lines before, during, and after D-Day. Between mission briefings bookended with footage from period newsreels, the player uses weapons authentic to the era to fight and kill hundreds of German *dock workers*, *Waffen-SS light* and *Waffen-SS heavy* soldiers, *kriegsmarine sailors*, *nefarious scientists*, and *Gestapo agents* in order to rescue Allied pilots, gather intelligence, and sabotage German infrastructure. Like Spielberg's cinematic production, *Medal of Honor* employed a military consultant who put the production team through a military-style boot camp and worked to ensure a high degree of authenticity to the arms, armaments, missions, and military culture characteristic of WWII (Tuttle 2005). And like *Goldeneye 007*, *Medal of Honor* managed to avoid controversy by anesthetizing killing. Though they cry out when shot, enemies do not bleed or lose body parts but simply fade away after falling to the ground.

Rather than take a comic stance on fantasy and science-fiction themes, FPS games from the late 1990s and early 2000s began incorporating more realistic elements by pitting players against human opponents in historical settings in which American interests are at stake. These traits are typical of a new type of FPS that rose to prominence in this period, the sub-genre of historical FPS games that includes another six unique iterations of the *Medal of Honor* series, four titles in the *Call of Duty* series, the first two games from the *Battlefield* series, and a slew of games set during the Vietnam War (*Vietcong*, *Men of Valor*, and *Shellshock: Nam 67*,) among others. Terrorists and soldiers clutched wounds and screamed in pain as they died, and graphics had come a long way since *Death Race's* stick-figure gremlins. But FPS games from this era avoided the intense criticism that *DOOM* received in the wake of Columbine, despite having been marketed and released more recently—just months afterward in the case of *Medal of Honor*.

They were aided, I argue, by their historical, military elements and their alignment with American strategic interests. As Aaron Hess' analysis of later iterations of the *Medal of Honor* series shows, the series both memorializes and celebrates American involvement in WWII. In this manner, playing *Medal of Honor* was figured in its advertising as a kind of auxillary service. The slogan, "You don't play, you volunteer," drove home the commemorative nature of the game and its glorification of American military prowess. Arguably, the player is fighting for either America or the free world, but metonymically the game makes America's interests the world's interests. As an adaptation of the previous summer's James Bond movie, *Goldeneye 007* was also clearly situated in a familiar context. It not only drew a bright-line between good government agents and bad criminals and terrorists, it positioned the player as one of the most recognizable champions of the West from the Cold War era. Equally significant, the player, as Bond, is caught in a decided post-Cold War struggle over the health of the global economy. While technically an English agent whose objective is to protect British wealth, Bond ultimately fights for the global economy of the neo-liberal world system. FPS games would soon narrow their focus and begin sending players into ongoing entanglements abroad to project American power and ensure continued access to strategic resources.

Shooting Tangos

In response to flagging recruitment numbers in the 1990s, *America's Army* (2002) was developed under the auspices of the US Army Office of Economic and Manpower Analysis. Ostensibly for the purpose of communicating the nature of army life, *America's Army* strongly emphasizes the US Army's core values during training, load screens, and even in certain aspects of gameplay. Links within the game interface take players to the US Army's recruiting website, goarmy.com, and copies of the game are given out for free at recruiting centers. *America's Army* allows players who downloaded the free software to create a soldier, complete single-player training scenarios, and join in online multiplayer matches. However, later iterations of the series would incorporate single-player campaigns with missions that reference contemporary affairs and are drawn from actual Army missions. In the 2005 Xbox release, *America's Army: Rise of a Soldier* (US Army, Ubisoft, and Secret Level), players found themselves defending oilfields from terrorist attacks, attacking terrorist training camps, and raiding drug processing facilities run by terrorists. Here, players kill "opfor" (opposing force) "tangos" (targets) in order to protect American access to strategic resources. Subsequent iterations of the series would model multiplayer scenarios on actual missions undertaken by special forces soldiers in Afghanistan and Iraq. Both a public relations tool and a recruiting effort, *America's Army* was criticized for its anesthetized representations of bloodless warfare and for enticing youth to consider military

Figure 4.5 Shooting "tangos" from afar in *America's Army: Rise of a Soldier* (US Army, Ubisoft, and Secret Level).

service. However, it was not upbraided for its depictions of violence as FPS games had been criticized in the past.

A number of other game franchises followed suit, positioning players as soldiers on contemporary battlefields facing off against terrorists of various stripes, but *Call of Duty 4: Modern Warfare* (Infinity Ward 2007) cemented the pre-eminence of this style. Set in the near future now past, the game is premised on a nuclear-armed paramilitary Russian ultranationalist organization's attempt to restore Russia to its Cold War hegemony. Roughly half of gameplay is set in Russia (and former Soviet republics), but the first half of the game's missions take place in an unnamed Middle Eastern country where the Russian ultranationalists have funded a *coup d'état* in order to destabilize the region and occupy the West's attention. While most of the action in Russia is played from the perspective of a British soldier, the player is sent into the Middle East as an American soldier to put down the coup d'état. Using weapons currently employed by soldiers in Iraq and Afghanistan, players hunt the would-be dictator, Al Asad across an unidentified Middle Eastern city and pursue him as he flees into Azerbaijan. Enemies in combat fatigues, some wearing ski masks and others wearing black-and-white checkered Keffiyeh

Figure 4.6 A firefight in an unnamed Middle Eastern village in *Call of Duty 4: Modern Warfare* (Infinity Ward 2007).

typical of traditional Arab fashion, are killed by the score as the player traverses each level and ultimately aids in the assassination of Al Asad. Despite its realistic graphics, contemporary setting, and resonance with the ongoing American engagements in the War on Terror, *Call of Duty 4: Modern Warfare* did not generate controversy.

But neither did any of the FPS games that took up contemporary conflict—real and imagined—as their conceit. Major franchises including *Tom Clancy's Rainbow 6: Vegas* (and its sequel), the *Soldier of Fortune* series, *Battlefield: Bad Company*, and *Battlefield 3*, as well as the low-budget but profitable *Terrorist Takedown* series and *Code of Honor* series, pitted players against terrorists and agents of rogue states from the Middle East, Latin America, and North Korea. With graphics described as photorealistic (McElroy 2010) and enemies who cry out and bleed when they die (except in the case of *America's Army*), this most recent wave of contemporary military FPS games depicts violence and killing of a previously unheard of quantity and quality.

However, this set of games also does an even better job of framing the conflicts in which the players are participating than those from the late 1990s. Instead of drawing from popular culture and history (or popular renditions of history,) these FPS games define their conflicts in terms that are circulating in contemporary culture. Fitting perfectly the ideological frame established by the Bush Administration's War on Terror war rhetoric, those doing the killing are American soldiers, and those killed are terrorists (Coe et al. 2004). Likewise, the missions are not battles in a war to ensure the security of the free world but rather police actions and interventions into the affairs of sovereign nations. Players no longer fight to save the world; instead they fight to bring stability to far-flung regions of the globe, protect strategic partners and preserve markets for American goods.

An Uncontroversial Conclusion

In this chapter, I hope to have shown that the FPS has become less controversial because games in the genre have more recently come to involve stories and themes that applaud American military intervention abroad. In this form, the FPS fits comfortably within the confines of the discursive formations that give shape to everyday life in America. Despite embracing violence against people – something that the early FPS games targeted by parent organizations and media watchdog groups never countenanced—they are intelligible statements within the discursive field of a nation embroiled in a War on Terror.

It is only in the last two years that FPS games have again attracted ire for their depictions of gun violence. In the early months of 2009, publisher Konami pulled funding for Atomic Games' development of *Six Days in Fallujah*, which promised to take players to the scene of the bloodiest battle of the Iraq War (for Coalition troops). Even though the developer began work on the game at the request of American marines who survived Fallujah, critics blasted its historically accurate account of the battle, particularly the deaths of American and British soldiers at the hands of insurgents (*Daily Mail* 2009). *Call of Duty: Modern Warfare 2* (Infinity Ward 2009) was widely criticized for its opening salvo, the level "No Russian," which positions the player as an American agent undercover with a Russian ultranationalist group on a shooting rampage in a Moscow airport. And the reboot of *Medal of Honor* (Danger Close and DICE 2010) also received negative attention for allowing players to play in multiplayer matches as Taliban fighters, though critics were largely pacified when the developers renamed the Taliban the generic "opposing force." In these instances violence was at issue, but not necessarily at the heart of the controversy; "who" the player kills and who does the killing in the game is more pressing than the act of shooting itself.

Indeed, this strategy can be seen in the first iteration of *America's Army*, which allowed online multiplayer matches between teams representing the US Army and terrorists. Significantly, every single player played from the perspective of a US soldier so that no one would ever willfully kill an American soldier. Such a permutation of the statement lacks intelligibility. It is the constitutive outside that highlights the boundaries of the otherwise open field upon which FPS players may kill without qualm.

Note

1 While AWE Productions' *Witchaven* series and Ravensoft's *Heretic* and *Hexen* used FPS game engines and mechanics, they also draw much from fantasy role-playing and are not typically discussed alongside the FPS games that represent gun violence. These games were, like contemporaneous FPS games, set in fantastic milieus populated by vicious creatures.

References

Butler, Judith. 1993. *Bodies that Matter: On the Discursive Limits of Sex*. NYC: Routledge.

Coe, Kevin, David Domke, Erica Graham, Sue L. John, and Victor W. Pickard. 2004. "No Shades of Gray: The Binary Discourse of George W. Bush and an Echoing Press." *Journal of Communication* 54 (2): 234–52.

Foucault, Michel. 1972. *The Archaeology of Knowledge & The Discourse on Language*. NYC: Pantheon.

—1990. *History of Sexuality, Volume 1: An Introduction*. NYC: Vintage.

Galloway, Alexander. 2006. "Origins of the First-Person Shooter." In *Gaming: Essays in Algorithmic Culture*, 39–69. Minneapolis, MN: University of Minnesota Press.

Gitelman, Lisa & Geoffrey B. Pingree. 2003. *New Media: 1740–1915*. Cambridge, MA: MIT Press.

Gross, Doug. 2011, June 1. "The 10 Biggest Violent Video-Game Controversies." *CNN.com*. http://articles.cnn.com/2011-06-29/tech/violent.video.games_1_sale-of-violent-video-mortal-kombat-entertainment-software-rating-board?_s=PM:TECH

Grossman, Dave and Gloria DeGaetano. 1999. *Stop Teaching Our Kids to Kill: A Call to Action Against TV, Movie & Video Game Violence*. NYC: Random House.

Hess, Aaron. 2007. "'You Don't Play, You Volunteer': Narrative Public Memory Construction in *Medal of Honor: Rising Sun*." *Critical Studies in Media Communication* 24 (4): 339–56.

"Iraq War Video Game Branded 'Crass and Insensitive' by Father of Red Cap Killed in Action." 2009, April 7. *Daily Mail*. http://www.dailymail.co.uk/news/article-1168235/Iraq-War-video-game-branded-crass-insensitive-father-Red-Cap-killed-action.html

Jenkins, Henry. 1993. "x Logic: Placing Nintendo in Children's Lives." *Quarterly Review of Film and Video* 14 (4): 55–70.

Kirsch, Steven J. 2011. *Children, Adolescents and Media Violence: A Critical Look at the Research*. Los Angeles: Sage.

Kohler, Chris. 2007, October 30. "How Protests Against Games Cause them to Sell More Copies." *Wired* http://www.wired.com/gamelife/2007/10/how-protests-ag/

Kushner, David. 2003. *Masters of DOOM: How Two Guys Created an Empire and Transformed Pop Culture*. NYC: Random House.

Lenhart, Amanda, Sydney Jones, and Alexandra Macgill. 2008, December 7. *Adults and Video Games*. Pew Internet & American Life Project. http://pewinternet.org/Reports/2008/Adults-and-Video-Games.aspx

Lumby, Catharine. 1997. "Panic Attacks: Old Fears in a New Media Era." *Media International Australia* 85: 40–6.

Marvin, Carolyn. 1988. *When Old Technologies Were New: Thinking About Electric Communication in the Late Nineteenth Century*. NYC: Oxford University Press.

McElroy, Justin. 2010, August 12. "Ken Levine explains why BioShock Infinite isn't photorealistic." *Joystiq.com*. http://www.joystiq.com/2010/08/12/ken-levine-explains-why-BioShock-infinite-isnt-photorealistic/

Miller, Toby. (2006). "Gaming for Beginners." *Games and Culture* 1 (1): 5–12.

Quinlan, Joe. (Producer) (1982, December 29). *The MacNeil/Lehrer Report* [Television Broadcast]. Educational Broadcasting and GWETA.

Springhall, John. 1998. *Youth, Popular Culture and Moral Panics: Penny Gaffs to Gangsta-Rap, 1830–1996*. NYC: St. Martins Press.

Tuttle, Will. 2005, June 12. "Dale Dye Interview." *GameSpy*. http://ps2.gamespy.com/playstation-2/medal-of-honor-st-nazaire/621891p1.html

Washington State Senate. 1994. Public Health & Safety Act 1994.SBR 6174

Games

3D Realms. 1996. *Duke Nukem 3D* [DOS]. GT Interactive Software.

Danger Close and DICE. 2010. *Medal of Honor* [Microsoft Windows, PlayStation 3, Xbox 360]. Electronic Arts.

Dreamworks Interactive. 1999. *Medal of Honor* [PlayStation]. Electronic Arts.

id Software. 1993. *DOOM* [DOS]. id Software.

Infinity Ward. 2007. *Call of Duty 4: Modern Warfare* [Microsoft Windows, PlayStation 3, Xbox 360]. Activision.

—2009. *Call of Duty: Modern Warfare 2* [Microsoft Windows, PlayStation 3, Xbox 360]. Activision.

Rare Interactive. 1997. *Goldeneye 007* [Nintendo 64]. Nintendo.

Secret Level, US Army and Ubisoft. 2005. *America's Army: Rise of a Soldier* [Xbox]. Ubisoft.
US Army. 2002. *America's Army* [Microsoft Windows]. US Army.

5

The Shameful Trinity: Game Studies, Empire, and the Cognitariat
Toby Miller

Blackwell is what his creators call an interactive virtual character—a life-sized, 3-D simulation of a person whose mission is to help train real soldiers. He inhabits FlatWorld, a kind of theme-park version of a war zone run by the University of Southern California's (USC) Institute for Creative Technologies [ICT].

At a time when Hollywood is often tagged by those on the political right as a liberal bastion, ICT teams the military and the entertainment biz for defense projects, funded by a five-year, $100 million grant from the Pentagon—the largest the university has ever received.

San Diego Union-Tribune (Hebert 2005)

Most of us who are outsiders to the field probably think of electronic games in one of two ways. They are either the newest means of rotting the brains of the young, or exciting new educational forms that will improve learning. In terms of the role that research universities should play in them, we perhaps imagine that scholars evaluate the potential harm caused in real life by players of violent first-person shooter games (hereafter FPS) alongside the potential benefit of conflict-resolution gaming or peaceful virtual worlds. We might even think about those wacky folks over in creative industries making their own games as part of the entrepreneurial spirit of small business that is supposedly enabled by their work in universities.

Meanwhile, there is a binary in game studies. At one antinomy stand omniscient, omnipotent technocrats plotting to control the emotions and thoughts of young people around the world and turn them into malleable consumers, workers, and killers. At the other stand omniscient, omnipotent players outwitting the efforts of capital, the state, and parents to understand and corral them (Tobin 2004). Psychologists who construct the former model replay their baleful contributions to attacking the popular that have stalked media innovations for over a century. New-media *savants* who construct the latter model invoke pre-capitalist philosophers, thereby dodging questions of state and capital by heading for aesthetics.

This second, boosterish group concerns me most here, because it contributes to the phenomenon I am addressing. The reliance on high art and high technology brokers a high neo-liberalism thanks to ludology (ignoring the work of professional associations such as the Association for the Study of Play or the North American Society for the Sociology of Sport) and narratology, returning to the non-materialist, non-medium-specific work of literary studies (ignoring the media studies parlayed by the International Association for Media and Communication Research or the Union for Democratic Communication). Drawing on the banal possessive individualism of neoclassical economics, reactionary game analysts study virtual environments to understand "whole societies under controlled conditions" (Castronova 2006), neglecting or caricaturing history and ethnography as they do so. At an epistemological level, game studies are therefore fractured between supportive insiders who play games, and hostile outsiders who do not.

Beyond that binary, the reality is that game studies churn out content for the military and workers for the industry, predicated on the boosterish antinomy. In response to those political-economic arrangements, this chapter interrogates twin tendencies: the powerful ties that link game studies to imperial militarism and precarious employment. I focus on the United States because it has been a prime mover in militaristic uses of games and innovations of precarious cultural work. Readers may wish to look at other chapters in this volume for additional accounts of games and the military, notably those by Lizardi, Moore, and Voorhees. Fisher offers an alternative vision.

Wider theoretical issues transcend these coordinates, and are guides to where I think game studies of FPS should be heading. The three levels of media studies—the political economy of cultural production, the textuality of meaning, and the creativity of audiences—all need to be central to game studies, even as they are modified to account for the specificities of FPS. We must connect the conditions of existence of games and play—how they came into being, what they are, and what they do—via institutional history, stylistic analysis, and audience research. All three tools are necessary as counters to the reductive celebrations and denunciations of FPS—a febrile yet familiar oscillation in public debates that ironically mirrors spectatorial positions in the games themselves.

Game Studies and the Military

The wider context to these issues is the geopolitical role of the US. And US imperialism poses many complexities for its opponents, analysts, and fellow travelers. Its different modalities have involved invasion and seizure (as per the Philippines and Cuba); temporary occupation and permanent militarization (think of Japan); ideological imperialism (consider the Monroe doctrine and Theodore Roosevelt); febrile anti-Marxism ("All the Way with LBJ" and "Win One for the Gipper"); and ideological anti-imperialism (for example, Franklin Delano Roosevelt and Barack Obama).

Yanqui imperialism differs from the classic nineteenth-century model exemplified by the UK. It's much harder to gain independence from the US than it was from Britain, because US imperialism is indirect and mediated as well as direct and intense. This produces fewer dramatic moments of resistive nation-building than the painful but well-defined struggles towards sovereignty that threw off conventional colonial yokes across the twentieth century. The difference arose because Yanqui imperialism began at a more fully developed stage of industrial capitalism and led into the post-industrial age as Washington sought to break colonialism down and gain access to labor and consumption on a global scale. This coincided with a Cold War that favored imperial proxies over possessions, due to both prevailing ideology and the desire to avoid direct nuclear conflict with an apparent equal. Once the Soviet Union collapsed, the free markets that had been undermined by classic imperialism in 1914 were re-established as rhetorical tropes, confirming the drive towards a looser model of domination.

None of the above means that the US variety of imperialism lacks the drive and the horror of old-world imperialism. The country that advertises itself as the world's greatest promise of modernity has been dedicated to translating its national legacy, a nineteenth-century regime of clearance, genocide, and enslavement as much as democracy—a modernity built, as each successful one has been, on brutality—into a foreign and economic policy with similar effects and, at times, methods. But it has principally done so through ideation rather than colonization, albeit underwritten by military and commercial power. Spain's *conquista de América*, Portugal's *missão civilizadora*, and France's *mission civilisatrice* saw these nations occupy conquered peoples then exemplify approved conduct up close; gringos invade if necessary, then instruct from afar. And game studies have been complicit with imperialism and state terror from the first.

Gaming has been crucial to core doctrines of neo-empire since the late nineteenth century, when the US Naval War College Game simulated Prussian and French field tactics. Such methods gained popularity when they predicted Japanese strategy in the Pacific from 1942. By the late '50s, computers were utilized to theorize and play war games (Der Derian 2003, 38–9). The links to audiovisual simulation were facilitated by the Armed Forces Communications and Electronics Association, a scholarly society that started in 1946 and thrives today.

Meanwhile, game theory in 1960s and '70s political science and warcraft scientized the study and practice of crisis decision-making. It was founded on a rational-actor model of maximizing utility reapplied to states, soldiers, and diplomats to construct nuclear-war prospects. Then, with the decline of Keynesianism, game theory's ideal-typical monadic subject came to dominate economics and political science more generally. Utility maximization even overtook parts of Marxism, which had tended to favor collective rather than selfish models of choice. Games were in, everywhere you looked.

That notion of individuals out for themselves remains in vogue, re-stimulated through electronic games (many of which have been invented or refined for the US military by defense contractors since the early days). The Pentagon worked with Atari in the 1980s to redevelop *BattleZone* as a simulator and established a gaming center within the National Defense University (Power 2007, 276). In the early 1990s, the end of Cold War II wrought economic havoc on many corporations involved in the US defense industry. They turned to games as a natural supplement to their principal customer, the military. The new geopolitical crisis of the twenty-first century has seen firms conducting half their games business with the private market and half with the Pentagon (Hall 2006).

Today's United States is a sovereignty-obsessed territorial state, a de-territorialized overlord, a doctrinaire free marketer, and an interventionist debtor nation—worried about immigration, terrorism, and credit and obsessed with its right to indirect rule of the globe's material resources and supply of labor and loans. The geopolitical segments of these identities merge in Washington's blend of discourse and warfare. And universities and FPS are crucial to that project by providing practical training in, and ideological support for, killing.

In 1996, the National Academy of Sciences held a workshop for academia, Hollywood, and the Pentagon on simulation and games. The next year, the National Research Council announced a collaborative research agenda on popular culture and militarism and convened meetings to streamline such cooperation, from special effects to training simulations, from immersive technologies to simulated networks (Lenoir 2003, 190; Macedonia 2002).

As part of these developments, untold numbers of academic journals and institutes on games have become closely tied to the Pentagon, generating research designed to test and augment the recruiting and training potential of games to ideologize, hire, and instruct the population. The Center for Computational Analysis of Social and Organizational Systems at Carnegie-Mellon University in Pittsburgh, for example, promulgates studies underwritten by the Office of Naval Research and the Defense Advanced Research Projects Agency (DARPA). DARPA's wonderful slogan is "Creating & Preventing Strategic Surprise." Similar work around the country and the globe is proudly paraded by the Association for the Advancement of Artificial Intelligence (another "scientific society") that matches professor to Pentagon.

In Los Angeles, USC's ICT was set up in 1998 to articulate faculty, film and television producers, game designers, and the Defense budget—to the tune of US$45 million in military money, a figure that was doubled with its 2004 renewal. The Secretary of the Army and the head of the Motion Picture Association of America opened the Institute and the set designer for the *Star Trek* franchise created its workspace. ICT proceeded to use Pentagon loot and Hollywood muscle to test out homicidal technologies and narratives under the aegis of film, engineering, and communications professors, collaborating on major motion pictures such as *Spider-Man 2* (Sam Raimi 2004) as well as numerous military applications. By the end of 2010, it could boast that its products were available on 65 military bases (Deck 2004; Silver and Marwick 2006, 50; Turse 2008, 120; Hennigan 2010).

The Institute produces imperial recruitment tools such as *Full Spectrum Warrior* that double as "training devices for military operations in urban terrain": what's good for the Xbox is good for the combat simulator. The utility of these innovations continues in the field. The Pentagon is aware that off-duty soldiers play games and wants to invade their supposed leisure time to wean them from the skater genre many currently favor and towards what are essentially training manuals. It even boasts that *Full Spectrum Warrior* was the "game that captured Saddam," because the men who dug Saddam Hussein out had been trained with it. And electronic games have become crucial tools as fewer and fewer nations allow the US to play live war games on their terrain (Burston 2003; Stockwell and Muir 2003; Andersen 2007; Turse 2008, 122 and 119; Harmon 2003; Kundnani 2004).

To keep up with the Institute's work, you can listen to podcasts from *Armed with Science: Research Applications for the Modern Military* via the Defense Department's website. You'll learn how the Pentagon and USC are developing *UrbanSim* to improve "the art of battle command" as part of Obama's imperial wars. It's described as a small shift from commercial gaming: "instead of having Godzilla and tornados attacking your city, the players are faced with things like uncooperative local officials and ethnic divisions in the communities, different tribal rivalries," to quote an Institute scholar in the pod (March 3 2010 edition). You might also visit its Twitter address (@usc_ict), blog (http://ict.usc.edu), or Facebook page (USCICT). In these purportedly "social media" sites, you'll find hortatory remarks of self-regard rarely seen in the post-War era: the Institute "is revolutionizing learning through the development of interactive digital media" because "[c]ollaborating with our entertainment industry neighbors, we are leaders in producing virtual humans," furthering "cultural awareness, leadership and health"—which means servicing the Pentagon. For despite the fact that ICT (which has stopped replying to my requests for a visit) says its "innovations help save lives," the enterprise is dedicated to renovating machinery of war.

Digging a little further, one can test out these life-saving technologies courtesy of the virtual recruiter "Lab TV Sergeant Star," developed by the Institute's marvelously if unconsciously named Mixed Reality Research and Development wing as a means of attracting gormless youth to serve. Sergeant Star is disingenuously described as "a new class of virtual human guide" animated by "Hollywood storytelling techniques" whose "personality matches his good looks" (Hint: white; square-jawed). Right.

For its part, the Naval Postgraduate School's Modeling, Virtual Environments and Simulation Academic Program developed *Operation Starfighter* based on the film *The Last Starfighter* (Nick Castle 1984). Across the armed forces, attempts were made to connect the ideology and technology of state violence through game studies and popular culture. *America's Army* was launched with due symbolism on the 4th of July 2002—dually symbolic, in that Independence Day doubles as a key date in the film industry's summer roll-out of features. The military had to bring additional servers into play to handle four hundred thousand downloads of the game that first day. *Gamespot PC Reviews* awarded it a high textual rating, and was equally impressed by the "business model." <http://americasarmy.com/community> takes full advantage of the usual array of cybertarian fantasies about the new media as a form of magical civil society, across the gamut of community *fora*, internet chats, fan sites, and virtual competitions. Plus the game is formally commodified through privatization—bought by Ubisoft to be repurposed for consoles, arcades, and cell phones, and turned into figurines by the allegedly edgy independent company Radioactive Clown. Tournaments are convened, replete with hundreds of thousands of dollars' prize money, and there are smaller events at military recruiting sites ("AA:SF" 2008; Power 2007, 279–80; Turse 2008, 117 and 123–4; Lenoir 2003, 175).

A decade after its release, *America's Army* remains one of the ten most-played games on-line, with millions of registered users. Civilian developers regularly refresh it by consulting with veterans and participating in physical war games. Paratexts provide additional forms of promotional renewal. With over forty million downloads, and websites by the thousand, its message has traveled far and wide—an excellent return on the initial public investment of US$19 million and US$5 million for annual updates. Studies of young people who have positive attitudes to the US military indicate that 30 per cent of them formed that view through playing the game—a game that sports a Teen rating, forbids role reversal via modifications (preventing players from experiencing the pain of the other) and is officially ranked first among the Army's recruiting tools (Nieborg 2004; Turse 2008, 118 and 157; Craig 2006; Shachtman 2002; Thompson 2004).

DARPA likes to spread the joy around beyond the ICT, of course, deploying its US$2 billion annual budget to examine how social networking of the game can uncover top *America's Army* players' distinct behaviors, the optimum size of an *America's Army* team, the importance of fire volume toward opponent, the recommendable communication structure and content, and the contribution of the unity among team members (Carley et al. 2005). And the Agency refers to Orlando as "Team Orlando," because the city houses

Disney's research-and-development "imagineers," the University of Central Florida's Institute for Simulation and Training, and Lockheed Martin (the nation's biggest military contractor, whose slogan is "We Never Forget Who We're Working For").

Virtual blowback is underway, with Al Qaeda reportedly learning tactics by playing these games and developing counters of their own (Power 2007, 283), Islam Games thriving, Hezbollah offering *Special Force 2* (Singer 2010), and the artist Joseph DeLappe creating counter-texts on-line by typing the details of dead soldiers into the game under the moniker "dead-in-Iraq." Chapters in this book by Welsh, Snider et al., and Duncan and Ohl address counter-hegemonic FPS gaming.

The upshot of this story must be the recognition that game studies as presently constituted are part of "technological nation-alism" (Charland 1986). They have a symbiotic ideological and material relationship with what is also, by the way, a leading polluter—the US Department of Defense. Military uses of electronics, information technologies, games, and special effects link our field to the Pentagon's orgiastic use of fossil fuels, destruction of terrain and infrastructure, radiation, conventional pollution, buried ordinance, defoliants, land use, anti-personnel mines, carcinogenic chemical deposits, and toxic effluents. Despite latter-day claims that it is "going green," the department remains the world's largest user of petroleum (Shachtman 2010; Corbett and Turco 2006; Leaning 2000; Jorgenson et al. 2010).

The game studies professoriate involved with these delightful paymasters would do well to read some scientific history. In his testimony to the US Atomic Energy Commission, the noted physicist J. Robert Oppenheimer, who led the group that developed the atomic bomb, talked about the instrumental rationality that animated the people who created this awesome technology. Once these scientists saw that it was feasible, the device's impact lost intel-lectual and emotional significance for them. They had been overtaken by what he labeled its "technically sweet" quality (United States Atomic Energy Commission 1954, 81).

Just such techno-saccharine is the lifeblood of the instrumental pleasure and exhilarating utopia that course through the affirmative culture of game studies. "Technically sweet" qualities animate innovation, adoption, and the mix of the sublime—the awesome, the ineffable, the uncontrollable, the powerful—with the beautiful—the approachable, the attractive, the pliant, the soothing. In philosophical aesthetics, the sublime and the beautiful are generally regarded as opposites. But game technologies have helped bring them together for denizens of the ICT and their counterparts across campuses.

That should lead us to a next step, one that transcends console critique or cybertarian acclaim. I clearly favor using political economy, textual analysis, and audience research to comprehend and teach how the media cover militarism. But our efforts should turn not only to publishing and pedagogy but the very fabric of gaming research, notably in the US. For example, the American Academy of Pediatrics denounces the mimetic force of violent electronic games on young people, yet fails to examine how the Pentagon preys upon it (2009). By contrast, as per the brave actions taken by professional bodies in anthropology and—belatedly—psychology against their co-optation by the US war machine, we must turn game studies against imperialism and militarism. For example, USC and Carnegie-Mellon academics should protest the bloody work of empire undertaken on their campuses, collectively and publicly. We must all contest DARPA's ideological incorporation of untenured faculty, whom it seeks to engage via a "Young Faculty Award" that aims "to develop the next generation of academic scientists, engineers and mathematicians in key disciplines who will focus a significant portion of their career on D[epartment]o[f]D[efense] and national security issues." Academics in other countries need to consider boycotts of military-endowed US game studies if we fail to contest our murderous paymasters, as per the struggles against the previous regime in South Africa.

Game Studies and the Cognitariat

In addition to an alliance with imperialism, game studies are also complicit with an industry that is destabilizing work life. Antonio Negri (2007) explains this phenomenon in his re-disposal of the Reaganite futurist Alvin Toffler's (1983) idea of the cognitariat. Negri uses the concept to describe people mired in casualized labor who

have heady educational qualifications and live at the complex inter-
stices of capital, education, and government. As we shall see, that
diagnosis applies to work for game companies and the way they are
boosted as signs of a new, improved economy in the Global North.

The UK's Arts & Humanities Research Council and National
Endowment for Science, Technology and the Arts identify gaming as
a prime "example of where the creative industries make a significant
contribution to the economy" and insist that they should be central
to national research priorities (Bakhshi et al. 2008, 9). The upshot
of this discourse is that market objectives overdetermine cultural
ones. The college-trained cognitariat plays key roles in the production
and circulation of goods and services by creating and coordinating
games, as musicians, directors, writers, journalists, sound engineers,
editors, cinematographers, and graphic designers. The cognitariat
also features audiences and consumers, who pay for content,
interpret it in order to give it living meaning, and elide real barriers
of entry to media production through their dubious anointment
as producer-consumers (prosumers). These groups operate within
institutional contexts: private bureaucracies, controlling investment,
production, and distribution across the media; public bureaucracies,
offering what capitalism cannot while comporting themselves in an
ever-more commercial manner; small businesses, run by charismatic
individuals; and networks, fluid associations formed to undertake
specific projects or represent players' interests.

The prevailing ideology of capitalist futurism that underpins the
cognitariat requires correction. As Marcuse predicted seventy years
ago, far from liberating all and sundry, technological convergence
has intensified managerial coordination (1941). Writing in this critical
neo-Marxist tradition, Herbert I. Schiller (1976, 8–9 and 16) recast
cultural and technological convergence as the "infrastructure of
socialization," designed to synchronize the interests of dominant
strata via "business cultures," organizational models, "institutional
networks," and modes of communication and cultural production.
How does this play out when eager undergrads who have learnt how
to design games enter the industry?

These willing cognitarians typically engage in practices of self-
exploitation and identity formation. They appear to be autotelic, such
that being part of the gentried poor and dedicated to the life of the

mind via play is fulfilling in itself (Gorz 2004). This makes them prey to predatory employers: big publishers develop exploitative work practices as their power increases via the destruction or purchase of small businesses. Consider the notorious case of Electronic Arts (hereafter, EA). EA is based in California, with "worldwide studios" in British Columbia and offshoots in Canada, Hong Kong, Tokyo, China, and Britain, *inter alia*. It makes *The Sims*, National Hockey League games, *FIFA World Cup*, and the John Madden "football" franchise. Trip Hawkins founded the company in 1982, dismissing television as "brain-deadening" and embracing "interactive media" as a development "that would connect people and help them grow." Not surprisingly, and in best cybertarian fashion, EA derives from a desire to emphasize art and technology under the sign of publishing. Its developers were initially promoted as authors. *M.U.L.E.* and *Murder on the Zinderneuf*, for instance, were marketed through their designers' names—rather like rock albums of the day. Several shining-white designer youths were celebrated in a famous 1983 advertisement called "We See Farther." But geek authorship was soon supplanted. By the mid-1980s, the "authors" of key games were no longer dweebs in black polo necks, but Doctor J and Larry Bird (basketball celebrities brought in as endorsers and *faux* designers). Creators lost their moment of fame as authors and became cognitarians (Cifaldi and Fleming 2007; for the general story of deauthorizing game designers, see Deuze et al. 2007).

EA bought development studios, set up design teams on an industrial model, and cut discounts to software distributors. Then it dealt directly with retailers, writing games for personal computers and consoles and becoming a distributor. In addition to continuing with console options, EA entered virtual worlds and awakened to female consumers in the late 1990s, buying advertising space and time across fashion periodicals and TV aimed at young women. The firm became massively successful—2007 revenues were US$3.091 billion, the company boasted almost eight thousand employees, and it began buying other studios. After losing pre-eminence to Activision-Blizzard in 2009–10, EA's stock price fell, but an early switch from a dependence on console games meant it was ready to deal with the desire of young men for virtual killing via mobile devices (Cifaldi and Fleming 2007; Cadin et al. 2006; Morris 2011).

Most importantly for our story, in 2004, the company became a byword for the poor labor practices that characterize the sector, because a blogger going under the *soubriquet* of ea_spouse posted a vibrant account of the exploitation experienced by her *fiancé* and others working for the firm (ea_spouse 2004). Eloquently ripping back the veneer of joyous cybertarianism from games development, she disclosed that EA's claim to blend aesthetics and technology, as per its name and corporate trademark—"Challenge Everything"—belied the company's treatment of employees. She interpellated "any EA executive that happens to read this" provocatively: "I have a good challenge for you: how about safe and sane labor practices for the people on whose backs you walk for your millions?"

The nature of such exploitation, across many companies, is this: a putatively limited "pre-crunch" is announced in the period prior to release of a new game. Forty-eight-hour weeks are required, with the alibi that months of this will obviate the need for a real "crunch" at the conclusion of development. The pre-crunch goes on beyond its deadline, and 72-hour weeks are mandated. That crunch passes its promised end, illness and irritability strike, and a new crunch is announced. Everyone must work 85- to 91-hour weeks, 9 am to 10 pm Monday to Sunday inclusive, with the (occasional) Saturday evening off, after 6.30 pm. There is no overtime or leave in return for this massive expenditure of talent and time (also see Dyer-Witheford and de Peuter 2006; Schumacher 2006–7).

At the very moment that ea_spouse blew the whistle on the corporation, *Fortune* magazine was ranking EA among the "100 Best Companies to Work For" (Levering et al. 2003). The firm went on to come 62nd in the magazine's "List of Industry Stars" and was declared 91st among firms that "try hard to do right by their staff" as measured by the Great Place to Work Institute in San Francisco (for depthless smiles, see the photo gallery at http://www.greatplacetowork.com). EA calls itself "a one-class society." Its Vice-President of Human Resources at the time of ea_spouse's revelations, Rusty Rueff, operated with the following dictum: "Most creativity comes at one of two times: When your back is up against the wall or in a time of calm." Today, EA Labels President Frank Gibeau reassures potential investors that "we're on the offensive. We're moving from a fire-and-forget packaged goods model to an online services model." In case readers find these jumped-up, pumped-up firing-squad analogies in any way alarming, *Fortune* magazine admiringly notes that cognitarians can "refresh their energy with free espresso or by playing volleyball and basketball." Despite these wonders, the exploitation begat class-action lawsuits that saw the funsters pay US$30 million for overdue overtime based on the fact that employees "do not perform work that is original or creative" and are "seldom allowed to use their own judgment" (Dyer-Witheford and de Peuter 2006; Morris 2011; Surette 2006; for additional scandal, see Bohannon 2008). EA's website continues to blather on about its labor record, but not in terms of the class action—rather, how well it fares on the Human Rights Campaign's Corporate Equality Index. So that's alright, then.

ea_spouse's bold intervention generated febrile and substantial responses, such as calls for unionization, appeals to federal and state labor machinery, confirmation that EA was horrendous but by no means aberrant, frustration that the bourgeois press was disinclined to investigate or even report the situation, denunciations of asinine managerialism and private-sector bureaucracy (for example, "[t]he average game company manager is quite possibly the worst qualified leader of people in the world"), and a recognition that intellectual property rights make labor disposable ("I'm beginning to think that EA is really nothing more than a licensing warehouse. They'll always be able to recruit naïve talent to slave away ... alienating talent is not a big problem for them"). ea_spouse went on to run a website replete with horror stories from angry former idealists across the globe who thought they were doing "cool stuff" until they experienced web-shop horror. Meanwhile, labor solidarity remains compromised by job threats from around the world and non-disclosure agreements, which send a chill wind across employment silos (Waters 2007).

Conclusion

The German cultural-policy advocacy group Kultur Macht Europa issued an instructive and sterling declaration following its Fourth Federal Congress on Cultural Policy in 2007 about protecting cognitarians as well as proprietors under copyright and other laws. Similar concerns appear in the *Jodhpur Initiative for Promoting Cultural Industries in the Asia-Pacific Region*, which was adopted by 28 countries in 2005 (*Jodhpur Initiatives* 2005). Inspired by such counters to the dominant discourse of game studies, analysts need to follow Vincent Mosco's reminder that real work begins once the utopic and dystopic rhetorics of new communications technologies and cultural genres have played out, the moment when alarm and fantasy give way to banality (2004, 19). Otherwise, we are left with the same tired choice: "the freedom to choose after all the major political, economic, and social decisions have already been made" (60). Mosco's imprecation provides a powerful corrective to the apolitical, ahistorical tendencies that characterize much of game studies.

Games are binding art to science as never before. Computing applications to narrative and art, and vice versa, are well known to professors from computing to dance. Faculty at opposite ends of the university write the same codes, analyze the same narratives, go to the same parties, take the same drugs, and sleep with the same people. Just like the cognitariat! In the US, a more powerful link between electronic games and universities brings science and art together. It's called the military. Let's challenge that nexus even as we strive for better working conditions for those laboring in this ultra-cognitarian industry.

References

"AA:SF Tops 9 Million User Mark!" 2008, February 10. <http://americasarmy.com/intel>.

American Academy of Pediatrics, Council on Communications and Media. 2009. "Policy Statement—Media Violence." *Pediatrics* 124 (5): 1495–503.

Andersen, Robin. 2007, February 12. "Bush's Fantasy Budget and the Military/Entertainment Complex." *PRWatch.org* <http://prwatch.org/node/5742>.

Bakhshi, Hasan, Philippe Schneider, and Christophe Walker. 2008. *Arts and Humanities Research and Innovation*. London: Arts & Humanities Research Council/National Endowment for Science, Technology & the Arts.

Bohannon, John. 2008. "'Spore' Documentary Spawns Protest by Scientists Who Starred in It." *Science* 322: 517.

Burston, Jonathan. 2003. "War and the Entertainment Industries: New Research Priorities in an Era of Cyber-Patriotism." *War and the Media: Reporting Conflict 24/7*, edited by Daya Kishan Thussu and Des Freedman, 163–75. London: Sage Publications.

Cadin, Loïc, Francis Guérin, and Robert DeFillippi. 2006. "HRM Practices in the Bohannon Video Game Industry: Industry or Country Contingent?" *European Management Journal* 24 (4): 288–98.

Carley, Kathleen, Il-Chul Moon, Mike Schneider, and Oleg Shigiltchoff. 2005. *Detailed Analysis of Factors Affecting Team Success and Failure in the America's Army Game*. CASOS Technical Report.

Castronova, Edward. 2006. "On the Research Value of Large Games: Natural Experiments in Norrath and Camelot." *Games & Culture: A Journal of Interactive Media* 1 (2): 163–86.

Charland, Maurice. 1986. "Technological Nationalism." *Canadian Journal of Political and Social Theory* 10 (1): 196–220.

Cifaldi, Frank and Jeffrey Fleming. 2007, February 16. "We See Farther—A History of Electronic Arts." *Gamasutra: The Art & Business of Making Games* <http://www.gamasutra.com/view/feature/1711/we_see_farther__a_history_of_.php>.

Corbett, Charles J. and Richard P. Turco. 2006. *Sustainability in the Motion Picture Industry*. Report prepared for the Integrated Waste Management Board of the State of California <http://www.ioe.ucla.edu/media/files/mpis_report.pdf>.

Craig, Kathleen. 2006, June 6. "Dead in Iraq: It's No Game." *Wired* <http://www.wired.com/gaming/gamingreviews/news/2006/06/71052>.

Deck, Andy. 2004. "Demilitarizing the Playground." *Art Context* <http://artcontext.org/crit/essays/noQuarter>.

Der Derian, James. 2003. "War as Game." *Brown Journal of World Affairs* 10 (1): 37–48.

Deuze, Mark, Chase Bowen Martin, and Christian Allen. 2007. "The Professional Identity of Gameworkers." *Convergence: The International Journal of Research into New Media Technologies* 13 (4): 335–53.

Dyer-Witheford, Nick and Greig S. de Peuter. 2006. "'EA Spouse' and the Crisis of Video Game Labour: Enjoyment, Exclusion, Exploitation, and Exodus." *Canadian Journal of Communication* 31 (3): 599–617.

ea_spouse. 2004, November 11. "EA: The Human Story." *Live Journal* <http://ea-spouse.livejournal.com/274.html>.

Gorz, André. 2004. "Économie de la connaissance, exploitation des savoirs: Entretien réalisé par Yann Moulier Boutang and Carlo Vercellone." *Multitudes* <http://multitudes.samizdat.net/Economie-de-la-connaissance>.

Hall, Karen J. 2006. "Shooters to the Left of Us, Shooters to the Right: First Person Arcade Shooter Games, the Violence Debate, and the Legacy of Militarism." *Reconstruction: Studies in Contemporary Culture* 6 (1) <http://reconstruction.eserver.org/061/hall.shtml>.

Harmon, Amy. 2003, April 3. "More Than Just a Game, But How Close to Reality?" *New York Times* <http://www.nytimes.com/2003/04/03/technology/more-than-just-a-game-but-how-close-to-reality.html>.

Hebert, James. 2005, November 6. "Band of Brothers." *San Diego Union-Tribune* <http://legacy.signonsandiego.com/uniontrib/20051106/news_lz1a06ictech.html>.

Hennigan, W. J. 2010, November 2. "Computer Simulation is a Growing Reality for Instruction." *Los Angeles Times* <http://articles.latimes.com/2010/nov/02/business/la-fi-virtual-reality-20101102>.

Jodhpur Initiatives. 2005. *Asia-Pacific Creative Communities: A Strategy for the 21st Century*. Bangkok: UNESCO.

Jorgenson, Andrew K., Brett Clark, and Jeffrey Kentor. 2010. "Militarization and the Environment: A Panel Study of Carbon Dioxide Emissions and the Ecological Footprints of Nations, 1970–2000." *Global Environmental Politics* 10 (1): 7–29.

Kultur Macht Europa. 2007, June 7. "Culture Powers Europe" <http://www.kultur-macht-europa.eu/47.html?&no_cache=1&L=1&tx_ttnews%5Btt_news%5D=138&cHash=d8fe0dfdce>.

Kundnani, Arun. 2004. "Wired for War: Military Technology and the Politics of Fear." *Race & Class* 46 (1): 116–25.

Leaning, Jennifer. 2000. "Environment and Health: 5. Impact of War." *Canadian Medical Association Journal* 163 (9): 1157–61.

Lenoir, Timothy. 2003. "Programming Theaters of War: Gamemakers as Soldiers." *Bombs and Bandwidth: The Emerging Relationship Between Information Technology and Security*, edited by Robert Latham, 175–98. New York: New Press.

Levering, Robert, Milton Moskowitz, Ann Harrington, and Christopher Tzacyk. 2003, January 20. "100 Best Companies to Work For." *Fortune*: 127–52.

Macedonia, Mike. 2002. "Games, Simulation, and the Military Education Dilemma." *The Internet and the University: 2001 Forum*, 157–67. Boulder: Educause.

Marcuse, Herbert. 1941. "Some Social Implications of Modern Technology." *Studies in Philosophy and Social Sciences* 9 (3): 414–39.

Morris, Chris. 2011, March 2. "Electronic Arts Goes 'On the Offensive.'" *CNBC.com* <http://www.cnbc.com/id/41875080>.

Mosco, Vincent. 2004. *The Digital Sublime: Myth, Power, and Cyberspace*. Cambridge, Mass.: MIT Press.

Negri, Antonio. 2007. *goodbye mister socialism*. Paris: Seuil.

Nieborg, David B. 2004. "America's Army: More Than a Game." *Transforming Knowledge into Action Through Gaming and*

Simulation, edited by Thomas Eberle and Willy Christian Kriz. Munich: SAGSAGA. CD-ROM.

Peichi, Chung. 2008. "New Media for Social Change: Globalisation and the Online Gaming Industries of South Korea and Singapore." *Science Technology & Society* 13 (2): 303–23.

Power, Marcus. 2007. "Digitized Virtuosity: Video War Games and Post-9/11 Cyber-Deterrence." *Security Dialogue* 38 (2): 271–88.

Schiller, Herbert I. 1976. *Communication and Cultural Domination*. New York: International Arts and Sciences Press.

Schumacher, Leif. 2006–7. "Immaterial Fordism: The Paradox of Game Industry Labor." *Work Organisation, Labour and Globalisation* 1 (1): 144–55.

Shachtman, Noah. 2002, July 4. "Shoot 'Em Up and Join the Army." *Wired* <http://www.wired.com/gaming/gamingreviews/news/2002/07/53663>.

—2010, May/June. "Green Monster." *Foreign Policy* <http://www.foreignpolicy.com/articles/2010/04/26/green_monster?page=full>.

Silver, David and Alice Marwick. 2006. "Internet Studies in Times of Terror." *Critical Cyberculture Studies*, edited by David Silver and Adrienne Massanari, 47–54. New York: New York University Press.

Singer, Peter W. 2010, March/April. "Meet the Sims ... and Shoot Them." *Foreign Policy* <http://www.foreignpolicy.com/articles/2010/02/22/meet_the_sims_and_shoot_them?page=full>.

Sisler, Vit. 2008. "Digital Arabs: Representation in Video Games." *European Journal of Cultural Studies* 11 (2): 203–20.

Stockwell, Stephen and Adam Muir. 2003. "The Military-Entertainment Complex: A New Facet of Information Warfare." *Fibreculture* 1 <http://one.fibreculturejournal.org/fcj-004-the-military-entertainment-complex-a-new-facet-of-information-warfare>.

Surette, Tim. 2006, April 26. "EA Settles OT Dispute, Disgruntled 'Spouse' Outed." *GameSpot* <http://www.gamespot.com/news/6148369.html>.

Thompson, Clive. 2004, August 22. "The Making of an X Box Warrior." *New York Times Magazine* <http://query.nytimes.com/gst/fullpage.html?res=9C02EEDD133FF931A1575BC0A9629C8B63&pagewanted=1>.

Tobin, Joseph. 2004. "Introduction." *Pikachu's Global Adventure*, edited by Joseph Tobin, 3–33. Durham: Duke University Press.

Toffler, Alvin. 1983. *Previews and Premises*. New York: William Morrow.

Turse, Nick. 2008. *The Complex: How the Military Invades Our Everyday Lives*. New York: Metropolitan Books.

United States Atomic Energy Commission. 1954. *In the Matter of J. Robert Oppenheimer. Transcript of Hearing Before Personnel Security Board* <http://universityhonors.umd.edu/HONR269J/archive/AEC540612.htm>.

PART TWO

Campaign

6

Bigger, Better, Stronger, Faster: Disposable Bodies and Cyborg Construction

Josh Call

"You, my cyborgs, are the product of my imagination and labor: living beings with the control and organization of a machine. Tirelessly, I will work to strip away the barriers that keep living beings from realizing their full potential … Humanity is on the verge of a new era, with me, SHODAN, as its god." Shodan, *System Shock 2* (Irrational Games 1999)

It's a Saturday evening at home, and I'm taking a rare chance to play a game. I'm making a vain attempt at a *Mirror's Edge* (DICE 2008) speed run, and the learning curve is surprisingly steep. My wife sits on the couch reading a book, avoiding looking at the game that tends to make her motion-sick. In the middle of attempting a relatively simple jump, I miss my mark. I mutter something to myself. My wife looks up to witness the slow free-fall of my character to her inevitable demise. As the avatar picks up speed, gradually reaching terminal velocity, my wife looks away and closes her eyes. Mistaking her reaction for a motion sickness response, I offer to shut down the game. She looks back at me and says: "It wasn't making me sick, I just don't want to think about what that fall feels like."

In some ways this kind of reaction seems surprising. After all, it was not my wife doing the falling. It was not someone she knows. It was not even a character she has any particular attraction to or identification with. FPS games are a tolerated genre in our house; something to be played after the kids go to bed and when there is nothing "more worthwhile" to watch. Much of this is rooted in the discomfort generated by the core gameplay mechanics. It is not a question of violence, or narrative structure, so much as it is a function of bodily presence. Her statement is suggestive of the ways in which the player is compelled to collapse the distance between the physical body and the game's point-of-view through the avatar. Effectively, when I missed my mark and failed the jump, the inevitable free-fall finale was perceived and interpreted by my wife as a visceral experience read through the lens and language of her own embodiment. The avatar's experience became co-present with my wife's.

Digital Bodies in FPS Games

There is considerable conversation about the role of the avatar in FPS games. This is hardly surprising given that the primary vehicle for FPS gameplay (not to mention the cinematic point-of-view) is the avatar's body. The introduction to this volume invests considerable time into naming the unique aspects of the FPS genre as rooted both in the visual perspective and the ontological orientations of "immersion" and "identification." These features are rooted in the primary apparatus of the avatar. It serves as a focal point for the player's actions and agency in the gameworld, ultimately encoding player choice through a dynamic of interactivity.

The degree to which games fully develop this kind of interaction is, to some extent, variable. Still, the general trend is to root the bulk of the player's lens to the items or weapons held in their hands. The recognition of the body is reduced then to whatever weapons or items the player uses. Notable exceptions to this trend exist, although they produce their own level of complication. Namco's conceptual FPS game *Breakdown* (2004) adds additional interactivity by providing inputs for the avatar to pick up items and interact with game objects. Unlike the more frequent practice of picking up items by simply "running over" them, Namco's more complicated construct requires players to center their gaze on the item and, using a sequence of button-pressing, actually witness the avatar picking up the object in question. There is a complex sequence of steps here. After centering the camera, the screen prompts the player to press the "use" button. One press brings up the avatar's hand (which can

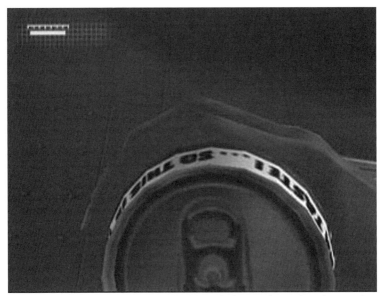

Figure 6.1 The player is provided with an intimate view when interacting with items in *Breakdown* (Namco 2004) There is even a memorable scene involving a toilet and some digestive pyrotechnics, thankfully not pictured here.

be adjusted slightly using the controller). A second press causes the hand to reach out and claim the item with a snatching motion. At this point, the player can control the hand holding the object, rotating it slightly to study our new find. Several objects reward the player for doing this by having writing on them that is ultimately inconsequential to the game beyond flavor context. A third and final press of the action button finally "uses" the actual item.

While this may seem a bit excessive by general FPS standards, it certainly pushed the level of game interaction in certain ways. While it clearly slowed down the pace of the game, forcing players to consider (if only briefly) the items they engaged with, it also reinforces a central element of the player/avatar relationship by re-centering the body as tangible element. As the above picture shows, the body does more in *Breakdown* than simply move and shoot. It also pushes keys (one button at a time), drinks soda (not without an animation for actually popping open the can), and carries food to the mouth (the image of which always changes in order to reflect the bite taken). This is an interesting example that pushes certain aspects of interaction and immersion in new ways. The increasing levels of interaction suggest a more involved player-avatar relationship by increasing both the frequency and tangibility of player action. Eating and drinking make sense, as bodily actions, and the rendering of these moves reflects their "realness." Alison McMahan (2003) theorizes this trend as a design consequence of games moving increasingly towards virtual reality simulation. Namco's experimental efforts here seem an appropriate expression of that trend in their attempt to make movements more contextualized, more "real." What is interesting is that the degree of immersion is drastically reduced in this interaction because of the steps involved. Our ability to suspend our disbelief here is challenged by the constant mechanic of pressing the "action" button at each step of interacting with the item.

This notion of avatar-based immersion is nothing new. T. L. Taylor (2002) imagines embodiment as a natural extension of gameplay environments: "Avatars form one of the central points at which users intersect with a technological object and embody themselves." This embodiment occurs as a result of viewing the game's avatar manifest player agency and action, "making the virtual environment and the variety of phenomenon it fosters real." While Taylor's analysis focuses on online environments and multiple user contexts, there are clear implications for avatar-based games in general, in particular FPS games, specifically for the ways that such games root inter-action in a body. Taylor further offers: "Users do not simply roam through the space as 'mind,' but find themselves grounded in the practice of the body, and thus in the world." Having a body serves as our primary mechanic and metaphor for understanding and inter-acting with gamespaces. The presence or absence of realistic body movements is a cornerstone of sound FPS game design, and also one if its greatest hurdles (as in the example of *Breakdown*). Peter Bayliss (2004) extends the player/avatar relationship by focusing on the gameplay as the locus of interaction between the two. Bayliss' argument centers on the ambiguity of terms like "immersion" and "engagement," preferring instead to discuss the qualities that determine the player's context for "being-in-the-game-world." This context, informed by the familiarity and ease with which players respond to digital inputs and contexts, serves as a function of our collapsed nature into the avatar; the digital self requires players to develop new literacies of play in order to effectively "be" in the game.

It is this characteristic of "being" that gaming bodies so neces-sarily explore in play. The player-avatar relationship is not simply a matter of control and extension, but serves in a much more intimate capacity. Bayliss further argues that "the experience of any particular player arises predominately from the attitude or position they take towards the activities a specific videogame affords." These affordances are made manifest through the ontological extension of the player's avatar – a participation in being between the player and the gameworld. This participation serves as a reflection of player action, indexing their active sense of self in gamespace. Bob Rehak's (2003) *Playing at Being: Psychoanalysis and the Avatar* extends this notion, arguing that:

> Through gaming then the concepts of avatar and interface become linked; part of what users seek from computers is continual response to their own actions—a reflection of personal agency made available onscreen for reclamation. (5)

James Gee (2008) offers a similar vision of the player/avatar relationship, extending the avatar to represent player agency and learning in digital space. He argues that:

> [P]layers inhabit the goals of a virtual character in a virtual world. At the same time, that virtual world is designed to be attuned to those goals. In these video games, the real-world player gains a surrogate, that is, the virtual character the player is playing (e.g. Garrett in *Thief: Deadly Shadows*). By inhabit I mean that you, the player, act in the game as if the goals of your surrogate are your goals. (6)

This is an important inversion on the player-avatar relationship as it suggests a kind of reciprocal nature between player and avatar, a further collapsing not only of bodies, but of intentions and actions.

Given the complex work of hybridizing the gaming body through the player-avatar, it should come as no real surprise that games overall have become increasingly complex. These games, though, work with cyborgs largely as a product of mechanistic construction and ludic genre through the presence of the avatar. Moreover, this has pushed the FPS as a genre into cyborg status. Its hybrid nature is exemplified in the cross-pollination between the FPS and the RPG. Games like *System Shock* and *System Shock 2* served as functional and ideological precursors to other titles like the *Deus Ex* franchise. While it is, perhaps, appropriate that these games ask players to engage with the social and ethical consequences of the cyborg in their narratives, it is their design elements that serve to highlight their hybrid nature.

Most fans of the FPS genre will recognize the name *Deus Ex*. Built on models established by the *System Shock* games (Oliver and Peltier 2005), *Deus Ex* broke new ground in player immersion as a consequence of choice, particularly as it relates to the construction of the body. Imagined from the beginning as a hybrid game built on the necessity of player choice (Spector 2000), a central feature of each of the three *Deus Ex* titles is the ability to customize the "body" to suit the needs of the player. Players enact their particular version of the cyborg body through the game's interface of inventory and upgrades. These upgrades, while cybernetic in nature, ultimately

Figure 6.2 *Deus Ex: Human Revolution* (Eidos Montreal 2011) has a significant series of options in upgrading and modifying the avatar body of protagonist Adam Jensen These choices serve to "augment" the player's abilities according to the strategies they wish to employ.

focus the accessible strategies that a player might adopt throughout the game. These features, while distinctly RPG in nature, serve to hybridize (and equally cyborgize) this FPS game by commodifying our bodily choices into game-based decisions (Lahti 2003).

These choices, while a function of the core gameplay, reiterate the nature of the body and its cyborg status. The body, however impermanent, becomes the site of political choice as a result of the ontology it generates through the play options it makes available. Gee (2008) offers up the idea of what he names the "projective stance," whereby players project themselves into the playspace via the avatar as a means to become consubstantial with the game. He argues that "virtual characters have virtual minds and virtual bodies. They become the player's surrogate mind and body" (6). This makes the act of playing games a political move, in the sense that it requires conscious action on choice, and construction of the player-avatar according to a design. This is rooted in an interaction and immersion that are reciprocal between game and player, and allows the avatar to exist as a cyborg body—a digital and mechanical extension of the player.

If, then, the avatar is to serve as the embodied locus of player interaction, the necessary question that follows is: "What kind of cyborg body is the player-avatar?"

Cyborg Bodies: Avatars and Hybrid Self

We are a culture obsessed with cyborgs. Whether an inevitable consequence of an increasingly technocratic culture, or a strict fascination with altering the nature of our body, cybernetics infuses our media in countless ways. From the mega-corp. information currency of Cyberpunk Fiction and *Shadowrun* (FASA Corporation) games, to the various visions of the cyborg as destroyers of humanity, the cyborg image permeates our popular media. Few readers will see the word "cyborg" and not think of *Star Trek* and the Borg. Others will undoubtedly remember James Cameron's *The Terminator* (1984), and the subsequent franchise of movies. Readers more familiar with the literary iterations of cyborgs might hearken back to the works of Isaac Asimov or Philip K. Dick. Regardless of what associations we draw, the cyborg has fully integrated with our cultural milieu as well as our technological reality. The trouble with these particular constructions is that their representations function as a more problematic counterpoint to genuine cyborg ontology; they reify an image of the cyborg as rooted in gender binaries (Devoss 2000), or colonial rhetorics of difference (Handlarski 2010). While a complicated construction, the cyborg serves as a focal point for understanding the complexities of the player-avatar relationship, particularly as it applies to FPS games and mechanics.

By now, many readers will be familiar with Donna Haraway's (1999) often-cited "A Cyborg Manifesto: Science, Technology, and Socialist Feminism in the Late 20th Century." The scope of the argument presents the idea of the cyborg as a viable extension of feminist political agency—one rooted in changing both the rhetorical and bodily politics of women. Drawing on a range of theories and discourses, Haraway offers a vision of human/machine interaction that serves as both scientific taxonomy and social metaphor. It is in this vision of the cyborg that the player-avatar relationship takes on new focus, specifically in FPS games. Haraway's central defining feature of the cyborg names it as both bodily construct and operative metaphor:

> A cyborg is a cybernetic organism, a hybrid of machine and organism, a creature of social reality as well as a creature of fiction. Social reality is lived social relations, our most important political construction, a world-changing fiction. (191)

And while our culture celebrates and reinforces cyborg images in popular media, the reality of such bodily constructions extends well beyond the products of action films into the political and bodily discourses of those who engage with it. In this regard, the player-avatar serves as a substantial example of a cyborg construction.

The avatar cyborg indexes its hybrid status in multiple ways. Given the reliance of the FPS genre on the embodiment of the player in the avatar, the mechanic of registering and reporting damage and

Figure 6.3 Players watch helplessly as Faith, the protagonist of *Mirror's Edge* (DICE 2008) falls to a frighteningly painful demise. While this simple image does not do justice to the visceral experience, it does highlight the perspective of the player as they experience the event.

pain is integral to successful "being-in-the-game." Much like my wife's reaction to the deadly free-fall of *Mirror's Edge* (see figure 6.3), FPS games have grown increasingly complex in their attention to detail concerning bodily damage. Early examples from the genre are noteworthy for their ability to highlight how things have changed over two decades of game design. Looking specifically at two early hallmarks of the genre, *DOOM* and *Wolfenstein 3D*, the player is presented with an interesting representation of the avatar as index of bodily distress.

Older FPS games relied on a more heavily stylized HUD as a means to represent mechanistic data for the player (see the introduction to this volume for more on this). One of the central features of this HUD was an image of the avatar's face. The primary purpose of this image is to represent the various and multiple emotional affects of the avatar and player. Throughout *DOOM* the player could witness the avatar's face register pain (when getting shot or wounded), rage (when firing at length with certain weapons), or even showing the effects of excessive damage (bleeding out of the eyes, ears, nose, and mouth). These expressive features serve as an index of game experiences, but also serve to illustrate the body in particular kinds of ways. The player experiences harm to the avatar self largely as a witness to an image (one that often looks nothing like the player). This complicates the kind of identification possible, as it clearly suggests that the player is playing a role, rather than embodying the avatar with their own essence.

This particular graphic has several familiar elements to it. First, and most obviously, is the red screen. FPS games (and other genres) have used a flashing red screen to represent to the player that the avatar body is under assault. Each red flash serves to signify injury. This is a traditional means of indexing damage mechanics for the player to react to. As games have grown increasingly complicated, this relatively simple system has evolved into a more robust semiotic system to convey contextual information. For example, looking at the *Call of Duty* franchise, we see the red flashes on the screen, but also a corresponding directional radius marker to indicate directionality for the incoming damage often accompanies them. Now we are expected to know not only that we are being wounded, but also where that corresponding injury and pain are

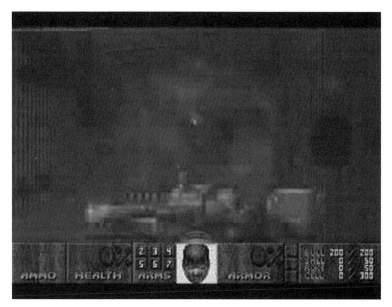

Figure 6.4 Players can watch as the avatar takes increasing levels of damage in *DOOM* (id Software 1993), ultimately seeing their bodies fail. These images often correspond to a more traditional percentage-based health meter This image shows the avatar representation at 0% health.

coming from and to react accordingly. In this regard the body has been alternately prioritized. Rather than simply providing us an image of our character to witness being injured, we are invited into the particulars of the body experience by knowing where the injury is resulting from, and the severity of the wounding (more intense red flashes and radial markers indicate more extensive injury). This level of injury signification functions as ludic, mechanistic, and dramatistic in nature, but also invites an embodied response from the player. The result is the collapsing of the avatar body into a cyborg construct—a hybrid of player and game interface. Haraway's metaphor here reinforces this hybrid nature, reminding us that our identity in this moment is bound to the interaction of body and technology (in this case, the game). This is a moment of telepresence made manifest.

Biocca (1997) invites similar analysis of interactive gaming as a cyborg ontology:

> The teleology of human-machine symbiosis in advanced commu-nication interfaces is towards total embodiment during key periods of information intensive communication (e.g. sensorimotor training in flight, battle, sports, etc.; certain forms of entertainment where simulations of the past places, telepresence to existing places, and the subjective experience of others is critical). (15)

Biocca's larger argument suggests that a more complicated level of awareness stems from increased levels of interactive requirement. In this case, the player is being asked to respond to the imminent threat of bodily damage to the avatar (and, by telepresence extension, the player). These reactions are contingent on the player's ability to respond to the complex series of signs communicated from the games interface, namely severity and directionality of damage. This model is largely representative of current shooter games (first-person) and otherwise. In addition to the *Call of Duty* games, we can see evidence of this current model in the *Halo* franchise, the *Battlefield* franchise, and the *Gears of War* games.

The complication here is that the actual trauma of injury and violence is not present in the moment of play. The tendency of the player to respond in visceral ways to the (tele)presence or antici-pation of injury to the avatar (as my wife does with *Mirror's Edge*) functions as a kind of rhetorical identification with the avatar's body. The perception of injury to the avatar's body is an imagi-native consequence of the immersion of the player in the game through the vehicle of the avatar. In short, the interface provides the means for this interaction while also denying the prospect of total consubstantiation. Bryan-Mitchell Young (2005) reinforces this complicated dualism, arguing that the player's physical self is ultimately "disembodied" in favor of the avatar self. This is a function of utility in gameplay because "The physical body disappears and, at least while playing the game, the body within the game is of much greater concern since it is the body most in use" (2). It is this "gaming body" that serves to highlight the cyborg nature of the player-avatar. Haraway's (1992) cyborg serves as the intersection of flesh and machine, not exclusively the symbiosis. She argues that "The cyborg is the figure born of the interface of automaton and autonomy" (139). This functionally serves as a systemic example of how player and game intersect. The digital game operates not only as a text, but as a "technocultural form" that is only understandable through careful examination of player agency, a kind of "reciprocal relationship between artifacts and social groups" (Gidding 2005). The larger point, that there is a kind of social constructivist link between society and the technologies they employ, functions in tandem with Haraway's vision of bodies as hybrid organisms – at once both biological and mechanical. The caveat is that their identity status (their ontology) is a direct consequence of the kinds of interactions or agency made available through digital immersion.

Disposable Bodies: Cyborg Regeneration and FPS Mechanics

The features of cyborg status are increasingly evident through mechanics specific to the FPS genre. For example, the mechanistic structures that govern simple factors like player health have evolved considerably to reflect a more hybrid vision of the player-avatar. Originally, players had to find items to restore lost health, particularly when health was represented as a functional percentage (as in the earlier *DOOM* image). Many games have moved to an alternate model, often named as a "regenerative health system." Many of the same games under discussion here utilize this method. *Halo* games and *Call of Duty* games (along with numerous others) put this to considerable use. As the player-avatar takes increasing damage, the wounding is no longer registered or reported as a function of numeric representation. Instead, we are presented with an ocularly privileged image of our view being increasingly bloodied, distorted, and hazy. This visual representation is designed to correspond to the severity of the damage registered through the game. The interface translates this for players as increased difficulty in performing tasks through visual hindrance. The irony here, of course, is that the more "damage" a player takes, the harder it is to prevent further damage from occurring. This particular game mechanic was imagined as a "real world" response system, mimicking the effects of wounding and trauma. As a result, players are forced to develop play strategies to account for this; what Martti Lahti (2003) calls a "sort of prosthetic memory ... to survive as we melt into electronic worlds" (166), or what Ted Friedman (1999) would name as the "cyborgian consciousness," the ability to think along with the machine.

What makes this particular system so pivotal for this analysis is the function of "regeneration" in gameplay. Players in these games no longer need to carry an inventory of health items, run over medkits, or worry about stockpiling resources. Instead, they are required to take cover and avoid injury for a short amount of time (usually a matter of several seconds), and the character health will slowly begin regenerating back to full. Assuming no continued injury takes place, players can resume the game in short order with minimal complication. Not surprisingly, games that employ these regenerative health models also frequently design maps and mechanics that reinforce systems of cover to facilitate this feature. This is not a product of a natural body, nor is it a function of any human ideology. Instead, this serves as what Mervyn Bendle (2002) terms a "posthuman ideology," wherein bodily rhetorics are reduced to transferable data. Bendle's larger worries about the ethical consequences of subsuming bodily rhetorics under a posthuman framework may seem grounded in light of this particular game implementation. In earlier examples like *DOOM* (id Software 1993) or *Wolfenstein 3D* (id Software 1989), and more recent titles like *Dead Island* (Techland 2011), *BioShock* (2K Boston 2007), and *Deus Ex: Invisible War* (Eidos Montreal 2011), the presence of significant harm produces particular responses from players. Many of us are familiar with the consequences of being too careless in our game, having no items to support us, and being in a situation that we simply can't surmount – the "no health, no ammo, no items, boss fight" experience. While artificial in some ways (does picking up a medkit really "fix" plasma burns or a shotgun blast to the face?), the structural consequences of a non-regenerating health model were more present to the player. The "body" had limits rooted in the available resources of the player.

This structural revision to the damage mechanic of shooting games (FPS games in particular) offers a bodily rhetoric rooted in a kind of trans-human status. The body becomes a self-replicating, self-sustaining form that exceeds the parameters of the flesh, reifying the possibilities of the mechanical and the digital. It reinforces the cyborg nature of the body by removing the permanence of injury and replacing it with "a self-regulating human machine *system*" (Bendle 2002). This represents a kind of parallel on the cyborg-freedom offered by Haraway (1992), who imagined:

> A cyborg exists when two kinds of boundaries are simultaneously problematic: 1) that between animals (or other organisms) and humans, and 2) that between self-controlled, self-governing machines (automatons) and organisms, especially humans (models of autonomy). The cyborg is the figure born of the interface of automaton and autonomy. (139)

The freedom from the permanence of bodily trauma is implicit in this newer mode of gameplay, making the representation of pain the touchstone of the data, rather than the damage. Pain, here, serves as a both signifier and digital signal, a communication of input independent of physical bodily consequence. In this way, pain is rhetorical. Elaine Scarry (1985) reinforces this idea in her work *The Body in Pain*, offering "physical pain is not identical with (and often exists without) either agency or damage, but these things are referential; consequentially we often call on them to convey the experience of pain itself" (15). Thus, the perceptual representation of pain in the game's damage mechanic translates (in this case) to agency rather than actual damage. The player's reaction is to move, hide, and "mitigate" the pain by regenerating rather than fleeing and "treating" the "damage." This is a reaction at once both biological and mechanical. It highlights the biological reception of pain while effacing the permanence of bodily damage in ways that reinforce the mechanical. The hybrid nature of the cyborg is both present and unavoidable.

This pattern of hybridizing the gaming body, of making it more cyborg, is equally a part of other mechanics central to the FPS game – specifically, the function of respawning. In what is perhaps the ultimate act of making the avatar a cyborg, the permanence of the gaming body can be removed entirely. Many FPS games still employ a traditional "checkpoint" or "save state" mechanic. If the

avatar body is destroyed, the game reverts (both bodily and temporally) to a previous state. Many games employ this method, even in
conjunction with regenerative health models. Still, there are recent
examples in the FPS genre that offer new ways to navigate this
mechanic. Both *BioShock* and *Borderlands* remove the final barrier of
bodily permanence in their ludic mechanics as well as their narrative
constructions. In each case, the gaming body of the avatar ceases
to have a physical ontological permanence, further highlighting the
ontological status of the gaming body. The avatar body is, in this
case, disposable, as an endless supply is readily available.

BioShock explores this mechanic though the inclusion of the
vita-chamber (see figure 5), a device developed by Rapture scientists to clone the body of those whose DNA is kept on file with
each individual device. As the player progresses through the game,
chambers are "unlocked" by proximity. If the player-avatar is killed,
the gaming body is instantly re-corporealized at the vita-chamber
with the necessary inventory and skills, and no loss of game
progress. While the body itself is not a cyborg in the traditional
sense (see Peaty in this collection for more on this) as it lacks a
mechanical/digital component, it is exclusively the product of cyborg
reproduction. The avatar body is the consequence of a mechanical
process governed by systems of code. The uniquely permanent
quality of the body is replaced by a series of bodily constructs,
mechanically produced. The game's narrative offers a complex articulation of this mechanic, arguing that the avatar protagonist is himself
a clone, a body reproduced from the original parent mechanically.
In this case, the city's founder, Andrew Ryan serves as the genetic
"parent" while the biological carrier of the body is derived from the
same technology that allows the vita-chamber. In effect, the game
employs a mechanic that is both ludic and narrative to account for
a process expected of FPS games, while simultaneously reinforcing
the cyborg image of the avatar body. *BioShock* builds this image on
the backs of its spiritual predecessor *System Shock* (Looking Glass
Studios 2004) and the "regeneration chamber." In an interesting
twist, the latter has a much more insidious complication with its
respawn mechanics. If the player is unfortunate enough to perish on
a floor where they have not yet reached the regeneration chamber
and altered its program (the protagonist is a hacker, after all), the

Figure 6.5 The *BioShock* (2K Boston 2007) vita-chamber serves as a familiar sight throughout the game. While functionally it operates like a checkpoint, its mechanics (both ludic and narrative) serve to extend the cyborg metaphor.

minions of the megalomaniacal A. I. Shodan will carry the avatar-body to it personally and convert it to a cyborg servant, devoid of will.

This process is ultimately unsurprising as it reinforces the mechanical nature of reproduction inherent to cyborgs. Haraway (1999) reminds us that "Cyborg replication is uncoupled from organic reproduction" (191). The feminist-social directive of Haraway's project takes on new dimensions here in the presence of the avatar body by de-prioritizing the avatar body in favor of the player-avatar's "gaming body." Bodies cease to be uniquely gendered and rooted in systems of biological reproduction, operating instead from an ontology established in the agency as established by the player. This simultaneously de-prioritizes the biological imperative of reproduction, favoring instead a reproduction rooted in digital performance as opposed to biological permanence. Bodies are disposable and mass-producible. Not only can we produce them, we can make them bigger, better, stronger, and faster.

References

Bayliss, Peter. 2007. "Beings in the Game-world: Characters, Avatars, and Players." IE '07 Proceedings of the 4th Australasian Conference on Interactive Entertainment.

Bendle, Mervyn F. 2002. "Teleportation, Cyborgs and the Posthuman Ideology." *Social Semiotics* 12 (1): 45–62.

Biocca, Frank. 1997. "The Cyborg's Dilemma: Embodiment in Virtual Environments." Second Cognitive Technology Conference, Aizu Japan.

Chee, Yam San. 2007. "Embodiment, Embeddedness, and Experience: Game Based Learning and the Construction of Identity." In *Research and Practice in Technology Enhanced Learning* 2 (1): 3–30.

Devoss, Danielle. 2000. "Rereading Cyborg(?) Women: The Visual Rhetoric of Images of Cyborg (and Cyber) Bodies on the World Wide Web." *Cyberpsychology and Behavior* 3(5): 835–45.

Friedman, Ted. 1999. The Semiotics of SimCity. *First Monday* 4 (4–5) http://frodo.lib.uic.edu/ojsjournals/index.php/fm/article/view/660/575

Gee, James Paul. 2008. "Video Games and Embodiment." In *Games and Culture* 3 (3–4): 253–63.

Giddings, S. 2005. "Playing with Non-Humans: Digital Games as Technocultural Form." In *Proceedings of DiGRA 2005 Conference: Changing Views – Worlds in Play*, 16–20. June 2005, Vancouver, British Columbia, Canada.

Handlarski, Denise. 1992. *Primate Visions: Gender, Race, and Nature in the World of Modern Science.* NYC: Routledge.

—2010. "Pro-Creation: Haraway's 'Regeneration' and the Post-Colonial Cyborg Body." *Women's Studies* 39: 73–99.

Haraway, Donna. 1999. "A Manifesto for Cyborgs: Science, Technology, and Socialist Feminism in the 1980s." In *Feminism / Postmodernism*, edited by Linda J. Nicholson, 190–233. London: Routledge.

Lahti, Martti. 2003. "As We Become Machines: Corporealized Pleasures in Video Games." In *The Video Game Theory Reader*, edited by Mark J. P Wolf and Bernard Perron, 157–70. NYC: Routledge.

McMahan, Alison. 2003. "Immersion, Engagement, and Presence: A Method for Analyzing 3-D G." In *The Video Game Theory Reader*, edited by Mark J. P Wolf and Bernard Perron, 67–86. NYC: Routledge.

Oliver, Martin and Caroline Peltier. 2005. "The Things we Learned on Liberty Island: Designing Games to Help People Become Competent Game Players." Proceedings of DiGRA 2005 Conference: Changing Views – Worlds in Play.

Rehak, Bob. 2003. "Playing at Being: Psychoanalysis and the Avatar."

In *The Video Game Theory Reader*, edited by Mark J. P. Wolf and Bernard Perron, 103–28. NYC: Routledge.

Scarry, Elaine. 1985. *The Body in Pain: The Making and Unmaking of the World*. Oxford: Oxford UP.

Shabot, Sara Cohen. 2010. "Grotesque Bodies: A Response to Disembodied Cyborgs." *Journal of Gender Studies* 15 (3): 223–35.

Smith, Harvey. 2001. "The Future of Game Design: Moving Beyond *Deus Ex* and Other Dated Paradigms." Keynote address of the game track at the Multimedia International Market, Montreal, October 2001.

Spector, Warren. 2000. "Postmortem: Ion Storm's *Deus Ex*." Gamasutra. http://www.gamasutra.com/features/20001206/ spector_01.htm.

Taylor, T. L. 2002. "Living Digitally: Embodiment in Virtual Worlds." In *The Social Life of Avatars: Presence and Interaction in Shared Virtual Environments*, edited by R. Schroeder, 40–62. London: Springer-Verlag

Young, Bryan-Mitchell. "Gaming Mind, Gaming Body: The Mind/Body Split for a New Era." Proceedings of DiGRA 2005 Conference: Changing Views – Worlds in Play.

Games

2K Boston. 2007. *BioShock* [MAC OS X, Microsoft Windows, PlayStation 3, Xbox 360] 2K Games.

DICE. 2008. *Mirror's Edge* [iOS, Microsoft Windows, PlayStation 3, Xbox 360] Electronic Arts.

Eidos Montreal. 2011. *Deus Ex: Human Revolution* [MAC OS X, Microsoft Windows, PlayStation 3, Xbox 360]. Square Enix.

Gearbox Software. 1989. *Wolfenstein 3D* [DOS] Apogee.

—2009. *Borderlands* [Microsoft Windows, PlayStation 3, Xbox 360] 2K Games.

id Software. 1993. *DOOM* [DOS] id Software.

Irrational Games. 1999. *System Shock 2* [Microsoft Windows]. Electronic Arts.

Looking Glass Studios. 1994. *System Shock* [DOS, Macintosh]. Origin Systems.

Namco. 2004. *Breakdown* [Xbox]. Namco Electronic Arts.

Techland. 2011. *Dead Island* [Microsoft Windows, PlayStation 3, Xbox 360]. Deep Silver.

7

"Hatched from the Veins in Your Arms": Movement, Ontology, and First-Person Gameplay in *BioShock*

Gwyneth Peaty

Set in a richly crafted underwater city, *BioShock* (2K Boston 2007) is a survival horror FPS that offers its players a number of unique gaming experiences. First and foremost among these is the ability to transform the virtual body by injecting and consuming Plasmids: mutagens that enable the player-character's genetic code to be "rewritten." Supplementing a more conventional assortment of guns, crossbows, and grenade launchers, Plasmids allow the player-character to incorporate and transform environmental features such as fire, ice, wind, electricity, and insects into a dangerous artillery of bodily forces. Beyond their purpose as weapons, the use of Plasmids represents a scenario in which the boundaries that separate the individual body from its surroundings are dissolved. Equipping, loading, firing, and exchanging these armaments involves transgressing the borders between the avatar and the gameworld. Couched in terms of genetic engineering, gameplay facilitates the interfacing of human and nonhuman components on multiple levels, all of which are mediated by the mechanics of first-person gameplay.

Focusing on *BioShock*, this chapter will argue that first-person gaming can facilitate a "playing-out" of contemporary anxieties regarding biomedicine, technology, and the body through genre-specific mechanics that are simultaneously functional and meaningful. Artist and game designer Mary Flanagan (2009) has pointed out that "as a cultural medium, games carry embedded beliefs within their systems of representation and their structures, whether games designers intend these ideologies or not" (223). It is these structures that this chapter is interested in. This chapter is not concerned with the question "do computer games tell stories or not?" (Carlquist 2002). Rather, it aims to take part in the timely shift that is occurring as researchers move towards a more nuanced consideration of the ways in which meaning is produced in videogames.

Highly acclaimed by gamers, press, and scholars alike, *BioShock* has inspired a steady stream of publication and discussion since it was released. The game has attracted analyses from a variety of perspectives, including art (Tavinor 2009), agency (Hocking 2009; Tulloch 2010), ethics and philosophy (Schulzke 2009; Sicart 2009; Packer 2010; Travis 2010). Few, however, have examined the ontological tensions that shape both form and function of its gameplay, and none have considered what the mechanics of this game might tell us about the role of expressive movement in contemporary FPS gaming. Exploring *BioShock* in these terms is intended to show how instrumental gameplay elements—while they may not resemble traditional storytelling apparatus—can generate meaning and have complex cultural resonance.

As Katie Salen and Eric Zimmerman (2004) have explained, any discussion of "meaning" in videogames must take account of the dynamic structures of the game design. "Meaningful play," they argue, "is the process by which a player takes action within the designed system of a game and the system responds to the action. The meaning of an action in a game resides in the relationship between action and outcome" (34). Unlike texts such as film, television, and literature, games take shape in response to the presence and participation of players. A game's ultimate form and "meaning" is therefore variable: dependent upon the goals, abilities, interests, and choices of different players as they negotiate their way through a specific gameworld. FPS games have a unique architecture and convey meaning in ways specific to the first-person point-of-view (hereafter POV). In the same way, role-playing games, real-time strategy games and adventure games have their own distinguishing structure. Different genres represent a variety of gaming technologies and designs, generating diverse player experiences. Attending to such genre-specific attributes allows for a more nuanced examination of how meaning is produced during gameplay, and reflects the fact that digital games "are not one form, but many" (Aarseth 2004, 47). Promoted as "the genetically enhanced shooter," *BioShock* adopts the rhetoric and imagery of genetic engineering in the course of creating a unique FPS gameplay system. While it taps into discourses of biomedicine and the posthuman, the game reformulates these concepts in the context of first-person gaming. The convergence of these elements raises some intriguing questions, especially when you consider the role of the body in first-person gameplay.

Shocking Biologies

BioShock begins in the immediate wake of an airplane accident over the Atlantic. The player-character must swim from the burning wreckage to a nearby island, where a bathysphere then provides transport down to the dystopian city of Rapture on the ocean floor. While the sounds of splashing and grunting suggest that a person is present, the player's POV is entirely disembodied at this point. It is not until the player-character finds a wrench to hold that a hand appears. In *BioShock*, like most FPS games, hands holding weapons are the only visible part of the avatar's anatomy during gameplay. Strategically placed at the lower corners of the screen, these appendages combine with the head-height perspective of the first-person POV to create a sense of immediate, subjective presence. In this way, "first person games bind the player directly into the gamescape" and "create the illusion that the game space extends beyond the screen to connect with and incorporate the bodies of players or the objects in their grasp" (King and Krzywinska 2006, 103). (For more on the FPS avatar and embodiment, see Victor Navarro's chapter in this volume.) After practicing wrench-based self-defense on some splicers (the violent, genetically modified citizens of Rapture), the player-character is invited to "power up" by injecting an unknown substance. This act is accompanied by a brief but spectacular cutscene in which the avatar inserts a large syringe into their left wrist. Both hands clench and spasm as blue electricity arcs through the veins and the avatar screams in agony. The significance of this event is explained by Atlas, the non-player character (hereafter NPC) who provides directions via radio: "Your genetic code is being rewritten. Hold on and everything will be fine." This is the first of many references to the body as a coded object, a conceit which punctuates and shapes the visual and technical aspects of gameplay.

Like any good tutorial stage, the first level of *BioShock* teaches the player about the game by providing instructive scenarios that illustrate not only the gameplay mechanics, but also the fundamental rules and relationships that structure the gameworld. In doing so, this stage introduces both the coded nature of the virtual body and the convergence of human, technological, and environmental elements that this kind of body enables. Having injected the first Plasmid, Electro Bolt, the player-character is in possession of a new weapon: "a fist full of lightning." When this power is in use, the left hand becomes visible. Its veins pulse with electricity. Blue light snaps and sparks between the fingers as they flex. When the Plasmid is fired, lightning arcs from the gesturing hand to strike targets with a satisfying "zap." What follows this acquisition is a series of learning moments, where the game provides explicit instructions as to how this power can be used. First, the player-character must use the Plasmid to open a door that blocks their way. The door's locking mechanism is clearly broken, and gameplay cannot continue until it is fixed with a bolt of electric current. In the next section, the player-character is attacked by splicers. "Zap 'em, then whack 'em" instructs Atlas. Hits of electricity temporarily freeze enemy bodies in place, allowing the player-character to run away or draw closer without danger. Finally, an encounter with a number of splicers in a shallow pool illustrates the active role of the environment. "Hit them with an Electro Bolt," suggests Atlas. This action demonstrates the conductivity of water, as the whole group is electrocuted simultaneously. Such practical strategy lessons set out the player-character's ability to interact with various elements of the environment. They also demonstrate a space in which players are made capable of traversing the distance between the virtual body and the rest of the gameworld.

In *BioShock*, the borders that separate biologies from technologies are blurred, allowing for exchanges between mechanical, corporeal, and environmental structures. Natural elements such as electricity are transformed from external to internal features of the body, able to be absorbed and converted into a conduit of the player's will. As the game continues, the player-character is increasingly able

Figure 7.1 Using Electro Bolt to open the door into *Rapture* (2K Boston 2007).

to interface with machines such as surveillance cameras, security bots, and gun turrets. Objects that would otherwise sense, target, and attack can be "hacked" and made friendly. The more the player-character rewrites their DNA, effectively hacking their own organic machinery, the further they are able to mesh safely with these and other objects. People in the game are likewise open to interference. Plasmids are available which allow the player to influence the emotions, perceptions, and behaviors of NPCs. Just as mechanical systems can be altered, human systems can be reprogrammed. Arcing between a variety of bodies, machines, and natural features, the use of Plasmids literally creates a bridge between virtual entities that might otherwise be considered distinct and self-contained.

Genetic Machines

The interactions described above are based on a particular concept of the virtual body. Specifically, the game draws on "the notion that the human genetic code may be rewritten or over-written by genetic engineers or that it was written into by some unseen engineer in the first place" (Clarke 2009, 6). This perspective borrows directly from biomedical science, a discourse whose contemporary modes of viewing and representing human biology have resulted in a "re-conceptualization of the body, from a morphological structure to a molecular organization, in effect converted flesh and blood into information" (Anker and Nelkin 2004, 18). Catherine Waldby (2000) describes how a wide variety of medical disciplines now "understand the body as a network of informational systems, working through code, signal, transcription, interference, noise, and the execution of programmes" (25). Framing the molecular and the cybernetic in identical terms, *BioShock* adopts this biomedical mode by presenting the virtual body as a "decipherable text" whose genetic structure can be "assembled according to instructions encoded in the chromosomes" (Anker and Nelkin 2004, 18). The ability to "upgrade" that is central to the game's Plasmid system is likewise enmeshed in the logic of biomedicine. If the body is conceived as a genetic machine, it follows that it can be engineered to improve performance. This is no fantasy, for the strategic manipulation of bodily systems has become a medical fact in contemporary biomedicine. "Treatment for certain diseases," Waldby explains, "now proceeds through gene therapy, which rectifies genetic 'deficits' or abnormalities like cystic fibrosis through the insertion of corrective genetic material directly into the patient's cells" (26). *BioShock* simulates and reformulates the process of gene therapy, presenting a gamespace in which the injection of new materials enables real-time enhancements of the virtual body.

The terms "posthuman" and "cyborg" are often used in reference to such augmented figures: anatomies whose organic architecture has been altered, extended, and technologized. While familiar domestic items such as reading glasses and hearing aids serve to augment and enhance the body, it is the more spectacular possibilities of the posthuman that capture our attention. It is "ideas of mutation, transformation, and body modification enabled by advanced medical technologies" that feature prominently in popular culture (Clarke 2009, 30). The spectacular interweaving of human and nonhuman that characterizes such imaginings induces a kind of ontological collapse. As Donna Haraway (1991) puts it, technologized bodies suggest that "any objects or persons can be reasonably thought of in terms of disassembly and reassembly; no 'natural' architectures constrain system design" (212). In a posthuman age, "no objects, spaces, or bodies are sacred in themselves; any component can be interfaced with any other" (212). *BioShock* adopts this notion as a foundational element of gameplay, constructing a world in which bodies, machines, and environments coalesce. The possibilities, hopes, and fears inspired by posthuman embodiment are thus embedded within the game's core apparatus.

Games are perhaps ideal texts to express the collapse of the body as a bounded object. (See Josh Call's chapter in this volume for further discussion of cyborg embodiment in FPS gaming.) As Anne Balsamo (1996) points out, virtual representations of the body "make it difficult to continue to think about the material body as a bounded entity, or to continue to distinguish its inside from its outside, its surface from its depth" (131). In the gameworld everything is made from the same basic material, formed from lines of code, part of the same integrated network. Games are not boundless border-free spaces, however, because these lines of code are used to construct objects and delimit the relationships between them. From the health and weapon systems to the virtual environment and physics engine, every aspect of the gameworld is carefully designed and determined. The fact that *BioShock* facilitates the blurring of ontological boundaries is not, therefore, an inevitable feature of the medium, but a deliberate design function.

Where biomedical and posthuman discourses place "the body" at the center of their visual fields, FPS games do just the opposite. In fact, the body of the player-character is largely invisible in first-person gaming. Ed Halter (2006) describes the early FPS *DOOM* (id Software 1993) as "a brutal mastery over the flesh: the gamer, whose muscles atrophied slowly as he sat near motionless at his PC for hours on end, became a disembodied gun, floating through tombs and destroying every warm body encountered" (159). Disembodiment would seem to be a requirement of the FPS genre, where the player is invited to stretch their mind across the boundary of the screen and into a world of subjective efficacy. But this view does not hold with contemporary games such as *BioShock*, because here the very qualities that encourage a sense of subjective presence are those that indicate the player's occupancy "within" a virtual body. From the sounds of footsteps and grunts of pain, to the gesturing hands and head-height position of the POV, gameplay is designed to communicate the existence of a body. (For more on affect and embodiment in FPS gaming, see Chris Moore's chapter in this volume.) The game solicits an imaginative optical extension, a convergence of mechanical and organic lenses that lends itself particularly well to the posthuman logic of the gameworld. Bryan-Mitchell Young (2005) argues that the mimicking of human movement is also key to the perception of embodiment in an FPS, as "the player is able to move in any direction, can turn, weave, walk in one direction while looking in another" (2). Motion, vision, and embodiment are intimately linked; the mediated gaze points up, down, and around as controlled by the player, mirroring the swivels of a human head. This invisible figure takes up space, has weight and volume, bumps into things and splashes through water. Stripped of these effects, the FPS perspective would indeed resemble a "virtual camera" floating through a three-dimensional space (Nitsche 2008, 92). The first-person POV therefore operates as a mode of embodied vision, a

Figure 7.2 Injecting the first Plasmid (2K Boston 2007).

mobile gaze actively invested with virtual form and presence. Despite first appearances, FPS games present a unique way of exploring and expressing specific ideas about the body, while situating the player as the driving force.

Cultural Moves

As the only visible portion of virtual anatomy, the FPS hands are a focal point for expressing ideas about the body. In *BioShock*, the color and shape of these hands suggest that the avatar is male and Caucasian. As shown in Figure 7.2, matching chain tattoos on the inside of each wrist add further detail, dovetailing with in-game references to both "the great chain" of industrial society and the body's status as a "slave" to genetic programming. These details are important because the hands are omnipresent during gameplay. Their movements accompany every action, while their appearance changes constantly in reaction to player choices. In his essay *Genre Trouble*, Espen Aarseth (2004) argues that the visual portrayal of such game elements is incidental, acting as a kind of interchangeable membrane draped across a game's most important feature: the rule system. From this perspective, the appearance of game bodies has little significance. Aarseth famously dismisses discussions of female anatomy in the *Tomb Raider* videogame franchise (Core Design 1996) by commenting that "the dimensions of Lara Croft's body, already analyzed to death by film theorists, are irrelevant to me as a player, because a different-looking body would not make me play differently. When I play, I don't even see her body, but see through it and past it" (48). The FPS genre might seem to provide the clearest evidence of this argument: proving the triviality of the body's appearance by rendering it largely invisible. Yet FPS games do not erase the body, but generate gameworlds that produce and endorse particular notions of embodiment. (Aaron Duncan and Jessy Ohl discuss the gendering of FPS gameplay in this same volume.) Far from being irrelevant, the FPS hands in *BioShock* blur the distinction between how game elements look (and potentially signify) and their practical utility during gameplay. They are not simply practical tools, but central to the meaningful and communicative architecture of the game.

The player-character's hands are a good example of how form and function can become enmeshed in the FPS genre. Instrumentally crucial, their purposeful actions represent an evolving sequence of possibilities and player choices. The hands are in constant motion, providing visual confirmation of whatever weapon is being utilized. Each weapon, in turn, is accompanied by a set of animations. When the player-character is holding the wrench, for instance, it is grasped in the right hand. When the weapon is used, the right hand lifts, striking out and downwards with the wrench. This action is accompanied by a swoosh of air, and a sound that indicates what kind of surface is being hit (smash, thud, squelch, clank). Movement also occurs independently. The hand constantly shifts up and down, as though in time with footsteps or human breath. This emphasizes the sense that the player-character has a lived body—grounded, rather than floating. At regular intervals the right hand rests the head of the wrench in the other hand. A clicking sound marks contact between the wrench and the left palm, which rises into view to hold the wrench, then disappears as the wrench is lifted away again. This action has no strategic purpose; it does not directly affect gameplay and cannot be controlled by the player. Instead, it serves to reinforce the impression that the player-character is embodied. The hands are not static; they fidget and respond to the weight of held objects, reacting to the movements and sensations of an unseen person.

The system that governs the possible actions and appearance of the FPS hands in *BioShock* also speaks to a particular vision of the body as a permeable object. The motions of these hands have utility in the sense that they provide the player with crucial information (such as "you are reloading" and "you have X weapon equipped"), while simultaneously conveying a more complex engagement with posthuman ontology. When Plasmids are in use, the movement of the hands takes on an overtly expressive quality that speaks to the porous nature of the virtual body. The hands do not simply move, but gesture, and the surface of the virtual skin is broken from within and without. In order to use Plasmids the player-character must continuously collect and inject hypodermic needles full of EVE, a "serum" which takes the role of genetic ammunition. A bar at the top left corner of the screen indicates how much EVE is left in the body, and how many spare syringes are remaining. Each time a Plasmid is used, the amount of EVE in the body decreases. When it runs out, the player-character must "reload" by injecting again. Both hands rise quickly during live gameplay, the right hand holding a needle which is plunged into the left wrist. These moments punctuate the action, working as a constant reminder that the enhanced game body requires maintenance and perforation in order to remain powerful.

Bernadette Flynn (2008) has argued that in-game movement should be understood as "a language enacted in embodied practice" (126). This notion is interesting to consider in relation to *BioShock*'s Plasmid system, in which actions are both instrumental and performative. Just as the player-character penetrates the skin of the hands with the hypodermic, the body is breached from the inside during Plasmid use. The Incinerate! Plasmid, for instance, gives the player-character the ability to generate fire from within. The left hand turns dark red, and its veins and fingertips burn with a fiery glow. The hand gestures reflexively at regular intervals, flames bursting from the palm and burning the skin black. When this Plasmid is fired, the fingers snap, shooting a spark that ignites the targeted object.

The Winter Blast Plasmid is similarly distinctive. When this power is equipped, the left hand freezes into a hard fist and sharp icicles erupt through bloody holes in the frozen skin. When firing, the hand gestures forward, shooting a cold breeze that turns enemies into living ice statues. Perhaps the most spectacular augmentation is Insect Swarm, which transforms the hands into a living beehive. When it is equipped, a honeycomb of holes opens up in the skin of the hands and forearms, and a large number of bees begin to crawl in and out. The surface of the skin swells and blisters as the creatures sting and buzz about the fingers. When the player-character fires this Plasmid, both hands gesture and the swarm erupts loudly from its human nest to attack whoever is nearby. In all of these cases, the surface of the virtual body is shown to be porous and easily transgressed.

Of all the organs, skin marks the outer limits of the body—its culturally charged perimeters. Tasked with separating inside from outside, body from environment, skin marks "the fleshy interface between bodies and worlds" (Ahmed and Stacey 2001, 1). The use of Plasmids during gameplay simulates a violent breaching of the

Figure 7.3 Attacking a splicer with Insect Swarm (2K Boston 2007).

skin, explicitly breaking down the perceived border that contains and defines the body in the gameworld. In this sense, the hands embody the posthuman notion that "the human body can no longer be figured either as a bounded entity or as a naturally given and distinct part of an unquestioned whole that is itself conceived as the 'environment'" (Smelik and Lykke 2008, x). The ontological disintegration of the body, fundamental to the dynamics of the larger game, is here played out across and through the surface of the first-person hands. Flynn (2008) contends that "game spaces always involve a particular way of thinking about the body" and that movements performed within these spaces should be understood as cultural acts (141). By utilizing *BioShock*'s FPS hands, the player is implementing a set of carefully designed, culturally meaningful gestures. Simultaneously embodying the operative functions of gameplay devices and the expressive movements of symbolic devices, these hands are "loaded" in more than one sense.

While individuals make different choices during gameplay, the expressive presence of the FPS hands is shared by every player. Likewise, Plasmid use is not a negotiable element. If a player refuses the invitation to power up at the start, the first door cannot be opened and the game will not continue. Players will find it increasingly difficult to survive if they stop injecting EVE or using Plasmids further into the game. In an early level, all conventional weapons are taken away for a short but challenging period, leaving Plasmids as the only defense. By requiring each player to utilize the Plasmid system, *BioShock* presents ontological collapse as an essential feature of posthuman empowerment.

Gene Play

Biomedical discourses are committed to exposing the internal. In particular, "anatomical medicine concerns itself with the identification of pathology as interior topography, which must be visually encountered in order to be fully known" (Waldby 2000, 24). Accordingly, medical technologies subject the body to "new orders of machine vision" that ultimately reproduce biological systems as "digitized information configured on a computer screen" (5). The mysteries of the body are unmasked before being transformed into data that is both readable and actionable. The absence of "the body" as a whole entity in FPS games would seem to subvert this preoccupation with internal mechanisms and their exposure. In *BioShock*, the focus on interiors appears to be entirely transposed onto exteriors via the skin of the hands. Further examination, however, suggests that supplementary elements of the gameworld are dedicated to representing and revealing the body's contents.

BioShock presents a gameplay system in which DNA "points" are used to purchase body modifications from genetic vending machines. The player-character must collect a substance called ADAM, which facilitates genetic modification. Taken from the Little Sisters (NPCs who roam the hallways of Rapture), ADAM is a valuable substance that shapes Plasmid use. The more points of ADAM you collect, the more Plasmids are available for purchase. ADAM can be "spent" at a Gatherer's Garden—a retail machine that sells a variety of Plasmids for a range of prices. Accessing these machines pauses the game, opening a full-screen interface which lists potential upgrades and their cost in ADAM. Once the merchandise has been selected and purchased, it must be allocated a place in the body. Rather than framing this process in organic terms, the virtual body's interior is represented by a grid of mechanized "slots." In the early stages of the game, only a few of these slots are accessible. The player-character must collect enough genetic currency to open new slots and equip the body with more powers.

Spare upgrades are stored in machines called Gene Banks —stations where the player can view and manipulate their own genetic composition. Accessing the Gene Bank opens another full-screen interface that depicts the interior of the virtual body as a mechanized system characterized by wires, valves, tracks, and panels. Using this apparatus, genetic components can be surveyed, exchanged, and added to the body in real time. Round icons representing Plasmids are selected and dragged to empty slots to equip, while existing slots are freed by removing and storing unwanted substances in the Gene Bank. In this context, the biological is explicitly conflated with mechanical and economic systems, as genetic units simultaneously operate as mechanized parts and set measures of value.

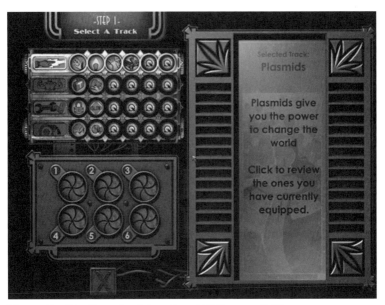

Figure 7.4 The Gene Bank interface (2K Boston 2007).

While in-game Gene Banks do not mimic the operation of real-world gene banks, they invite the player to explore the implications of biomedical databases. A gene bank or biobank "can be defined as a stored collection of genetic samples in the form of blood or tissue" (Austin, Harding, and McElroy 2003, 37). As the term "bank" suggests, these collections are mapped in terms of cultural, medical, and economic value. Organic samples are preserved, encoded, and "linked to databases of medical, genealogical and lifestyle information" (43). Material samples become units of data that can be cataloged, rated, compared, and manipulated. Participation allows the individual contributor "to bank DNA, to be coded or anonymized, to allow cell lines to be made, to allow access to others and to participate in future research" (Knoppers and Chadwick 2005, 76). This process suggests a profound kind of disembodiment, whereby the body's genetic formula is distilled and the subjective realities of living beings are effectively jettisoned. Gene banks frame DNA as a quantifiable resource, ultimately situating genetics in the realm of economics. The commercialization of genetic materials in *BioShock* plays directly upon the logic of such "banking." The player buys gene upgrades from vending machines in the same way they purchase first-aid kits and bags of chips. Like other products, these mutagens have a specific value and price. Only those with the requisite amount of ADAM can afford to upgrade and benefit from the advancements of genomic research. Yet the potentially sinister ramifications of such a system are transformed, during gameplay, into a useful source of agency. *BioShock's* Gene Banks are numerous and fully accessible, allowing for greater choice and flexibility when strategically modifying the virtual body. Nothing left in the Gene Bank is lost, simply preserved until it is needed. In this way, the game presents a space in which gene banking has a practical utility—a limited, definable purpose that is controlled by the player.

Plasmids are not the only genetic resource available for purchase at Gatherer's Gardens. Gene Tonics are also offered as supplementary body modifications. Tonics participate in the merging of the body with its surroundings, decreasing the vulnerability of the virtual body by increasing its integration with nonhuman game elements. Combat Tonics such as Armored Shell, Human Inferno, and Electric Flesh protect the body from external damage; Engineering Tonics such as Clever Inventor, Safecracker, and Hacking Expert improve interactions with machines; and Physical Tonics such as SportBoost increase speed, power, and agility. The transformative effects of these substances are explicitly framed in terms of the coded body. As Atlas explains, taking the Security Evasion Tonic "adjusts the thermal signature of your epidermal layer" to help the player-character go undetected by cameras and bots. Another Tonic facilitates electromagnetic synthesis between the avatar and machines: "your personal EM signature becomes altered to interact uniquely with alarm sensors." Like Plasmids, Tonics are assigned a series of slots in the body, and are equipped by selecting and dragging icons around the Gene Bank. Many of these icons emphasize the natural origins of the modification. For instance, Armored Shell is represented by an armadillo, Electric Flesh by an eel, and SportBoost by a hummingbird. By extension, Tonics do more than enhance human genetics; they allow for the adoption of animal traits via the insertion of nonhuman DNA into the body.

Tonics are rarely as spectacular as Plasmids, yet they are central to the player-character's strategic manipulations of the gameworld.

Integrating elemental, mechanical, human, and animal structures, *BioShock*'s vision of genetic play collapses the borders of the human form externally and internally. Posthuman selfhood is imagined as a thrilling extension as the player is invited to "biologically modify your body: send electric bolts storming from your fingertips or unleash a swarm of killer hornets hatched from the veins in your arms." The further the virtual body is assimilated within its environment, the safer and more powerful the player-character will become during gameplay. This phenomenon is epitomized by one of the most useful Tonics: Natural Camouflage. Represented by an image of a chameleon, this modification enables the player-character to become invisible when standing still. Hands and weapons turn translucent as the body blends into its environment. The absorption of the human into its surroundings appears complete in these moments.

Gatherer's Gardens, Gene Banks, Plasmids, and Tonics all depend upon the idea that the human anatomy is a mechanized system in which separate but interrelated components are located. In this sense they resemble medical monitoring devices that segment the body "into functional parts and molecular codes" and allow individuals to

Figure 7.5 Approaching a Gene Bank with Incinerate! (2K Boston 2007).

"technologically witness, if not yet manage, the molecular functioning of bodily processes" (Balsamo 1995, 216). *BioShock* takes the next step by inviting the player to not only view their genetic topography, but reach in and alter it, optimizing the structure of the virtual body as best suits their unique gameplay preferences. Mechanized interiors are subject to strategic reassembly via "the masterful touch of the cursor or virtual scalpel" (Waldby 2000, 158). Tapping into the imagined transparency of the technologized body, this vision of human anatomy allows for the production of meaning "through the composition and editing of actual human components (cells, genes, gametes)" (Burfoot 2003, 49). Such interfaces are not, of course, specific to FPS games. But in this scenario they reveal how different gameplay elements can combine to produce a specific notion of the body. *BioShock* provides an example of how first-person gameplay can facilitate particular "visions" of embodiment that come together via a complimentary network of design and gameplay features.

Cultural Visions

First-person gaming invites players to experience action through the eyes of a virtual body. As Alexander Galloway (2006) points out, this visual architecture is the definitive characteristic of FPS games: "the first-person subjective perspective is so omnipresent and so central to the grammar of the entire game that it essentially becomes coterminous with it" (63). The screen mediates player sight, framing virtual space and simulating an ocular field of vision. Staring at and through the screen, the player adopts the mechanized gaze, creating the sensation that this digitized outlook "is not held separate from the body, but embedded behind the eyes" (Brooker 2009, 128). Yet, as *BioShock* illustrates, this first-person POV is more than "just" a generic feature. In practice it manifests an ideological perspective, a way of seeing and doing that positions the player in culturally implicated ways. In the context of contemporary biomedicine – which typically constructs individuals as coded objects vulnerable to external regimes of knowledge and surveillance – this game strives to situate players in a position of subjective mastery. The first-person POV reinforces the primacy of the individual, effectively co-opting the "new orders of machine vision" (Waldby 2000, 5) by situating the player as both origin and administrator of the posthuman gaze. In doing so, *BioShock* betrays a profound disquiet regarding the effects of science and technology upon the human body – that entity whose "natural" limits are shown to be easily transgressed.

In this game the coalescence of the human and the nonhuman, biology and technology, is explicitly presented as a source of efficacy – a new stage of evolution that shifts power literally into the hands of the individual. As the Gene Bank opening screen (visible in Figure 7.4) states, "Plasmids give you the power to change the world." However, accompanying this empowerment is the constant presence of tortured flesh. The hands that "change the world" are punctured, electrified, stung, frozen, and burnt as they do so. The body's most symbolic border exists in a state of perpetual disintegration, its spectacular torment an ever-present marker of the importance and vulnerability of ontological boundaries. Furthermore, such damage is unavoidable. Gameplay forces the player to transform and mutate. Without the requisite genetic currency to do so, you are rendered powerless within the gameworld.

As a dynamic system, *BioShock* signals both fear and desire. The exhilaration of upgrading one's body is accompanied by its loss: the evaporation of the human as a distinct category of being. In this sense the game registers social unease over the growing power of biomedical science, in particular those genetic interventions that breach the shielding skin. Invited to splice their own virtual anatomies at a genetic level, players experience the extent to which this new power depends upon a vision of the penetrable, controllable body – a body that is both vulnerable to, and dependent upon, external forces. *BioShock* thus facilitates a playing-out of cultural anxieties surrounding the biotechnologized body, foregrounding the importance of ontological boundaries and individual agency by simulating the loss of each.

Exemplifying the expressive nature of first-person gaming, *BioShock* highlights the potential for gameplay mechanics to be both practical and meaningful. The distinctive architecture of the first-person POV offers unique formulations of embodiment and vision, providing a genre-specific structure that generates particular relationships between bodies, objects, ideas, and the player. While features such as the weapons system, Gene Bank interface, and gesturing hands may not resemble traditional storytelling devices, their utility forms part of a larger communicative structure. A greater critical focus on such aspects of FPS gaming could expand our understanding of how meaning is produced in this genre, taking into account the complexity of the playable apparatus. Approached on its own terms, through its own structures, first-person gameplay offers a fruitful site of analysis that speaks to wider sociocultural evolutions and preoccupations.

References

Aarseth, Espen. 2004. "Genre Trouble." In *First Person: New Media as Story, Performance, and Game*, edited by Noah Wardrip-Fruin and Pat Harrigan, 45–55. Cambridge, MA: MIT Press.

Ahmed, Sara and Jackie Stacey. 2001. "Introduction: Dermographies." In *Thinking Through the Skin*, edited by Sara Ahmed and Jackie Stacey, 1–18. London: Routledge.

Anker, Suzanne and Dorothy Nelkin. 2004. *The Molecular Gaze: Art in the Genetic Age*. New York: CSHL Press.

Austin, Melissa, Sarah Harding, and Courtney McElroy. 2003. "Genebanks: A Comparison of Eight Proposed International Genetic Databases." *Community Genetics* 6 (1): 37–45.

Balsamo, Anne. 1995. "Forms of Technological Embodiment: Reading the Body in Contemporary Culture." In *Cyberspace/Cyberbodies/ Cyberpunk: Cultures of Technological Embodiment*, edited by Mike Featherstone and Roger Burrows, 215–37. London: Sage.

—1996. *Technologies of the Gendered Body: Reading Cyborg Women*. Durham: Duke University Press.

Brooker, Will. 2009. "Camera-eye, CG-eye: Videogames and the 'cinematic.'" *Cinema Journal* 48 (3): 122–8.

Burfoot, Annette. 2003. "Human Remains: Identity Politics in the Face of Biotechnology." *Cultural Critique* 53: 47–71.

Carlquist, Jonas. 2002. "Playing the Story: Computer Games as a Narrative Genre." *Human IT* 6 (3): 7–53.

Clarke, Julie. 2009. *The Paradox of the Posthuman: Science Fiction/ Techno-horror Films and Visual Media*. Saarbrücken, Germany: VDM Verlag.

Flanagan, Mary. 2009. *Critical Play: Radical Game Design*. Cambridge, MA: MIT Press.

Flynn, Bernadette 2008. "The Navigator's Experience: An Examination of the Spatial in Computer Games." In *The Pleasures of Computer Gaming*, edited by Melanie Swalwell and Jason Wilson, 118–46. London: McFarland.

Galloway, Alexander. 2006. *Gaming: Essays on Algorithmic Culture*. Minneapolis: University of Minnesota Press.

Halter, Ed. 2006. From *Sun Tzu to Xbox: War and Video Games*. New York: Thunder Mouth Press.

Haraway, Donna. 1991. *Simians, Cyborgs, and Women: The Reinvention of Nature*. New York: Routledge.

Hocking, Clint. 2009. "Ludonarrative Dissonance in BioShock: The Problem of What the Game is About." In *Well Played 1.0: Video Games, Value and Meaning*, edited by Drew Davidson, 114–17. Pittsburgh, PA: ETC Press.

King, Geoff, and Tanya Krzywinska. 2006. *Tomb Raiders and Space Invaders: Videogame Forms and Contexts*. New York: I. B. Taurus.

Knoppers, Bartha Maria and Ruth Chadwick. 2005. "Human Genetic Research: Emerging Trends in Ethics." *Nature Reviews: Genetics* 6 (1): 75–9.

Nitsche, Michael. 2008. *Video Game Spaces: Image, Play, and Structure in 3D Game Worlds*. Cambridge, MA: MIT Press.

Packer, Joseph. 2010. "The Battle for Galt's Gulch: *BioShock* as Critique of Objectivism." *Journal of Gaming and Virtual Worlds* 2 (3): 209–24.

Salen, Katie and Eric Zimmerman. 2004. *Rules of Play: Game Design Fundamentals*. London: MIT Press.

Schulzke, Marcus. 2009. "Moral Decision Making in *Fallout*." *Game Studies* 9 (2). http://gamestudies.org/0902/articles/schulzke.

Sicart, Miguel. 2009. *The Ethics of Computer Games*. Cambridge, MA: MIT Press.

Smelik, Anneke and Nina Lykke. 2008. "Introduction." In *Bits of Life: Feminism at the Intersections of Media, Bioscience, and Technology*, edited by Anneke Smelik and Nina Lykke, ix-xix. Seattle: University of Washington Press.

Tavinor, Grant. 2009. "*BioShock* and the Art of Rapture." *Philosophy and Literature* 33 (1): 91–106.

Travis, Roger. 2010. "BioShock in the Cave: Ethical Education in Plato and in Video Games." In *Ethics and Game Design: Teaching Values Through Play*, edited by Karen Schrier and David Gibson, 86–101. Hershey, PA: IGI Global.

Tulloch, Rowan. 2010. "A man chooses, a slave obeys: Agency, Interactivity and Freedom in Video Gaming." *Journal of Gaming and Virtual Worlds* 2 (1): 27–38.

Waldby, Catherine. 2000. *The Visible Human Project: Informatic Bodies and Posthuman Medicine*. London: Routledge.

Young, Bryan-Mitchell. 2005. "Gaming Mind, Gaming Body: The Mind/

Body Split for a New Era." *Proceedings of the Changing Views – Worlds in Play DiGRA Conference*, June 2005, University of Vancouver, USA. http://www.digra.org/dl/db/06278.12199.pdf

Games

2K Boston. 2007. *BioShock* [Mac OS X, Microsoft Windows, PlayStation 3, Xbox 360] 2K Games.
Core Designs. 1996. *Tomb Raider* [DOS, Microsoft Windows, PlayStation, Sega Saturn] Eidos Interactive.
id Software. 1993. *DOOM* [DOS] id Software.

8

Meat Chunks in the Metro: The Apocalyptic Soul of the Ukrainian Shooter
Dan Pinchbeck

I Said Come In, Don't Just Stand There ...

Here's the thing. The guy is sitting with his back to me at the fire, talking to his friend, who is quietly strumming his guitar. I stroll right up to him, casual as you like, then out comes the knife and I drop him before he has a chance to react. None of this because I'm in a kill-or-be-killed situation. No heroics. I'm killing for bread because I'm broke and can't afford any and I'm starving to death. And I'm using a knife because I ran out of bullets.

Here's another scenario. I'm in a deserted, ruined library, the windows are all blown out and the whole place is scattered with debris and destroyed shelves. The filter on my gasmask is running out and I'll choke to death pretty soon if I don't find another one. I'm trying to run from the Librarian, and I'm panicking because I'm nearly out of bullets. All I've got left are seventeen ball-bearings and I don't know if it's going to be enough to take him down. If I'm lucky and I get through this, I might be able to barter them for a clip of bullets at the next station. If I make it there at all.

This chapter examines the recent Ukrainian shooters *S.T.A.L.K.E.R.* (GSC Game World 2006, 2008, 2009)[1] and *Metro 2033* (4A Games 2010). It focuses on the transitions to games from the idiosyncratic apocalyptic visions of the source material: the novels *Roadside Picnic* (Strugatsky & Strugatsky 1971) and *Metro 2033* (Glukhovsky 2002–5). In doing so, it provides some insights into how these games create their worlds, moods, and gameplay and navigate the constraints of the medium as opposed to the written word. This process is normally referred to, after Bolter and Grusin (2000), as "remediation." Much has been written on the subject of the relationship between games and other forms of media, and it doesn't need repeating again here. More to the point, rather than reiterating generic, high-level theory, what this chapter will demonstrate is that by looking in detail at these quite idiosyncratic games, points of interest emerge that raise really interesting, specific points about FPS design. That's not to completely discredit or ignore the body of work surrounding remediation, but I would argue that while it may be useful for *game studies*, it is of limited use in understanding *game design*. This is a chapter about FPS design, and for this, it is better to go directly to the games themselves and let what we find determine our understanding (Pinchbeck 2009).

The franchise of *S.T.A.L.K.E.R.*, covering three games over six years, a number of international awards, a series of novels, and a TV show, not to mention over four million units sold (GSC Game World 2011), should be familiar to anyone with a passing interest in first-person gaming. *Metro 2033* is perhaps less well-known, but has still secured a cult following, critical acclaim, and somewhere around half a million sales – VGChartz puts Xbox 360 sales at approximately 380,000 and the game is also available on PC. Both games mix classic shooter combat with a strong emphasis on horror and RPG elements. Both draw inspiration from novels, and we should quickly introduce these: although we can assume at least a working knowledge of the existence of the games, the reader may be less acquainted with their source material.

Boris and Arkady Strugastky's *Roadside Picnic* (hereafter *RP)* takes place in a near-future Canada at The Zone, the site of an alien visitation full of anomalous entities with mysterious properties and evocative names. It's a bleak vision of the limits of human understanding: while a scientific institute attempts to understand The Zone, Stalkers smuggle entities out at night to sell on the black market. The novel focuses on Red Schuhart, a Stalker driven into The Zone to fund a cure for his daughter Monkey, who is losing her humanity as a result of Schuhart's exposure to The Zone. As Monkey's condition deteriorates, Schuhart makes a desperate attempt to locate a wish-granting Golden Ball, somewhere in the center of The Zone. In 1979, Andrei Tarkovsky re-imagined the novel in his film *Stalker*, transposing The Zone back to Russia and dropping the overt science-fiction of the novel. Instead, an unnamed Stalker agrees to guide a Writer and a Professor into The Zone to find the Wish Granter. Arriving at its location, the Professor reveals he has come to destroy it, believing it can only bring misery to mankind. Similarly, in *RP*, the despairing Schuhart, reduced to murder-by-proxy, drenched in filth, bellows his wish of "Happiness! For everyone, and no-one shall go hungry!" (145) at the novel's conclusion, yet the reader is left with the uneasy sense that the very worst thing in the world may have just occurred.

Metro 2033 (hereafter *M33)*[2] is a highly philosophical work set in the Moscow underground, where a few thousand humans eke out an existence following an apocalyptic nuclear conflict. The novel follows Artyom, whose home station is being attacked by "Dark Ones" (ghoulish creatures that serve as a metaphor for the extinction of humanity), as he journeys across the Metro to Polis, the last beacon of civilization in the dying world. Refused help, he instead gains access to a secret military metro system and eventually nukes the Dark Ones at the very point he realizes they come bearing salvation, not death. *M33* is as much a product of its age as *RP*, created episodically for online publication, free from censorship but cynical of all political and theological systems. If *RP* swims in ambiguity and lack of reason, *M33* fires philosophies and ideas into the air and simply records their failure to land satisfactorily. Similarly, if the conclusion of *RP* is a strangely horrible vacuum that fails to erupt into either apocalypse or paradise, then *M33* presents the utter failure of humanity to escape its own fear and isolation, with Artyom left to return to his bunker and the dying squabble of ideologies.

Normalization and Virtual Expansion

M33 is structured geographically: Artyom travels from station to station, line to line, each distinct and existing to enable a philosophical discussion of ideology and reality. Along one line, Communism has taken hold, elsewhere a Fourth Reich. The Hansa represent the dying light of capitalism; Park Pobedy is a new society of near-blind cannibals created as a social experiment. The Metro also appears, like The Zone (in *SoC* not, critically, *RP*), as almost sentient; there is a supernatural world woven around the brutal, prosaic one. There are explicit monsters that everyone can see: the Librarians, the beasts at Paveletskaya, the Dark Ones, "pterodactyls" hunting on the surface. But there are also more ambiguous elements: demons hidden in the stars of the Kremlin (271–3), ghosts trapped in pipes that sing the living to their deaths, visions of trains, and shadows of the apocalypse. The Metro's inhabitants exist in a hinterland, already dead and damned, forced to co-exist with the otherworldly. Finally, there is the legendary Metro 2, a network that links military sites, the Kremlin, and government bunkers (drawn from the "real" urban myth). This plays a relatively small role in the novel, and is primarily the domain of Pobedy's cannibals, though it does lead Artyom's Stalker comrades to the D6 missile silo.

In terms of its transition to the FPS, the first thing to note is that *M33* is a vast, sprawling novel and it's no surprise to find the game's Metro scaled down considerably. However, what is interesting is that although the overall actual size of the environments explored during the game are reduced, this process actually serves to create a sense of place that the book sometimes lacks. This may be due to the psychogeographic, rather than realistic, core of the novel. Although Glukhovsky does spend some time visually describing the locations, this is normally shot through with heavy symbolism and metaphor: the stations always represent something else. In contrast, the game is inevitably required to have a consistent graphical identity, and this actually serves to stabilize the locations of the Metro, earthing them to a greater sense of reality and "normality." In other words, if *M33* uses the Metro as a metaphor for the human condition, *Metro 2033* presents it as a genuine, existent place. The game was praised for its ability to convey a sense of life in the stations, particularly in its early sections, as Artyom travels through Exhibition (VDNKh), Riga (Rizhskaya), and Market (Prospekt Mir), although it does drop two of the stations with the most detailed social descriptions in the novel (Kitai Gorod and Dobryninskaya) along with the far stranger Smolenskaya/Pobedy events and environments. It goes without saying that complex social interactions are exceptionally hard to simulate computationally.

The player is also frequently presented with incomplete environments that can never be fully explored, which virtually increases the sense of scale of the Metro. This is a difficult thing to balance against the potential frustration of a player wanting to break out of the linear corridor, but *Metro 2033* uses a number of simple design tricks to achieve it. The gasmask filter limiting available exploration time in surface sections is one; in the Metro itself, several levels use vertical depth as a way of faking this scale. For example, Artyom and Bourbon cross a bridge over a deep abyss as they head for Market, suggesting

Figure 8.1 Inaccessible vertical vistas increase the sense of scale in *Metro 2033* (4A Games 2010).

that the Metro runs much deeper than is initially apparent. This trick is repeated elsewhere during the crossing of the Red/Nazi frontlines. Equally, shifting the action between train tunnels, maintenance areas, and much older obsolete transit systems, not to mention the huge military base of D6, all invite the player to fill in the blanks between the limited points of representation the game provides. In many ways, the sense of a convincing, engaging world in a game is often a product of how well the vacuum *between* represented environments is handled as is it of the environments themselves – similar to McCloud's (1993) argument that it's all about what happens *between* the frames of a comic book.

SoC opts for an entirely different strategy, presenting linear quests in a persistent non-linear world. The background to The Zone begins historically, with the Chernobyl nuclear accident in 1996. Following this, a shadowy government science group sets up shop in the Exclusion Zone, experimenting with the noosphere. As a result, a second incident is triggered, creating an area of altered physics and genetic mutation. Within the newly created Zone, lethal anomalies spawn unearthly artifacts with strange powers, and it is not just an ecosystem that is born but an economy, as competing ideological powers fight over the secrets and exploitable resources. This origin story of the game's world is profoundly different to *RP* and thinking about the consequences of the shift is illuminating.

Simply put, The Zone of *SoC* is the product of human science, not alien intelligence. *RP* presents a world visited by aliens; if it is a political allegory, as Marsh argues (1986), the cause of The Zone is nevertheless accidental. As Lem (1983) puts it, "something has fallen from the sky" (321). If the central mystery of *RP's* Zone is the identity and motives of the visitors, then the central political theme of the book is the ethics of the exploitation of science, particularly when function and effect are largely unknown. In *SoC*, by contrast, the worst has, in a very real sense, already happened. The accident at Chernobyl is already established as a cultural marker for developers and players, and, in a way, GSC Game World extend this question of culpability and responsibility by having the group that creates C-Consciousness conduct their experiments in the one place in the world unlikely to ever be reclaimed. Equally, *RP* presents a broadly urban Zone, an industrial quarter of the city of Harmont, whereas

SoC is mainly rural, with only Pripyat (and Limansk in *CS*) as once-highly populated spaces. This is inverted during the course of both novel and game: The Zone in *RP* is so lethal no one can live in it, and only Stalkers make swift raids into it. In the game, there is a thriving population, and the dangers of The Zone are relatively visible and known. It is this difference in how habitable and predictable the world is, the way in which *SoC* handles anomalies and artifacts, that has most to tell us in terms of what games apparently require of their environments, and how *SoC* and *Metro 2033* undermine some well-established design ideas.

Anomalies and Integer-based Causality

SoC relies upon distortions of physics and chemistry to give The Zone its unique flavor. Lava pits and nukage have, of course, been staples of the genre since *DOOM* (id Software 1993), but *SoC* forces players to engage with lethal entities by making them the source of artifacts that provide much-needed cash and superhuman abilities. *SoC* presents seven standard anomalies, ranging from jets of fire to patches of enhanced gravity or wind, pools of toxins, and electrical discharges. These are all static, occupy set locations, have distinct areas of effect, and semi-randomly produce artifacts. The artifacts have a range of positive and negative effects, tiered in intensity, and are associated in both name and effect with specific anomalies. For example, the Vortex anomaly produces the artifacts Wrenched, Gravi, and Goldfish, all of which give a bonus to defense from rupture damage but irradiate the player slightly. In addition to these standard artifacts, there are five unique artifacts that offer benefits without adverse effects. A player can concentrate on artifact hunting, building cash reserves, and hopefully accumulating more powerful and rare artifacts. Of course, obtaining artifacts is difficult and requires the player to enter into high-risk areas. *SoC* therefore makes the process of enhancing the player's abilities very dangerous. While some anomalies are easy to exploit, others are harder to spot. The Fruit Punch has distinct visible edges, but the lethal Whirligig can only be identified by swirling leaves. The subtlety of some of these cues mean a careless player, particularly in low-light, runs a heavy risk of

Figure 8.2 A generically placed Springboard anomaly in *SoC* (GSC Game World 2006) An animated visual distortion, just visible at the center of the image, is all that gives away the anomaly to the player.

hitting an anomaly. Even with the most powerful armor and a belt full of artifacts, a Vortex or Whirligig will usually kill the player in one hit. The Zone retains a menace and forces the player to travel respectfully, even at their most amped-up.

However, all of the anomalies are predictable and their effects are instant. This is very different from the silver web in *RP* that apparently causes Kirill to die of a massive heart attack hours after brushing against it (42–3). A player can learn to avoid them, or which artifacts are the most useful for counteracting their effects (a Pellicle renders Fruit Punches little more than a nuisance, for example). Equally, all artifacts have the same effects, and these are explicit: a Pellicle offers +30 Chemical Burn defense. It is interesting that in *CoP*, anomalies are less evenly distributed and based around weird environmental features, such as the Oakpine or Circus, which creates a greater sense of uniqueness even if everything retains an unambiguous basis in integer adjustment. *RP* might have relatively common artifacts like So-Sos and Black Sprays being brought from The Zone, but their properties are far from explicit or even understood. This raises an interesting design question: the degree to which players will tolerate a break or absence in causality. The grouping of both anomalies and artifacts in *CoP* is potentially significant as it attempts to make both more unique and break the immediate association between them and a purely structural form of gameplay. In other words, redistributing threat to fewer, more dangerous entities creates a greater scope for ambiguity; the anomalies of *CoP* are without doubt weirder than scattered Springboards around *SoC*, even if the actual objects they contain are as integer-based as ever. The approach to the Oasis might be slightly ham-fisted as a puzzle, but there is no precedent for it elsewhere in the game. The player is not able to apply prior knowledge and this reduces their sense of power and security, preventing them from applying pre-existing knowledge. Howell (2011) calls this process of deliberate undermining "schematically disruptive", arguing that whilst not as explicitly disruptive as Wilson & Sicart's Abusive Design (2010), it has a power to force the player out of their comfort zone and to engage with a game on a heightened level. Causality and predict-ability are, of course, fundamentally important to games, particularly to the traditional model of gameplay loops, and challenging them is therefore a high-risk but potentially powerful means of changing a player's engagement with the game in a dramatic way.

Equally, *Metro 2033* shifts the novel's supernatural elements towards predictable, explicitly causal manifestations. The invisible threats of deathly voices and tunnel fear are represented only fleet-ingly, although one might argue that tunnel fear finds its natural counterpoint in the inherent anxiety of survival horror games. However, we do find sequences such as Ghosts, possibly the most successful chapter of the game, in which Artyom follows Khan through firstly a haunted tunnel, and then one that is home to a strange electrical anomaly. In both cases, the intangible is rendered visual, seeming to affirm the age-old arguments about games being primarily a visual medium. Likewise, the demonic entity living in the book's Kremlin station is reinvented as a mutant "biomass" in the game. In the latter case, the effect of translating something profoundly alien and apparently sentient into a gameplay challenge reduces the impact of the scene considerably. The novel's biomass

Figure 8.3 The unique Oakpine anomaly in *S.T.A.L.K.E.R.: Call of Pripyat* (GSC Game World 2009).

may be eventually scared away by fire (a perfectly replicable game event), but it is a living sea that sings its victims to suicide. Instead, the game gives us rolling balls of plasma to shoot at, and a fleshy mountain dispatched with a crane. Comparing this to the Ghost sequence, when the only action available to the player is slowly following Khan through a crowd of silhouettes, is an interesting case study. The D6 biomass is less emotionally effective because it follows a long build-up without combat, as Artyom descends into a military complex with Miller's team, in an atmosphere loaded with dread. This is earthed by the combat sequence that follows, which refocuses the player back to the question of skilled response, not interpretative questioning. In contrast, Ghosts requires no skill to complete, and retains an openness and ambiguity throughout. It is completed with a sense of "what was that?" rather than "I did it." This turning away from the sense of a goal achieved towards something more ambiguous, a lack of explicit resolution to a game episode, is returned to in *Metro 2033's* ethereal ending sequences and saturates several other parts of the game. Although it is largely forced to make the supernatural elements explicit and integer-based, by making the encounter with the ghosts both unique and non-skill-based, predictability and causality are undermined, forcing the player away from standard modes of play and attention.

Combat, Threat, and Familiarity

In a very similar way, traditional gameplay leads design, in terms of the agents populating the environment, in a very specific direction. Both *Metro 2033* and *SoC* are shooters first and foremost; combat is a central aspect of gameplay. What is interesting, however, is how both games work to protect both the mystery and sense of threat of their worlds while allowing this to define play. As noted above, the biomass section of *Metro 2033* is a good example of how combat inevitably shifts the model of engagement from an interpretative to a challenge-solving orientation. This potentially flattens out the diegetic properties[3] of an entity to its structural characteristics. We pattern the challenge and hone our skills in beating it, and this has an inevitable effect on how we engage with the delivery device. This is encapsulated by the Librarians of *Metro 2033*. The semi-sentient wraith-ape creatures of the novel are replaced with giant brutal beasts. Librarians can soak up huge amounts of damage which may lead the player to the panicked and erroneous conclusion that they are, contrary to nearly every other FPS monster ever created, immune to bullets. Discovering that you can in fact kill a Librarian changes the way in which they are engaged with. Rather than being something that just needs running from (remembering that running in an unknown environment is, of course, not something you really

Figure 8.4 A Librarian from *Metro 2033* (4A Games 2010).

want to be doing, particularly if there might be another Librarian just around the corner), the central issue becomes whether killing them is worth the bullets, a distinctly pragmatic concern. Similarly, the Flying Demons are altered by the discovery that enough firepower will eventually kill them. Until this point, the stress of moving through the streets of Moscow is amplified by the knowledge that something you cannot kill can drop from the sky at any moment, making it a desperate run from cover to cover, shelter to shelter.

Despite the disappointment that both Demons and Librarians can be killed, the sheer weight of ammunition required to do so means they are prevented, to an extent, from simply becoming obstacles as opposed to sources of serious anxiety. Killing them severely compromises the player's ability to cope with subsequent encounters, and what is interesting about the game's design is the general difference in difficulty in terms of taking on the Metro's mutant inhabitants. Compared to human opponents, mutants soak up a large amount of damage and are extremely fast. This compounds the relatively low quantity of ammunition available to the player, making mutant encounters substantially more stressful than gunfights with Nazis and Bandits. Not only is there rarely time to plan a tactical approach, as these are profoundly reactive instances, but each bullet is artificially increased in value: it needs to count, because you need more of them to drop each agent. It means that signs of mutant activity immediately increase the sense of tension and fear for the player and keep the Metro seeming far more dangerous than its human inhabitants[4]. Because the game does not offer a progressive increase in the avatar's power, mutant fights are stressful to the very end; there is never a particular sense of mastering them. This is in keeping, to an extent, with the novel, although, not surprisingly, actual fights with mutants are more often replaced with the threat of their attack. Artyom is party to defending Paveletskaya, has a running engagement (albeit defined mostly by him being the one doing the running) with creatures on the streets of Moscow as he heads for Smolenskaya, and kills a Librarian more through instinct than judgment, but the only real combat in the novel is between human protagonists. The novel relies to a far greater extent on ambiguous and unrepresented threats to life; it is always what lurks in the dark, not what crawls from it into the light. Just as with *RP's* Zone, it is what cannot be expressed or described that is the most threatening.

What is interesting about *Metro 2033* and *SoC* is how they attempt to co-opt this traditional device of fear of the unknown by undermining standard shooter behavior. *Metro 2033* makes mutants much harder to kill and questions the point of doing so, as the trade-off in terms of ammunition is rarely worth it, which makes forced battles seem all the more nihilistic. *SoC* opts for keeping mutant encounters predominantly zoned and limited, making human-on-human conflict the mainstay of gameplay. The more dangerous mutants – Snorks, Bloodsuckers, Poltergeist, Pseudogiants, and Controllers – are generally located in underground labs. They are associated with dark, cramped spaces where anomalies are harder to avoid and, like *Metro 2033*, tactical approaches to combat, including whether or not to avoid it, cannot be exploited as effectively; once again, they are *reactive* fights, rather than ones where the player can adopt a *proactive*, strategic approach[5]. They are also introduced via set-pieces: the Bloodsucker's first, invisible charge in the Agroprom basements; the attack by the Controller on exiting the basements;

Figure 8.5 A poltergeist in *S.T.A.L.K.E.R.: Call of Pripyat.* The poltergeist is represented by the glowing blue light, but even when this is not visible, it can still pick up objects and hurl them at the player, meaning they may not have any idea what the attack is caused by (GSC Game World 2010).

and the terrifying lower levels of X18, where initially the player has no idea whether the flying debris is an as yet unknown anomaly or a sentient attack. Mutants, relying on close-range attacks, are at their most dangerous in cramped spaces – exactly where we find them. Players rapidly learn to associate underground sequences with mutant attacks, and by separating mutants, as tougher and rarer enemies, from the rolling battles with human agents, *SoC* protects the real terrors of The Zone from over-familiarity[6]. The sense of power of the player is subtly undermined by this. With the exception of what appears to be some kind of invisible entity in the first foray into The Zone: "a shimmering, a trembling, sort of like hot air at noon over a tin roof" (21) and Pilman's mention of "Dick the Tramp and the jolly ghosts" (107), all the dangers of *RP's* Zone are purely environmental. Equally, in Tarkovsky's film, everything about The Zone is immaterial and inferred, never actual; in fact, *RP* is arguably more normalized than *Stalker* in that the threats may not be tangible but they are demonstrably real. Kirill backs into the silver web and drops dead of a heart attack several hours later, and there is a proven statistical correlation between resettled Zone survivors and the occurrence of natural disasters in their new homes, even though how the causality operates is a mystery.

Prediction, Power, and the Avatar

Like most games, shooters tend to co-opt the fairly standard narrative model of a world jolted from normality, with balance being restored by the actions of the protagonist. The idea of resolution is important for carving a dramatic arc, long-term goal, and reward for play, and is certainly ingrained as an industry standard. How a world enables such a transformative arc is inherent to its design; it is uncommon to simply string visually diverse locations together to serve as a non-integrated backdrop any more. Just as the requirements of a dramatic arc impact the development of central characters, and just as the traditional gameplay model requires the avatar to increase in power as a game progresses, so the world must yield to the player as well. The player learns to master the space; they improve at navigating the world, understanding the world, beating what the world throws at them, and this is fundamentally tied to prediction and causality, which allow skills to develop. In a sense, *RP's* Red is a master of The Zone; he survives where many other Stalkers have fallen. But this mastery has two important caveats. Firstly, he has mainly learned from experience—more specifically, from the mistakes of others. "That was Four-Eyes," he tells Artie, "And on the left hill, you can't see from here, lies Poodle. In the same condition" (135). In a way, the quicksave function of a game could arguably serve a similar purpose to the piles of rags and bones dotting the novel's Zone, but this leads us to a trial-and-error style of game design that is anachronistic and dated. So without this blind-evolution method of learning, a game requires its hazards to be predictable and repeatable, as does the more prosaic question of cost-per-asset, something we should never overlook. As we have seen, these two factors converge to necessitate that *SoC's* Zone is fundamentally normalized. In *RP*, many hazards are highly ambiguous and individu-alized. In *SoC*, learning to predict where an anomaly might be, how it behaves, and how to neutralize its effects is a hardwired aspect of the learning process, just like getting access to better guns and armor.

The second major caveat is that, a little like Artyom, Red's survival in The Zone frequently comes down to a kind of sixth sense. In the book's first expedition, he finds himself simply unable to throw a path-finding nut forwards, but cannot explain why. This is completely separate and distinct to the skill he demonstrates in spotting the altered trajectory of a bolt caught in Mosquito Mange. Games are built, fundamentally, for the player to learn and then exploit skills like this second instance. A highly ambiguous sense of danger, without any representation, is much more difficult because we are dealing with systems of computational causality, and this lies at the heart of the schematic expectations of players too. While games are actually very good at creating anxiety and fear, ambiguity is much harder to pull off, particularly if a player is trying to progress. Red remains fearful of The Zone right until the last. The player, via Strelok, probably retains a healthy respect for The Zone but towards the end of the game is no longer subject to unknown anxieties: the fear of moving forwards for what the next step may provoke. And, critically, in *RP* we are talking about non-causal, often invisible entities that can kill you hours or even months later without you even knowing you'd been affected. The Zone is not just alien in origin, it is fundamentally unknowable: Red, Pilman, Kirill, and the reader, will never understand it, or be able to predict what lies ahead. For Gomel (1995), "The Zone remains an empty signifier" where "the Apocalypse is left pending" (14). In contrast, *SoC's* Zone is a human, or post-human, creation. It can be controlled, beaten, outsmarted. Despite the inferences of sentience, The Zone is first and foremost a dangerous environment and, as such, it can be conquered. In *SoC*, Strelok changes The Zone. This is unambiguous: he turns off the Brain Scorcher, he opens the path to Pripyat and the NPP. Equally, in *CS*, The Zone responds to Strelok's intrusion with Blow Outs; it protects itself. Both instances prove that The Zone is susceptible to further human influence. Its power is therefore earthed and this gives the player a degree of control and power and freedom from fear that is fundamentally and profoundly different to the book. Like the Metro, the inherent requirements of gameplay force a normalization of The Zone.

Like Red, Artyom is no fighter, although he exhibits quite a temper, and even kills twice in the novel. Neither occasion, however, is particularly heroic. He kills a Librarian through a combination of terror and to put Daniel out of his dying agonies, and he shoots a Nazi officer while the man's attention is elsewhere. The game's Artyom, by contrast, is a one-man killing machine, cutting through Nazis, Communists, Bandits, and mutants, even if there is reduced scope of power-ups compared to *SoC* (*Metro 2033* has a more limited weapon set and only two instances where the avatar's armor can be upgraded). Both versions of Artyom, however, are inconsistent visionaries. In the novel, what stands Artyom apart is his ability to hear "the song of the Metro," a heightened sensitivity to the super-natural elements of the world. However, he is neither privileged nor protected from these forces, with the exception of the voices that render his VDNKh compatriots comatose and kill Bourbon. He is just as susceptible to the biomass in the Kremlin station, and tunnel fear elsewhere, and when the Brahmins of Polis send him to retrieve a sacred tome and prove himself the chosen one, his abilities desert him completely. What he is, however, is a conduit for the Dark Ones, which Artyom only realizes as the missile barrage he has unleashed rains down on the Dark One city, destroying them all. Likewise in the

Figure 8.6 The vision in the playground in *Metro 2033* (4A Games 2010).

game, the vision sequences (of both a pre-apocalyptic playground and the entity that nearly kills Artyom and Bourbon in the catacombs) are disconnected from the rest of the game, offering at best a chance to continue living, rather than any reward for achieving a desired resolution. By not letting the player know what to aim for, power is replaced with only the "reward" of staying alive.

In keeping with *SoC*, the game offers a choice of endings, one following the course of the novel and a hidden, positive end, accessible only if the player acts in a moral way at an assortment of broadly unsignposted events during the game. This is, in itself, an interesting design choice, given the great lengths Western developers go to in foregrounding ethical or moral choice in their games. You simply have to act in a good way, without reward, in *Metro 2033*, in order to achieve the good ending. Likewise, the choice of Wish Granter "bad" endings in *SoC* is determined by factors ranging from wealth amassed to a karma index that is never available to the player. Unlike a game like *inFamous* (Sucker Punch 2009) or *Fallout 3* (Bethesda 2008), moral behavior is not an explicit integer to be played with, but a hidden consequence.

Aside from his ability with an assortment of battered and improvised weapons, the game's Artyom has explicit visions on several occasions (the novel's are more abstract and not always explicitly visual). Aside from these, he has no apparent special abilities on display. This is interesting, as we are not talking about having to represent any extraordinary abilities in-game; in the novel, Artyom is not capable of anything other than being aware of a deeper sense of life in the Metro, and even this is something he doesn't trust himself. But the game's protagonist appears, at least on the surface, less sensitive. Partially this may be due to the inherently problematic question of an avatar's interior life in a game, something normally avoided in FPS games. Certainly, on the occasions where it has been foregrounded, such as with *Prey's* Tommy (Humanhead Studios 2006), it has been less than successful. Outside cutscenes, avatars may occasionally vocalize, but internal monologues are extremely rare and usually found in older games (Pinchbeck 2009). Artyom may offer some glimpses into his interior life in the short voice-overs of the loading screens, but we never are given any sense of his reactions to the more supernatural experiences he has.

RP's Schuhart in many ways is an ideal FPS protagonist. He is libertarian, socially distant and physically competent; a resourceful, hands-on everyman, just trying to make his way in the world. Strelok, the amnesiac anti-hero of *SoC*, is not dissimilar in many ways. We begin the game with no self-knowledge, a common trait in FPS games. This is an extremely useful way of allowing the player to assimilate a lack of local knowledge into their general gameplay schema. The only clue is a mysterious message on an otherwise blank PDA: "Kill the Strelok" (which translates as "shooter" and may be either a nickname, or just a generic description). As the game progresses, we learn that this Strelok is the leader of a group of Stalkers, highly driven, ambitious, and obsessed with reaching the center of The Zone. In later games he is also described as secretive and manipulative (*CS*), although he later assists military personnel out of The Zone, becoming a scientific advisor to the government (*CoP*).

For Csicery-Romay (1986), Schuhart's journey through the novel is one of stripping away: he loses his job, his freedom, his dignity, and is driven to the Golden Ball by his desperation to not lose his daughter. Csicery-Romay argues that when Schuhart "arrives at the Golden Ball, nothing is left of him... He stinks with the slime and burns of his ordeals; by sending the boy Arnie to his certain death, he has abandoned the morality that set him apart from others" (33). In contrast, Strelok arrives at the Wish Granter a superman, toting the best armor and weaponry, powerful artifacts, and an unquestionable supremacy over The Zone. Schuhart has lost everything, but Strelok has won. What is interesting, however, is that whilst *RP* ends on the ambiguous raging prayer of a desperate man, the Wish Granter in *SoC* is a pure folly; no good can come of it, much as the Professor

Figure 8.7 The 'false' endings of *S.T.A.L.K.E.R.: Shadow of Chernobyl* (GSC Game World 2006) Strelok is (clockwise, from top left) turned to stone, disintegrated, crushed, and blinded. In a fifth ending, he sees visions of a nuclear apocalypse.

argues in Tarkovsky's film. In all five versions of the endgame at the Wish Granter, Strelok is doomed: blinded, crushed, turned to stone. It is only by following a sub-quest two-thirds of the way through the game that Strelok can make his way *past* the Wish Granter, seeing it for an illusion, a last-ditch booby-trap to protect the C-Consciousness entity at the heart of The Zone. Unlike Csicery-Romay's understanding of the close of *RP* as a "utopian prayer" (23), in *SoC* the Wish Granter is a malignant illusion. This, in itself, goes one step further than Tarkovsky, who simply renders it impotent, redundant.

The central point here is that Red and Strelok embark on opposite journeys. Red starts with ambition, optimism, potential, and ends the novel on his knees, a desperate and shattered murderer. Strelok enters The Zone knowing nothing, penniless, vulnerable, lost, but at the game's fake conclusion, just prior to the Wish Granter, he is probably the most powerful figure in The Zone. He may not walk on water, but he strides across toxic waste without hesitation.

In all cases, we find heroes: self-reliant and resourceful outsiders, who make journeys into unknown lands where normal rules of society and reality break down. The core differences are ones of power; games are predicated upon the gradual increase of mastery over the presented space, kept in check by an increasingly difficult set of obstacles. But the final outcome is normally a more powerful position than the start. Both Glukhovsky's Artyom and the Strugatskys' Red end their respective journeys at points of absolute loss. 4A's Artyom and GSC's Strelok strive upwards in knowledge, mastery, and capacity to survive these hostile worlds and end stronger. This raises an intriguing question for game design: can the clearly powerful design tool of stripping a protagonist bare find form in a medium where even the most nihilistic of worlds embed a rise to power?

Get Out of Here, Stalker!

Even a limited examination of these books and games, such as is possible here, offers insights into the constraints and opportunities created by the remediation process in relation to FPS design. Key considerations are normalization, virtual expansion, predictability and causality, uniqueness and familiarity, managing combat to undermine or shift normal expectations, and an attempt to offer alternative ways of working with ambiguity and power in relation to the avatar. To conclude, let me summarize these once more to offer a fully rounded picture.

The cost of representing an image in a game is greater than in a novel, while, at the same time, games require representation rather than inference if the image in question is to be factored into gameplay. This tends to force a reduction in scale or volume of diversity and abstraction, particularly in the case of *Metro 2033* or *RP*, which are fundamentally based on ambiguous imagery. In both, this reduction is counterbalanced by the inference of a wider environment than is accessible to the player. In other words, rather than incomplete imagery, game designers are more or less forced to either *present in full* or *show but deny*. This runs hand-in-hand with the normalization; computational and ludic entities share a base requirement of stable behaviors, although for different reasons. This normalization and "integerisation" may run contra to the deep ambiguities that give *M33* and *RP* much of their power, but the tendency to engage with such entities on a structural, goal-orientated level may be offset by introducing unique events or reducing the overall number of such entities while increasing their unique properties. Both games handle mutants this way, making a conceptual divide between these encounters and "normal" gunplay. Finally, the common trick of stripping either power or humanity from a protagonist simply runs in the opposite direction to traditional game avatar development, both diegetically and structurally. Introducing mystery to keep gameplay interesting is a common-enough trick, but these Ukrainian studios display an idiosyncratic lack of need to ever bother getting to the bottom of these mysteries. If the narratives of *SoC* or *Metro 2033* are resolved, the worlds retain an unfathomable distance. The biomass in D6 can be killed, but we never know what it is or why it is there and, critically, the Stalkers just chalk it up to one of the many weird, inhuman facets of a world that extends far beyond human understanding. At the same time, however, both games add a greater human element to their worlds. The Zone is the creation of a human endeavor. *Metro 2033* is the product of a human apocalypse, like the book, but its existence as a psychogeographic environment is downplayed.

In their attempts to inject a greater sense of ambiguity, both in reality and morality, and their particularly bleak outlooks, *Metro 2033* and the *S.T.A.L.K.E.R.* games stand apart from other shooters. The design tricks to rob the player of a sense of power, whether by the realization that fourteen ball-bearings are not enough to make it to the next station, or by blinding, crushing, ossifying, or disintegrating the player at their moment of victory, make these games particularly apocalyptic in nature. *SoC* and *Metro 2033* make *Fallout*'s post-nuclear world look like Sesame Street. There is little comedy or redemption to be found in either, just a bitter scrabble for power and survival.

Finally, these games raise intriguing questions. What happens when ambiguity and unique events form the mainstay of gameplay? Is it possible to create games based around the loss of power, not its gain? Can the hiding of moral integers be extended to other areas of gameplay? Can we build a game with eroded causality? Worlds where the most terrifying things are never seen, but only inferred; where there is no reward other than the fleeting sense of surviving just for a minute longer: a profound shift in the deployment of significance of entities and actions, and the concept of goal and reward in games – are such things possible in this medium? *Metro 2033* and *S.T.A.L.K.E.R.* offer us tantalizing glimpses that they are, even as we gasp for oxygen, kill for bread, run in terror, die alone in the dark.

Notes

1 A three-game franchise abbreviated as follows: *Shadow of Chernobyl* (2007) – SoC; *Clear Sky* (2008) – CS; *Call of Pripyat* (2010) – CoP. We will focus primarily on *SoC* here, as it is the immediate source of the remediated material; however, we will consider *CS* and *CoP* occasionally, where relevant.

2 The novel will be abbreviated to distinguish it from the game. *M33* means the novel, *Metro 2033* the game.

3 Meaning the way it is represented and understood as a symbolic, or narrative, object, rather than a gameplay one, although I have argued before that we should remember that this separation is artificial and should only be applied as an analytical tool (Pinchbeck 2007).

4 All of these tricks are, of course, classic survival horror design tactics. It's their mix with more generic FPS combat that marks these games apart.

5 The difference between *reactive* and *proactive* shooters is one of the major ways in which the genre has developed since *DOOM*. I discuss this in more detail in Pinchbeck (2013).

6 It's also worth noting that in all the *S.T.A.L.K.E.R.* games, not only are the environments really substantial, but there are many empty buildings serving little or no function in quests or plot. This sense of isolation, loneliness, and emptiness is what Sakey (2010) sees as being central to his concept of environmental alienation and fuels the impact of mutants we are discussing here.

References

Bolter, Jay David and Richard Grusin. 2000. *Remediation: Understanding New Media.* Cambridge: The MIT Press.

Csicsery-Ronay Jnr, Istvan. 1986. "Towards the Last Fairy Tale: On the Fairy-Tale Paradigm in the Strugatskys' Science Fiction, 1963–72." *Science Fiction Studies* 13 (38): 142.

Glukhovsky, Dmitry. 2007. *Metro 2033* (trans. Natasha Randall). London: Gollancz.

Gomel, Elana. 1995. "The Poetics of Censorship: Allegory as Form and Ideology in the Novels of Arkady and Boris Strugatsky." *Science Fiction Studies* 22 (1): 87–105.

Howell, Peter. 2011. "Schematically Disruptive Game Design." In *Proceedings of DiGRA 2011: Think, Design, Play.* Utrecht School of the Arts.

Lem, Stanislaw. 1991. "About the Strugatskys' Roadside Picnic." In *Microworlds*, 243–78. London: Mandarin.

Marsh, Rosalind. J. 1986. "Soviet Fiction and the Nuclear Debate." *Soviet Studies* 38 (2): 248–70.

McCloud, Scott. 1993. *Understanding Comics: The Invisible Art.* New York: HarperCollins.

Pinchbeck, Dan. 2007. "Counting Barrels in *Quake 4*: affordances and homodiegetic structures in FPS worlds." In *Proceedings of DiGRA 2007: Situated Play.* University of Tokyo.

—2009. *Story as a function of Gameplay in First Person Shooters and an analysis of FPS diegetic content 1998–2007.* Doctoral Thesis, University of Portsmouth, UK. Available from *www.thechineseroom. co.uk/thesis.pdf*

—2013. *DOOM: Scarydarkfast*. Ann Arbor, MI: University of Michigan Press.

Sakey, Matthew. 2010. "Alone for All Seasons: Environmental Estrangement in S.T.A.L.K.E.R." In *Well Played 2.0: Videogames, Value and Meaning*, edited by Drew Davidson. Lulu.com

Strugatksy, Arkady and Boris Strugatsky. 1977. *Roadside Picnic* (trans. Antonina W. Bouis). Newton Abbot: Readers Union.

Wilson, Douglas and Miguel Sicart. (2010). "Now it's Personal: On Abusive Game Design." In *Proceedings of the International Conference on the Future of Game Design and Technology*, 40–7.

Games

4A Games. 2010. *Metro 2033* [PC, Xbox 360]. THQ.

Bethesda Game Studios. 2008. *Fallout 3* [Microsoft Windows, PlayStation3, Xbox 360]. Bethesda Softworks and Zenimax Media.

GSC Game World. 2006. *S.T.A.L.K.E.R.: Shadow of Chernobyl* [Microsoft Windows]. THQ.

—2008. *S.T.A.L.K.E.R.: Clear Sky* [Microsoft Windows]. Deep Silver.

—2009. *S.T.A.L.K.E.R.: Call of Pripyat* [Microsoft Windows]. Bitcomposer Games.

Humanhead Studios. 2006. *Prey* [Microsoft Windows]. 2K Games.

Sucker Punch. 2009. *inFamous* [PlayStation 3]. Sony Computer Entertainment.

9

More Bang For Your Buck—Hardware Hacking, Real Money Trade, and Transgressive Play within Console-Based First-Person Shooters

Alan Meades

I ignore the insults and posturing challenges coming over the voice chat, instead focusing on where I'll position myself once the game starts. I decide on one of the bunkers that'll give me good visibility over the dusty Afghan battleground. I've got my custom load-out, a holographic scoped assault rifle and a stock of claymore mines that I'll use to cover my back as I look out over the wreckage of the downed transport plane for insurgents. The game starts and I spawn on the south end of the map. I sprint past the Humvees, watching out for potential hiding spots in the wrecked fuselage and instinctively scan the ridge to the north for the silhouette of enemy snipers. Finding nothing I break off into the poppy field, I'm seconds away from the entrance to the bunker … then it all goes wrong. Rockets rain down unexpectedly from the sky and I am killed in a plume of smoke, dust and debris; I spawn somewhere else on the map and die almost instantaneously. Each of my attempts to escape the rockets fails, but my opponents aren't on the ridge, nor in the wreckage of the plane, they're in none of the usual hotspots, instead they appear to be flying through the air firing streams of rockets that are conventionally restricted to one or two per spawn. It is clear that the rules of the game have been ruptured, the game has been "modded." Despite the frustration and disorientation, I feel compelled to stay in the match even after many of my teammates disconnect. Perhaps after a minute more, a klaxon sounds, a towering mushroom cloud erupts on the edge of the screen, the map is engulfed in flames, and the match comes to its grim and jarring conclusion.

Having experienced an event like this, one would normally begin to question the motives: why would somebody do this, what might they gain, what would be the point? Perhaps they simply enjoy ruining other people's fun? Perhaps they feel a temporary elevation of power and importance? Perhaps they wish to undermine and break the game? Perhaps they have nothing better to do but to waste other people's time and their own? Yet what if these interpretations are incorrect; what if the transgressive events described above serve an express purpose, but one that is concealed to many who play or study the game?

For those unfamiliar with the *Call of Duty* franchise (henceforth COD), or its sixth iteration, *Modern Warfare 2* (henceforth MW2) in particular, I should stress that the match described was atypical —it had been modified without consent of the developers (Infinity Ward 2009). The modification occurs in direct violation of the game end user license agreement (EULA), the consoles' terms of service

(TOS), and copyright law such as the US 1998 Digital Millennium Copyright Act.

As such, this modification represents an expression of non-normative play, a field that has garnered significant academic attention over the last decade, e.g. Consalvo's extensive work on cheating (2007), Koivisto and Foo's research on grief play (2004), and Wright, Boria, and Breidenbach's taxonomy of "creative player action" in *Counter-Strike* (Valve 2000). Similarly, a number of academics have focused more closely on the process of modding from a PC perspective, e.g. Olli Sotamaa (2004), Julian Kücklich (2005), and Hector Postigo (2007, 2008). In comparison to existing literature within the field, perhaps due to its illicit nature and the somewhat elusive nature of the communities of production, console modding has received little attention despite the size of the console gaming audience and the existence of modding as a cultural practice within it; a notable exception is that of Jordan's 'From Rule-Breaking to ROM Hacking' (2007). Interestingly, by looking the archetypal console FPS franchise, COD, and its sixth iteration, MW2, we can begin to map out the complexities of console modding and the relationships that underpin it.

The Xbox LIVE activity chart for the week beginning November 8th 2010 (Hyrb 2010) lists four iterations of the COD franchise in its top nine slots. Not only is the COD franchise deeply generic, representing the iconic console-based FPS, one could argue that it constitutes the definitive Xbox LIVE experience – simply put, the COD franchise has consistently entertained greater numbers of players for longer periods of time than other equivalent FPS game. The latest iteration of the series, *Call of Duty: Black Ops* (Treyarch 2010) (hereafter BLOPs), generated $1 billion dollars'-worth of revenue for Activision within six weeks (Fahey 2010). It boasts the best opening month of sales for any game in American history, and is already the seventh best-selling piece of videogame software (Matthews 2010). At peak usage on its first day of release, BLOPS had 2.9 million simultaneous Xbox 360 players on its multiplayer mode, in addition to 1.5 million PlayStation 3 players and 55,000 PC players for the same period (Patterson 2010). In comparison, the previous iteration, MW2, boasted 2.2 million Xbox LIVE players on day one (Crecente 2009).

MW2 "modded lobbies" as described above are fortunately comparatively rare on the Xbox 360 console, with the vast majority of players never experiencing them first-hand. Yet despite this, the modded lobby and its perpetrators have become the practitioners of witchcraft and sorcery of the gaming culture in which the current generation of FPS games are embedded. The skills that the modder or hacker can unlock, and the underhand play styles they can deploy, have captured the imagination of players who speak of them in contempt, disgust, and perhaps a little fear.

It is the primary aim of this paper to illuminate the transgressive practices that surround modded lobbies, considering the ways in which they can be viewed not as rebellion or resistance, but as indices of the seduction of the contemporary FPS.

If we step back from the initial spectacle and audacity of the modded lobby and consider what purpose it serves, apart from that of willed resistance, a web of mutually interdependent relationships are exposed. We discover a ludic ecosystem in which different groups are entertained and supported by the game in different ways depending on their position on a continuum of affinity with the game text and the technologies that surround it. The herbivorous majority of player base consume the text as intended, while a smaller number of predatorial players gaze across the digital territory as a space for domination. Simultaneously a small number of entrepreneurial and technically astute poachers seek out ways of fulfilling those predatorial desires, through the delivery of digital equivalents of big-game trophies or carefully orchestrated safaris in which they dominate their quarry. Each takes what they wish from the same digital terrain—whether it is financial income, increased status, or the ability to (perhaps illegitimately) claim an alignment with a concept of authentic or pure-play, as intended by the game developers.

While the ecosystem metaphor may be too tenuous for some, it offers us some perspective to begin to read the apparently anarchic and disruptive event that opened this chapter as a corollary of the ways in which hardware hackers, software modders, and videogame players converge on the FPS as a way of furthering their various needs. Originating from both the developer and player base, the demands to meet the expectations of an idealized notion of what the player should do have led to the development of emergent illicit ecosystems. Rather than being viewed as damaging wanton acts of digital vandalism, signaling a player's antagonism towards the text, such transgressive events, I argue, should be considered antithetically, as unintended indices of the sheer seduction of the FPS genre as well as indicative of the steps that player are willing to take to be co-opted and embraced by the cultures that are seen to surround the game. By approaching the modded lobby from this perspective, while still jarring and in clear violation of EULA and copyright law, it represents a fascinating example of the evolution of the peculiarities of videogame culture.

In "I Fought the Law: Transgressive Play and The Implied Player", Espen Aarseth (2007) defines "transgressive play" as any behavior that goes against the notion of the "idealized player." This is the concept of the player that is used during game development, which he argues creates a "prison-house of regulated play" (133). Applying Wolfgang Iser's concept of implied reader and Gadamer's games that "master the player" to videogames and their development, Aarseth presents transgressive play as a natural reaction to overly rigid conceptions of play and the player (player as "player function") and a fleeting assertion of a player's "true" identity and individuality.

> Transgressive play is a symbolic gesture of rebellion against the tyranny of the game, a (perhaps illusory) way for the played subject to regain their sense of identity and uniqueness through the mechanisms of the game itself … These marginal events and occurrences, these wondrous acts of transgression, are absolutely vital because they give us hope, true or false; they remind us that it is possible to regain control, however briefly, to dominate that which dominates us so completely. (132–3)

While Aarseth's notion of the implied player is of use in the analysis of non-normative play tropes in their broadest sense, the notion of transgressive play as a temporary resistance to the "tyranny of the game," which one assumes either passes or is crushed, is nonetheless problematic. Playing a game that so deeply intrudes upon the sovereignty of agency and identity that it necessitates an act of rebellion (symbolically or otherwise) doesn't sound particularly fun and raises the question of why it is that the transgressive player simply doesn't stop playing that game and do something less domineering? Yet, if one considers transgressive play from a more contemporary model of power-relations and resistance, such as that outlined by Hardt and Negri's (2000) biopolitical multitude, the ways in which the modded lobby can be seen as a selective resistance— such as against some of the means of playing the game, but not the game itself—has greater clarity. From such a perspective the transgressive act needn't represent a direct resistance to the tyranny of the game or its developers, but provides a much more contemporary reflection of the expectations and concerns of the videogame culture and our relationships with media texts more generally.

Building upon Michel Foucault's notion of biopower and the biopolitical empire, Hardt and Negri present the multitude as the members of contemporary society in which mechanisms of control and censure have been divested and interiorized by the individual:

> The behaviors of social integration and exclusion proper to rule are thus increasingly interiorized within the subjects themselves. Power is now exercised through machines that directly organize the brains (in communication systems, information networks, etc.) and bodies (in welfare systems, monitored activities, etc.) toward a state of autonomous alienation from the sense of life and the desire for creativity. (24)

Within the biopolitical environment, where the multitude is unable to confidently identify the lines of influence and domination, who is oppressing or needing opposition, resistance becomes entirely symbolic and abstracted. From this perspective the multitude simultaneously perpetuates the mechanisms of control and represents the power that can undermine them. The multitude thus ultimately maintains and holds the potential to challenge the biopolitical empire, while in turn the biopolitical body equally becomes the source of tensions and joys for those it controls. If we consider contemporary entertainment products as biopolitical mechanisms, videogames such as COD represent an opportunity for control and freedom in equal measure—one may find release and freedom within a videogame that demands contrition in its players and consumers.

Returning to the subject of videogames, which are seen as "a paradigmatic media of Empire" (Dyer-Witheford and de Peuter 2009, xv) transgressive play need not be viewed as directly oppositional to the text on which it manifests itself. The transgression can be against any one of the empirical structures that impose order on the player; in addition, from such a perspective there is no apparent contradiction (at least in terms of biopower) between the notion of a player breaking a game in order to play it better, or in a more authentic way. A transgressor may in fact be seduced by the text they appear to be attacking, such are the apparent paradoxes of agency in the biopolitical terrain.

Aarseth expressly explores transgressive play from a single-player perspective, such as his experiences in *Elder Scrolls: Oblivion*'s (Bethesda Game Studios 2006) world of Cryodiil, but it becomes more fully useful when applied to multiplayer gaming such as online FPS games. In single-player games, any mismatch between the implied player and the actual player could be accounted for on the player's terms by adjusting the difficulty setting or resorting to cheat codes, walkthroughs, or publicly known glitches. Consalvo (2007) explores some of the ways in which players have justified this deviation from the implied player model, including "because I was stuck," "for the pleasure of the experience," "time compression," and "simply being an ass" (95–103).

Consalvo goes on to question the perception of cheating from these contexts, suggesting that while some saw cheating as forming identity, "... it is more helpful to examine cheating as a practice, particularly one that is ludic, situated, and iterative in its expression" (127). While one assumes that, from the perpetrator's perspective, deviance from the expected manner of play is an activity rather than an identity – that is, it is a way that someone plays, rather than signifying a type of player – by contrast in multiplayer games the luxury to choose the implication of deviance is removed from the individual and placed in the hands of the masses.

In the contemporary generation of console FPS games, where play is increasingly placed in the biopolitical gaze of multiplayer matches, those perceived as playing in ways that deviate from the implied player model, even if this is simply a lack of ability, are singled out as noobs, or cheats, and are often ostracized by the player community. For these misfits there is little choice but to seek out alternative means of meeting these expectations if they wish to play in any (externally defined) meaningful sense or extract value in a conventional reading of the game; if they simply wish to access the equipment and play options reserved as rewards for players that subscribe to the implied player model.

If videogames demand certain behaviors and ideological positions from their players in order to enjoy the game and create enjoyable adversaries for their foes, they do so through a process of rhetorical indoctrination and persuasion. Dovey and Kennedy (2006) see the alignment of players to the rhetoric of the game "... not only as a desired quality for the production of active, engaging and meaningful experiences, but also simultaneously as the means through which the gameplayer is most likely to be exploited in the interests of monster conglomerates" (9).

In *Persuasive Games* Ian Bogost suggests that videogames, by their nature, are particularly suited to mounting arguments and influencing players through "procedural rhetoric," whereby a code is written that "... enforces rules to generate some kind of representation, rather than authoring the representation itself" (Bogost 2007, 4). Games therefore become mechanisms for persuasion through finesse. Building upon Fogg's (2003) seven types of persuasive technology, Bogost argues that videogames persuade procedurally in the following ways:

- Reduction – altering the level of complexity something is modeled with, inferring significance – e.g. damage modeling on MW2 where opponents must be hit multiple times.

- Tunneling – sequencing events in a specific non-negotiable order, inferring causality – e.g. offering access to weapons after a specific level of experience is attained.

- Tailoring – presenting information relevant to individuals to change their behavior or attitudes – e.g. offering player data related to their use of specific weapons in MW2.

- Suggestion – on-screen prompts in specific situations – e.g. the button-press reminder when near a useable item.

- Self-monitoring – allowing users to monitor performance through the creation of a metric – e.g. experience points or a user's kill/death ratio.

- Surveillance – the ability to observe the behavior of others in order to modify play – e.g. kill-cams that show the location and load-out of a victor.

- Conditioning – offering greater reward for some ways of play, while comparatively punishing others – e.g. rewarding head-shots with additional experience. (Bogost 2007, 60)

Gonzalo Frasca (2003) suggests that these persuasive technologies can be seen to work on three conceptual levels: the representation of the game (what it presents), manipulation rules (what the player can do within the game), and "goal rules" (what players must do to win):

> Games with goal rules provide both a personal and social reward: whoever reaches the end of a game will be recognized as a good player. (232)

In turn, these rhetorical statements signal the rules and parameters of the game to its potential players; they signal what they must contract themselves to in order to play. Many find themselves naturally aligning their behavior with the demands of the implied player, picking up the persuasive cues through the technologies detailed above; they learn to play the game as intended and appreciate its various pleasures. The player is persuaded in what she should do, how to play, and the lens through which the play of others should be viewed. This creates a persuasive rhetoric that contextualizes and produces both sanctioned and illegitimate play, distilling into an idealized kind of "pure play" and a transgressive opposite – a cotangent to be avoided at all costs. Play is therefore productive of biopower.

For players whose play styles or ability deviate from the implied player model, the game will be an experience of almost constant frustration and negative reinforcement, both as a product of the goal rules ("game-over" screens, or in the case of multiplayer FPS, straggling at the bottom of the leaderboard) and the biopolitical context of play (ridicule, ostracism). Similarly, power-gamers or dedicated players who see through the rhetorical framing of the game and gaze at the systems of conditioning underneath it are viewed to play in too efficient, non-normative ways and also face censure. Their play, as Taylor (2003) notes, "... looks and sounds quite unlike how we usually speak of gaming in general" and is often regarded as "corruption of authentic game space" (310).

It is the nature of biopower to deprive and emasculate that which is deviant. As such, transgressive play is conceptualized as an unfortunate and tiresome symptom of the social nature of multiplayer videogames. It is frequently conceptualized as conducted by the incompetent, the deviant, the criminal, and the malicious – these are the ways in which the biopolitical machine rationalizes those who do not comply, making them "other" and deficient in either effort, ethics, observation of law. Such exclusion not only negates the claims of the transgressor, but also reinforces the authority of a defined model of play. The biopolitical machine uses the transgressive act as a means of further strengthening the sense of belonging and meaning of the center.

Returning to Aarseth's tyranny of the game, we can begin to see how the FPS game ecosystem is intolerant to behavior that deviates from that of the implied player. Those players that are unable or unwilling to dedicate the necessary resources or to play in certain, sanctioned ways are treated with suspicion and contempt by the player body and are persuaded to play correctly, or not play at all. This represents a persuasive and powerful motivational factor to contrition—in order to experience the game, to be accepted by the community of players, in order to access all of the content in the game, and ultimately to have fun, one must play in a relatively restrictive manner.

While expectations of fair play and the like exist in practically all forms of play, the super-complex and globally networked manner of online multiplayer FPS games has created a blueprint for play that is both remarkably coherent and persuasive. Whereas there may be kick-abouts in the park, five-a-side, and premiership matches of football, according to skill and investment, for the majority of MW2 players there is one prototypical benchmark for play, which is enforced through the biopolitical nature of videogames.

> By accepting to play, the player subjects herself to the rules and structures of the game and this defines the player: a person subjected to a rule-based system; no longer a complete, free subject with the power to decide what to do next. (Aarseth 2007, 130)

Returning to the specifics of MW2 and the COD franchise, we can begin to see how the implied player and the goal rules have influenced what players regard as important in play. Each COD release has included both a single and multiplayer component; however, the fourth release, MW, introduced elements of avatar development and persistence unseen within multiplayer FPS gaming. It rewarded players with experience points that unlocked increasingly potent weapons and skills that remained persistent across the matches they played. In addition to the weapons the player unlocks as experience is gained, progress is marked with military rank and medals that are displayed when playing in multiplayer matches, indicating a player's expertise and service record. In the journey from the first rank, Private First Class, through to Commander (level 70) the player accrues all of the weapons and perks in the game, typically taking a player around 60 hours of online play to achieve (Piston Heads 2010). This focus on long-term goal shifted the temporal focus and social significance of multiplayer gaming from a short blast of competitive fun against immaterial opponents to a long-term process of accrual in a culture of competition, much more akin to traditional MMO "grind" mechanics. In addition, the user interface which tracked experience and the medal system that displayed attainment for all to see brought systems of surveillance and self-monitoring unseen within the FPS genre.

When playing the COD franchise online it is common to find yourself being repeatedly killed by opponents using more accurate and powerful weapons that you simply do not have access to, or using weapon attachments or perks (such as moving silently) that are unlocked at far higher rank. It feels that there is a conspiracy where other, more powerful players collude to kill the comparatively weak and uninitiated, and attempt to prevent the player from gaining access to the equipment and perks that are so effective. During instances of split-second twitch gameplay, such as when you stumble into an opponent around a corner, one learns that there is simply a better combination of weapon, perk, and strategy often only available to the most experienced, and that shot-for-shot you will lose. Over time such a model created a schism within the player base – creating a mass of players being dominated by others who, due to the way in which their skills were rewarded, far exceeded the potency and strategic capability of their prey. Despite this apparent inequality it is certainly the case that the persistent unlocks, while creating rhetorics of power and status, have made the multiplayer element increasingly engaging and entertaining. It is a predatory model of social jockeying where one asserts their power on the weaker, while avoiding the powerful.

Yet even in this model, the progress ends; the player that reaches Commander rank has no more weapons, perks, or attachments available to unlock. It would be entirely logical for the player then to continue playing using the most effective weapons and strategies, dominating matches *ad nauseum* or until interest in the game wanes. Equally it would be inevitable that all players would eventually reach Commander rank and that the game would become something different – a different equilibrium would establish itself that no longer focuses upon progression, attainment, and status. However, efforts have been made to avoid such stagnation or reinterpretation through the introduction of "prestige status." Once a player has reached rank 70 a previously greyed-out menu option becomes selectable; through a clear example of suggestion an on-screen prompts invited players to "[t]rade all your accomplishments for a bit of prestige …" and emphasizes that "[p]restige has a price … There's no going back" (Infinity Ward 2009).

By going "prestige" the players abandon their accumulated weapons, perks, and experience points, starting as if new to the game, in exchange for a "prestige emblem" visible in multiplayer matches. This process can be repeated ten times (up until 10th prestige), with a different and more desirable emblem awarded each time. By going prestige the player indicates their mastery of the multiplayer game to their peers; it becomes an act of asceticism, a rite of passage, where the powerful veteran warrior renounces all accumulations in order to start their battle again. For a group of players so effectively inducted into the persuasive rhetoric of the game (through the application of reduction, tunneling, suggestion, self-monitoring, surveillance, and conditioning) and convinced of a mode of pure-play as defined by the implied player, the suggestion to "go prestige" takes on a powerful totemic significance. Prestige becomes the mark of legitimate play and therefore Frasca's good player.

This is reflected in the ways that players refer to prestige on Fora: we are told that it prolongs the game as was intended by the designers, that one becomes a better player and that this is a more authentic way of playing the game. "... Get better playing tougher competition. Play the game the way it was meant" (Deeled 2010). This further exposes the anxieties many players have of being regarded as playing incorrectly, like a "noob." "Kids think you're all 1337 seeing you with a cool rank" (GameSpot 2009), "its worth it u unlock new titles and emblems and you don't look like a noob," "Show everyone that you're not a noob," "you gain unfathomable honor and respect by prestiging. It is the ultimate sacrifice!" (Big Dog 2010). Members of the community of play mock those who are yet to prestige with similar enthusiasm: "Well, if you're just a little wuss and can't man up, don't do it ... If you want to show some balls … go for it," "Sack up and do it" (Letterthatstates 2010).

These isolated examples of player discourse surrounding prestige and MW2 more specifically provide some indication of the nature and persuasiveness of the social expectation to play in certain, sanctioned ways. For some, prestige has become abstracted from the in-game activity itself, a mark of the right way to play which needn't be authenticated by any observed behavior. It becomes a trusted measure of inclusion; a marker of subcultural style (Hebdige 1979). It represents a compelling example of the extent to which players genuinely have become seduced by the game – willing to allow the procedural rhetoric of the game to filter good and bad players, which in turn is used to assert hierarchy and status. While this is a natural and fitting outcome for those who genuinely engage with the game, accruing the experience points as was intended, the "social goods" or cultural capital at stake such as social inclusion and status are so compelling that many are prepared to seek alternative, and often illegal, methods to meet this need—including the use of modded lobbies. In the following examples, due to the illicit nature of the activities being explored, attempts have been made to anonymize the data where appropriate.

Modded lobbies are reliant on illegally modified Xbox 360 console systems, known as JTAGs, and manipulated instances of the COD software to give players radically altered affordances and experiences within the game. Modded lobbies allow entire reprogramming of the game code and adjustment of the player experience, from user interface to constitutive rules of the game. However, typically the changes are limited to alteration of strings and integers that control access to items, the number that are available, movement and elements such as experience points. Modded lobbies that have been built to inflate the accumulation of experience points and access to MW2 prestige are commonly known as "10th prestige" lobbies, or simply 10th lobbies.

Modders advertise the availability of 10th lobbies and their respective entrance fees on various auction websites, bulletin boards, and specific gaming forums. At the time of writing, access to MW2 10th prestige lobbies is available for between $6.99 and $14.99 (eBay.com 2010); websites that specifically offer modded lobbies as a service such as 10thprestige.com (2010) and xbox360xperts.com (2010) charge higher rates, between $30 and $50. In comparison, modder community sites such as The Tech Game (2010) and their reciprocally linked Youtube accounts present a market price of 10th prestige at around $25.

Other models of gaining access to a modded lobby exist, such as lobby rental services, where players are free to use the modified game however they wish for a set period of time. Lobby rentals can be found for as little as $23 per 30 minutes, or $150 for four hours (2010). Lobby rentals allow the player to adopt the model used by internet hosting resellers, by buying modded lobby access in bulk then selling smaller portions to other users to make a profit. This shows that the costs involved in accessing a modded lobby fluctuate significantly, largely dependent on the signals that indicate the reputation of the modder and the likelihood of the modded lobby transpiring. As these are illicit acts, a user has little recompense if the modder does not deliver, and as such they undertake significant investigative work before paying to access a 10th prestige lobby.

The anxieties over non-existent lobbies can be seen on the Xbox360xperts forums' "shout box," on which customers publicly communicate directly with site administrators (2010). Over the course of 15 minutes on 4 January 2011 three individuals posted questions to the administrators detailing that they had recently paid for prestige services and were keen to know when the next lobby would be taking place. Interviews with players and individuals within the modding community give some indication of the number of players willing to use a modded lobby, suggesting that at peak demand lobbies can generate in excess of £3000 per active window, although due to its anecdotal (and illicit) nature this cannot be verified. Similarly, ongoing interviews with active COD players expose a number of instances where players have admitted to used modded lobbies, although in each case this was justified through a dismissive reference to time along the lines of "I just did it once just to get the weapons because I didn't have time – I didn't need to do it ..."

Having arranged the financial terms and paid them via Paypal or similar, the player is into the modded lobby, whereupon killing an opponent or pressing buttons on the controller when prompted award the player inflated experience points allowing them to reach rank 70 in one match. During the intermission between games the player "goes prestige" and then repeats the process when it commences a maximum of ten times. The player then leaves the lobby (or is booted by the host), carrying the experience points and the relevant prestige icon into all of the subsequent games they play.

The actual process of running a modded lobby requires significant co-ordination, interaction, and transaction between hardware hackers, software modders, and players wishing to obtain prestige through subterfuge. This complex relationship is illustrated by considering the process in depth.

The JTAG requires significant electronics skill to produce, and a botched procedure often results in an entirely inoperative console. As a result JTAGs are frequently sold to those wishing to create modded lobbies by individual adept hardware hackers, commanding values of around $200 per JTAG. The modder then installs the game software (from a legal or illegal source) and attempts to compile a list of modifications to the code by referring to "managed code" lists held on websites such as Se7ensins.com and the patch-making tutorials on the same sites. The managed code list consists of snippets of code and a corresponding explanation of the impact on the MW2 game environment, including entries for "Wallhack," "God Mode," "Auto Aim," "Spawn Projectiles," "Invisibility"—and those related to 10th prestige "Complete All Challenges without Challenge Progression and Experience" (2010). Once the patch has been applied the hacked COD lobby is ready to be played; however doing so on Xbox LIVE, which is mandatory to accrue experience points, is not without its repercussions.

That a patch applied to a lone JTAG console, perhaps in a different continent, has any bearing on other players in a multiplayer match is due to the specific architecture of the Xbox LIVE system. MW2 games rely upon a hosted match system, whereby the player determined to have the least latency, or who instigates a private match, becomes the host. This host's hardware coordinates the match and synchronizes the packets of data for the match. Crucially, this synchronization includes specific game settings such as weapon damage and the experience conferred for each kill, which if taken from a modified console are utterly at odds with those on a conventional public match. In addition, similar modifications can control which console hosts the match, and therefore the rules by which all players are restricted.

When a player uses a modified console to join Xbox LIVE it is automatically detected as illegitimate, instigating a 3- to 5-hour process that bans both gamertag and the console (The Tech Game 2010). The invalidated JTAG does have secondary value as an offline JTAG, or as a base system that can be modified further to take on the credentials of an unbanned system through a process known as "keyvaulting." However, in relation to modded lobbies the console is only viable for perhaps four hours per investment, during which a modder must recoup the cost of the JTAG console or face financial loss.

In addition to the relatively toothless threats of gamertag and console "permabans" there is the risk of legal challenge. Microsoft make it clear that they "… may take any legal action it deems appropriate against users who violate Microsoft's systems or network security," which appears to have begun to occur (Microsoft

Corporation 2010). In 2008 Matthew Crippen was accused of violating the DMCA on two counts of performing a JTAG modification for $60, facing a penalty of up to five years' imprisonment for each violation (USA v. Crippen 2009). Fortunately for Crippen the prosecution abandoned the indictment "based on fairness and justice" (Kravets 2010), not because of innocence but because of the inadmissibility of evidence. It is interesting to consider that while the production of a JTAG appears in violation of the DCMA, so too would the injection and manipulation of Xbox software on a JTAG required to setup a modded lobby.

We have finally reached the point at which we can return to the example of the modded lobby first introduced in the open paragraphs of this chapter. One begins to ask the question—if a modded lobby is such a contentious and legally precarious event, then why would a modder ever take the risk of exposing this to the public? By raising the profile of such behavior the modder will have increased the likelihood of the biopolitical nature of the player body to demand censure.

If the modder has set up modded lobbies as a serious commercial concern, they will need to replace any invalidated JTAGs with functioning equivalents and seek new customers. If conducted effectively, repeat trade is relatively unlikely (at least until the next iteration of the COD franchise a year later) and as a result the modder must find ways to maximize the visibility and perceived integrity of their services. The offering must remain coherent and distinct across the few sporadic hours that a lobby is operational for, while the proposition must appear sophisticated, authentic, discrete, and good value for money. To complicate matters further, this must all be done anonymously if the modder is to mitigate against any legal censure or social response. In effect the modder is engaged in the process of the creation of an illicit brand, complete with its own recognizable product name and unique features which are adver-tised in the various websites, forums, and online videos. Instead of "Colonel Sanders' Kentucky Fried Chicken," we encounter "GODx's Mega GUN Game," "Team XEX's Mod" and "Mofos Modz," whose logos are clearly visible in the user interface design of the mod and serve as the touchstone that allows a potential customer to ascertain a modder's reputation before purchase. These videos are simultaneously used as advertisements, assertions of status within the modding communities, and as way in which the modder tracks and establishes an identity across the disparate and apparently unrelated instances of modded lobbies that appear from time to time on Xbox LIVE—it becomes an advert, a résumé, a business card.

Figure 9.1 User interface of the "XEX Mofos Mod" – note the squares indicating the presence on an opponent, irrespective of walls (Codxboxgaming 2010).

Figure 9.2 In-game display of maximum experience being awarded for a kill (SeibR1990 2010).

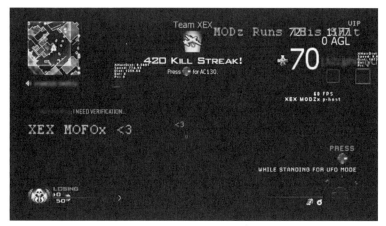

Figure 9.3 The "XEX Mofos Mod" (Codxboxgaming 2010).

Figure 9.4 The "GODx Mega GUN Game mod" (XeXMOFOx 2010).

Figure 9.5 Point-of-view of the player flying through the air using "Boody's Hacked Lobby" (Boody234 2010).

Figure 9.6 A scoreboard from a modded lobby on a public match – note the small size of the defeated team and the non-normative kill/death totals (SeibR1990 2010).

What this leads to is a curious replication of advertising and copyright, where modders heavily brand the user interfaces of the modded lobbies that they create and simultaneously cast aspersions on the other modders as imposters or competitors. In this regard the very design of the mod becomes crucial to the status within the techno-culture communities of the modder, who, with one eye on the financial implications of their mod and another on their status with the community, simultaneously assists with the accrual of status by players, the raising of their social status within modding communities, and the denigration of other modders that have incurred their ire. Perversely, while not based on any "implied modder," the modded lobby becomes a rhetorical device that attempts to persuade players of the merits and idealized features of the right way to mod.

While the modder must record video of the lobby in action as evidence to drive future income, they daren't risk implicating any of the customers on their matches. In effect they need to populate a modded lobby with players that the modder has no interest in, has no concern whether or not they receive censure or reprimand from their peers. The modder does this, ideally once a list of paying customers has been exhausted but the Xbox and gamertag not yet invalidated, by "forcing host" and joining general public matches in MW2. With this setup unsuspecting players around the world enter the modded lobby and are governed by its rules, which brings us back to the events described in the opening paragraph.

The unsuspecting players who are in the match suddenly find that they and their teammates can fly through the air, shoot missiles for bullets, release unlimited numbers of attack helicopters, and generally play havoc with the conventional order of the game. Understandably, so seduced by the power now randomly conferred upon them, they experiment and revel in the fleeting omnipotence, all the while playing an unwitting role in a calculated secret marketing campaign. This continues until that Xbox is finally banned and the lobby ceases to exist, at which point the modded lobby becomes net-lore, to be vilified or exalted according to the type of audience and their relationship to the tyranny of the game.

Conclusion

This chapter has exposed the ways in which transgressive play, such as the modded lobby, can be understood as being motivated by rational demands for social acceptance, access to otherwise inaccessible elements to the game, and by financial profit. These are in addition to the other rhetorics that traditionally define transgression. By exposing the ambiguous and heteroglossic nature of the transgressive act—simultaneously an act of rebellion, a step in a path of seduction, a clandestine temporary release from rules, a creation of identity, a revenue generator, a reputation builder, and an advert—this chapter has attempted to challenge a simplistic reading of non-normative play. It has illustrated the sophisticated technical, social, and economic contexts to the creation of modded lobbies, although, it should be noted, not the legal significance in any depth. From this perspective the demand that fuels the transgressive play is not one of resistance as suggested by Aarseth, but one of seduction for the player and profit for the modder within the context of contemporary perspectives on notions of readership and what people do with texts. Similarly, within multiplayer environments the transgressive act can be seen as neither solely an activity nor an identity, but an activity that has significant bearing on the way that individuals are regarded and understood.

This can be seen with the illicitly obtained status of the player reunited with the community after surreptitiously using a modded lobby, brandishing the trophies of their black-market safari. It is also present with the player who fails to meet the normative expectations of the group, is identified as a deviant "noob," and is consigned to individual or unrewarding play. Yet another invocation of it is the modder that uses imagery in modded lobbies and the filigree trail of forum entries across the internet to project an identity of distant (but not too distant) "arch cyberpunk." Each of these activities is fundamentally engaged in actions where identity is a significant factor.

Whether one views the modded lobby as emergent creativity, inevitable outcome of overly restrictive coding, black-market entrepreneurialism, the product of unhealthy obsession with a game, or perhaps a mix of all of the above, its ambiguous and multivalent nature illustrates the compelling nature of the contemporary FPS and the way in which the design and expectations of the game resonate across ludic, social, economic, and legal realms. In turn this raises questions about not just what it means to play "correctly," but to be a consumer of contemporary FPS videogames.

References

10thprestige.com. Leveling and Prestige. 2010. www.10thprestige.com/prestige-leveling.html.

Aarseth, Espen. 2007. "I Fought the Law: Transgressive Play and The Implied Player." Situated Play, *Proceedings of DiGRA 2007 Conference*, 130–3. Digital Games Research Association (DiGRA).

Big Dog. 2010. "Should I prestige on mw2?" September 2010. *Yahoo Answers.* http://uk.answers.yahoo.com/question/index?qid=20100830081556AAXBeJw.

Bogost, Ian. 2007. *Persuasive Games: The Expressive Power of Videogames.* Cambridge, Massachusetts: MIT Press.

Boody234. 2010. "Boody234's Modded lobby." 4 April 2010. http://www.thetechgame.com/Forums/viewtopic/t=101087.html.

Codxboxgaming. 2010. "XEX MODZx's MW2 10th Prestige Lobby." 29 June 2010. http://www.youtube.com/watch?v=GPmpPPKA4jg&feature=fvw.

Consalvo, Mia. 2007. *Cheating: Gaining Advantage in Videogames.* Cambridge, Massachusetts: MIT Press.

Crecente, Brian. 2010. "Modern Warfare 2 By the Xbox Live Numbers." 18 November 2009. http://kotaku.com/5407371/modern-warfare-2-by-the-xbox-live-numbers.

Deeled. 2010. "Should I go prestige?" *Yahoo Answers.* March 2010. http://uk.answers.yahoo.com/question/index?qid=20100325081238AAFlgXK.

Dovey, Jon and Helen W. Kennedy. 2006. *Game Cultures: Computer Games as New Media.* Berkshire: Open University Press.

Dyer-Witheford, Nick and Greig de Peuter. 2009. *Games of Empire: Global Capitalism and Video Games.* Minnesota: University of Minnesota Press.

eBay.com. 2010. "10th Prestige eBay Search." 6 January 2010. www.ebay.com.

Fahey, Michael. 2010. "You've Purchased $1 billion Worth Of *Call Of Duty: Black Ops.*" 21 12 2010. http://kotaku.com/5715720/youve-purchased-1-billion-worth-of-call-of-duty-black-ops.

Fogg, B. J. 2003. *Persuasive Technology: Using Computers to Change What We Think and Do.* San Francisco: Morgan Kauffman.

Foo, Chek Yang and Elina Koivisto. 2004. "Defining Grief Play in MMORPGs: Player and Developer Perceptions." *Proceedings of the 2004 ACM SIGCHI International Conference on Advances in Computer Entertainment Technology.* New York: ACM.

Frasca, Gonzalo. 2003. "Simulation versus Narrative: Introduction to Ludology." In *The Video Game Theory Reader*, edited by Mark J. P Wolf and Bernard Perron, 221–35. London: Routledge.

GameSpot. GameSpot Forums – why prestige? 4 December 2009. http://uk.gamespot.com/xbox360/action/modernwarfare2/show_msgs.php (accessed 30 December 2010).

Hardt, Michael and Antonio Negri. 2000. *Empire*. New York: Harvard University Press.

Hebdige, Dick. 1979. *Subculture: The Meaning of Style*. London: Routledge.

Hyrb, Larry. 2010. "Activity for week of Nov 8." 18 November 2010. http://majornelson.com/archive/2010/11/18/live-activity-for-week-of-nov-8.aspx.

Jordan, Will. 2007. "From Rule-Breaking to ROM-Hacking: Theorizing the Computer Game-as-Commodity." *Situated Play, Proceedings of DiGRA 2007 Conference*, 708–13. DiGRA.

Kravets, David. 2010. "Prosecutors Dismiss Xbox-Modding Case Mid-Trial." 2 December 2010. http://www.wired.com/threatlevel/2010/12/crippen-dismissed/.

Kücklich, Julian. 2005. "Precarious Playbour: Modders and the Digital Games Industry." *Fiberculture* 5. http://five.fibreculturejournal.org/fcj-025-precarious-playbour-modders-and-the-digital-games-industry/.

Letterthatstates. 2010. "Should I go prestige?" *Yahoo Answers*. March 2010. http://uk.answers.yahoo.com/question/index?qid=20100325081238AAFlgXK.

Matthews, Matt. 2010. "Exclusive: Black Ops For Xbox 360 Sells Nearly 5 Million In U.S." 10 December 2010. http://www.gamasutra.com/view/news/31995/Exclusive_Black_Ops_For_Xbox_360_Sells_Nearly_5_Million_In_US.php.

Microsoft Corporation. 2010. "Xbox LIVE and Games for Windows LIVE Terms of Use." October 2010. http://www.xbox.com/en-us/legal/livetou.

MW2 10th Prestige lobby rentals. 22 June 2010. (accessed 4 January 2011).

Patterson, Patrick Scott. 2010. "Call of Duty: Black Ops on XBox Live sees 2.9 million Simultaneous Players." 10 November 2010. http://www.examiner.com/arcade-game-in-dallas/call-of-duty-black-ops-on-xbox-live-sees-2-9-million-simultaneous-players.

Piston Heads. 2010. "MW2: lvl70 how long did it take you?" 12 January 2010. http://www.pistonheads.com/gassing/topic.asp.

Postigo, Hector. 2007. "Of Mods and Modders: Chasing Down the Value of Fan-Based Digital Game Modifications." *Games and Culture*, 2 (4): 300–13.

—2008. "Video Game Appropriation Through Modifications: Attitudes Concerning Intellectual Property Among Modders and Fans." *Convergence*, 14 (4): 59–74.

Se7enSins.com. Se7enSins. 2007–11. http://www.se7ensins.com/ (accessed 4 January 2011).

SeibR1990. 2010. "MW2 Xbox360 New God Mode, Wall hack, Unlimited Ammo, Online Ranked After Patch." 18 November 2010. http://www.youtube.com/watch?v=US3qma-P6Xc&feature=fvst.

Sotamaa, Ollii. 2004. "Playing it my way? Mapping the modder agency." Internet Research Conference 5.0, Sussex, UK.

Taylor, T. L. 2003. "Power Gamers Just Want To Have Fun? Instrumental Play in an MMOG." In *Level Up Games Conference Proceedings*, edited by M. Copier and J. Raessens, 300–12. Utrecht: Utrecht: Universiteit.

TheTechGame Network LLC. www.thetechgame.com. 2008–11. www.thetechgame.com (accessed 4 January 2011).

USA v. Crippen. CR09-00703 (United States District Court, Central District of California, 24 July 2009).

Wright, Talmadge, Eric Boria, and Paul Breidenbach. 2002. "Creative Player Actions in FPS Online Video Games." *Game Studies* 2 (2). http://www.gamestudies.org/0202/wright/

Xbox360xperts.com. 2010. "Call of Duty: Black Ops Modded Lobbies." 11 December 2010. http://www.xbox360xperts.com/forums/index. php.

XeXMOFOx. 2010. "MW2 | Gun Game | XEX MOFOx." 11 August 2010. http://www.youtube.com/watch?v=7opbHAPJChs&feature=related.

Games

Bethesda GameStudios. 2006. *The Elder Scrolls IV: Oblivion* [Xbox 360, Microsoft Windows]. ZeniMax.

Infinity Ward. 2009. *Call of Duty: Modern Warfare 2* [Microsoft Windows, PlayStation 3, Xbox 360]. Activision.

Treyarch. 2010. *Call of Duty: Black Ops* [Xbox 360, PlayStation 3, Microsoft Windows, Wii]. Activision.

Valve. 2003. *Counter-Strike* [Xbox, Microsoft Windows]. Valve.

10

"Tips and tricks to take your game to the next level": Expertise and Identity in FPS Games

Daniel Ashton and James Newman

"Think you're a big boy? You think that just because you've gotten a few headshots through a wall, that you're some kind of a hotshot? Wrong."

(Lono and Animathias 2008)

So begins the introduction to the third installment of Lono and Animathias' (2008) "Call of Duty 4 Expert's Multiplayer Guide Series." The guides in this series are examples of a type of game text known variously, and often interchangeably, as "walkthroughs," "FAQs" (Frequently Asked Questions) or "Strategy Guides" and are produced by players for players, and distributed through fansites and online repositories such as GameFAQs.com, which hosts many hundreds of thousands of walkthroughs dedicated to all manner of games (and often quite specific aspects of particular games). These texts present game scholars with a rich and detailed insight in the ways in which players apprehend and continue to engage with gameplay as well as revealing and creating contexts within which play is performed and mastery, status, and expertise are constructed and negotiated. We proceed, then, from a position that sees player-produced walkthroughs as key sites through which games are encountered and made sense of by players. However, more than this, we are also keen to cast light on walkthroughs as a discursive space in which considerable gameplay takes place.

Player-produced walkthroughs are not merely documents of extant understanding and apprehensions of gameplay potential or codifications of ludic opportunity. Nor even are they, as we shall see, simply instructions that help players in difficulty overcome challenges that hold back their progress in the game. While they are both of these things, without doubt, we believe that by considering the production and distribution of player-produced walkthrough texts, they are revealed as operating at an (inter)active, ludic rather than a documentary level and as exploratory investigations that open up gameplay and continue engagement with games rather than as solutions to problems which play on notions of completion and construct the game as a finite series of challenges. The first-person shooter (FPS) often appears to be a genre of videogame defined by its viewpoint, even being named to reflect the presentation of the gameworld on-screen. In turn, while there are examples of changing experiences associated with FPS, such as Bogost's (2006) discussion of how *Thief* (Looking Glass Studios 1998) challenged the discursive mode of FPS from "slaughter" to "sneak," FPS games are held to be highly controlled linear experiences (see Kline, Dyer-Witheford, and de Peuter 2003). We argue that the playing of an FPS, like any game, takes place off-screen as well as on-. Our interest in exploring this issue is twofold.

First, we wish to explore the operation of the walkthrough in itself. Second, we are interested in beginning to document the dialogical relationship between the on- and off-screen spaces of gameplay. This is not simply a matter of considering the walkthrough as a pedagogical or didactic resource to be drawn on in order to improve one's play. Rather, we are interested in understanding how the discussions that take place in and around walkthroughs, the reflective and synthetic nature of walkthroughs that respond to and incorporate strategies and techniques drawn from a wide constituency of players, come together. Importantly, it is not our intention merely to present the walkthrough as a space of unbridled creativity, though without doubt the exploration of the boundaries and potentialities of gameplay is the focus of much walkthrough writing and discussion. Indeed, it is key to our understanding of the ludic function and operation of the walkthrough that the restrictive, regulatory nature of walkthroughs is foregrounded. Just as they might be seen as explorations of gameplay potential, so too are they simultaneously spaces through which control is exerted and specific approaches to play or particular techniques become normalized and (dis)allowed. We offer some commentary also on the ways in which walkthroughs are used to demonstrate, confirm, and perform gameplay expertise. The presentation and management of identity, both through the processes of authorship but also through comparison of one's own performance with the benchmarks set out in the text, are vital to understanding the ways in which the walkthrough functions as a key site in which mastery and gamer status are produced and negotiated.

Central to our position is a notion that cuts to the very heart of academic game studies as a discipline and concerns both the contours and location of gameplay. Here, we suggest that "gameplay" is not simply a negotiation between player and system. Nor even is it simply framed by off-screen discussions that shape and restrict on-screen activity. Rather, we want to suggest that gameplay operates both on- and off-screen. As we will demonstrate, much of the ludic pleasure and performance of videogames operates through online forums, fansite discussion boards and through conversation and talk. Only sometimes do these playful, investigative discussions result in a return to the joypad and we note many instances where this "off-screen gameplay" effectively constitutes self-contained performances of mastery and expertise. Our consideration of walkthroughs seeks to highlight one formal means of codifying and capturing these discursive off-screen gameplay practices and the performances of expert gamer identities.

The Videogame Walkthrough

Given the significance and embeddedness of player-produced walkthroughs in gaming culture, it is surprising to note that they have been subject to comparatively little academic enquiry. More worryingly, perhaps, however is the fact that even among those beginning studies, there is often some confusion over exactly what the walkthrough is, what function it plays in relation to gameplay and how it relates to other objects, artifacts, and practices of gaming. Our brief discussion here aims to begin to set out some of what, for us at least, is distinctive about the production, form, and function of player-produced walkthroughs. Importantly, we seek here to distinguish these player-produced walkthroughs from the "Official Strategy Guides" that are the products of commercial publishing and which, while bearing some superficial similarities, are not only materially different in terms of their form and format, but reveal markedly different relationships between their authors and the creators of the games that are their subjects as well as between authors, gameplay, and players.

At their simplest, we might argue that videogame walkthroughs provide instructions on various elements of gameplay in relation to specific digital games, and exist as text-based documents and, to a lesser extent, as recorded moving image game footage. Walkthroughs present a variety of functions and a range of uses that include extended instruction manuals, virtual tour guides, and explorations of the boundaries of the logic and integrity of the game code and simulation models. Mia Consalvo's (2003) study of *The Legend of Zelda: Ocarina of Time* walkthroughs describes the texts as "detailed guides to how a player should play a game sequence to find all of the hidden bonuses and surprises, how to avoid certain death, and how to advance past difficult puzzles or trouble spots to best play and win the game" (327–8). Similarly, Burn (2006) suggests that the interest of the walkthrough is in "relaying the procedural demands of the game system" (90). Both Consalvo (2007) and Newman (2008) have subsequently gone on to explore the ways in which walkthrough use might be considered "cheating" within specific gaming cultures and contexts.

In fact, the conceptualization of player-produced walkthroughs as documents primarily concerned with delivering "solutions" to specific games ("how to advance past difficult puzzles or trouble spots to best play and win the game" as Consalvo [2003] has it) is something of a mischaracterization. As Newman (2008) has noted, the idea of player-produced walkthroughs existing as solutions to be turned to in much the way that StuckGamer's videos might be sought out for demonstration of successful technique, is typically a product of the equation of commercial Strategy Guides with player-produced walkthroughs. Without doubt, player-produced walkthroughs can more than adequately serve the function of purveyors of hints and tips to assist gamers during times of difficulty. Indeed, if we broaden, for a moment, our discussion of walkthroughs to encompass video-based site StuckGamer.com, which swaps plaintext for full-motion video walkthroughs, we see this "completion" imperative take center stage. The very name of the site, "StuckGamer," alludes to the point at which the materials it hosts will be turned to, while its full-length videos are oriented around singular journeys through the gameworld in which a particular, distinctive player/playing is center stage and effectively becomes coded as definitive. However, any investigation of the scope and extent of the kinds of text-based walkthroughs that are collected at hubs such as GameFAQs.com, and which are the focus of our study, reveals a considerably wider array of potential functions than presenting definitive solutions. The walkthroughs collected at repositories such as GameFAQs speak of a more diverse range of motivations among authors and readers alike and which are based more around exploration and exchange than definitive didactic statements. Indeed in relation to FPS, Reeves, Brown, and Laurier (2009) investigate the "intricacies of deft gameplay" and suggest that "a core component of FPS experiences is the pleasure obtained from the player's engagement and gradual mastering of the game mechanic" (206). Documenting in-game mastery is Reeves et al.'s main concern and while we are also interested by situated gameplay, the focus here is on the discursive production and display of mastery within walkthroughs.

Our decision to focus on player-produced walkthroughs reflects our interest in the status of these texts not simply as presentations of solutions for gamers unable to progress beyond a particular point, but as foci for discussion and experimentation with games and gameplay. This resonates with Reeves et al.'s (2009) study into *Counter-Strike* from which they highlight how "CS players became experts in large part through differentiating repetition, trying out small variations on the 'same' response to the enemy, the 'same' probing and the use of the 'same' weapon" (224). We have chosen not to consider commercially produced Official Strategy Guides, often published in close consultation with game development teams and publishers, as these tend to legitimize a limited range of ways to tackle the game; demonstrating only "approved" tactics, strategies, and approaches to gameplay. The player-produced walkthroughs, FAQs, and guides we consider here, on the other hand, are more concerned with documenting games and gameplay opportunity in completist and exploratory terms. As such, discussions about mechanisms for exploiting inconsistencies or glitches in games fall within the remit of the fan-author who is liberated from the demand to deal only with "officially sanctioned" gameplay and technique.

Text/Paratext—Access and Inflection

Walkthroughs are a common means through which gamers mediate games for other gamers. As Burn (2006) suggests in his discussion of Kao Megura's walkthrough for *Final Fantasy VII*, "for this fan, the thrill of the game seems very much bound up in his exhaustive expertise in the properties of the puzzle maze, and in the game as system" (90). In this respect, walkthroughs can be conceptualized as ancillary materials that inform engagement with texts (Barker 2004; Caldwell 2008; Gray 2010). According to Martin Barker, ancillary or satellite texts "shape in advance the conditions under which interpretations of film are formed." Barker (2004) highlights "publicity materials, Press Kits and EPKs, contractually-required interviews and photo opportunities and so on … [that] … constitute more or less patterned discursive preparations for the act of viewing." In relation to *Call of Duty*, the range of such materials could include the Activison website, the retail space through which the game is displayed through posters and other promotional materials, and reviews found in magazines, on the television, and on the web.

As Barker (2004) observes, these ancillary materials are "foreknowledge" that can shape "expectations," and that "constitute a discursive framework around a film, a kind of mental scaffolding giving it particular kinds of 'support' and providing the means by which people may 'climb inside.'" Rather than interpretations of the film or discursive preparation for viewing, we can see the scaffolding potential of walkthroughs as a blueprint encouraging new styles of play. In his discussion of spoilers, spin-offs, and other paratexts, Jonathan Gray (2010) suggests that for analytical purposes, paratexts can be divided into those that "control and determine our entrance to a text – entryway paratexts – and those that inflect or redirect the text following initial interaction – in medias res paratexts" (35). Walkthroughs can provide both an entrance to a game by providing insights into how the game is constituted and the designed experience, and a means to inflect players' interaction.

Rare's (2001) lauded *Goldeneye 007* FPS is particularly illustrative of the scope of player-produced walkthroughs and the way in which they comprehensively mine games, providing multiple access points and encouraging self-conscious re-play. GameFAQs hosts 39 English language walkthroughs for *Goldeneye* (with a further two "Foreign Language walkthroughs" in Swedish and Portuguese). Fourteen of these (including the foreign language texts) explicitly set out to address the full extent of the game, providing comprehensive coverage of every level and meticulously documenting each weapon, collectible, and narrative branch. However, what is perhaps most notable are the "In-depth" guides that either focus on specific moments of the game or deliberately subvert its apparent logic or structure. Both Ernest64 and HHuang's guides center their attentions on the Aztec level precisely because it is hard.

2) Aztec Level Walkthrough (00 Agent mode)

This level is for the expert-advanced player, i.e. it is TOUGH, and that means also, you'll have trouble with it... (Ernest64)

In drawing players to this level in the game and focusing on the heightened difficulty of its gameplay challenge, which is further amplified by the imperative to tackle it in all of its available difficulty settings, the differences between which are keenly documented, this guide homes in on and constructs a specific challenge. We might argue here that *Goldeneye 007* is reduced to a series of distinct tasks to be mastered. Beyond rising to the challenges set by the game, and flagged within walkthroughs as particularly worthy, we find in other walkthroughs an altogether more subversive intent. Super Nova's "Mission Failure FAQ" guide seeks to extend gameplay by documenting every point at which a *Goldeneye 007* mission may be failed. The opening of the guide lays out the motivations for the creation of the guide and gives a sense of its intended usage as a means of adding longevity to the game by exploring the entirety of its operation.

```
===============
))))2. The Concept((((
===============
```

The object of this short FAQ is to explain how to fail every objective it is possible to fail in the game. When you have finished everything, and are bored with Goldeneye in general, see if you can fail a mission as fully as possible. It's always more fun to kill Natalya rather than protect her, or to set off the alarm and go all out when stealth is supposed to be employed.

I got the idea for this FAQ off Split Infinity, who wrote a similar guide for Goldeneye's unofficial sequel, Perfect Dark. For each mission you will find all objectives listed, and an explanation of how to fail them.

Please note that this FAQ is entirely for fun – it is not intended to

be useful, but to give ideas of how to improve the lifespan of the most classic First Person Shooter of all time.
(Super Nova)

The desire to comprehensively apprehend the extent of gameplay is manifestly clear here and it should be noted that the In-depth guides considerably outnumber the more "traditional" guides that address the entirety of the game. Proceeding from a position that places the conquering of the game's challenges as routine or matter-of-fact, the exploration of failure rounds out the players' understanding. It is interesting, then, that part of the pleasure of continued, extended play in this most-decorated of FPS games has little to do with the ostensible action or objective. In the production of walkthroughs, gameplay is less concerned with first-person shooting than playing with the narrative structure itself. Here, then, the game itself, its structures and its branches, become the object of playful engagement. What is curious to note about this arrangement is how much of what makes the game pleasurable in replay, in the first person and even as a single-player experience, is delivered and accessed through out-game encounters with other players, through the exchange of knowledge and promotion of new ways of playing. We will return to the idea of identity and the collaborative nature of authorship that are also foregrounded in Super Nova's introductory comments and the situation of these practices within the context of other walkthroughs/walkthrough authors. However, for now, it is useful to consider other ways in which walkthroughs frame engagement and present sites for playful engagement.

The *Goldeneye 007* walkthroughs also reveal self-consciously investigative forms of play. It is for this reason that Newman (2008) suggests that walkthroughs can be understood as the documentation of form of play that resembles reverse-engineering. In analyzing the revelation of bugs, glitches, and other coding/implementation anomalies that might give rise to unpredictable or unanticipated gameplay or audiovisual artifacts or, in extreme cases, might even crash the game outright, Newman notes the ways in which walkthroughs renegotiate the player-designer relationship and encourage (perhaps even demand) deliberately investigative, resistant, and deviant strategies of gameplay. As in the case of revealing (and reveling in the revelation of) glitches, these modes of engagement frequently involve playing beyond performative norms and technical limits. We might consider the revelation of "rocket jumping" techniques in *Quake* (see *Quake Terminus*, for instance <http://www.quaketerminus.com/quakebible/adv-rjump.htm>) as a particularly pertinent and now utterly normalized result of this imperative. Similarly, to ascertain the multiple points of mission failure in *Goldeneye 007* requires an approach to play which is motivated not by a desire to move through the game's narrative to its conclusion, or to solve its "trouble spots," but rather by an interest in understanding most fully what the entire extent of the narrative could be. In fact, following the twisted logic of the walkthrough, in setting failure as its goal, Super Nova's "Mission Failure FAQ" elevates the trouble spots to moments of gameplay objective. Chris Schultze's "Goldeneye 007 Glitches FAQ" is a case in point. While proudly identifying 229 glitches spread across various parts of the game, there is no sense of criticism and no note of disappointment:

--Table Of Contents--
1) Freezing Glitches (12)
2) Weapon/Item/Ammo Screw-Ups (49)
3) Floating Weapons/Ammo (8)
4) Cut-Scene Glitches (30)
5) Sound Glitches (10)
6) Misc. Glitches (120)

In fact, far from registering concern for or expressing any kind of indignation about the programming anomalies that in some (in fact, 12) cases can bring the gameplay to cessation, there is an evident glee and relish in the description of the sometimes game-stopping glitches:

1.) Crash The Game In The Archives
In Archives on multiplayer play with remote mines. Fire a remote mine at the glass. Go to the other side of the glass, and fire a mine on the back of that mine. Shoot out the glass and the mines will float. If you fire a mine at the floating mines the game will freeze

It should be noted that not all glitches have terminal consequences and some may even be harnessed to enhance and alter gameplay. For instance,

5.) Exploding Bond
Turn on invincibility and set off a plastique in the Silo or let the one-minute timer run out in the Bunker. Explosions follow you around wherever you go and you can kill enemies like that.

In even these brief descriptions, we note the complexity of gameplay activity that gives rise to the identified glitch. Two things are significant here. First, it is clear that readers are being asked to re-perform complicated series of gameplay maneuvers that both test their gaming mettle in the face of another player's demonstrable expertise. We will return to this point later in the chapter. However, second, and equally critical, is that the play that revealed these glitches is self-evidently exploratory. The desire to locate as many glitches as possible (the 229 total is proudly displayed at the very top of the guide) drives players into play that seeks to push at and beyond the boundaries of the game's tolerances and design. Most interestingly, this frequently means discarding the ostensible objective of the game. So, where we might think of walkthroughs as instructional materials that aid gamers dealing with troublesome moments, we just as easily view them as materials that encourage a reconfiguration of the game as a ludic space. In the case of *Goldeneye 007*, the first-person shooting is effectively stripped from the gameplay engagement and the environment is foregrounded as a place to play in and with. Essentially, the FPS is recast as a kind of sandbox game.

The focus on specific aspects of gameplay, even those that seem counter-intuitively based on performative failure or the disintegration of the game's system, perhaps puts us in mind of Gray's discussion of how in medias res paratexts "focus attention on specific actions, themes, or issues." In exploring in medias res paratexts, Gray (2010) suggests a move away from "questions of textual ontology – what is the text? – to questions of textual phenomenology – how does the text happen?" (41). This approach usefully signals how walkthroughs may be used in partial ways over a space of time. Rather than providing a prescriptive "start to finish" guide that directs each action the player makes, walkthroughs might be dipped into and used in fairly distinctive and personal ways. As research into reception studies and everyday practices of engaging with media texts demonstrates (Hermes 1995), care should be taken in making assumptions and generalizing experiences. Similarly, a particular walkthrough might not exist as the single or exclusive source of information and walkthroughs do not exist in isolation from other paratexts, whether they be promotional materials or fan art. As Gray suggests (2010), "for texts that stabilize any one media platform as central, each platform serves as a paratext for the others" (42). Highlighting the capacity of walkthroughs to inform the playing experience should not be at the expense of recognizing the capacity of other paratexts. To do so would prompt the kind of narrowly focused analysis that we are extending beyond.

Peter Lunenfeld's suggestion, as outlined by Mia Consalvo (2007), that "we are in an age where the backstory to the creation of objects is often more interesting than the texts themselves" points to diverse histories and motivations that go into the creation of walkthroughs (22). By analyzing the contexts and meta-commentary that surround walkthroughs, we are examining the backstory to perhaps the most widely used player-produced texts—in other words, the backstory to the ancillary texts that can shape, inform, and structure gameplay. While seemingly far removed from the world of guns, grenades, and grunts, the analysis of walkthroughs in fact reveals specific forms of play, the motivations for these, and how they are communicated to and engaged with by their audience of players. As such, although it might seem curious, even somewhat perverse, to note that the performance of FPS play might be as much a transaction between reader and plaintext document as it is a frenetic journey through corridors with all guns blazing, once we conceive them as more than instructional guides, walkthroughs reveal their ability to not only shape but also virtually host gameplay.

Identity and Expertise

Key to our position on walkthroughs is the understanding that they exist not as static texts but rather are the products of an ongoing discursive process situated with communities or constituencies of players. The significance of FPS professional gaming leagues (see Taylor 2010) presents a further example of the wider social and discursive processes of engaging with the game that exist off-screen. The following draws on walkthroughs posted on GameFAQs for the *Call of Duty* franchise (2003–10) and examines how for walkthrough authors, meanings and associations extend beyond the unfolding of the game on-screen to how they sit with a community of walkthrough experts, establish relationships with authors, and enact the performance of authorship through credits, acknowledgments, biographies, and logos and the pseudo-legal boilerplate that has become a common fixture.

Biographies, Expertise, and Reader Relationships

The construction of "expert" and "non-expert" positions entails forming relationships with readers of mutual appreciation. The construction of 'expert' and 'non-expert' positions entails forming relationships wuth readers who share a mutual appreciation and developing a rapport with a loyal fan base for the game. For example, in forming a relationship with their readers, walkthrough authors will often offer comments on their gaming preferences: "I decided to write this guide because this is my most favorite fps game ever. Even though its not too unique weapon and story wise it still has a whole lot of fast paced action packed into the 5 hour game" (Rata1). This was often furthered by "thank you" comments to readers and an explicit receptiveness to recognition: "Any critics, suggestions, spelling mistakes, contribu-tions are welcome, so please send them at the following e-mail […] since feedback is the best reward of all" (vinheim). Recognizing appre-ciation could also translate into requests for donations, such as: "If you feel like you want to compensate me somehow for doing this guide or any of my other guides. I accept paypal.com donations. All donations will help me with school, so I do appreciate whatever you send" (Omegamustard). In turn, there is a balance between seeking further information and contributions, and a confidence and security in their own offering: "Email me with tips, suggestions, or strategies for veteran difficulty at g---@yahoo.com. I have no plans of including intel locations since every other guide I've seen contains that information, so do not bother telling me where to find it" (drgrady). This can also be seen in the way that access might be restricted and certain protocols have to be followed, such as not sending friend requests or Xbox LIVE messages, ensuring email subject lines are appropriately worded (at risk of being deleted as spam) and the main body is short and not "a wall of text." The inclusion of questions from readers works to distinguish the author as a notable presence whose views are of interest and significance.

The development of the walkthrough "expert" persona is contextually established and maintained, and walkthroughs exist as a form through which specific identities are actualized. The prowess and ability of the walkthrough author is established in the register adopted in addressing "their audience." The simple fact of accessing a walkthrough suggests a lack or deficiency and sets up a hierarchy of expertise between the author and reader. Walkthrough authors outline their credentials to their readership through the "meta-commentary," usually the preamble and summary notes that accompany the diegesis or blow-by-blow account of gameplay. The often-extensive introductions indicate what is covered and provide points of definition and clarification, and outline mutual understanding. This approach sets up the mentor/expert and mentee/player relationship by outlining what will happen and to what extent. Such statements provide little specific information about the game, but instead signal experience and authority on the part of the author. Rather than an explicit statement on gameplay progress, comments can point to the ethos or approach to gameplay that the author adopts. Whilst the walkthrough author is positioned as an expert and has the potential to shape encounters, this is not to say that a limited number of encounters or ways of playing are advocated, and analysis of player-produced walkthroughs reveals a wide diversity of advice, suggestions, and guidance. Unlike the commercially produced Official Strategy Guides, such as Bradygames' *Signature Series Call of Duty: Black Ops*, that legitimize a limited range of ways to tackle the game and demonstrate only "approved" tactics, strategies and approaches to gameplay, the player-produced walkthroughs can be much more varied in their content.

A further means to establish expertise is through identification and alignment with other walkthrough author "experts." Positioning oneself with other walkthrough authors works to establish the boundaries of credibility and entitlement. This is not necessarily a case of drawing up a list of "best" authors, but rather indicating that comparisons and differences may be drawn between players/readers and experts/authors. In establishing the presence of expert groups, it follows that authors would then rhetorically position themselves within it. For example, this author indicates their specific knowledge and understanding of walkthrough writing and aligns themselves with and speaks for other walkthrough writers:

> Gbness, Mighty Oracle, Super Slash, PeTeRL90, Truly Dexterous, warfreak, IceQueenZer0, BSulpher, Da Hui, DBM11085, Snow Dragon: All those who I consider online friends. These guys are really cool and I always have a blast talking to them on AIM, MSN and the FCBS. They all inspire me in writing more and more FAQ's. Note that all these fellows are FAQ writers as myself, so I thank them too for supporting me in my FAQing (vinheim)

"Vinheim" makes clear that this is a select group of walkthrough writers who provide support and inspiration. In references both to themselves and other walkthrough writers, there is a sense of reverence. This also comes across in comments on Facebook referring to their status and reputation:

> I created a Facebook page for you to check it […] This was made because several people like to add me on Facebook and since I'm not accepting people I don't know, and I removed the people that added me (sorry for that), I created this page, so enjoy. (vinheim)

The presence of a Facebook "support" page helps to further illustrate how the actual walkthrough text dealing with gameplay can be mediated, contextualized, and engaged with through a range of reference points and ancillary materials. Moreover, as a number of commentators have highlighted (for example Hills 2009), Facebook emphasizes the presentation of the self. For Vinheim, Facebook presents a means to maintain their public profile. Similarly, in his discussion of Megura, Burn (2006) suggests that "the social motivation for this particular development of players preference is clearly bound up in the very public status that such a position wins in return for his hard work" (90). The presence of a Facebook page also indicates how savvy walkthrough authors can be alert to their status and might seek to secure it. The inclusion of acknowledgements is also revealing for assessing how the walkthrough is understood as a personally significant piece of writing. Dedications to fiancées and friends mark out the establishment of a walkthrough author persona of note and standing.

The identification and invitation to join a Facebook page sits closely with the establishment and maintenance of "walkthrough" author biography. As part of their biography, walkthrough authors will often present an overview of the games worked. For example, JediMeister states, "this is my fourth game walkthrough. I haven't written a walkthrough for a couple years but since I'm about to start working again, I decided to give it one last go." Along the same lines, authors will often include a list of completed walkthroughs as part of their biography. The construction of expert status is bolstered by the evidence-base of completed walkthroughs. Wide-ranging game completed lists suggest that walkthrough writing is a distinctive form of engagement and that the relationship with FPS games might not be particularly important. The breadth of walkthroughs documented by authors suggests that FPS-orientated players do not undertake writing walkthroughs exclusively for these games. While the walkthrough content is specific to the content of a particular game, the process of documenting gameplay and the further processes of attempting to follow and enact this walkthrough content encourages a reconceptualization of the status of these as "another walkthrough challenge." The specificity and distinctiveness of FPS becomes less apparent when it is stripped down to mechanics and simulation within the textual walkthrough.

Legal Notices

The inclusion of "legal" notices is a principal means by which walkthrough authors attribute value to their work. While the game copyright will often be with the publisher, the inclusion of notices highlights that a walkthrough can be a distinct object demanding recognition and protection. The standard version employed by a number of walkthrough authors is as follows:

> This document may not be reproduced under any circumstances except for personal, private use. It may not be placed on any web site or otherwise distributed publicly without advance written permission. Use of this guide on any other website or as a part of any public display is strictly prohibited, and a violation of copyright

Whilst the standing and enforceability of these notices is unclear, they exist as much to make clear the commitment and work undertaken in the process of writing, publishing, and maintaining a walkthrough. This can be seen in comments included with the "legal notice" along the lines of: "The creation of this Guide took a lot of time, please respect that." The following notice emphasizes restrictions on publication and distribution in terms of personal enterprise and plagiarism:

> I, [...] dbcification, am the sole writer, and owner of all of the things in this guide that are not directly mentioned to be from someone else. I am giving permission for this to be on GameFAQs/ GameSpot, Neoseeker, IGN, Supercheats, Cheat Code Central, MMGN, and the Shadow Elites clan site for the time being. If you want to post it elsewhere, email me with the subject "MWR Guide Posting," and I'll get back to you ASAP. Don't plagiarize me, bro (dbcification)

In this notice, there is an appeal to "rights" discourses and to notions of social acceptability around plagiarism and authorial control over their work. As Burn (2006, 91) notes in his discussion of Kao Megura's response to those who use his FAQs to "increase sales," the importance full and accurate crediting can operate in terms of personal investment, professional aspirations, and fan community contributions: "[Megura's] disillusionment seems to proceed partly from aspirations to professional status, in which intellectual property rights become more of an issue [...] yet, it also seems to proceed from an idealistic desire to serve the fan community" (91). These notices point to the significance and value of walkthrough authors' activities and practices, and a key factor in the establishment, recognition, and protection of walkthrough authors' reputation.

Versions, Updates, and Mastery

As seen, walkthrough authors would often include sites that are allowed and disallowed, and the importance of context is apparent through the naming of GameFAQs as confirmed host for the walkthrough. GameFAQs' format and organization has an instructive role in presenting information and data that, while aside from the gameplay that unfolds on screen, is a significant means by which walkthrough author expertise is communicated and by which decisions on walkthrough selection are made. For example, the version history provided by "dbcification" outlines 13 versions with specific details, such as "1.7.1 Added the guide onto Cheat Code Central. Fixed wrong information about RPGs and choppers. Also fixed Expert challenge numbers for Shotguns." The version history communicates authors' levels of dedication, detail, and proficiency. Apparently minor changes, such as fixing grammar and presenting, can contribute to a larger collection, record and recognition of walkthrough materials. The significance of completeness is highlighted by notes for the final version, "2.0", provided by "dbcification": "Added Cubfan's Multiplayer Guide, added a new strategy, indexed the entire guide, streamlined and edited and rewrote a lot, and made it generally awesome and undoubtedly the best MWR guide in existence!"

Providing information on updates and new walkthrough releases is a further means in which walkthrough author status is constructed. Furthermore, version numbers, update statuses, and attached .txt file sizes are all central to GameFAQs' architecture and provide crucial navigational assistance for walkthrough users in search either of specificity, comprehensiveness, evidence of the walkthrough's "completion" or its status as an ongoing investigation. (See Ashton and Newman 2010 for more on the discursive work of these data/metadata in the lists presented at walkthrough repositories such as GameFAQs.)

Similarly, the "what's next" section included in walkthroughs outlines the completion stage and gameplay strategies and further content will be added. The "when ready" aspect of walkthroughs in which authors make clear what can be expected of them and their ability to perform, subject to a range of considerations such as school/work and availability of hardware/software, highlights the potential expectation on the part of the reader and that author has given consideration to when they will practically be able to add further material. This can be in comments that anticipate the release schedule of games and assess the time needed to complete and publish the walkthrough. For example, in expectation of a forth-coming release, walkthrough author "The Gum" states that "it will take a few months past the release date to get it sorted out […] So, look for that around January of 2011." The information on updates and versions signify commitment as well as status. It can be clear from version numbers that there is an investment in the quality of walkthroughs. Walkthrough texts are not simply presentations of solutions for gamers unable to progress beyond a particular point, but are also foci for discussion and experimentation with games and gameplay. The following walkthrough author comments illus-trate an ethos of "working to the limit" and a process of sustained engagement and experimentation:

It's now at 7,993 lines of text in the formatted version [and] there's really not that much left for me to add in that can be added into a plain text guide (dbcification)

Each mission walkthrough has an average of about 900 words, which is pretty incredible compared to the 300 or so my CoD1 missions had (Psy)

The player-produced walkthrough text is a comprehensive record of investigative play. It is not the product of idle or casual engagement with a game, but the result of a systematic attempt to interrogate and document the extent of the game's potential. Paramount for authors is the complete mastery of the game and the acquisition of the most complete knowledge of its systems and operation. Commentaries on the writing process evidence and reveal the process of work involved.

For example, in the following walkthrough author Psy documents the time invested in completing the walkthrough: "After four long, hard days of writing, I've finally completely finished the guide for all of the missions in *Call of Duty 2*. It probably took me 20–30 hours to finish." In providing a record of working hours and time spent completing the walkthrough, the author is signaling both their mastery of the game and their own personal investment. On one hand, this may be viewed as a passionate engagement with this particular game. In turn, the actual game for which a walkthrough is being written can matter less than the process of walkthrough authorship. This approach to walkthroughs recognizes the multiple ways in which authors comment on the status of their work, for example through legal notices, and the completeness of their work, for example through documenting version and updates. These aspects contribute to and are part of the construction of a walkthrough—a biography of expertise. (See also Taylor in this volume on player expertise.)

Summary

What we hope to have shown in our discussion of player-produced walkthroughs is the multifaceted ways in which they operate and the different functions they perform for authors and readers alike. On one hand, they might be seen as instructional materials that guide stuck players through gameplay, allowing them to traverse complex problems. In this way, walkthroughs reveal what is often a linearity of game structure effectively gives rise to bottlenecks that bar progress to the remainder of the game's ludic potential. However, while their name suggests a more didactic function that literally walks players through gameplay, we are keen to foreground the discursive spaces that walkthroughs open up and exist within. Unlike their commercially published counterparts, player-produced walkthroughs are as concerned with thorough explorations of gameplay potential as they are the completion of ostensible objectives. To this end, they frequently present glitches and gameplay anomalies as viable and inseparable elements of the ludic menu that the particular game offers. By mining the potentiality of the game's system, we see player-produced walkthroughs as explicitly stated attempts to extend the longevity of titles by revealing new modes of engagement. As such, walkthroughs demonstrably offer academic game studies practitioners a rich resource that documents gameplay as lived experience drawing attention to the variety of ways in which games are played and played with, explored and interrogated, often to and even beyond breaking point.

It is key to our understanding of player-produced walkthroughs that they be seen not merely as codifications or even regulations of gameplay but rather as extensions of the gameplay that occurs in-game or on-screen. The identity play that we have seen in relation to discussion of and within the texts as well as the encouragement to enter into a dialogical relationship between the outlines of play potential, discussions of expertise and mastery, and one's performances provide, for us, evidence of the walkthrough as part of gameplay rather than "merely" a paratextual adjunct. The walkthrough, then, sits between on- and off-screen bridging the in- and out-game.

It is perhaps curious to note that these most resolutely non-interactive texts comprised of lines of almost code-like plaintext and that seem a world away from the audiovisual richness and real-time performance-orientation of contemporary FPSs are among the most important sites wherein the potential for first-person shooting is simultaneously captured, negotiated, and reshaped. Declarations or definitions of expertise and mastery in a given FPS are, in our assessment here, as likely to be discursively produced in the textuality of a player-produced walkthrough as they are in a real-time deathmatch or measured through the completion of missions and objectives meted out in the game.

The player-produced walkthrough opens up a space in which the game may be encountered in new ways precisely because it is always encountered in the context of other players' playings. In this way, the first-person performance always and already exists in relation to the performances of others, even if they are encountered not in-game but through the networked context of electronic text.

References

Ashton, Daniel and James Newman. 2010. "Relations of Control: Walkthroughs and the Structuring of Player Agency." *Fibreculture* 16. http://sixteen.fibreculturejournal.org/relations-of-control-walkthroughs-and-the-structuring-of-player-agency/

Barker, Martin. 2004. "News, Reviews, Clues, Interviews and Other Ancillary Materials – A Critique and Research Proposal." In *21st Century Film Studies: A Scope Reader*, edited by James Burton. Nottingham University. http://www.scope.nottingham.ac.uk/reader/chapter.php?id=2

Brady Games. 2010. *Signature Series Call of Duty: Black Ops*. Indianapolis: Brady Games.

Burn, Andrew. 2006. "Reworking the Text: Online Fandom." In *Computer Games,* edited by Diane Carr, David Buckingham, Andrew Burn, and Gareth Schott, 88–102, Cambridge: Polity Press.

Bogost, Ian. 2006. *Unit Operations: An Approach to Videogame Criticism*. Cambridge, Mass: MIT Press.

Caldwell, John Thornton. 2008. *Production Culture: Industrial Reflexivity and Critical Practice in Film and Television*. London: Duke University Press.

Consalvo, Mia. 2003. "Zelda 64 and Video Game Fans: A Walkthrough of Games, Intertextuality, and Narrative." *Television and New Media* 4 (3): 321–34.

—2007. *Cheating: Gaining Advantage in Videogames*. Cambridge, MA: The MIT Press.

Gray, Jonathan. 2010. *Show Sold Separately: Promos, Spoilers and Other Media Paratexts*. New York: New York University Press.

Hermes, Joke. 1995. *Reading Women's Magazines: An Analysis of Everyday Media Use*. Cambridge: Polity Press.

Hills, Matt. 2009. "Case Study: Social Networking and Self-Identity." In *Digital Cultures: Understanding New Media*, edited by Glen Creeber and Royston Martin, 107–21. Maidenhead: Open University Press.

Kline, Stephen, Dyer-Witheford, Nick, and De Peuter, Greig. 2003. *Digital Play: The Interaction of Technology, Culture and Marketing*. London: McGill-Queen's University Press.

Lono and Animathias. 2008. "Call of Duty 4 Expert's Multiplayer Guide Series." Last modified October 16. http://sarcasticgamer.com/wp/index.php/author/animathias-and-lono

Newman, James. 2008. *Playing with Videogames*. London: Routledge.

Reeves, Stuart, Brown, Barry, and Laurier, Eric. 2009. "Experts at Play: Understanding Skilled Expertise." *Games and Culture* 4 (3): 205–27.

Taylor, T. L. 2010. "Playing for Keeps: The Rise of Professional Computer

Gaming." Paper presented at *Clash of Realities*, Cologne, Germany, April 21–3.

Games

Looking Glass Studios. 1998. *Thief: The Dark Project* [Microsoft Windows]. Eidos Interactive.
Rare. 1997. *Goldeneye 007* [N64]. Nintendo.

PART THREE

Multiplayer

11

"A Silent Team is a Dead Team": Communicative Norms in Competitive FPS Play

Nick Taylor[1]

This paper documents the discursive practices of an emergent domain in digital gaming: the world of professional videogame play, or "e-Sports"[2]. Through analyzing audio-visual recordings of competitive FPS players' verbal communications with one another in the context of team-based tournament play (and in players' training sessions), the paper documents the ways in which particular communicative forms are positioned as central to the execution—and, crucially, the performance—of cyber athleticism, as it is practiced by a community of competitive North American *Halo* players.

My case study is based on fieldwork from an eight-month audio-visual ethnography of *Halo 3* tournaments in three very different sites: a small-scale local area network (hereafter LAN) club called "NerdCorps," the 2008 Major League Gaming (hereafter MLG) Toronto Open, and the 2008 World Cyber Games (hereafter WCG) Finals in Cologne, Germany. My ethnography followed a core group of approximately twenty competitive *Halo 3*[3] players who regularly attended monthly NerdCorps events in order to train for the far more lucrative MLG and WCG tournaments, where they competed against other *Halo 3* gamers in the hopes of attaining "professional" status[4] and even sponsorship opportunities. The exploration I undertake here, of players' verbal communications during team-based *Halo 3* competition, constitutes part of this larger study of emergent forms of competitive digital gaming, and FPS play specifically, that are directly modeled upon the transformation of other participatory activities into high-stakes, low-participation spectator-driven sports. In particular, this analysis of how players use particular communicative forms to choreograph each others' in-game activities, as well as to craft and perform their own (and others') identities as "cyber athletes", illuminates one means by which these players enact the transformation of FPS play into a professional spectator sport through their embodied practices.

This exploration begins with an overview of speech act theory (Austin 1975; Searle 1976), which offers a conceptual framework for analyzing the performative dimensions of speech. Following Bronwyn Davies and Rom Harré's reformulation of speech act theory (1990) to account for the ways we perform inclusion or affiliation with particular discourses, I develop a broad taxonomy of the speech acts uttered most often from competitive *Halo 3* gamers at the tournaments I attended. This taxonomy separates "instrinsic" speech acts, those directed explicitly towards choreographing players' in-game activities during play, from "extrinsic" speech acts, which are directed more towards signaling or performing inclusion in a discourse that links competitive gaming to the domain of professional, male-dominated spectator sport. Analyses of specific speech acts uttered by research participants during tournament play are drawn from my audio-visual data. In each instance, I provide a still image taken from the audio-visual data, describe the context of the utterance, the speakers and audience, and the apparent effects of the utterance.

Background

In a 2008 interview with ESPN, Chris Puckett, a play-by-play commentator for Major League Gaming's Pro Circuit tournaments, offers this advice to aspiring competitive *Halo 3* players: "put in the practice, focus on communication first, then your shot." In Puckett's opinion, verbal interactions between teammates are more important to success in team-based competition than one's "shot"—the dexterity and hand-eye coordination normally associated with game-based competency, and with FPS games specifically[5]. This advice about what it takes to become an elite competitive *Halo 3* player highlights a central aspect of the professionalization of team-based digital play as I saw it practiced by the gamers I studied: players' performance of *specific* forms of verbal, game-related communication and the regulation of these performances by other players, as well as organizers and spectators. As one player described to me when asked about the importance of communication, "a silent team is a dead team": knowing how, when and what to speak in the context of team-based play are as important to the performance of professional *Halo 3* play as (for example) the ability to re-load a weapon at just the right time, aim while running and jumping, or seek cover from enemy fire.

The particular focus in this paper is to develop an analysis of players' verbal communications with one another. I draw from audio-visual data to discuss the following kinds of utterances: a system of game-based descriptors used during play to coordinate team action (called "map callouts" by players); verbal encouragement, critique, and mentorship among players (which often focused on how and when to use map callouts); and rebukes and taunts between players and the homophobic and misogynistic language used to do so. In documenting these different types of utterances, I make a distinction between speech acts that directly pertain to in-game events and are intrinsic to team-based play, and speech acts that are extrinsic to play and whose effects relate more to players' public performance of a particular kind of subject position made possible by the transformation of play into sport.

Methodology

Between early 2008 and late 2009, I served as NerdCorps' videographer, producing promotional audio-visual materials to recruit more people to their competitive LAN events in exchange for the opportunity to interview players, collect surveys, and record LAN play. This involvement in a socio-technical community that very much relies on audio-visual technologies and the spectatorial opportunities they represent, gave me the opportunity to travel with NerdCorps teams as they participated in larger, more lucrative *Halo 3* tournaments.

Video ethnography allowed me to explore, and represent, the choreography between players and non-human "agents" within the socio-technical apparatuses of the LAN tournaments I attended. In doing so I deployed one of the core insights developed by other games researchers working with Actor-Network Theory: that gaming competency is as much a product of a game or genre "training" its players as it is about players' mastery over the game (Giddings and Kennedy 2008, 19).

For my video ethnography, I employed audio-visual recording, alongside written accounts of my non-participant observation at each tournament, to generate textual and audio-visual data. I collected over 50 hours of audio-visual data (including four hours of video recorded interviews) that I edited into approximately 400 individual clips, between 30 seconds and four minutes in length. Following a set of coding protocols developed and refined through my involvement in previous, large-scale ethnographic projects employing audio-visual recording tools, I edited and coded data through an iterative and inductive process informed by grounded theory methods (Glaser & Strauss 1967).

Theoretical Framework: Word Play

In order to more meaningfully differentiate between the communicative forms players used, I draw upon speech act theory, first articulated by John Austin (1975) and then refined/re-worked by John Searle (1969; 1976), Kent Bach and Michael Harnish (1979), and Bronwyn Davies and Rom Harré (1990), among others. Speech act theory offers a framework for categorizing and analyzing the "performative" aspects of spoken language, asking how speakers "do things with words" (Austin 1975): formalize relationships, coordinate the actions of others, commit to a particular intent, and so on. In a series of lectures collectively titled *How To Do Things With Words*, Austin (1975) articulates an understanding of spoken language where the utterance "is, or is a part of, the doing of an action" (5). According to Austin, a performative utterance can be analyzed in three ways: as "locutionary" act, in terms of its ostensible meaning and content; as "illocutionary" act, in terms of its intended effect on the speaker or listener(s); and as "perlocutionary" act, in terms of its actual effects on the speaker, the audience, and the context of the utterance (98–103).

Working from this distinction, Austin asserts that analyzing the illocutionary sense of an utterance—what the speaker does or intends to do through the speech act—is of primary importance to social studies of language. John Searle re-formulates Austin's rough taxonomy of illocutionary acts, a project he sees as crucial in accounting for the "limited number of basic things we can do with language" (Searle 1976, 22)[6]. Briefly, this taxonomy includes: "representative" illocutionary acts, which describe a set of conditions; "directive" utterances, intended to coordinate the actions of the person(s) to whom they are addressed; "commissives," which consign the speaker to a particular goal or plan; "expressives," to communicate the speaker's state of mind; and "declaratives," such as "you're fired," that bring about the conditions to which they refer (10–14). This taxonomy (and its further refinements and extensions: Alston 1991; Bach and Harnish 1979; Harnish 1990; Sbisa 2002) has been used to carry out focused analyses of discrete talk segments (see, for example, Kubo 2002; Moulin and Rousseau 2002; Recanati

1987; Yamada 2002). In these approaches, statements are often represented in symbolic and/or schematic form as sequences of syntactic elements, in order to examine their mechanics: the force with which they are expressed, for instance, or the presumed sincerity of the speaker.

Rather than apply Searle's taxonomy to formal analyses of individual talk fragments, however, I employ it as a set of concepts for expressing and organizing the effects of different speech acts in the contexts of their use. In doing so, I follow attempts to bring speech act theory in line with a post-structuralist notion of discourse as dynamically realized and socially reproduced systems of meaning, through which subjects regulate and negotiate acceptable identities, activities, and practices (Davies and Harré 1990, 45). In this post-structuralist formation of speech act theory, and similar to Snider, Lockridge, and Lawson's approach (this volume), the aim is not to decode individual speech acts in order to reveal the speaker's intention or psychological state of mind; rather, speech acts are regarded as means through which individuals take up and rehearse particular subject positions within a given domain (46).

Going Pro

Following this re-working of speech act theory[7], the different performative utterances documented here constitute one set of resources (alongside non-verbal forms of communication such as gesture, proximity, gaze, and gameplay) through which players engage in and reproduce a discourse around what constitutes professional *Halo 3* play: here, mastery of a highly codified lingo, as well as an ability to trash-talk, are as important as abilities related to navigation and targeting. Silence is associated with incompetence and inexperience. This discourse is further characterized by an acceptance (celebration even) of misogynistic and homophobic banter between players—banter that has far more to do with rehearsing particular hyper-masculinized subject positions than with executing gameplay. These speech acts form one part of the discursive matrix through which competitive gaming is legitimated as (male-dominated) spectator sport.

In contrast to recent studies of e-Sports, which either provide rationales for competitive gaming's status as sport (Hutchins 2008), or accept this as fact (Rambusch, Jakobsson, and Pargmann 2007), my aim in this paper is to regard the professionalization of gaming as a process carried out through the deliberate appropriation of imagery, media production practices, and discourses from the domain of spectator sports (Taylor 2009). In this regard, I see in the professionalization of digital play a shift that is similar to the rise of professional sports beginning in the early twentieth century (albeit on a different scale and under different socio-economic and techno-logical conditions), and continuing with the emergence of a sports media industry that caters primarily to heterosexual men (Messner 2007). The legitimation of competitive gaming as spectator sport carries with it similar gender effects: it elevates and rewards partici-pants in a typically masculinized domain, while relegating others to the sidelines (McDonagh and Pappano 2009).

Intrinsic and Extrinsic Speech Acts

The utterances analyzed here are organized in two general theoretical categories. I differentiate between speech acts *intrinsic* to play, those that immediately relate to events in the game and direct players' efforts to a particular strategy or course of action, and speech acts *extrinsic* to play, those that address other *players* rather than the minutia of *play*, including taunting, trash-talking, mentorship, and motivational speech. The intrinsic speech acts I examine enable team members to choreograph their efforts with each other in real time, and constitute part of the domain of embodied competencies elite players draw upon in team-based play. Extrinsic speech acts, by contrast, involve the "discursive positioning" of participants in relation to notions of what being a pro *Halo 3* gamer entails (Davies and Harré 1990). These categories are not mutually exclusive; the distinction is intended to illustrate that participation in this pro-gaming community has as much to do with affecting a particular subject position—one which traffics in the kinds of homophobia, misogyny, and hyper-masculinization commonly associated with professional sports (Curry 2002; Waitt 2008; Taylor, Jenson, and de Castell 2010)—as it does with playing FPS games expertly.

Map Callouts: Choreographing Play

Following the distinction between intrinsic and extrinsic speech acts, the first set of utterances I look at involves a specialized vocabulary for competitive *Halo 3* play, generally referred to by players as "callouts." These constitute a highly codified terminology for describing and identifying on-screen events among teammates, referring to specific areas in specific game arenas (or "maps") where enemies, power-ups, and/or objectives appear during the course of gameplay. To show how they are used and what they accomplish within competitive team *Halo 3* play, I will refer to an audio-visual clip[8] recorded during the first day of competition at the 2008 MLG Toronto Open (Figure 11.1). The clip shows a high-ranked American team in the foreground, playing against another team. As in most instances of team-based play I observed, players repeat each map callout two or three times, although one player is the more vocal and audible team member throughout this clip. Here, the more vocal teammate is "Slice," on the left side in the image (the other two teammates are not visible in the shot).

Unlike the systems of specific pre-scripted plays or formations used in organized team sports (as engineered, for instance, by the quarterback in football, or the midfielder in soccer), map callouts are not often used as "directives" to explicitly regulate other players'

Figure 11.1 "Slice," on the left, shouting callouts during MLG tournament play.

actions. Rather, they are used more as "representatives": they describe, in a codified and concise way, the action unfolding in a particular part of the game environment, which other teammates might not be in a position to see on their screens. For instance, when Slice yells "Two dead in their lobby! Two dead in their lobby!" he describes a specific set of conditions that he is viewing/taking part in: two opposing players have been killed (by one of Slice's teammates) in the opposing team's lobby, the area of the arena where opposing players re-spawn[9] after being killed. Similarly, when Slice's teammate proclaims "One shot our snipe, one shot our snipe" he is notifying other teammates of two conditions: he has spotted an enemy player on their side of the map close to the area on their side of the arena where the sniper rifle power-up appears ("Our snipe"), and this player has been weakened (presumably, though not necessarily, by the player himself) to the point where he is only one direct shot of the battle rifle (the default weapon for MLG competitive play) away from being eliminated. As these examples show, callouts are used to instantiate a shared virtual topography through a pre-determined system of verbal cues.

While most commonly used as "representative" utterances, I also observed callouts being used as directive utterances on occasion, in players' instructions to one another. In the same clip, Slice alerts his team members to "Joker," an opponent. At first, he exclaims "Joker one shot Joker one shot," his representative utterance indicating that this player has been weakened; in the next instance, he yells "Joker is one shot, just jump up and shoot him once," a directive utterance aimed at no teammate in particular. A second later, Slice comments "I got him I got him." In a matter of seconds, Slice identifies an enemy's weakened status, urges his teammates to finish the opponent off, does so himself, and then alerts his teammates that he's done so. From my observations of competitive *Halo 3* play across various tournaments, this rapid-fire narration, in which callouts are repeated several times in quick succession to describe unfolding events in-game, marks a standard, even mundane competitive gaming moment. At the same time, the use of callouts in directive utterances is less common in my audio-visual record than their use in representative utterances. While each player on the team engages in uses of callouts as representative utterances, only

Slice seems to use callouts as directives—perhaps indicating (and/or instantiating) his status as team leader. This was consistent across the majority of teams I observed: while all team members engaged in callouts, typically only one member employed them in directive speech acts.

Verbal "Screen Looking"

Callouts constituted the majority of players' verbal communications with their teammates during the *Halo 3* play I observed, and were regarded by players and commentators as an essential part of the repertoire for competitive team play. At the elite levels of 4v4 team-based play I observed, *Halo 3* is intensely fast-paced and chaotic; the difference between killing another player or being killed by them is often a matter of who sees who first. Knowing the location of teammates and opponents offers considerable strategic advantage. As a communicative system for representing on-screen events, then, callouts are a means of *verbally* extending players' field of vision, allowing them to overcome two constraints on their ability to see, and react to, on-screen action. The first limitation is virtual, and relates to the design of the game arenas used at the tournaments I attended (the four most popular arenas at the NerdCorps, MLG, and WCG events I observed are named "The Pit," "Construct," "Narrows," and "Guardian"). These spaces are comprised of dark corridors, multiple, disjointed platforms, and sharp, blind corners: they are designed to curtail and confound players' in-game lines of sight. The second limitation concerns the material layout of televisions and consoles at LAN tournaments: because a team of four has to use multiple television sets (either two televisions running in split-screen mode, accommodating two players each, or four televisions, one for each player on the team), players usually have to look away from their own television in order to see where their teammate(s) are and what they are doing—called "screen looking" by players. In the 1v1 training sessions I observed at the local NerdCorps events, screen looking was a much-maligned practice in a setup where players usually had to sit beside or share screens with other opponents. Screen looking your opponent is a means of gaining strategic advantage, and over the course of my fieldwork at NerdCorps I observed several instances of players accusing one another of cheating, or in some cases defending their screen looking as a legitimate tactic[10].

In team play, however, screen looking is an encouraged and even habitual act: when a player dies, they look at their teammates' screens during the seconds before they re-spawn, often shouting out encouragements and/or warnings as they do so. When their avatars are alive, however, the rapid pace of competitive team play makes it almost impossible to look at other teammates' screens. Because of this physical limitation as well as the design of virtual arenas, callouts constitute "verbal screen looking": a kind of collaborative "lateral surveillance" (Andrejevic 2005) that extends players' awareness of on-screen actions beyond what their limited line of sight, constrained by the configuration/design of both virtual and material technologies, allows for[11].

Community Artifacts: Mapping Speech

Callouts are regarded as central to the skill repertoire required for competitive team-based *Halo 3* play, as I learned from observing the local, national, and international LAN tournaments I attended, as well as talking with players and organizers. Like the hardcore gaming communities around other games (particularly massively multiplayer online games; see Steinkuehler 2008; Taylor 2006), these practices are also articulated and debated in online game-related forums (the most prominent among competitive *Halo* franchise players in North America are MLG's forums, at http://www.mlgpro.com/forums). On these sites, players produce and publish diagrams of callouts, identifying the locations and communally regulated codenames for weapon and power-up spawn points, elevators between platforms, team re-spawn points, and so on[12]. As resources made explicitly to instruct other players in not only where certain points on the map are located, but how to call them out to teammates in online and LAN-based matches, these digital artifacts are one means through which a codified set of verbal/textual referents is regulated and standardized.

Regulating Talk: "Be Loud!"

As with T. L. Taylor's (2006) look at in-game communication tools for participatory surveillance in *World of Warcraft*, a player's use or misuse of this technical register is subject to regulation and critique from other participants—whether teammates, spectators, or opponents. In another clip from the 2008 MLG Toronto Open, a NerdCorps participant, "Shadow," is watching a local Toronto squad lose to an American team (Figure 11.2). After the match, Shadow criticizes one of the team's members for not being loud enough. "When you do badly don't be quiet – you weren't talking!" he says, leaning in after some seconds trying to get the other player's attention. When the other player defends himself, claiming "I *was* yelling," Shadow replies that the only player he heard making callouts was "OldSchool," another player on the team. This interaction suggests a shared conception about the importance of "being loud" to successful play: Shadow's critique, and the other player's defense, suggests that the team lost in part because one player wasn't audible enough in his callouts.

Here, a player critiques his peer for his perceived silence during play; the player accused of not communicating properly insists that he *was* being loud (perhaps just not loud *enough*), signaling his recognition of and participation in the discursive equation between

Figure 11.2 "Shadow" (left) telling his peer to "be loud."

"being loud" and competent team play. It is not enough *that* this particular player utilizes map callouts; it is also *how* he produces these utterances (being "loud enough") that matters to his participation in a pro-gaming community. This instance demonstrates the extent to which the *performance* of callouts is central to not only successful team strategy, but also to the discursive construction of professional *Halo 3* play.

Extrinsic Speech

The use of standardized callouts is regarded as an integral part of elite team-based *Halo 3* play, so much so that a player's misuse of callouts can be blamed as a primary reason for his team losing. In this section, I examine speech acts that are not directly related to in-game events or to the real-time choreography of effective team play, but may be just as important to players' performance, in public, of the subject positions associated with this emergent e-Sport. This includes forms of encouragement and motivation between players, as well as the various ways taunts and insults are deployed: whether to distract, provoke, or alienate other players. I argue that although each of these communicative forms is related to and often triggered by participants' gameplay, they are largely extrinsic to in-game events—that is, they concern the regulation and certain subject positions regarded as acceptable within a community heavily invested in the links between gaming competence and a (sports-related) hyper-masculinity.

"Keep This Pace Goin' Guys"

Among the more common kinds of extrinsic speech acts are instances where players (as well as spectators) congratulate each other for specific in-game achievements (i.e. "Nice shot") or spur each other on (i.e. "Let's go"). Audio-visual footage of training tournaments at NerdCorps LAN events offers examples. The instance I examine here is from the 4v4 team finals of an event in Spring 2008 (Figure 11.3): "Reach," in the middle, encourages his teammates on as they play another team of NerdCorps regulars in the tournament

Figure 11.3 "Reach" urging his teammates (not depicted) to "keep this pace goin'."

finals. Widely regarded as less skilled than other NerdCorps players, Reach was heavily involved in helping the organizers run monthly events, and at the time of my study was volunteering for MLG Canada in hopes of being hired on as a play-by-play commentator for MLG tournaments. One of the NerdCorps organizers described these activities as attempts by a less competent player to "make a name for himself" in the competitive gaming industry.

At the start of the clip, Reach exclaims "Let's keep this goin' guys, we got a good pace goin' here." Moments later, Reach again shouts "Keep this pace goin' guys" as the camera pans from his teammates to him. As illocutionary acts, Reach's comments appear as directive utterances, in so far as he is urging his teammates towards a stated goal, however vaguely described. In contrast to the more substantive directives made by Slice, however, Reach's comments seem more deliberately performative, as if he is rehearsing a more motivational role for his team (and possibly for the camera). His directive utterances have no noticeable impact on his teammates, as they continue to focus intently on their screens and shout callouts to one another. "Keep this pace goin' guys" may be *framed* as a directive utterance, but not in the same way as Slice's intrinsically oriented utterances. Instead of coordinating the play of his teammates, Reach seems more intent on rehearsing a particular identity in relation to his more competent teammates, that of a motivator or coach rather than captain.

Taunts, Trash-talk, and Put-downs

Taunts and insults were a common occurrence throughout my fieldwork, and seem to be integral to the discursive repertoire of many players[13]. In looking at specific moments of players mocking, teasing, and/or provoking one another, I argue that inclusion in a competitive gaming community involves, for these players, participating in a kind of verbal antagonism: trash-talking between opponents was regarded by most players I interviewed at NerdCorps and MLG events as a legitimate tactic, and some players at the World Cyber Games felt that play suffered as a result of the tournament's strict rule against it. Players used taunts and insults not only to trash-talk, but to marginalize less competent play(ers) and, specifically, to describe their play in misogynistic or homophobic terms. Once again, the discursive parallels between competitive *Halo 3* play and masculinized sports practices and institutions is significant: across both, competence is often associated with heteronormative masculinity, and expressed in violent and hyper-masculinized language, while incompetence is equated with femininity and homosexuality (Atencio and Wright 2008; Curry 2002; Waitt 2008).

Here, I examine three clips in which participants at NerdCorps training events engage in antagonistic speech acts. In the first instance, players on opposing teams engage in trash-talk during heated 4v4 play, which can be regarded as a kind of belligerent but harmless verbal sparring. The second clip shows novice players being punished and marginalized through the speech acts of their teammate; here, put-downs are used to disassociate an accomplished participant from the incompetent players she has been teamed up with. In the third clip, which is perhaps qualitatively different in ways worth pursuing, a successful and popular male player loudly but "jokingly" threatens a female player after she reacts to his sexualized comments during Free-for-All play at a NerdCorps event. Unlike the first two clips, the exchange is wholly unrelated to on-screen action, and demonstrates that much of the discursive practices this community engages in has far more to do with players' embodied and gendered identities than what they are doing, or capable of doing, in the game.

"Sit Down With That Shit, Man!"

In the first clip I examine here, two teams of NerdCorps regulars are playing one another in round-robin 4v4 play during a training event in the summer of 2008. During play, "Focus," the player closest to the camera, and on the team that is currently behind by a match in the best-of-three format, engages in a two-minute exchange of taunts and provocations with a player on the other team who is off-camera. The following is a partial transcript of their exchange:

> Focus: Suck on that!
> Focus: Sit down with that shit man!
> Other player: Are you winning?
> Focus: Sit down with that shit!
> [15 seconds later]
> Focus: You wanna play that buddy?
> Other player: I'm gonna play that cuz I'm winning – and I've already won a game. Where's your win?
> Focus: It's comin' baby, it's comin'.
> Other player: I'm waitin' for it, any day buddy.
> [90 seconds later]
> Focus: Oh baby ooooh baby! Is everybody dead?

This transcript does not represent a full record of what is said over the three-minute clip; their dialogue is only part of a complex, multi-layered soundscape as players from both teams shout callouts, encouragements, and taunts. Their exchange of provocations is antagonistic, but not hostile; the participants seem more concerned with distracting and teasing, rather than provoking one another, and notably, it stops abruptly as soon as the match ends, at which point each team member shakes hands and/or congratulates opposing team members. This sort of trash-talking is the most common type of verbal antagonism I observed, and according to many players I talked to (as well as the NerdCorps organizers), it constitutes as legitimate a gameplay tactic as callouts; while callouts work to choreograph the actions of team members, trash-talking is regarded as a way of disrupting this choreography. The almost playful verbal sparring between the two opponents in this clip stands in contrast to the following account of novice players being alienated through a dismissive exchange between more accomplished NerdCorps regulars.

"These Guys Have So Much Awareness"

The interaction I examine next, from another NerdCorps tournament during the summer of 2008, involves "Fatal Fantasy" (hereafter Fatal), the lone female regular at the events, and her friend "Burns," who are teamed up with two unfamiliar and novice young men, whom I had not seen before and did not see afterwards (Figure 11.4). One of them is not visible in the camera shot. "Mad Hatter," another NerdCorps regular, watches their round-robin team play. Both Fatal and Burns engage only sporadically in callouts, demonstrating what seems like a lack of enthusiasm for, and disengagement from, their match. Their teammates appear to be silent the entire duration of the clip. At the beginning of the clip, Fatal tries to coordinate the other two players, explicitly turning to look at them twice as she utters map callouts. Halfway through the clip, Fatal shakes her head and

Figure 11.4 Mad Hatter, Burns and Fatal (from the left edge of the clip), disparaging novices.

exclaims that the match is the "Most epic choke I've ever seen, I kid you not," presumably in response to her team's struggles. Moments later, Mad Hatter comments, sarcastically and in earshot of the whole team, "Wow, these guys have so much awareness," referring to the novice play of Fatal's teammates. She replies by stating, "These kids? No they don't." She appears to avoid looking their way for the rest of the clip. After the round comes to a close, another spectator off-camera exclaims "You got raped guys, so hard," and Fatal shakes her head again[14].

In my reading of this exchange, Fatal distances herself both verbally and non-verbally from the poor play of the two inexperienced players. She replies to Mad Hatter's comment in a way that both alienates and infantilizes the two novices ("These kids? No they don't"), effectively positioning those sitting directly beside her as unworthy of any further direct contact. Where the trash-talk between Focus and his opponent involved two NerdCorps regulars relatively equal in skill, this exchange involves the outright dismissal of two new and less competent players by a group of more expert regulars.

"Slap You Across the Throat"

Whereas the previous exchange depicts a player distancing herself from the poor play of her teammates, the next audio-visual clip I discuss depicts male participants marginalizing a female player for reasons *wholly* extrinsic to her play—her gender, in a community in which women are not regarded as legitimate participants (Taylor, Jenson, and de Castell, 2009). The clip is from the NerdCorps event directly before the 2008 MLG Toronto Open (Figure 11.5). It begins with "Vik Vicious" (hereafter Vik), regarded by NerdCorps organizers and participants as the club's most successful player and one of the best *Halo 3* players in Canada, shouting racialized and homophobic remarks, to no one in particular, during an otherwise quiet period of Free-for-All play[15]. Moments into the clip, Vik begins to yell "Suck my bird, nigga!" in a loud and deep voice, to no one in particular. "Hopper," seated beside him, laughs, and Vik continues "why can't you talk, is there a bird[16] in your throat?" Seconds later, Vik again yells "Eat my bird, nigga!" more loudly, at which point Fatal, seated several feet away with her back to Vik, leans back and looks at Vik

Figure 11.5 Vik (left) telling Fatal (right) "I'll slap you across the throat."

until he catches her gaze, then turns back to look at her screen, shaking her head. Vik responds "Oh what, you got a problem with that [Fatal]? I'll slap you across the throat," after which he comments "No really, I don't hit girls."

None of the other players around Vik or Fatal (including Hopper, Vik's teammate, who had laughed at the initial outbursts) seem to visibly or audibly respond to the exchange. Vik's outburst is encouraged by his teammate Hopper, also a well-respected player, who laughs out loud after the first two remarks. His response to Fatal, the only one to visibly take offense at his remarks, is to threaten physical violence against her, before assuring her (and the other participants, as well as the camera and possibly myself) that he doesn't "hit girls." His threat against her is certainly problematic, but so is his following claim that he doesn't hit girls; this comment re-emphasizes Fatal's gendered identity within a male-dominated space. Here, the marginalization of a player affected through the utterances of others has little to do with Fatal's gaming competence, as is the case with the novice players Fatal dismisses in the previous clip, and everything to do with the maintenance of a discourse that problematizes Fatal's attempts at legitimate participation, on the grounds of her gendered identity.

Instances of utterances involving misogynistic, homophobic, and/ or racialized language occurred frequently throughout the tournaments I observed. As in other leisure and sport-related contexts dominated by young males (Curry 2002; Pascoe 2007; Waitt 2008), such speech acts arguably function to alienate "other" subject positions; in this instance, Vik's utterance and its sanctioning by other players (as well as myself) serves to (re)create a space that is unfriendly, and potentially unsafe, to female gamers. The interaction I examine between Vik and Fatal clearly illustrates that affirmations of heteronormative masculinity are a significant part of this community's discursive practices. The forms of extrinsic speech sanctioned in this community, and deployed to marginalize particular players, demonstrate that the ability to perform professional gaming has as much to do with players' gender as their abilities to shoot one another in *Halo 3*.

Conclusion

The categorization and interpretation of verbal interactions offered in this account of competitive *Halo 3* players' discursive practices is a representative but not exhaustive sample of the communicative patterns I observed. Excluded from this account are the forms of communication employed by *Halo 3* coaches, participants whose function, from what I observed at MLG Toronto[17], is to take on the role of shouting map callouts for the entire team, so that individual players do not have to. I also did not take up players' use of the term "rape," and the issues the use of this term raises in a male-dominated community where women are most often positioned in supportive and sexualized roles.

The analysis offered here, however, plays up what appears to be a crucial characteristic of the emergent discourse around profession-alized *Halo 3* play, expressed through the sentiment that "a silent team is a dead team": that the competencies required to participate in this community not only involve game-based skill, dexterity, hand-eye coordination, and a familiarity with the game formats and maps used in tournaments, but also the routinized deployment of a codified speech system that both accomplishes and demonstrates successful team coordination. The communicative forms that I have defined as intrinsic to play, then, are as much the repertoire for elite players as the ability to aim and fire while running or jumping, rapidly navigate virtual space, and memorize when and where on each game terrain certain power-ups appear. As my exploration of extrinsic speech acts makes clear, however, callouts constitute only part of the ways players verbally participate in a pro-gaming discourse. Players' verbal enactment and regulation of a pro-gamer masculinity seems as important to competitive *Halo 3* play as the cultivation and execution of game-based competencies, including callouts.

This analysis contributes to a growing body of research that examines the competencies and practices associated with competitive FPS play (Reeves, Brown, and Laurier 2009) and e-Sports (Rambusch, Jakobsson, and Pargman 2007; Taylor 2009). In following *Halo 3* players' own understandings of what constitutes elite, indeed professional play with regards to competitive FPS gaming, this work extends current accounts of what expert FPS play entails and requires, in two primary ways. The first concerns the inclusion of linguistic competencies in the repertoire of expert *Halo 3* players; the second is the acknowledgement that expertise, however defined, is certainly not the most important qualifier for success, or even inclusion in this emergent e-Sport. Equally important for this community of competitive FPS gamers is the ability to occupy a particular gendered subject position—to "talk the talk" that links competitive FPS play to the domain of male-dominated, professional spectator sports.

Notes

1 Thank you to the organizers of NerdCorps, and the players with whom I worked between 2008 and 2009, without which this research would not have been possible.

2 The term has primarily been used to refer to tournament-based and league-sponsored play in either team-based or one-on-one games (Rambusch, Jakobsson, and Pargmann 2007; Taylor and Witkowski 2010). Popular genres include real-time strategy (*Starcraft* and *Starcraft II*); fighting games (*Street Fighter IV*, *Super Smash Brothers Brawl*); sports games; and FPS games, both PC-based (*Counter-Strike*) and on consoles (the *Halo* and *Gears of War* franchises). The name of this organization, and the nicknames of its participants, have been altered to protect their anonymity.

3 At the time of my study, *Halo 3* was the most recent installment of the *Halo* franchise, and the one most played in the competitive tournaments I documented, including the Major League Gaming (MLG) tournaments. It has since been replaced by *Halo: Reach*.

4 Teams that place eighth or higher at Major League Gaming tournaments are given "professional" designation.

5 See, for instance, Reeves, Brown, and Laurier (2009); Thompson (2002).

6 Searle, like Austin, maintains that the intended effects of a speech act cannot be conflated with its actual effects, and preserves Austin's distinction between illocutionary (intended) and perlocutionary (actual) effects of speech.

7 A similar framework is offered up in James Gee's articulation and application of discourse analysis (1999), in so far as inclusion in a particular "affinity group" is partially a matter of mastering the group's discursive practices.

8 Throughout this chapter I will refer to moments in my audio-visual record as clips, in order to emphasize the selective and specific audio-visual ethnographic techniques by which such moments are made visible: e.g. through setting up a recording and positioning the camera, to editing and annotating particular instances in the data.

9 When they are killed, players must wait a certain set amount of time (depending on particular tournament rules) before they reappear—"re-spawn"—back in a designated part of the game arena (their "lobby"), usually on the far side from their opponents' lobby.

10 Most players played far more *Halo 3* online, over Xbox LIVE's online gaming service, than they do in LANs, meaning screen looking is only an issue at LAN play. The regulation of screen looking is, therefore, part of a more general negotiation between players, organizers, and promoters about what counts as "legitimate" tournament play, particularly as the e-Sports industry positions LAN events as the primary arenas for professional gaming (see, for instance, Taylor 2009).

11 T. L. Taylor, examining user-created software modifications to *World of Warcraft,* makes a similar comment regarding experienced players' deployment of software tools for monitoring teammates' in-game actions. Taylor claims such practices perform "important work in assisting collaborative play, especially at the high end of the game" (Taylor 2006, 329).

12 See, for instance, the *maps* published on http://www.freewebs.com/competitiveonlinegaming/mapsandcallouts.htm.

13 Significantly, the only site/event where taunting among players is not present is at the World Cyber Games, where trash-talking was disallowed as part of a mandate to promote "good sportsmanship" at events styled as competitive gaming "Olympics."

14 Participants' frequent use of "rape" to describe in-game events is an issue that demands further and separate analysis, beyond the limits of this paper.

15 At NerdCorps events, Free-for-All (or FFA) play involved up to eight players in a single map fighting one another; the organizers regarded it as a means to hone players' game-based skills.

16 "Bird" in this context is a euphemism for penis.

17 My primary reason for not discussing this role is because I only observed them at the MLG event I went to, and not at NerdCorps tournaments or the World Cyber Games.

References

Alston, William P. 1991. "Searle on Illocutionary Acts." In *John Searle and His Critics*, edited by Ernest Lepore and Robert van Gulick, 57–80. Oxford: Blackwell.

Andrejevic, Mark. 2005. "The Work of Watching One Another: Lateral Surveillance, Risk, and Governance." *Surveillance and Society* 2: 479–97.

Atencio, Matthew, and Jan Wright. 2008. "'We be Killin' Them': Hierarchies of Black Masculinity in Urban Basketball Spaces." *Sociology of Sport Journal* 25: 263–80.

Austin, John. 1975. *How to do Things with Words*. Oxford: Clarendon Press.

Bach, Kent and Robert M. Harnish. 1979. *Linguistic Communication and Speech Acts*. Cambridge, MA: MIT Press.

Bjork, Staffan and Jonas Linderoth. 2010. "Pickup Groups as Situated Activity Systems: Game Design and Social Rules in *Left 4 Dead*." Paper presented at the Association of Internet Researchers, Gothenburg, Sweden, October.

Curry, Timothy J. 2002. "Fraternal Bonding in the Locker Room: A Profeminist Analysis of Talk About Competition and Women." In *Gender and Sport: A Reader*, edited by Sheila Scraton and Anne Flintoff, 169–87. New York: Routledge.

Davies, Bronwyn and Rom Harré. 1990. "Positioning: The Discursive Production of Selves." *Journal for the Theory of Social Behaviour* 20 (1): 43–63.

Gee, James P. 1999. *An Introduction to Discourse Analysis: Theory and Method*. New York: Routledge.

Giddings, Seth and Helen Kennedy. 2008. "Little Jesuses and *@#?-off Robots: On Cybernetics, Aesthetics, and Not Being Very Good at *Lego Star Wars*." In *The Pleasures of Computer Gaming: Essays on Cultural History, Theory and Aesthetics*, edited by Melanie Smallwell, 13–32. Jefferson, NC: McFarland.

Glaser, Barney.G. and Anselm L. Strauss. 1967. *The Discovery of Grounded Theory: Strategies for Qualitative Research*. Chicago: Aldine.

Harnish, Robert M. 1990. "Speech Acts and Intentionality." In *Speech Acts, Meaning and Intentions*, edited by Armin Burkhart, 169–83. Berlin: de Gruyter.

Hutchins, Brett. 2008. "Signs of Meta-change in Second Modernity." *New Media & Society* 10 (6): 851–69.

Kubo, Susumo. 2002. "Illocutionary Morphology and Speech Acts." In *Essays in Speech Act Theory*, edited by Daniel Vanderveken and Susumo Kubo, 209–24. Philadelphia, PA: John Benjamin.

McDonagh, Eileen and Laura Pappano. 2009. *Playing with the Boys: Why Separate is Not Equal in Sports*. New York: Oxford University Press.

Messner, Michael A. 2007. "Sports and Male Domination: The Female Athlete as Contested Terrain." In *Out of Play: Critical Essays on Gender and Sport*, edited by Michael A. Messner, 31–44. Albany: State University of New York Press.

Moulin, Bernard and Daniel Rousseau. 2002. "An Approach for Modeling and Simulating Conversations." In *Essays in Speech Act Theory*, edited by Daniel Vanderveken and Susumo Kubo, 175–205. Philadelphia, PA: John Benjamin.

Rambusch, Jana, Peter Jakobsson, and Daniel Pargman. 2007. "Exploring e-Sports: A Case Study of Gameplay in *Counter-Strike*." Paper presented at the Digital Games Research Association Conference, Tokyo, Japan, September 2007.

Recanati, Francois. 1987. *Meaning and Force: The Pragmatics of Performative Utterances*. New York: Cambridge University Press.

Reeves, Stuart, Barry Brown, and Eric Laurier. 2009. "Experts at Play: Understanding Skilled Expertise." *Games and Culture* 4 (3): 205–27.

Sbisa, Marina. 2002. "Speech Acts in Context." *Language and Communication* 22: 421–36.

Searle, John R. 1969. *Speech Acts*. New York: Cambridge University Press.

—1976. "A Classification of Illocutionary Acts." *Language and Society* 5 (1): 1–23.

Searle, John R. and Daniel Vanderveken. 1985. *Foundations of Illocutionary Logic*. New York: Cambridge University Press.

Steinkuehler, Constance A. 2008. "Cognition and Literacy in Massively

Multiplayer Online Games." In *Handbook of Research on New Literacies*, edited by Julie Coiro, Michele Knobel, Colin Lankshear, and Donald Leu, 611–34. Mahwah, NJ: Lawrence Erlbaum.

Taylor, Nicholas, Jennifer Jenson, and Suzanne de Castell. 2009. "Cheerleaders, Booth Babes, *Halo* Hoes: Pro-gaming, Gender, and Jobs for the Boys." *Digital Creativity* 20 (4): 239–52.

Taylor, T. L. 2006. "Does *WoW* Change Everything? How a PvP Server, Multinational Player Base, and Surveillance Mod Scene Caused Me Pause." *Games and Culture* 1 (4): 318–37.

—2009. "Negotiating Play: The Process of Rule Construction in Professional Computer Gaming." Paper presented at the Digital Games Research Association Conference, Uxbridge, England, September 2009.

Taylor, T. L. and Emma Witkowski. 2010. "This is How We Play It: What a Mega-LAN Can Teach Us About Games." Paper presented at Foundations of Digital Games Conference, Monterey, CA, June 2010.

Thompson, Clive. 2002. "Violence and the Political Life of Videogames." In *Game On: The History and Culture of Videogames*, edited by Lucien King, 22–31. London: Laurence King.

Waitt, Gordon. 2008. "'Killing Waves': Surfing, Space and Gender." *Social and Cultural Geography* 9 (1): 75–94.

Yamada, Tomoyuki. 2002. "An Ascription-based Theory of Illocutionary Acts." In *Essays in Speech Act Theory*, edited by Daniel Vanderveken and Susumo Kubo, 151–74. Philadelphia, PA: John Benjamin, 2002.

Games

Blizzard. 1998. *Starcraft* [Microsoft Windows]. Blizzard Entertainment.

—2010. *Starcraft II* [Microsoft Windows]. Blizzard Entertainment.

Bungie. 2007. *Halo 3* [Xbox 360]. Microsoft Game Studios.

—2010. *Halo: Reach* [Xbox 360]. Microsoft Game Studios.

Capcom. 2009. *Street Fighter IV* [Xbox 360, PlayStation 3]. Capcom.

Epic Games. 2008. *Gears of War 2* [Xbox 360]. Microsoft Game Studios.

Nintendo. 2008. *Super Smash Brothers Brawl* [Nintendo Wii]. Nintendo.

Valve. 2000. *Counter-Strike* [Microsoft Windows]. Valve.

12

Challenging the Rules and Roles of Gaming: Griefing as Rhetorical Tactic

Evan Snider, Tim Lockridge, and Dan Lawson

"**G**reetings," a player says to his teammates, "Welcome to another episode of *Team Fortress 2* trivia. If you can answer my trivia questions correctly, I will let you out." He has trapped his teammates in the game's spawn point, refusing to let them pass until they swear allegiance to Ron Paul, promise to support a gold standard, or correctly answer a handful of trivia questions. The player is a member of Team Roomba, a clan devoted to disrupting games whose *YouTube* videos (with millions of views) are wildly popular. Their videos also dispel one major assumption about griefing: that it's solely about cheating or bad play or harassment.

The above incident also challenges assumptions that griefers simply disrupt a game and leave, that the gameworld continues normally without them. During the quiz show, the teammates at first resist the grief but then begin to play along, searching for and arguing over correct answers. For instance, one quiz show participant is asked what organ of the body produces bile. That participant persistently argues for the gall bladder, even after another teammate correctly answers (the liver), and the griefer moves to allow the teammates past. Then, after a round, another player begins to parody (in a sense, griefing) the griefer, repeatedly asking "What is the thing of the thing?" Through the intervention of the griefer, the game itself is changed: the terms of engagement are modified, opening new spaces and styles of play within the game. When teammates use the in-game voice chat to argue over biological trivia rather than communicate game strategies, the griefer has effectively shifted play away from standard modes.

In this chapter, we argue that griefing is better understood not as isolated instances or actions but as an approach to playing games and even to the concept of play itself—what we call a rhetorical tactic. Similar to Alan Meades' discussion of modding in this same volume, rather than defining griefing solely in terms of intentionally detracting from another's enjoyment of a game—as antisocial behavior—we seek to expand notions of griefing as an ideological activity and posit it as an approach to gameplay that challenges culturally prescribed notions of play. However, whereas Meades examines transgressive play in terms of mods and altering the game itself, we focus more on how players transgress expectations about the game while operating within the game's mechanical parameters.

In particular, we explore griefing in FPS games. Griefing differs across games and genres, and it takes on a particular flavor in FPSs. FPS griefers have their own unique toolkits for griefing, including exploiting team dynamics and mechanics (such as teamkills), as well as game modes, map boundaries, and character roles. Broadly, griefers are extremely adept at locating game mechanics or implicit assumptions about gameplay that they can exploit or disrupt. Griefers in FPSs, however, are particularly skillful in this regard, perhaps because FPS games, as a genre, share a significant number of features.

But griefing involves far more than game mechanics. It is an entire style of play, and as such it serves as a response to the gameworld and in-game situations. As James Paul Gee (2007) writes in *What Video Games Have to Teach Us About Learning and Literacy*, most FPSs "play on cultural models that treat heroes as superhuman people and that see warfare (for the 'right' cause) as heroic" (153). What Gee calls cultural models, others might call ideologies; as a genre, first-person shooters are overdetermined by militaristic ideologies and social formations. Griefers in FPSs—intentionally or not—subvert these ideologies and social formations by disrupting teamwork and the end goal of the game, namely victory over an enemy. This in turn not only draws attention to the way subjects are formed in these digital environments but also invites the potential for redefining new subject formations and models of being in the game. As Gee acknowledges, "there is something wrong when these sorts of models are never challenged or overtly reflected on," and griefing presents one such challenge to the cultural models of FPS games (153).

This chapter presents the results of a qualitative study of griefers. Though the researchers conducted interviews, this study is not necessarily ethnographic but rather an extended analysis of discourse. We posit griefing as a discursive practice—a way to interact within and between social worlds through symbols and symbolic action. Instead of limiting our examination to one instance through one method, we have examined several instances through several methods.

Our primary method is rhetorical criticism, through which we work toward a theory of griefing. And while our use of rhetorical criticism focuses on artifacts (forum posts, interviews, and videos), we agree with Sonja Foss's (1989) assertion that the work of rhetorical criticism "moves beyond the particularities of the artifact under study in an effort to discover what that artifact suggests about symbolic processes in general" (6). By focusing on griefing texts, we hope to develop a theory of griefers' rhetorical tactics—the ways in which players move through and respond to the value and reward systems of the FPS. Given the post-structural bent of our theoretical lens, we are less interested in divining griefers' motivations (which, given the doubtless variety and emphases, would ultimately prove impossible and likely uninteresting) than we are in identifying the larger ideological and rhetorical situations to which they respond.

In developing this rhetorical approach to griefing, we began by reading griefing discussion threads in the Something Awful forums, a site long associated with the practice of griefing (Bakioglu 2009; Dibbell 2008). We analyzed those forum posts—recording griefing narratives and collecting links to *YouTube* videos—studying the way that griefers discuss their practices in the context of an "in-group." We then contacted FPS griefers who regularly contributed to the discussion, working from the premise that regular posters would have specific understandings of and insights into griefing. We conducted interviews with willing participants, paying particular attention to the ways they articulate and understand their own actions, and we've used those interview transcripts to supply context to the act of griefing (as a text) itself. While the griefing stories we heard from our participants provide an important element in our analysis, as rhetoric is always already contingent, we found watching videos particularly productive for understanding how griefing operates in context. In our study of these artifacts, we saw three major patterns: griefing as a challenge to genre, griefing as performance, and griefing as a disruption of the win-focus. We use these patterns to develop a theory of the rhetorical tactic.

In what follows, we describe how the disciplinary language of rhetoric serves as a frame for our analysis of griefing. We then discuss how our research supports, extends, and challenges the existing literature on griefing, most of which has not necessarily accounted for the potentially generative aspects of griefing. After that, we propose an alternative framework for understanding griefing as a rhetorical tactic, a term we adapt from Michel de Certeau's *The Practice of Everyday Life*. Finally, we present the data that convinced us to reposition griefing as rhetorical and productive. Griefing, we argue, exploits genre knowledge and game mechanics in order to parody privileged modes of play and disrupt or shift the end goal of the game.

The Rhetoric of Griefing, the FPS, and Ideology

To examine how griefing parodies privileged modes of play, we must first define how those modes are privileged. To do so, we rely on James Berlin (2002), who situates rhetoric within ideology, as a function of ideology. That is, rather than the global notion of rhetoric arbitrating competing ideological claims, rhetoric is "always already ideological. This position means that any examination of a rhetoric must first consider the ways its very discursive nature can be read so as to favor one version of economic, social, and political arrangements over other versions" (54). In short, examining griefing as a rhetorical practice assumes that rhetoric—discourse in the service and deployment of power—is always already ideological.

Berlin, in connecting rhetoric to ideology, relies heavily on Goran Therborn's (1980) formulation, which sees ideology not as false consciousness (in that it assumes one can stand outside of ideology), but as a more constitutive and interpellating influence. According to Therborn, "Ideologies subject and qualify subjects by telling them, relating them to, and making them recognize: 1. *what exists*... 2. *what is good*... 3. *what is possible* and impossible" (18). In so doing, ideologies argue for a certain sense of the world through and by symbolic action.

A cursory examination of the ways in which first-person shooters "qualify subjects" reveals several ideological characteristics. For example, opposition and tribalism are hardwired into the game. Players can only be in the gameworld as members of teams that are defined primarily (in some games, solely) through their opposition to other teams. As James Manning observes in this volume, the playing pieces (characters) in the game are distinct from the gamespace they inhabit, distinct from each other in terms of their rules and frequently (as in the case of *Team Fortress 2* [Valve 2007]) the differences manifest in color palettes and aesthetic cues.

Features such as headquarters, drop zones, extraction points, and map layouts have less to do with any sort of objective verisimilitude and more to do with how they figure into team play. The world itself is ostensibly three-dimensional, though there are boundaries that are (usually) tacitly understood by its participants. Other features depicted in the world (such as the sky, certain doors, or banal items on a table such as paper or coffee cups) are decorative—that is, they signify only that players are part of a realistic larger world; they cannot be interacted with because they serve no function in the larger tasks of the game (which revolve around killing other players' avatars). Clearly defined roles within the teams also exist, typically as kits or skill sets. These roles are not simply socially understood but rather have a constitutive effect on the player's experience of and interaction with the gameworld. For example, a player choosing a sniper kit (as opposed to demolitions or assault) will experience the game in a very different way than a counterpart with a different kit might, regardless of social expectations.

What exists, then, tacitly endorses and argues for, in Therborn's terms, "what is good." In the case of the FPS, the objective is winning a given scenario; thus, what is good is whatever happens to further that objective. This may consist of the most basic task of the game (defeating the other team), but can also manifest in other features: gaining points, accomplishments, reputation, etc. Further, enacting one's role for the good of the team while at the same time pursuing individual concerns is also rewarded through these built-in features of the genre, as individual pursuits and accomplishments often yield boosts and equipment upgrades. In short, *doing*—that is, working toward a goal, whether it be victory in a particular scenario or longer-term individual advancement—rather than *being*, is the normative approach to play in the implied world of the standard FPS. In this respect, it shares many of the key configurations of militaristic ideologies in that it emphasizes pre-configured struggle, specialized roles, accrual, and accomplishment—above all, winning.

Finally, analyzing what is possible and impossible in the ideology(-ies) inherent in the gameplay experience of the FPS is particularly important because, as (in another context) James Berlin points out, "recognition of the existence of a condition ... and the desire for its change will go for nothing if ideology indicates that a change is simply not possible" (56). In this sense, the practice of griefing is particularly potent as a rhetorical tactic; by transgressing the assumed rules and roles of the game through such means as challenging map boundaries, the very notion of team play, established objectives and more, griefers highlight the ways in which subjects in this genre are qualified.

In this respect, we also analyze FPSs as a rhetorical *genre*. Rhetoricians have pushed genre beyond traditional definitions as a constellation of features and conventions—or, worse, a rigid form to be followed—to recognize genre as "typified rhetorical ways communicants come to recognize and act in all kinds of situations" (Bawarshi 2000, 335). In this view, genres are not simply texts, but what is *done* with those texts. Genre, like ideology, has a constitutive function in that it enables, privileges, or precludes discursive realities. From a rhetorical perspective, then, the genre of first-person shooters is marked by more than just its visual, story, and gameplay conventions; it is marked by typical ways of playing and tacit assumptions about how the game should be played. In discussing griefing practices, we use the term *genre knowledge* to refer to an often tacit and embedded knowledge of both formal conventions (rules, gameplay mechanics, game modes, etc.) and the social action enabled and reinscribed by those conventions.

Griefing and Ideology in Game Studies

While our work suggests that griefing might open a space for rethinking the work of ideology in the FPS, game studies scholars have already identified masculinity and militarism as two particularly pervasive ideologies in the FPS. For example, even in this volume alone, Gerald Voorhees discusses the normalization of FPS play through its increasing militarization, and Aaron Duncan and Jessy Ohl further explore the problems of feminized performances of hegemonic masculinity in trying to thwart patriarchy.

Andrew Kurtz (2002) uses an Althusserian lens to analyze interpellation and ideology in FPSs. Kurtz points to ideologies of masculinity and violence, but also to the "domination of uncharted space" (117). Importantly, he also calls attention to the ways videogames function differently from other media, which are, he argues, "filtered through larger discursive structures such as humanism, democracy, and globalization" (107). FPSs, Kurtz argues, lack these filters, and as such provide a more "unfiltered" version of these ideologies: they are "degree zero ideology" (108). In FPSs, masculinity and militarism are difficult, bordering on virtually impossible, to separate.

Similarly, analyzing chat logs from *Quake Online*, Natasha Chen Christensen (2006) found that the game reinforced masculine gender roles as embodied in aggression, violence, misogyny, and homophobia. Of particular interest is her claim that players

exaggerated wins and justified losses, further reinforcing the importance of victory in the ideological structure of the FPS. Terri Toles
(1985), however, in her study of 100 contemporary games, found
a prevalence of militaristic themes and ideologies. Toles suggests
that violence is not, in fact, the primary motivator in war games, but
rather obedience: Players are taught to obey, much as they would be
in a military situation.

Most such studies evoke either discussions of "militainment"
or the "military-entertainment complex" and/or arguments over the
causal connections between videogame violence and real-world
violence. For instance, drawing on Said's concept of Orientalism
and Lenoir's formulation of the military-entertainment complex,
Johan Hoglund (2008) argues that players of first-person shooters
are "enlisted" (read: interpellated) both through marketing strategies and the semiotics of the gameworld into subject positions
as willing soldiers. Similarly, engaging in the long-standing debate
over videogame violence, Karen Hall (2006) observes that FPSs "are
produced by and work to support a highly militaristic imperial culture"
(ABSTRACT).

One of our primary arguments is that griefing opens a space for
resisting ideologies of masculinity and militarism. Particularly, by
challenging the assumptions of the gameworld—the primacy of the
win, the value of teamwork and cooperation, and the utilitarianism
of in-game communication—griefers begin to call into question
ideological structures. We should note that, particularly when it
comes to masculine ideology, resistance can reinforce hegemony;
resistance to an entrenched ideology is often a distinctly masculine
move that simply reinscribes power. Still, we see a strong connection
between the ideological structures of the FPS and griefing, and,
through this connection, hope to extend existing studies of griefing
within the field of game studies. In particular, we would like to shift
the conversation beyond the perspective of the griefed, asking what
griefing accomplishes, exploring the situations in which griefing
arises, and examining the larger ideological frameworks to which
it—intentionally or not (or directly or not)—responds.

To examine exactly what constitutes griefing, or how such activity
might disrupt ideological frameworks, we first turn to existing
definitions of griefing. Mulligan and Patrovsky (2003), for example,

describe a griefer as "a player who derives his/her enjoyment not from playing the game, but from performing actions that detract from the enjoyment of the game by other players" (299). Foo and Koivisto (2004) point out that key to this definition is that the "act is intentional, it causes others to enjoy the game less, [and] the griefer enjoys the act" (246). This explication of the act of griefing points to the purposeful component of rhetorical action. Intentionality (the question of "why?"), however, is difficult to assess; as Foo and Koivisto, as well as Lin and Sun (2005), point out, what other players perceive as grief play may not be intentional at all; it may result from "greed play" (249), from inability, or from a lack of awareness of the conventions and expectations of the game (Lin and Sun 2005).

One of the easier assumptions to make about griefing is that it somehow grants the griefer an in-game advantage or is tied to cheating. Mia Consalvo (2007), for example, describes the often fine and implicit distinctions between cheating and other sorts of play. She discusses a category of players who define cheating only in relation to other players—that is, "cheating is necessarily social (or anti-social) … Cheating means the introduction of deception and possible chaos into the game world" (93). For these players, one does not cheat "the game" itself, but instead other players' game experiences or even the social order of the gameworld.

Cheating and griefing, however, are not coterminous. Our respondents consistently defined their actions in opposition to cheating. Several defined cheating in terms of the code: glitching and hacking are cheating, but anything that the hard code of the game allows is acceptable. One respondent claimed that griefing is not cheating, "unless you're actively circumventing rules to do so. Most of the time it's just either playing badly on purpose or using a method of play that is known to make other players mad." If it's in the game, this view suggests, why not use it? Nor do griefers necessarily gain an advantage from their actions; many of our respondents typically lost matches while griefing or sabotaged their own individual statistics for the sake of the grief.

To many, griefing and bullying are synonymous. This is by far the most predominant theme that emerges in the literature, and it covers many different styles of griefing and theoretical perspectives. Foo and Koivisto categorize this perspective as "harassment," the purpose of which is "to cause emotional distress to the victim. Aside from the enjoyment of seeing the victim suffer, the griefer does not benefit from the action otherwise" (248). So, while purposeful, the act of griefing does not necessarily grant any sort of advantage. Instead, it is a social practice seeking to induce some form of social action or response. While some griefers' actions could be characterized as bullying, this is only one small subsection of griefers.

Among gaming studies literature, Burcu Bakioglu's (2009) article "Spectacular Interventions in Second Life: Goon Culture, Griefing, and Disruption in Personal Spaces" is most pertinent to this research. Bakioglu distinguishes grief play (which he describes as a type of gameplay) from griefing (which he defines as a disruptive cultural activity). Similar to our work, Bakioglu uses a lens lent by Michel de Certeau to examine how griefers engage in this subversive practice. Bakioglu's work, however, is more informed by cultural studies approaches and focuses on griefing in *Second Life*. For Bakioglu, griefing is an organized and explicit cultural practice. Many of our respondents affirm that they participated at least peripherally in griefing culture, but griefing is a tactic that does not necessarily occur in an organized manner.

Griefing as a Rhetorical Tactic

We draw our primary theoretical framework from French theorist Michel de Certeau (1984), whose book, *The Practice of Everyday Life*, was one of the first and most prominent attempts to shift cultural studies away from studying cultural artifacts and toward studying "the use to which they are put by groups or individuals" (xii). Consumers of culture, de Certeau asserts, are not simply passive; rather, they make and do things with the products of the culture. In doing so, de Certeau redescribes passive consumers as "users" whose everyday acts of creativity are generative and productive, not of new cultural products but of new ways of acting and doing things with those cultural products. De Certeau characterizes creative user action as hidden but still organized by an internal logic, "a logic of the operation of actions relative to types of situations" (21). Griefing, seen in this light, serves as a form of creative user action.

De Certeau also distinguishes between strategies, or those forces employed when "a subject with will and power (a business, an army, a city, a scientific institution) can be isolated," and tactics, or those forces which work to disrupt those power systems (35–6). Strategies set the terms of engagement and establish their own spaces whereas tactics must work within the constraints of those terms of engagement and operate on and with the terrains established by strategies. Strategies "produce, tabulate, and impose," while tactics "use, manipulate, and divert" (30). Tactics are fragmentary, situational, and contingent. Tactics are simultaneously uses *of* a system and operations performed *on* that system. Perhaps most strikingly, tactics are unexpected; de Certeau eloquently calls a tactic "a guileful ruse" (37).

Throughout the remainder of the chapter, we read griefing as a tactic that responds to the strategy of the gameworld as determined by the game developers and traditional forms of usage. Griefing is a creative player action that, as de Certeau says of tactics, traces "the ruses of other interests and desires that are neither determined nor captured by the systems in which they develop" (xviii). We borrow the term creative player actions from Wright, Boria, and Breidenbach (2002) because it echoes de Certeau's creative user actions. Many of the griefing tactics we recount later, though, parallel their observations about playing with game rules and popular culture references.

In order to posit an alternative system of goals, griefers must always be on the lookout for strategies and possible tactics. They are attuned to the structure of a gameworld and its implied goals, even if they cannot articulate that knowledge. As de Certeau writes, "because it does not have a place, a tactic depends on time—it is always on the watch for opportunities that must be seized 'on the wing.' ... It must constantly manipulate events in order to turn them into 'opportunities'" (xix). Griefers' continual awareness—of the game's constraints, of genre knowledge, and of the community—implies that griefing is a way of *being* in the game that extends beyond playing the game; it is an approach to the concept of play itself.

Genre, Griefing, and Performance

FPSs constitute a genre, both in the traditional literary sense of a group of artifacts with common qualities and in the rhetorical sense. For example, one could look at specific mechanics of the first-person shooter—the player's perspective, HUDs, mini-maps, Deathmatch, objective-driven gameplay, weapon upgrades—as key identifiers of the genre or aspects that differentiate an FPS from a role-playing game (hereafter RPG) or platformer. From a rhetorical perspective, which considers the recurring systems and networks that are at work in the production and consumption of artifacts, the genre of first-person shooters also includes the social organization of players (e.g. through voice chat), standard forms of play, and assumptions about the game and gameplay.

In watching videos and reading accounts of griefing, we've noticed that the exploitation of genre knowledge—and often the *assumptions* of that knowledge—constitute a primary griefing tactic. For example, a seasoned FPS gamer knows that the map has specific boundaries designed to drive players into designated areas and generate specific types of battle zones and actions. These boundaries are often disguised as minefields or oceans, areas fatal to the player's avatar (in a game based on fatality/mortality). By pretending to be unaware of these boundaries (often to the detriment of their teammates), griefers make obvious how tacitly and unreflexively these boundaries are frequently accepted. In other words, by publicly challenging these boundaries, griefers confront their audience with questions of "what exists?" and "what is possible?"

For example, one *YouTube* griefer known as the Lollipop Prince regularly exploits these genre conventions and assumptions in his gameplay. In "Lollipop Prince's 1st game of Left4Dead2," the griefer begins the match by walking away from the gameplay area and promptly jumping into the body of water at the map's edge. Before the Lollipop Prince jumps into the water, he announces "Okay, this is my first time playing this game." And then, after his character has died and his team is hindered, a teammate quickly admonishes him, calling him stupid, assuming that a player participating in online play should understand the game's conventions. The Lollipop Prince replies that the game is brand new; no one has played it before, so how should he know that he can't swim? In this case, the griefer plays against the genre assumptions at work in the FPS, exploiting and challenging a knowledge base shared by many players. In doing so, he makes what is normally tacit and embedded knowledge—the knowledge that one simply cannot jump into the water and expect to live—explicit and available for commentary and critique. Boundary griefs like this are not entirely unique to FPSs, but they are particularly present, since map boundaries are a major component of the genre.

Viewed rhetorically, genre conventions—and the resistance to them—represent a complex system of interactions between players and developers. From one angle, these genre conventions allow for the development of franchises like *Call of Duty* or *Halo*, game series with frequent updates and incremental changes in gameplay. While each new update might present a new set of weapons or multiplayer variation, the core game mechanics remain intact. These conventions, however, also offer griefers a means of disrupting gameplay. One griefer, for example, told us that the recurring mechanics of the FPS facilitate griefing: "The thing about shooters is that a lot of developers stick with the same rules. No matter what game or franchise or studio, there will always be that basic set of rules," and "whenever a new shooter is about to come out, I already know the basic rules it is going to have." While the rules are often similar, the *roles* that players assume, including their patterns of behavior, are also highly rigid in FPSs. This common base across games allows griefers to predict how players will react in a given circumstance, and it also facilitates locating *differences* in gameplay and mechanics that will allow for griefing.

Even if a griefer knows a genre particularly well, though, successful griefs often include an element of opportunity, a moment in which an opening occurs where a particular tactic would be most effective. Most of our participants said that they discovered the majority of griefs by experimentation, finding them through the observation that a certain mechanic or pattern of behavior could be manipulated in a certain way. It is often a confluence of events that enabled the moment of griefing. For instance, one griefer related a grief he discovered in *Call of Duty: Black Ops* (Treyarch 2010). After noticing that teammates blinded by a flash bang grenade tended to hug walls or stay in a corner, he began to deliberately flash bang his teammates, then block them in a corner by standing in front of them, forcing them to kill him (and thus receive a teamkill penalty). This combination of factors includes several game mechanics (flash bangs that blind teammates, the inability to move from a corner when blocked in by another player, teamkills), a discernible pattern of behavior (blinded players move to corners), and a social system supported by mechanics (teamkills are punished).

Griefs such as this are spurred on by the genre conventions of the FPS, using genre conventions to disrupt those very conventions. Often, griefers are clearly aware of the conventions, but they are also purposefully ignorant (e.g. the Lollipop Prince) or willfully dismissive of them (e.g. rejecting the unwritten rule that you do not flash bang your own team). This willful ignorance or dismissal requires griefers to take on a particular persona, as well. In the case of the Lollipop Prince, his persona is the driving force of the grief; he adopts the persona of an annoying twelve-year-old boy and stays in that persona, even in interviews with his fan club. From a rhetorical perspective, this kind of symbolic action is clearly a performance for an audience, even if the audience isn't aware of the performance or does not appreciate it as such. In so doing, because they redefine the power relationships in play (between players, between players and developers), griefers perform the potentiality inherent in imagining the ideological question "what is possible?" in new ways.

Styles of Play: The Rules and Roles of Gaming

These performances can also be viewed as different styles of play, and this consideration is particularly important in the genre of the FPS, in which the constraints of the gameworld are especially rigid. The title of our chapter points to a tension between the social and technological constraints of the gameworld, and we see player roles as determined by both factors: players are forced to choose character classes and specializations by the game, but are also slotted into roles by the social dynamics of collaborative activity. Rules, too, are social and technological, with both hard-coded rules and player-imposed rules shaping the gameworld.

Griefers, then, are engaged in both role-play and rule-play. Griefers, particularly in FPSs, often exploit the constraints of heavily determined role systems to sabotage their own teams and/or disrupt traditional team dynamics. Griefing is even more clearly a form of rule-play: griefers will exploit bugs and other technological rules that the social world of the game should not allow; they will feign ignorance of social and technological game rules; they will exploit the rules of the gameworld to disrupt other players' activities; they will even posit alternative rules that call attention to the often tacit rule-based structure of the game world. The rigid constraints of FPSs are productive in this sense; they are "a body of constraints stimulating new discoveries, a set of rules with which improvisation plays" (de Certeau 1984, xxii).

The griefers we talked to all pointed to playing with rules—while still following them—as a characteristic of griefing. "I take pride in griefing," one of our respondents said, "by following the rules and abusing them." By adopting different styles of play, griefers often work to parody privileged or standard styles of play. For instance, in one *YouTube* video, a griefer drops into a game of Search and Destroy in *Black Ops* (Treyarch 2010). He begins by looking directly at a door that is very clearly decorative—an inconsequential part of the environment—and saying "All right, team, we need to blow this door up. I need one of you to find the detonator." He is immediately greeted with a response similar to that received by the Lollipop Prince: "Are you high?" He continues, placing significance and meaning on random objects in the environment (such as a hand truck) that other players clearly *know* have no importance in the gameworld. The griefer in this example posits an entirely different set of rules and objectives for the *Black Ops* (Treyarch 2010) Search and Destroy mode, and his grief serves as a parody of the traditional style of play in Search and Destroy. By assigning significance to otherwise insignificant objects, he confronts other players with the seemingly arbitrary nature of signification in the traditional style of play—what exists in the gameworld.

Griefing, then, offers a different perspective on the game; griefers look at the (game)world aslant. Anything that is different is enough to be at least the kernel of a grief. Take these quotes from our participants:

"[There's] something about using game mechanics the way developers didn't intend."

"I love finding new ways to play games."

"When I start getting bored of a game or it starts getting too easy [...] I start looking for non-standard ways of play to keep it interesting."

Boredom with a game was one of the most common exigencies for griefing we found; nearly all of our participants mentioned griefing once they got bored with playing a game the "traditional" way.

What do these "non-standard" or "new" styles of play look like? While almost any grief could be read as a non-standard style of play, we turn here to a particular style of play that is prominent in FPSs and helps illustrate our point. Some griefers serve as entertainers, both for themselves and for other players in the game. The Lollipop Prince video discussed above is an example of this style of play: the Lollipop Prince's running commentary serves as a form of entertainment for players in the game. Even if the griefer is completely useless otherwise, the entertainment he/she offers is enough to justify his/her place on the team. The Lollipop Prince's fan club is evidence of the popularity of this style of play, as is the number of hits (currently over 100,000) for his videos.

This style of play is particularly interesting for the schism it creates between different audiences. Some targets of this style of griefing find it amusing; as one of our participants said, "You get a lot of people who are immediately in on the joke." But others are infuriated by it; this is particularly true if they feel left out of the joke. For instance, one of our respondents related the story of using sound clips from the television show *Ren and Stimpy* through the game's chat system. The targets, usually younger players who did not have the cultural knowledge to understand where the clips were from, became angrier and angrier, which only served to up the entertainment value for the other targets. This griefer called his tactic "a survival thing," because if some of the targets are "in on the joke" and support the griefer, they are far less likely to band together to work around the griefing or kick the griefer from the game.

This particular style, which revolves around balancing entertainment with annoyance, is one of many different styles. When we look closely, these styles of play are akin to what de Certeau calls "tactics": they are patterns of use that go against the grain of the artifact and traditional modes of consumption and the ideologies that inform and underwrite the genre. De Certeau emphasizes the fact that the producers of cultural artifacts cannot control what users do with those artifacts. We found that all of our participants responded to this notion. "There are things developers can control the outcome with," one griefer told us, "but they can't control how a player is going to play their game." Another referred to his practices as "definitely not an intended use in the game." In the Team Roomba video, one of the griefers can be heard saying: "If developers didn't want players to do it, why would they put it in the game?" While there is something of an intentional fallacy in statements like this, they highlight the fact that griefing serves as a tactic that is a direct response to the strategy of the developers. In this light, actions like those described above are a productive response to a game universe with strict and implicit directions about the nature, progression, and types of gameplay.

Disrupting the End Goal: Victory in First-Person Shooters

A key component of griefing in FPSs is the win-focused nature of online play in the genre. Since *DOOM* (id Software 1993), Deathmatch has been the defining mode of online FPS gameplay, pitting players against each other, tallying points based on kills, and awarding wins and losses. In most contemporary shooters, Deathmatch variants simply add some sort of strategic structure to the Deathmatch model—Capture the Flag, King of the Hill, Search and Destroy—but still reward players based on a win or loss outcome. And more recent additions to the genre, like the RPG-esque leveling structure found in *Call of Duty*, only reinforce the importance of the win to the acquisition of weapons, perks, and player ethos. This all fuels what Joe Bisz (2009) sees as the problem with competition-heavy gameplay: "The win, like a test score, is a difficult-to-reject assessment of self-worth" (4.4). In shooters, the strategy of the win influences endless facets of player perception—for example, the measurement of

gameplay skill through statistics like accuracy and kill:death ratios—
and enforces a singular form of gameplay.

Griefing offers a means of disrupting the competitive win-focus,
of challenging a game's prescribed outcome. If the FPS presents
a win/loss dichotomy, privileging a win as the ideal scenario, the
griefer plays within a different paradigm—disrupting the win and
valuing the loss, or, perhaps, disregarding the entirety of the win/
loss structure. "The best griefs are always when you don't care about
winning," one griefer told us, adding that "I actually lose when I'm
doing it." Many griefs focus on teamkilling, a play style that functions
in opposition to the win. One griefer told us of how, in *Left 4 Dead
2* (Turtle Rock Studios and Valve 2008), he trapped his teammates in
the safe room (the room which all players must enter before the level
will successfully end) until a friend on the other team became The
Tank (a powerful enemy). He then allowed The Tank player to enter
the safe room and attack the griefer's teammates, while the griefer
quickly closed the safe room door whenever a teammate tried to run
away. In this scenario, the griefer only challenged the *outcome* of the
game; the team had traveled from the game's start point to its end
point, but the griefer disrupted the concluding tone—scheming and
valuing the loss.

Within win-disruption, it's important to note that griefing isn't
necessarily nihilistic or anarchistic; many griefers talked to us about
the difference between "good griefs" and "bad griefs." "A good
grief," one griefer said, "ends with results," while a bad grief is
one that results in the griefer being kicked from the game "before
seeing how you were able to affect the outcome or even getting
to hear a reaction from the other players after you were kicked."
Since a grief is a move to somehow shift the game's outcome, a
griefer must know the boundaries of the win-focus (specifically, the
actions—like excessive teamkilling—that will result in the griefer's
removal from the game server) and work within those confines.
Players unconcerned with the game's outcome would simply disrupt
until they were removed from the game, but this is what our participants referred to as a "bad grief." A "good grief" works toward an
outcome—griefers want to see how the grief changes the game
world. In this way, griefers don't simply eliminate the game's end
goal; instead, they shift the game's focus to a different goal.

There are countless ways in which that end goal might be shifted. One group of *Call of Duty* griefers described a style of play—what they call "Hush"—in which each member of the team equips a Sniper class (so they visually blend in with the scenery) and a radar jammer (so they aren't visible to the enemy), finds a grassy corner of the map, and lays prone for as long as possible. If the enemy discovers the group, they find a new corner and repeat the process, attempting to end the round with the lowest score possible. This type of gameplay uses specific FPS conventions—in this case, tools that allow a sniper to operate with a minimum level of detection —to generate a new style of play. Here, the work of the griefer is productive: it offers new ways of being in the game, it presents new goals that are in tension with the game's pre-defined goals, and it uses genre conventions to resist the genre. Hush gameplay also completely dismisses the win-focus and scoring conventions by not allowing either team to win, working toward an ideal score of zero. In short, it seeks to address and reevaluate the ideological assumptions in the game that posit what is good.

Another griefer told us how some of his griefs hinge on using the teamkill punishment system to remove other players from the game, splintering the team and working against the prescribed objective. He spoke of an elaborate *Battlefield 2* (DICE 2005) grief in which he would have teammates board a Black Hawk helicopter. He would then crash that helicopter onto an aircraft carrier, bailing out at the last minute. By bailing out, he did not receive any teamkills; rather, those teamkills passed to the second person to enter the helicopter. The griefer used the game's punishment system to generate a new outcome, one in which his teammates were slowly removed from the game—but he remained. While the griefers we spoke to all had different approaches, each had a serious interest in seeing the realization of their grief and the game's conclusion, particularly if that conclusion was something other than the developer-prescribed outcome. In so doing, they can observe the effects of confronting other players with the question, "what is possible?"—or perhaps rather, "what did we previously consider possible?"—in that gameworld.

Conclusion

When we began this project, we were surprised by the amount of scholarship that seemed to focus on the question of "Why would a player engage in griefing practices?" rather than considering what griefing practices might accomplish. Between those two questions, however, we see the blurry boundaries of motivation and entertainment. We've conceptualized griefing as a rhetorical tactic, as a means of challenging FPS conventions and maneuvering within rather rigid developer-driven strategies and rule systems. And we believe that griefers, regardless of motivation, are working within larger power systems and discursive structures, rejecting game guidelines and norms.

Still, we're struck by the importance griefers seem to place on their own amusement and gameplay experience. All of our participants spoke to the importance of humor, a position succinctly summarized by one griefer who said "It's hard to explain, but I get a sense of joy when I ruin someone's gaming experience." Another stated that "a high quality grief" is one "you laugh about." Herein lies the difficulty of griefing as an area for academic inquiry. It's easy to argue that griefers are simply game hedonists who change rules and social conventions to best match their own sense of amusement. But such a perspective, we'd argue, is that of the *griefed*, of the individual whose game experience is disrupted. Focusing on the *griefer*, however, allows us to consider the complicated relationship of the strategy and tactic, of highly prescribed gameworlds that are coded for a very specific set of outcomes. And while FPS griefing might indeed attract gaming sadists—two of our participants directly spoke of griefing's "schadenfreude" appeal—the practices of those griefers say much about the value and reward systems at work in the FPS. To confuse the two, the griefer's motivation and the griefing practice, is to misunderstand a powerful and tacit set of strategies at work in the contemporary FPS.

References

Bakioglu, Burcu S. 2009. "Spectacular Interventions of *Second Life*: Goon Culture, Griefing, and Disruption in Virtual Spaces." *Journal of Virtual Worlds Research* 1 (3): 1–21.

Bawarshi, Anis. 2000. "The Genre Function." *College English* 62 (3): 335–60.

Berlin, James. 2002. "Rhetoric and ideology in the Writing Classroom." In *Teaching Composition: Background Readings*, edited by T. R. Johnson and S. Morahan, 53–72. Boston: Bedford/St. Martin.

Bisz, Joe. 2009. The Birth of a Community, the Death of a Win: Player Production in the *Middle-earth Collectible Card Game. Transformative Works and Cultures* 2. http://journal.transformativeworks.org/index.php/twc/article/view/90

"Black Ops Griefing – How to Play Search and Destroy Part 1." 2010. *YouTube*. December 1. http://www.youtube.com/watch?v=zeOL2SVZNeo

Christensen, Natasha Chen. 2006. "Geeks at Play: Doing masculinity in an Online Gaming Site." *Reconstruction: Studies in Contemporary Culture* 6.1. http://reconstruction.eserver.org/061/christensen.shtml

Consalvo, Mia. 2007. *Cheating: Gaining Advantage in Video Games.* Cambridge: MIT Press.

De Certeau, Michel. 1984. *The Practice of Everyday Life.* Berkeley: University of California Press.

Dibbell, Julain. 2008. "Mutilated Furries, Flying Phalluses: Put the Blame on Griefers, the Sociopaths of the Virtual World." *Wired* 16 (02).

Foo, Chek Yang and Elina M. I. Koivisto. 2004. "Defining Grief Play in MMORPGs." *Proceedings of the 2004 ACM SIGCHI International Conference on Advances in Computer Entertainment Technology.* 245–50.

Foss, Sonja K. 1989. *Rhetorical Criticism: Exploration & Practice.* Prospect Heights, IL: Waveland Press.

Gee, James Paul. 2007. *What Video Games Have to Teach us about Learning and Literacy.* New York: Palgrave Macmillan.

Hall, Karen J. 2006. "Shooters to the Left of Us, Shooters to the Right: First Person Arcade Shooter Video Games, the Violence Debate, and the Legacy of Militarism." *Reconstruction: Studies in Contemporary Culture* 6 (1). http://reconstruction.eserver.org/061/hall.shtml

Hoglund, Johan. 2008. "Electronic Empire: Orientalism Revisited in the Military Shooter." *Game Studies* 8 (1). http://gamestudies.org/0801/articles/hoglund

Kurtz, Andrew. 2002. "Ideology and Interpellation in the First-person Shooter." In *Growing Up Postmodern: Neoliberalism and the War on the Young*, edited by Roland Strickland, 107–22. Lanham, MD: Rowman and Littlefield Publishers.

Lin, Holin and Chuen Tsai Sun. 2005. "The 'White-Eyed' Player Culture: Grief Play and Construction of Deviance in MMORPGs." *Proceedings of DiGRA 2005 Conference*, 1–12.

"Lollipop Prince's 1st game of Left4Dead2." 2009. *YouTube*. November 4. http://www.youtube.com/watch?v=hUtoaGIMDJ0

Mulligan, Jessica and Bridgette Patrovsky. 2003. *Developing Online Games: An Insider's Guide*. Indianapolis, IN: New Riders Publishing.

Sanford, Kathy and Leanna Madill. 2006. "Resistance Through Video Game Play: It's a Boy Thing." *Canadian Journal of Education* 29 (1): 287–306.

"TEAM ROOMBA PRESENTS: More Team Fortress 2 Griefing." 2001. *You Tube*. December 21. http://www.youtube.com/watch?v=JUPzN7tp7bQ

Therborn, Goran. 1980. *The Ideology of Power and the Power of Ideology*. London: Verso.

Toles, Terri. 1985. "Video Games and Military Ideology." *ARENA Review* 9 (1): 58–76.

Wright, Talmadge, Eric Boria, and Paul Breidenbach. 2002. "Creative Player Actions in FPS Online Video Games: Playing Counter-Strike." *Game Studies* 2 (2): http://www.gamestudies.org/0202/wright/

Games

Digital Illusions CE (DICE). 2005. *Battlefield 2* [Microsoft Windows]. EA Games.

id Software. 1993. *DOOM* [DOS]. id Software.

Treyarch. 2010. *Call of Duty: Black Ops* [Xbox 360, PlayStation 3, Microsoft Windows, Wii]. Activision.

Turtle Rock Studios and Valve. 2009. *Left 4 Dead 2* [MAC OS X, Microsoft Windows, Xbox 360]. Valve.

Valve. 2007. *Team Fortress 2* [Microsoft Windows, PlayStation 3, Xbox 360]. Valve.

13

The Best Possible Story? Learning about WWII from FPS Videogames

Stephanie Fisher

As artifacts of youth and popular culture, history-themed video games are likely resources used by today's students to construct interpretations of past events. A diverse body of literature that examines commercial history-themed videogames continues to grow each year (Baron 2010; Crogan 2003; Gish 2010; Kingsepp 2006; Squire 2004; Schut 2007; Schott 2008; Uricchio 2005), but for the most part these works are textual analyses that examine how the interactive nature of the medium can communicate history in ways that differ from older media such as text and/or film. They also provide players with an unprecedented opportunity to "replay" or actively immersive themselves in history. While this research offers valuable insight on these topics, it does not specifically address what players might learn by engaging in historically themed gameplay.

This chapter addresses the gap within the small niche of history-themed game-based learning that overlooks the educative potentials of the FPS genre thus far. I begin with a review of the literature to provide context for readers who are not familiar with this field of research. Then, following Kee's (2008) "history games and learning" framework, I demonstrate how World War II (hereafter WWII) FPS games make use of a "best possible story" (hereafter BPS) epistemology for engaging with history. In the last section, I discuss how a player-centered analytical framework that not only considers the game, but also the players and context, can demonstrate the different way in which players understand and make use of WWII FPS learning history.

Learning History Through Play

Over the past decade, digital games have garnered global recognition for their current and potential relevance in equipping the current generation of students with "21st century skills" (Ananiadoui and Claro 2009), prompting educational jurisdictions and policymakers worldwide to pay serious attention to the affordances of digital game-based learning (Jenson, Taylor, and Fisher 2010). In opposition to the direct transmission methods that dominate public schooling, videogames "teach" players how to play using an indirect instructional approach in which players develop skills that connect and manipulate information in the virtual space of digital gameworlds. Here learning is considered to be incidental, a by-product of the player's actions and interactions with rule structures, tasks, and activities in the gameworld as well as outside of the gameworld through competition, collaboration, and discussion with peers (de Castell and Jenson 2003; Prensky 2001). This chapter is concerned with the incidental "history education" that can occur while playing history-themed games, in particular WWII FPS games.

Examining the possibilities of digital games in regards to history education is a relatively small and unexplored area of research in comparison to the large body of scholarly work of each of these respective fields. An exception here is Squire (2004), who examined how players made use of the commercial game *Civilization III* to learn history in classroom and after-school club contexts. Generally, however, research that is specifically conducted to examine how players learn through historically themed gameplay does not usually use commercially available games. Rather, the focus of these studies is on the development of educational games from scratch. This work primarily examines how to best express history in virtual environments or design games that help players to develop historical inquiry skills (Kee et al. 2009; Neville and Shelton 2010; Schrier 2007). The educationally promising affordances of "process-oriented" games (e.g. simulation games) are of particular interest because the player's engagement with history is viewed as an authoring process, where their decisions have a direct impact on the in-game historical outcomes (Kee et al. 2009; Schrier 2007; Squire 2004; Uricchio 2005). The flexible, open-ended nature of these types of games affords multiple forms of play, allowing players to model complex historical relationships and "play out" history however they choose. This approach to "doing history" breaks away from heavily criticized, traditional notions of the discipline as being fixed in the past and unalterable or unchangeable. Because players can actively shape history, these researchers contend that process-oriented games are valuable educational tools.

In contrast to this excitement surrounding process-oriented games, the educational affordances of history-themed "narrative-oriented" games, such as WWII FPS games[1], receive far less scholarly attention. Within a narrative-oriented game, it is the storyline that bears the brunt of communicating history to the player, and "efforts are taken to maximize historical accuracy, allowing the settings, conditions and period details to constrain game play" (Uricchio 2005, 334). Similar to print or film-based media, history in these games is considered to be a closed event, primarily conveyed by the cinematics that frame and punctuate the interactive gameplay experience (Gish 2010). Opportunities to intervene or change the course of history are (nearly) non-existent and the player has no choice but to temporarily accept the historical narrative proposed if they want to progress.

This privileging of a historically authentic, realistic, fixed narrative over a player-authored (or learner-centered) historical experience parallels formal school-based history education (Loewen 1995;

Uricchio 2005; Wineberg 2000). School-based history education continues to replicate what Cohen (1988) refers to as an "old inheritance" notion of teaching where "teachers are active; they are tellers of truth who inculcate knowledge in students. Learners are relatively passive; students are accumulators of material who listen, read, and perform prescribed exercises. And knowledge is objective and stable" (10). This approach to teaching and learning history in the classroom is viewed as the source of numerous disciplinary issues, from students' inability to create meaningful historical interpretations to the marginalization of minority histories. Many scholars advocate for the abandonment of this instructional approach in favor of ones that are sensitive to the socio-cultural position of today's multicultural student, and facilitate the development of second-order history knowledge (Grant 2003; Levesque 2008; Loewen 1995; Seixas 2000; Wineberg 2000). That is, understanding the skills of historical practice such as generating, corroborating, representing, and assessing interpretations of the past.

In light of this negative portrayal of how history is taught and learned in schools, researchers' interest in using or developing process-oriented history-games for educational purposes is understandable, as some have already demonstrated how these games can help address these issues (Kee 2009; Squire 2004; Uricchio 2005). It may also explain why the educational value of more narrative-oriented genres, like history-themed FPS, continues to be overlooked despite their widespread popularity within the gaming culture.

FPS & BPS

The communication and representation of history in a videogame is constrained by the nature of the medium as well as by the demands and expectations of the gaming culture (Schut 2007; Uricchio 2005). Game developers are tasked with creating an immersive historical experience that adheres to the expected conventions of the genre, which can encourage particular historical interpretations (Schut 2007). As players interact with the representations and rule systems of a game, they come to understand the assumptions and values of a particular identity and develop what Shaffer (2005) refers to as an "epistemic frame." Shaffer argues: "participation in a community of practice involves developing that community's ways of doing, being, caring, and knowing, and that this … is organized by and around a way of thinking. That is, practice, identity, interest, understanding, and epistemology are bound together into an epistemic frame." This connection between epistemology and practice makes epistemic frames a potentially powerful tool for educational game designers.

Epistemic frames can guide designers in creating digital learning spaces where a player learns "how to be" in a particular community through their repeated performance of actions viewed as acceptable practice by members of that community. Learning how to "do" history in the real world through playing an epistemic game, for example, would have the player carry out historical inquiry in a manner that replicates the work of real historians. In lieu of a real historian or teacher, it is the game that acts as the "expert" community member and assesses the player's actions through feedback. In sum, an epistemic frame can be viewed as a mechanism through which players can use their game-based experiences to help them deal with related situations outside of this original context of learning. Because this chapter seeks to examine how *commercial* WWII FPS games can inform how a player might "do"/approach/perform/view the discipline of history when not playing the game, it follows that consideration should be paid to the built-in epistemic framing of history in these games.

WWII FPS games are primarily developed with profit in mind, not education, meaning that the epistemic frames of these games are not obligated to align themselves with the ones recommended or employed by historians or history educators. This is not to suggest that WWII FPS games *cannot* or *do not* share an educationally valuable epistemic frame due to their origins in entertainment; in fact, drawing on the work of historians, narratologists, and ludologists, historian and educator Kevin Kee (2008) shows how certain historical epistemologies can be mapped onto specific game genres due to similarities in mechanics and end goals.[2] By examining the narrative forms and rule systems of three popular digital game genres (action, adventure, simulation) and mapping them onto the goals of three historical epistemologies (best possible story, disciplinary, and post-modern/structuralist), Kee's (2008) framework demonstrates how each of these genres can communicate history.

As part of the "action" game genre, WWII FPS videogames are supposedly well suited to reflect and convey a BPS epistemology.[3] Frequently employed by schoolteachers and popular culture media, the purpose of a BPS epistemology is to use a single perspective, chronological narrative (usually of the evolution of a country) to provide a common understanding of the past for a unified social purpose (Kingsepp 2006; Levesque 2008; Loewen 1995; Morton 2006; Seixas 2000; Wineberg 2000). Because BPS is supportive of the "old inheritance" instructional model discussed in the previous section, it has been similarly criticized for presenting a very specific domain of historical content with which many cannot identify. It also excludes the historical accounts of minority groups in favor of the dominant one, namely the history of white, straight, upper-middle class males. Moreover, this epistemology is further criticized for presenting the learning of history as the exclusive memorization and regurgitation of facts that bolster this narrative, not second-order history knowledge (Levstik and Barton 2001; Seixas 2000; Stearns, Seixas, and Wineberg 2000).[4] In this context, undertaking historical inquiry that goes beyond or counters the presented narrative is not rewarded. This is because within a BPS epistemology, the narrative is specifically constructed to create a sense of unity among those who encounter it, and so it is not amenable to modification. Thus, a concern here is that learners who engage with history through a BPS epistemology may come to understand history as a discipline where the past can be "uncovered," communicated accurately, and agreed upon, not one where the past can be interpreted in multiple ways or studied from multiple perspectives through different lenses.

The framework connects action videogames to a BPS episte-mology through similarities in narrative and rules. Action games typically make use of a story structure marked by a clear and defined ending, often moving from a negative to a positive state, where the player spends the game trying to achieve goals outlined at the beginning of the narrative (Kee 2008). To complete an action game, players are expected to follow the predetermined narrative through to the end. Scholarly analyses of WWII FPS games appear to validate Kee's (2008) pairing of these games with a BPS historical epistemology. For example, historical narratives that are employed in these games follow a traditional linear sequence of events: each story node builds upon and references earlier story nodes and moves from a negative to a positive state with only one possible conclusion (Gish 2010). Here, history is presented as a straightforward sequence of events, with no competing interpretations or viewpoints. Each time one plays the game, the events unfold the same way, excluding player agency from the construction of the historical narrative (Baron 2010; Rejack 2007).

The interactive nature of the medium suggests that players of history-themed games can potentially change the course of in-game history; however, this is only to the degree that the game allows, and this differs between games and especially between genres (Uricchio 2005). WWII FPS games in general place players in a limited situation where they can react to events in the course of the war but have no direct control over the broader historical arc. Even in games like *Brothers in Arms* where the game features differ slightly from regular FPS norms,[5] players are unable to affect the historical outcomes of the game. Play in this sub-genre is highly constrained and players' decisions are often restricted to choosing between predetermined options that lead to the same result.

A player's movements through the game are also highly controlled—retreating, exploring, or searching for alternate ways around enemy lines is an unproductive activity and sometimes made impossible after passing a checkpoint. The only way to keep ammunition supplies well stocked the player is to defeat and loot enemy soldiers. This leaves the player with no choice but to continually advance forward and commit violent acts against enemy non-playable characters (hereafter NPCs) who stand in their way. In sum, players of WWII FPS games are limited to performing actions that support the progression of the historical narrative, which cannot be changed. The next section provides a more in-depth analysis of the history that is presented to players and the ways these games use a BPS epistemological perspective to communicate this history.

Allies v. Axis: The Biases of WWII FPS-BPS History

One oft-noted criticism of WWII FPS history is how it is a grossly biased historical narrative that privileges an Allied—particularly a Western/American—perspective of the conflict (Baron 2010; Gish 2010; Kingsepp 2006). Using the *Call of Duty* series as an example, Gish (2010) claims that within the campaign mode of play, WWII FPS games employ a "tripartite narrational [sic] layering of history," two of which are meant to provide context and give meaning to the players' actions within the game. The first layer is the "foundational narrative" of WWII in its totality, communicated primarily through cinematic trailers. The second layer is the "localized" narratives of specific events that are primarily communicated through the cutscenes that partition instances of actual gameplay.

It probably comes as no surprise to those familiar with WWII FPS games released in North America that the history communicated in these two layers maintains a Western (specifically American) perspective of the conflict. The foundational narrative layer foregrounds an understanding of Allied military force as heroically necessary to counter the Axis powers' malevolence (Baron 2010; Gish 2010). For instance, using a combination of animated images and archival footage, the opening cinematic of the best-selling game *Call of Duty: World at War* (Treyarch 2008) depicts Nazi Germany and Imperial Japan as aggressively relentless in their territorial expansion and subjugation of other nations and indifferent to committing war crimes against civilians.[6] No attempt is made to provide any counter-arguments to this narrative or alternative perspectives from an Axis point of view. While the player is fully informed on Allied motivations for going to war, Axis motivations remain unknown.

The absence of an Axis perspective arguably allows the player to play through the normative (and expected) "good vs. evil" dichotomy of FPS games without experiencing guilt or moral conflict from killing a human who is technically equivalent to the other soldiers in the game except for their affiliation. Axis soldiers are not viewed as regular people in an extraordinary situation like Allied soldiers; rather, they are portrayed and talked about as if they are somehow different ontologically. In WWII FPS games, players come to know and even relate to the backstories of Allied soldiers by watching cutscenes, yet there are no attempts to humanize the Axis soldiers in a similar way. Moreover, encounters with enemy NPCs always occur within "kill or be killed" scenarios. The absence of any other situations, even probable ones such as surrendering or capturing prisoners of war, leaves little wiggle room for an interpretation of Axis soldiers as anything but mindless killing machines. Historically, while hostile sentiments towards those fighting under the Axis banner certainly existed, these soldiers were not necessarily conceived of as being less than human or as inherently evil as they are portrayed in the game. For instance, a Canadian WWII veteran described the Axis soldiers he encountered while serving overseas as "just regular guys, like us." This statement was, ironically, made during an interview that can be found in the "extras" section of the WWII FPS game *Call of Duty 3* (Treyarch 2006).

Axis soldiers are further "othered" within the "localized narrative" layer, supporting the good vs. evil dichotomy set out in the overarching narrative. In the cutscenes for the game *Call of Duty 3* (Treyarch 2006), for example, Allied NPCs refer to and address their Axis counterparts using ethnic slurs such as the Bosch, Jerry, Krauts, Fritzy, but never German. While these speech acts reflect the pervasive racist overtones of that era, where identity was intricately linked to race, it is important to note that within *Call of Duty 3* (Treyarch 2006), racist slang is not used to reference Allied soldiers of a different nationality, even in cutscenes that portray heated arguments between these groups. By not referring to Axis soldiers in the same manner as Allied soldiers, ethnic slurs reinforce this portrayal of Axis soldiers as something *other* than human.

The "othering" of Axis soldiers has been a part of WWII-themed FPS play since the earliest games in the genre like *Wolfenstein 3D* (Apogee 1992), where the player assumes the identity of an American soldier and must escape Castle Wolfenstein, a Nazi stronghold. However, the difference between *Wolfenstein 3D* (Apogee 1989) and the more recent games in this genre is that the former does not lay any claims to historical authenticity, whereas WWII FPS games released in the past decade like the *Medal of Honor*, *Call of Duty*, and *Brothers in Arms* series do. The following section discusses the ways in which WWII FPS actually makes these claims and how it may encourage players to adopt a BPS epistemology when thinking about WWII history.

Historical Authenticity and the Encouragement of a BPS View of History

The stakes are high for any media work setting out to portray WWII, the most devastating worldwide conflict of the twentieth century, yet WWII FPS games are often marketed as providing players with an immersive, historically authentic WWII experience. The historical fidelity of many in-game elements cannot be denied, including weapons, vehicles, strategies, landscape, setting and more. These elements are notably the ones that aid in the construction of what Jenkins (2004) calls "environmental" or spatial storytelling (123). Here, WWII history is presented across a range of different artifacts and spaces to reinforce a historical sense of gameplay and provide a staging-ground that enacts narrative events. WWII FPS play is first and foremost supposed to be an enjoyable and entertaining experience, thus it is likely that the historical fidelity of said narrative events and the elements that drive them (e.g. characters and their backstories) will be compromised. This is similar to a novel or film set in the WWII era but revolving around fictional characters, such as the movies *The Thin Red Line* (1998) and *Inglourious Basterds* (2009). In campaign mode, for example, players usually assume the role of a low-ranking soldier who embodies all the stereotypical, valued qualities of a military hero who is dedicated to fighting for his country. The existence of such a soldier cannot be denied, however this identity is a construction based more on historical fiction, not fact, calling into question the authenticity of the history presented in the game. Thus, developers of these games validate their claims of historical fidelity in other ways.

It is not unusual for developers of WWII FPS games, for example, to publicize their consultation efforts with WWII veterans and/or historical advisors, or visit locations where these battles took place. While these are promotional tools, they are also a means for legitimizing the games' claims for historical authenticity.[7] Certain WWII FPS games also make use of archival footage or photographs to bolster these claims (Baron 2010; Rejack 2007). In the game *Brothers in Arms: Road to Hill 30* (Ubisoft 2006), for example, players can unlock archival photographs that document the real WWII locations and events played out in the game as a reward for level completion. As detailed by Rejack (2007), these unlockables include composite pictures that juxtapose a real photograph with its matching in-game screenshot, which is practically identical. Moreover, according to Baron (2010), the manner in which archival media is presented in WWII FPS games can discourage players from critically reflecting on the in-game history that is presented. The archival footage used in the opening cinematic for *Call of Duty: World at War* (Treyarch 2008), for example, appears and disappears so quickly that its inclusion functions more as a citation to authenticate the narrative that is being conveyed, in turn promoting a notion of history as teleological and that it could have only happened one way (Baron 2010).

All of these tactics—interviewing veterans for eyewitness accounts, consulting historical advisors, replicating environments or scenarios based on archival photos, and the inclusion of archival material within the game—are meant to legitimize the game's gestures toward providing the player with a "genuine" historical experience. Referencing a source vested with the authority to validate or refute "what happened" encourages players to view history as a "closed" event: WWII happened, and it happened this way, according to these historical authorities (Gish 2010; Rejack 2007). The employment of and reference to these historical authorities for promoting a notion of WWII history as a closed, agreed-upon narrative clearly demonstrates how these games espouse a BPS epistemology for communicating history.

Player-Centric Analytical Findings

It would be naïve to believe that the primary goal of any commercial games developer is to educate, not to make money, and it is not the intention of this piece to chastise developers of WWII FPS games for being "educationally irresponsible" in their use of BPS. Despite this demonstration of how WWII FPS games support and promote a highly criticized historical epistemology, it would be naïve for scholars to rely solely on textual analysis to assume what players learn when they engage with these games. Kee's (2008) organizing framework, although useful for examining how history is communicated to the player, is inherently limited for examining the complex act of game-based learning. This is because it does not account for the important external factors that come into play when players construct their historical interpretations. Examining the ways in which players use WWII FPS games for their own informal history education requires player-centric methodologies. Without asking the players themselves what they learn (or what think they can learn) from playing WWII FPS games, anything else is, at best, speculation.

Although they may share similar interests in gaming preferences, players of WWII FPS games are not cut from the same cloth, and should not be discussed or examined as if they were a homogenous group. There are a myriad of external/socio-cultural factors that will affect how players appropriate these games for learning, including their interest in WWII history, the frequency and intensity of their WWII FPS play, demographic variables such as sex, age, and geographic location, the context of their gameplay, and so on. While there are numerous variables that coalesce to shape how an individual will (or will not) make use of WWII FPS games to learn history, some will be more influential than others. For example, in a small-scale ethnographic study that sought to examine the ways in which players of WWII FPS games used these games as learning tools, two variables appeared to have considerably more influence in this regard: 1) the role of WWII FPS gaming in the player's daily life, and 2) the extent and quality of their existing, factual WWII knowledge learned from other resources (Fisher 2011).

The relative significance and importance of WWII FPS gameplay in the everyday lives of the study participants influenced how they considered, evaluated, and used historical game-based infor-mation. For example, participants who considered themselves to be advanced or expert WWII FPS players engaged with the history presented in these games more intensely and with a more serious disposition than someone who played WWII games more casually. Moreover, this heightened investment on a personal level made WWII FPS gameplay more memorable and as a result, players frequently chose to reference game-based historical information when talking about WWII history over information learned from other sources, even in non-game contexts such as their history classroom.[8] Another key variable identified in this study was the participants' existing knowledge about WWII history, as it appeared to function as a prerequisite for appropriating these games for learning in certain ways. For instance, a player who knew more about WWII history in general made use of WWII FPS games for learning history in more ways than a player who was less knowledgeable about the event.

In this study, WWII FPS videogames clearly played a contributing role in shaping how the participants thought and talked about WWII history. They were even aware of this happening to some degree. Even though it was not intentional or obvious to them at the time, one of the ways in which participants used these games for educational purposes was for practicing and developing skills essential to historical inquiry. These are skills that professional historians employ such as critically analyzing the historical fidelity of certain representations, scrutinizing the context in which texts were produced to uncover biases, and using evidence from a variety of sources.

At times during the group discussions, the participants, all self-proclaimed WWII gaming experts, would use very specific, detailed, game-based information from a variety of WWII FPS games as evidence while debating the accuracy and authenticity of different historical accounts, found in these games as well as films, documentaries, books, and novels. In a discussion about D-Day, for example, specifically the Allied invasion of Normandy's beaches in 1945, one participant made a case for how the FPS series *Medal of Honor* accurately portrayed this well-known campaign. He described how after landing on the beaches of Normandy, the player must attempt to run across the beach and up the hill through a barrage of heavy German gunfire while trying to shoot enemies with limited opportunities for cover and not be distracted by their computer-generated teammates being "gunned down." *Medal of Honor*'s representation of D-Day, he contended, appeared to be historically accurate as it mirrored the other accounts of D-Day he had encountered in non-fictional books, documentaries, and theatrical movies like *Saving Private Ryan* (1998). Another participant further commented that the emotions that are evoked when playing that level (fear, anxiety, disorientation, and so on) were likely reflective of how these soldiers probably felt amid this chaos, making the historical authenticity of the *Medal of Honor* account more likely. It was in these discussions where I observed participants engaging with WWII history from a "disciplinary" history epistemology, which seeks to provide learners with opportunities to evaluate accounts and interpretations of the past (Donovan and Bransford 2005; Seixas 2000). Moreover, not only were WWII FPS games used by participants as historical texts that they could examine and consult for information, but also these games were instrumental in constructing a space for them to engage with history.

As a form of entertainment, history-themed videogames are perceived as uncertain and highly contestable sources of information, in turn creating conditions for players to critically engage with the history presented in these games. For example, in their discussions of the storylines of WWII FPS games, the participants in this study examined the circumstances surrounding the creation of these games, employing a post-modern epistemology, where learners assess the criteria underlying the construction of historical arguments (Seixas 2000). The participants rejected, and were quite critical of, information that had been re-purposed to function as a typical FPS game convention. For instance, they took into account the inescapable subjectivities of the game developers to explain the overt, American-dominated narratives that are communicated by most WWII FPS videogames. Because videogames are intended to be exciting and fun, the participants also considered the games' origins in entertainment in their analyses of historical fidelity. For example, while the participants agreed that hand-to-hand combat could have been a plausible experience for a soldier, they viewed the inclusion of this in games like *Call of Duty 3* (Treyarch 2006) or *Call of Duty: World at War* (Treyarch 2008) as a gameplay feature meant to give the player a break from the predictable "shoot-em-up" scenario, and were likely not historically accurate. Here the participants demonstrated what Wertsch (2000) calls "knowing but not believing" (39). This means that while the participants knew and used game-based information, they did not necessarily accept this information as true.

The findings discussed above elucidate how players of WWII FPS games can use them to learn about WWII history in ways that are characteristic of disciplinary and post-modern historical episte-mologies. This extends the educative potentials of WWII FPS games beyond a BPS epistemology. WWII FPS videogames can provide an engaging, immersive historical experience and can be appropriated by players to develop skills that are highly valued by the historical community and necessary for performing historical inquiry in the same way as professionals. In sum, just because WWII FPS games promote and utilize a BPS epistemology, it does not mean that players will necessarily approach or engage with WWII history this way, either while playing or outside of the game.

Envisioning a Future for the Past

WWII FPS games have been developed consistently since the early 1990s and—the quality of graphics notwithstanding—have changed very little in terms of rules and narrative. Although players do not necessarily take up the BPS epistemology promoted by these games, the ways in which WWII FPS games portray and present history can be improved upon, at least from an educational standpoint.

One such way would be to modify the classic dichotomous structure employed in FPS games by including multiple, competing historical narratives and introducing alternative gameplay options. Currently, WWII FPS games claim to present multiple national perspectives of the war. However, these are all Allied perspectives and do not provide alternative or competing versions of events for the player to consider. One way to circumvent the promotion of a one-sided, victors' narrative would be to make players take on the identity of an Axis solider. This would provide a more comprehensive portrayal of WWII history and explicitly encourage players to take on a disciplinary epistemology for engaging with history. Modifying gameplay to include historically plausible scenarios such as the presence of non-military characters or capturing prisoners of war is another suggestion that game developers might consider. This would shake up typical FPS gameplay and allow players to exercise their options for interacting with NPCs. Because predictability and conti-nuity between games is a major selling feature in the commercial games industry, these suggestions are not likely to be taken up by commercial game developers. They might, however, be useful for educational game developers seeking to create an immersive historical gameplay experience that actively seeks to address the issues associated with BPS discussed in this chapter.

The inconsistencies that arise between the game-based analyses presented in this chapter and the learning outcomes observed from and reported on by players demonstrate the limits of textual analysis when investigating a game's educative potentials. This is not to say that researchers should not employ this methodology when analyzing games. Rather, because these analyses have traditionally relied on the play of a single person, differences between players are not accounted for (Weber et al. 2009). The findings of the ethnographic study mentioned above (Fisher 2011) are based on four players and this is not enough critical mass to make any general claims about learning through FPS play. Research that employs player-centric analytical framework is needed to continue the discussion of the educative potentials of WWII FPS for learning history.

Notes

1 While players do not necessarily have to follow the narrative presented in FPS games to enjoy gameplay, because these games make use of narrative to give meaning to the actions that players undertake in the game they fall closer to the "narratively oriented" pole of Urrichio's (2005) spectrum.

2 Although Kee's (2008) framework is intended as a guide to improve the design of games specially developed to teach history, the categories/pairings were constructed based on commercial game genres and can thus be applied to commercial history-themed videogames as well.

3 This pairing of action games with a BPS epistemology originates from Kee (2008). There may be larger implications of this pairing beyond WWII FPS videogames – for instance, applying this analysis to videogames where shooting and/or killing is de-emphasized, such as first-person stealth games, or when players attempt to complete the game without killing anyone (known as "pacifist runs").

4 Despite this criticism, a BPS epistemology is often employed by teachers as a sort of coping mechanism to appease the demands and constraints of formal schooling – a large amount of teachable

content coupled with too many tests and limited class time (Grant 2003).

5 The focus on mastering "fire and maneuver" tactics over "run and gun" play of typical WWII FPS games distinguishes the *Brothers in Arms* series from other games within this sub-genre (Rejack 2007, 414).

6 For an excellent and comprehensive analysis regarding the use of archival footage throughout *Call of Duty: World at War* (Treyarch 2008), refer to Baron (2010).

7 These sources also arguably function as a sort of built-in defense mechanism against those seeking to challenge the historical accuracy of what is being portrayed in the game as well as a shielding tactic against criticism regarding the games' high levels of graphic violence.

8 As well, it should be noted that the participant's investment in WWII FPS play and their enfranchisement with this particular sub-genre formed the criteria by which they were able to identify and self-proclaim, at the researcher's request, as a "history-gamer," and thus take part in the study in the first place.

References

Ananiadoui, Katerina and Magdalean Claro. 2009. "21st Century Skills and Competences for New Millennium Learners in OECD countries." *OECD Education Working Papers* 41: 32. doi: 10.1787/218525261154.

Baron, Jaimie. 2010. "Digital Historicism: Archival Footage, Digital Interface, and Historiographic Effects in *Call of Duty: World at War*." *Eludamos. Journal for Computer Game Culture* 4 (2): 303–14.

Cohen, David K. 1988. *Teaching Practice: Plus Ça Change*. East Lansing, MI: Center for Research on Teacher Education. http://www.eric.ed.gov/PDFS/ED299257.pdf.

Crogan, Patrick. 2003. "Gametime: History, Narrative and Temporality in *Combat Flight Simulator 2*." In *The Video Game Theory Reader*, edited by Mark J. P. Wolf and Bernard Perron, 275–302. New York: Routledge.

de Castell, Suzanne and Jennifer Jenson. 2003. "Serious Play." *Journal of Curriculum Studies* 35 (6): 649–65.

Donovan, M. Suzanne and John D. Bransford. 2005. *How Students Learn: History, Mathematics and Science in the Classroom*. Washington, DC: National Academies Press.

Fisher, Stephanie. 2011. "Playing with World War II: A Small Scale Study of Learning in Video Games." *Loading. The Journal of the Canadian Game Studies Association* 5 (8): 71–89.

Gish, Harrison. 2010. "Playing the Second World War: *Call of Duty* and the Telling of History." *Eludamos. Journal for Computer Game Culture* 4 (2): 167–80.

Grant, S. G. 2003. *History Lessons: Teaching, Learning, and Testing in U.S. High School Classrooms*. Mahwah, New Jersey: Lawrence Erlbaum.

Inglourious Basterds. DVD. Directed by Quentin Tarantino. Los Angeles, CA: Universal Pictures, 2009.

Jenkins, Henry. 2004. "Game Design as Narrative Architecture." In *First Person: New Media as Story, Performance, and Game,* edited by Noah Wardrip-Fruin and Pat Harrigan, 122–30. Cambridge: MIT Press.

Jenson, Jennifer, Nicholas Taylor, and Stephanie Fisher. 2010. "21st Century Skills, Technology and Learning." Toronto: Ontario Ministry of Education. http://www.edu.gov.on.ca/eng/research/Jenson_ReportEng.pdf

Kee, Kevin. 2008. "Computerized History Games: Options for Narratives." *Simulation and Gaming*. Prepublished December 24, 2008 doi: 10.1177/1046878108328087.

Kee, Kevin, Sharon Graham, Pat Dunae, John Lutz, Andrea Large, Michael Blondeau, and Mike Clare. 2009. "Towards a Theory of Good History Through Gaming." *The Canadian Historical Review* 90 (2): 303–26.

Kingsepp, Eva. 2006. "Immersive Historicity in World War II Digital Games." *Human IT* 8 (2): 61–90.

Levstik, Linda. S. and Keith C. Barton. 2001. *Doing History: Investigating with Children in Elementary and Middle Schools*. 2nd ed. Mahwah, NJ: Lawrence Erlbaum.

Loewen, James. W. 1995. *Lies My Teacher Told Me: Everything Your American History Textbook Got Wrong*. New York: Touchstone.

Morton, Desmond. 2006. "Canadian History Teaching in Canada: What's That Big Deal?" In *To the Past: History Education, Public Memory, and Citizenship in Canada,* edited by Ruth W. Sandwell, 23–31. Toronto: University of Toronto Press.

Neville, David O. and Brett E. Shelton. 2010. "Literary and Historical 3D Digital Game-based Learning: Design Guidelines." *Simulation & Gaming* 41 (4): 607–29.

Prensky, Marc. 2001. *Digital Game-based Learning*. Toronto: McGraw-Hill.

Rejack, Brian. 2007. "Toward a Virtual Reenactment of History: Video Games and the Recreation of the Past." *Rethinking History* 11 (3):411–25. doi: 10.1080/13642520701353652

Saving Private Ryan. DVD. Directed by Steven Spielberg. Los Angeles, CA: Paramount Pictures, 1998.

Schott, Gareth. 2008. "Language-GAME-Players: Articulating the Pleasures of 'Violent' Game Text." *Loading: The Journal of the Canadian Games Studies Association 2*(3). http://journals.sfu.ca/loading/index.php/loading/article/view/41/39.

Schrier, Karen. 2007. "Reliving history with 'reliving the revolution': Designing Augmented Reality Games to Teaching the Critical Thinking of History." In *Games and Simulations in Online Learning: Research and Development Frameworks*, edited by David Gibson, Clark Aldrich, and Marc Prensky, 250–69. Hershey, PA: Information Science Publishing.

Schut, Kevin. 2007. "Strategic Simulation and Our Past: The Bias of Computer Games in the Presentation of History." *Games and Culture* 2 (3): 213–35.

Seixas, Peter. 2000. "Schweigen! Die Kinder! or Does Postmodern History Have a Place in the Schools?" In *Knowing, Teaching and Learning History: National and International Perspectives*, edited by Peter Stearns, Peter Seixas, and Sam Wineberg, 19–37. New York: New York University Press.

Shaffer, David. 2005. "Epistemic Games." *Innovate* 1 (6). http://www.innovateonline.info/pdf/vol1_issue6/Epistemic_Games.pdf

Squire, Kurt. (2004). "Replaying History." Unpublished doctoral dissertation. Indiana University, Bloomington.

Stearns, Peter, Peter Seixas, and Sam Wineberg, eds. 2000. *Knowing, Teaching and Learning History: National and International Perspectives*. New York: New York University Press.

The Thin Red Line. DVD. Directed by Terrence Malick. Los Angeles, CA: Fox 2000 Pictures, 1998.

Uricchio, W. 2005. "Simulation, History, and Computer Games." In *Handbook of Computer Games Studies,* edited by Joost Raessens and Jeffrey Goldstein, 327–38. Cambridge, MA: MIT Press.

Weber, R., Katharina-Marie Behr, Ron Tamborini, Ute Ritterfeld, and Klaus Mathiak. 2009. "What Do We Really Know about First-person Shooter Games? An Event-related, High-resolution Content Analysis." *Journal of Computer-Mediated Communication* 14: 1016–37. doi:10.1111/j.1083-6101.2009.01479.x

Wertsch, James. V. 2000. "Is It Possible to Teach Beliefs, as Well as Knowledge About History?" In *Knowing, Teaching and Learning History: National and International Perspectives,* edited by Peter Stearns, Peter Seixas, and Sam Wineberg, 38–50. New York: New York University Press.

Wineberg, Sam. 2000. "Making Historical Sense." In *Knowing, Teaching and Learning History: National and International Perspectives,* edited by Peter Stearns, Peter Seixas, and Sam Wineberg, 306–26. New York: New York University Press.

Games

Gearbox Software. 2005. *Brothers in Arms: Road to Hill 30* [Microsoft Windows]. Ubisoft.
id Software. 1989. *Wolfenstein 3D* [DOS] Apogee.
—1992. *Wolfenstein 3D* [DOS]. Apogee Software.
Treyarch. 2006. *Call of Duty 3*. [PlayStation 2, PlayStation 3, Xbox, Xbox 360, Wii]. Activision.
—2008. *Call of Duty: World at War* [Microsoft Windows, PlayStation3, Xbox 360]. Activision.

14

Taking Aim at Sexual Harassment: Feminized Performances of Hegemonic Masculinity in the First-Person Shooter *Hey Baby*

Jessy Ohl and Aaron Duncan

Since their inception, FPS games and other violent computer games have been overwhelmingly created, marketed toward, and played by men (Scharrer 2004, 394).[1] The previous emphasis on male gaming audiences has corresponded with a general under-representation of women characters and a stigmatization of women gamers. When women are featured in FPS games, such as "Cortona" in *Halo* (Bungie 2001), "Jonna Dark" in the *Perfect Dark* (Rare 2001) series, and "Lilith" in *Borderlands* (Gearbox 2009), they are often relegated to secondary roles dependent on men for survival, or as fetishized sex objects equipped with small waists and enormous breasts. When provocatively dressed women characters fall victim to what Inness (1999) calls the "pseudo-tough heroine," which consists of an emphasis on the heroine's physical appearance in order to make her actions appear less threatening to the gender status quo.

Interactive violence and aggression (often toward women) are cornerstones of FPS games, which have led many scholars and feminists to question their emotional and cognitive value (Flanagan 2003, 369). Conversely, the centrality of patriarchal values and norms in FPS games leads Beavis and Charles (2007) to contend that the genre contains a generative space for feminist resistance (702). As the social pervasiveness and cultural significance of computer games continues to expand with the increasing number of women players, FPS games can no longer be conceived as the exclusive domain of men.

This chapter investigates the appropriation of the FPS format toward social change and gender equality through the controversial online FPS *Hey Baby* (LadyKillas, 2010). Designed by New York artist and producer Suyin Looui in 2010, the game was purportedly created as a "playful and provocative project designed to spark conversations about women's everyday experiences of public space" (LadyKillas 2010c, par. 1). The title, "Hey Baby," references the game's primary adversary, the form of sexual harassment commonly referred to as "cat-calling" or street harassment. In the game, the female protagonist is assailed by a multitude of men who deploy a variety of real-life "cat-calls" ranging from the seemingly innocent "Hey sweetheart," to the overtly aggressive, "I want to rape you bitch" (LadyKillas 2010c, par. 11). Street harassment, or what Elizabeth Kissling (1991) refers to as "sexual terrorism," has become a growing concern for feminist scholarship and has inspired a number of activist organizations (454–6). As Holly Kearly (2010) explains, street harassment is a significant challenge for global feminists because "as many as 80 percent of women around the world face at least occasional unwanted, harassing attention in public places from men they do not know"[2]. *Hey Baby* is rhetorically intriguing due to its political objectives of spreading awareness on sexual harassment in public spaces through the medium of the FPS, as well as the public discourse resulting from this choice.

Hey Baby's creation initiated intense debate concerning feminist appropriations of violence, because players are encouraged to respond to sexual harassment by executing the verbal attackers with a machine gun. Kate Whittle (2010) of *Ms. Magazine* succinctly summarizes the game by stating: "You walk down the street, harassers appear and say icky things and you gun them down. The harasser-corpses freeze in blood-spattered positions of agony and a tombstone appears bearing their creepy phrase, such as 'RIP, I Want To Lick You All Over'" (par. 4). The character is never physically harmed by the digital harassers, nor are there multiple levels or any discernible "end" to the game. Rather, participants fire at male chauvinists as long as desirable. Looui argues *Hey Baby* provides an unrestrictive arena where women can "act out their ridiculous revenge fantasies and have a laugh about it" (Gibson 2011, par. 8). Looui's aspirations for *Hey Baby* raise concerns over the efficacy of simulated violence in advancing women's rights, as well as the role of FPS games in communicating socially appropriate forms of gender behavior.

In this chapter we offer a gender and critical third-wave feminist analysis of the FPS game *Hey Baby*.[3] Gender and critical feminist scholarship presents a range of useful analytical tools for examining how computer games rhetorically constitute, express, and critique gender identities, due to the interconnectivity between gender and gaming as types of performance. We conceive gender not as an ontologically stable category, but instead in line with Judith Butler's (2006) view that gender is given substance performatively "through a sustained set of acts, posited through the gendered stylization of the body" (xv-xvi). From this perspective, gender is not something that people "have," but rather, like playing a computer game, is something people "do." Gender is a vital consideration for understanding the symbolic and socializing impacts of FPS games because, as Helen Kennedy (2006) notes, computer games are cultural practices "where the popular meanings of technology, play and gender converge" (183). Computer games are interactive media where gender is articulated and inculcated through the presentation of specific stylized bodies, discourses, and activities. In other words, playing computer games is one way people learn to "play" gender in the outside world.

Although *Hey Baby* aims to empower women, our analysis contends the game jeopardizes its political objectives by offering agency through traditionally masculine channels. Specifically, we argue *Hey Baby* represents a feminized performance of hegemonic masculinity. We use this term deliberately to reflect the scholarship of Judith Halberstam (1998) in *Female Masculinity*, which is useful for this analysis for several reasons. Initially, Halberstam views masculinity as a performance that scholars must not reduce exclusively "to the male body and its effects" (1). Rather, masculine performances do not necessitate that the agent, gamer, or computer game character be male. Second, Halberstam (1998) theorizes multiple forms of masculinity providing both emancipatory and oppressive functions (16). We contend *Hey Baby* exemplifies one specific type of masculine performance, hegemonic masculinity, which is feminized by positioning the player and main character as a woman fighting against patriarchy. In this way, *Hey Baby* hybridizes feminist goals of empowerment and equality with traditionally hegemonic masculine performances of aggression and violence as acceptable forms of political agency.[2] We continue this essay by discussing in greater detail previous research on gender in gaming scholarship. Next, we argue *Hey Baby* functions as a feminized performance of hegemonic masculinity. Finally, we discuss the implications of *Hey Baby*'s approach for future gaming scholarship and the creation of catharsis for women in the global conflict against street harassment.

Viewing Computer Games through Gender and Feminist Lenses

Analyzing the form and function of gender in FPS games is necessary because, as gender performances themselves, computer games contain a significant relationship to gender inequality in the material world. Computer games have held a historic relationship with women's liberation in the digital age. Although computer games are sometimes perceived as mere entertainment, Nola Alloway and Pam Gilbert (1998) are quick to note that computer games "implicitly speak a politics of gender" in terms of both inclusion and representation (100). As computers and video-gaming consoles grew in economic and political stature in the 90s, feminist activists became concerned that the exclusion of women from the development and enjoyment of these technologies would contribute to new structural inequalities. One the most important works in this area was Justine Cassell and Henry Jenkins' (1998) book *From Barbie to Mortal Kombat: Gender and Computer Games*, which examined numerous facets of the emerging computer game industry through the lens of gender. Concerning the threat of a technological gender gap, Cassell and Jenkins (1998) assert "[t]he relationship between boys' comparatively higher interest in computer games and their comparatively larger representation in high-power computer jobs is not accidental" (11). Since their publication in 1998, women have experienced a significant increase in attention by marketers and researchers as a gaming demographic. Yesmin Kafia et al. (2008) note that women now comprise 38 percent of all players and 42 percent of online game players. The growth in the number of women gamers in recent years promoted Gee (2003) to suggest that discussions of the role of gender and gaming be put to rest. Gee argues that enough progress has been made with regards to women and gaming that it is no longer an important societal issue and is only of interest to academics. However, Kafia et al. (2008) disagree in their follow-up book to the work of Cassell and Jenkins, arguing that simply increasing the number of women who play games is not enough and that more substantive analysis of the genre is needed in order to fully understand the role of gender in gaming. Laura Fantone (2009) agrees, noting that gender stereotypes and social divisions within computer games are stronger than ever.

Gender norms and stereotypes are continuously reified and strongly contested in the FPS genre. Helen Kennedy (2006) illustrates in her study of women gamers in the FPS *Quake* community that there exists a social anxiety that enjoying violent shooting games contributes to gender confusion in women and is "symptomatic of the final decline of civilization" (193). This has made FPS games a site for cyberfeminist action where "feisty, fearless and transgressing female gamers [...] perform a kind of gender insubordination" by achieving recognition and aptitude in spaces traditionally reserved for men (196). Feminist responses to the addition of women FPS gamers have been considerably mixed. While some have classified FPS games as irrelevant or counterproductive to feminist progress due to their negative representations of women, others have underscored the liberation many women experience from playing (Labre and Duke 2004, 145). The work of Royse et al. (2007) reveals that many women gamers prefer the FPS format because its emphasis on competition provides the opportunity to "define and extend their definitions of self and gender" (563). Furthermore, Catherine Beavis and Claire Charles' (2007) study of Australian cyber-cafés shows that women use FPS games to shuffle and merge traditional notions of femininity and masculinity. Despite passionate resistance against negative gender stereotypes by women gamers, the ethnographic study of Nicholas Taylor, Jen Jenson, and Suzanne de Castell (2009) concludes that professional FPS communities construct an environment where women are positioned as inferior inside the game and relegated to the sidelines on the outside. Thus, unequal inclusion into gaming communities and problematic representations of femininity forwarded by FPS games continue to be considerable political challenges for the advancement of women in contemporary society.

The majority of early research on gender and gaming was social-scientific in methodology. As the above discussion illustrates, recent scholarship has reflected a growing sophistication and diversification of critical approaches as well. In general, most previous research on gender in game studies has focused on gender representations found in games and the observation or interviewing of women gamers (Royse *et al.* 2007, 556). While these strategies have produced excellent research, conceptualizing gender and computer gaming as inter-connected performances requires a heightened attention to discourse. As John Sloop (2004) contends, critics must "reenvision rhetoric as a constructor of gender rather than as constructed by gender" (82). Therefore, centering this analysis on the discourse of *Hey Baby* creates the opportunity to explore how FPS games articulate, elevate, and consubstantiate gender identity.

Performing Hegemonic Masculinity

Once masculinity and femininity become conceptually detached from a naturalized anchor, it becomes possible to investigate how these performances are rhetorically facilitated and enacted in material and digital environments (For further discussion on masculinity in FPS games consult the pieces by Taylor and Snider et al. in this volume). Of course, masculinity and femininity are not all-encompassing gender categories. Rather, as Karen Lee Ashcraft and Lisa Flores (2000) illustrate, there exists a vast variety of masculinities and femininities constantly adapting to changes in economic, cultural, and communicative conditions (3). In the following section we argue *Hey Baby* favors one such version of gender performance—hegemonic masculinity. Hegemonic masculinity is a dominant and unapologetic performance of masculinity which "systematically dominates femininities and alternative masculinities" (Ashcraft and Flores 2000, 3). *Hey Baby* symbolizes a feminized performance of hegemonic masculinity through its hybridization of feminist goals of empowerment and opposition against street harassment with traditionally masculine approaches to conflict and agency.

To support these claims we examined a variety of discursive formations relating to *Hey Baby*. These texts included *Hey Baby*'s official website, the rhetoric and symbolism within the game itself, and public discourses in print and electronic media representing the game's release and reception. We assert *Hey Baby* channels the gamer through three performative embodiments of hegemonic masculinity; polarization of agency, erasure of difference, and individualist orientations to social change. It is important to remember these are by no means comprehensive or determinative tenets of hegemonic masculinity. Indeed, one of the enduring features of masculinity is its difficulty to be defined or isolated. According to Todd Resser (2010), "there is no single or simple origin to masculinity [...] There are only innumerable copies of masculinities floating around in culture, copies that can never be brought back to an originary masculinity that invented them" (18). Therefore, because masculinities are contextual performances, they cannot be defined or isolated in absolute terms. However, we believe these three rhetorical features of *Hey Baby* reflect several dominate themes and logics of hegemonic masculinity.

Love Them or Kill Them: The Polarization of Agency

Sexual harassment in public spaces is an all-too-common problem for women, and often results in considerable psychological and emotional trauma. Yet despite the seriousness and prevalence of such offenses, most girls and women "are not encouraged to confront street harassers or to take harassment seriously" (Sullivan, Lord, and McHugh 2010, 241). *Hey Baby* was created to mitigate these feelings of powerlessness by giving women an opportunity to vent their frustrations, quite literally, by "arming" them with a way to digitally eliminate sexism and patriarchy. The website advertises the game to women audiences by declaring: "Ladies are you sick and tired of catcalling, hollering, obnoxious one-liners and creepy street encounters? Tired of changing your route home to avoid uncomfortable situations? IT'S PAYBACKTIME, BOYS...." (LadyKillas 2010, par. 5). This "payback" takes shape through the medium of the FPS, which designer Suyin Looui purposefully selected in order to "repurpose the mechanics of the first person shooter, and transform this typically male form into a space for women to transgress" (Ramos 2011, par. 8). The reappropriation of the FPS format provides an opportunity for empowerment by granting women access to a gaming experience typically used to marginalize them. As one anonymous gamer proclaimed on the *Hey Baby* website, "YES! Finally a video game I want to play. Thank you!" (LadyKillas 2010, par. 3). In the case of *Hey Baby*, control and mastery are achieved primarily by murdering male oppressors. We contend *Hey Baby* functions as a performance of hegemonic masculinity by polarizing agency between digital violence and approval, rather than providing multiple possibilities for resistance.

As previously noted, the game positions the player as a female in an urban landscape during a beautiful sunny day. As you walk around, however, you are relentlessly cornered by men who all embody a variety of different sexual epithets which can be quickly disbanded with the use of your "3' long .80 caliber machine gun that's locked and loaded" (LadyKillas 2010a, par. 4). This violent and destructive response to conflict is symptomatic of hegemonic masculine performances, because as Nick Trujillo (1991) theorizes, "masculinity is hegemonic when power is defined in terms of physical force and control" (291). It would be problematic to assert that the use of violent resistance, simulated or otherwise, was completely inappropriate for women. Veena Cabreros-Sud (1995) contends that often in academic and social contexts "women's response to violence with violence is not viewed as one of the many expressions of resistance nor as a natural, human response to daily humiliation, but as a sociopolitical faux pas" (45). However, it is not the support of violence as an option for resistance alone that makes *Hey Baby* a performance of hegemonic masculinity, but also its restriction and polarization of acceptable forms of agency.

When the player is confronted by sexual harassers the game allows for only two diametrically oppositional choices. The player can either use their machine gun to brutally murder the men, or they can push "2" in order to "shower them with love" (LadyKillas 2010b, par. 3). This action results in the game's only vocalization of the otherwise silent protagonist who sweetly responds "Thank you! Have a great day!" As figure 14.1 shows, if the player elects to "shower them with

Figure 14.1 Showering a harasser with love and hearts (LadyKillas 2010)

love" an assortment of large red hearts floats around the screen and the man strolls away as if pacified by the approval; therefore, allowing for acceptance to be interpreted as a suitable and useful reaction to the verbal attacks. The participant is forced to select exclusively between violence and praise as available methods for coping with street harassment. Furthermore, verbal responses are only possible when the player actively embraces the sexist remarks, which undermines the legitimacy of dialogue and discussion as forms of resistance. This bifurcation of agency between death and approval explicitly restricts the player's ability to address simulated and real-life street harassment with personalized, intricate, or complex approaches.

Hey Baby's oversimplified depiction of confrontation asserts hegemonic masculinity by constraining choice and resolving powerlessness only through violence against others (Labre and Duke 2004, 153). Hegemonic masculinity limits individual choice, because as Resser argues, "[t]he only freedom, in actuality, is the freedom to accept or to reject" hegemonic masculinity's totalizing and absolute worldview (25). *Hey Baby's* FPS format allows women to conceive of themselves as warriors against street harassment rather than helpless victims; however, by polarizing and stratifying the methods of activism, some players became confused about the game's message (Whittle 2010, par. 5). After playing *Hey Baby*, feminist writer Amanda Hess (2010) asked: "What is the point of this game? I killed half a dozen dudes and couldn't figure out if I was making any progress toward some sort of discernible goal" (par. 5). In an interview with *NPR,* Looui was questioned if she thought "blowing kisses or shooting them dead" were the only real choices for women (NPR 2010, par. 28–30). Looui responded that while the game represents extreme measures, she wanted it to illustrate the range of possible strategies available to combat street harassment (par. 31). Unfortunately, none of the alternative tactics she discusses in the interview are present in the computer game or mentioned on its website. Since murdering street harassers in the outside world is not permitted, the only "real life" strategy *Hey Baby* supports is loving approval. As *Hey Baby* supplies gamers with a unique opportunity to express emotion without real-world consequences, empowerment is simultaneously undermined as a result of the game's polarized articulation of agency.

Erasure of Difference

The second performative feature of hegemonic masculinity exemplified in *Hey Baby* is the erasure of individual difference and diversity. One attribute of hegemonic masculinity is a disregard and disrespect for difference. Due to its supposed superiority, hegemonic masculinity views multiple perspectives as inferior, unnecessary, and threatening. Thus, performances of hegemonic masculinity elevate what Audre Lorde (1980) refers to as the "mythical norm," usually defined in Western society as "white, thin, male, young, heterosexual, Christian, and financially secure" (116). The actual achievement or embodiment of this subjectivity is incredibly rare; nonetheless, it is viewed as culturally normative and desirable (Connell and Messerschmidt 2005, 832). Gender and gaming scholars are interested in discursive and digital representations of the human body, because as Butler (2006) argues, bodies are how we read, perceive, and interpret social constructions of identity and difference (185). Significant criticism has been leveled at computer game creators for manufacturing fetishized representations of women, and this is especially true with FPSs (Flanagan 2003, 361). In response to the gaming industry's hyper-sexualization of women characters, Esther MacCallum-Stewart (2009) has observed a growing post-modern relationship between gamer and avatar in which players sometimes embrace stereotypical body images for the purposes of irony. (For an alternative reading on the role of the body in FPS games, see the Peaty and Call chapters in this same volume.)

Hey Baby's attempts to empower women against patriarchal forces make the game's digital construction of the body a paramount concern. *Hey Baby*'s tactic for opposing stereotypical representations of women's bodies is through removal. During gameplay, the participant is entirely unable to view or modify their digital self, which was a welcomed addition for some. "I'm eternally grateful," writes Amanda Hess (2010), "that players aren't forced to watch sexy avatars of themselves do the harasser-murderin' so as to satisfy the erotic requirements of any dudes who might be playing the game (all you see of yourself is the machine gun you're wielding)" (par. 8). Figure 14.2 illustrates the point-of-view for a player of the game. No parts of the protagonist's body are shown, only a large

Figure 14.2 Point of view for players of *Hey Baby* (LadyKillas 2010)

gun can be seen. *Hey Baby*'s movement away from the player's digital body forces gamers to focus on the character's actions, rather than outward physical appearance. However, this erasure of the player's body can also be read as the removal or essentialization of a significant source personal identification. *Hey Baby*'s presumption digital embodiment is less relevant to player subjectivity functions as a performance of hegemonic masculinity by resulting in a collapsing of diversity.

Even though *Hey Baby*'s FPS perspective frames street harassment as a problem for all women through its universalizing view of the digital environment, not all women experience street harassment similarly, or have equal access to forms of resistance. Deirdre Davis (1997) contends street harassment is relationally contingent on numerous social, cultural, and historical factors. For instance, she explains that when black men verbally assault black women they are often seeking to claim a level of whiteness (197). Attempting to create cohesion among women through the digital formation of shared lived experience is certainly an admirable goal. However, *Hey Baby*'s strategic ambiguity functions as a performance of hegemonic masculinity by erasing difference and multiple perspectives in the fight against street harassment.

Individuals of assorted genders, races, classes, abilities, and sexualities certainly approach *Hey Baby* from unique social, cultural, and political circumstances. Nevertheless, *Hey Baby* positions players within a totalizing subjectivity where identity is reducible to the phallic-shaped gun-barrel on-screen. Furthermore, although players are unable to see their digital selves during gameplay, they are provided several indications of their likely outward appearance. In order to play *Hey Baby*, individuals must navigate the game's official website which contains several visual advertisements for the game. For example, *Hey Baby's* cover-art, as shown in figure 14.3, consists of an image of a beautiful, thin, white, woman with flowing dark hair and red lips. She is wearing a short white dress, red shoes, and is holding a large gun behind her back (LadyKillas 2010a). In other sections of the game's website, the top portion of the interface showcases another image of the woman from the waist down, highlighting only her long white legs, red high-heels, and a penis-shaped weapon held between her legs (LadyKillas 2010b). Moreover, one of the game's cat-calls is "Oh my God. I hope you like

Figure 14.3 *Hey Baby* Cover-Art (LadyKillas 2010)

Black men" (LadyKillas 2010). These visual and verbal representations imply *Hey Baby*'s protagonist is a beautiful, thin, white, woman, and therefore function rhetorically to homogenize the experiences of those who do not share that subjectivity.

Michael Butterworth (2007) argues that hegemonic masculinity's suppression of difference functions as an ideological vehicle through which "whiteness is affirmed in everyday cultural practices" (232). It is possible *Hey Baby*'s removal of the body is effort toward solidarity. On the other hand, by not acknowledging complex overlapping sources of identity formation, *Hey Baby* implicitly prioritizes the experiences of white, heterosexual, US women (Crenshaw 1997, 220).

Forsaking Fellowship: The Individualist Paradigm

A consequence of hegemonic masculinity's disinterest in difference is a general disdain for collaboration. Mythic narratives of the "self-made man" and "rugged individualist" remain potent ideological fixtures which frame collaboration as feminine and weak (Rotundo 1994, 292–3). Young boys and men are often trained not to ask for help so as to appear strong, capable, and masculine (Addis and Mahalik 2003, 7–9). Conversely, Labre and Duke (2004) argue, in their analysis of the violent fighting game *Buffy the Vampire Slayer,* that traditional feminine heroism is associated with selflessness, relationship management, and the ability to work effectively in teams (138). These tensions between masculine and feminine approaches to problem-solving are present in modern feminist debates as well. Many feminist organizations have called for stronger domestic and transnational ties among women, while conversely, other third-wave discourses suggest women should "assert power as individuals in private and professional spheres rather than work for social change collectively" (Anderson and Stewart 2004, 601). The final enactment of hegemonic masculinity in *Hey Baby* is an individualist orientation to the issue of street harassment.

Most FPS games define success based on personal achievement. However, even in popular FSPs such as *Halo* (Bungie 2001) and *Call of Duty* (Activision 2003), players are unable to progress without teamwork and collaboration. *Hey Baby* differs in this regard because of an absence of interaction and reliance on others. There are no mentors, sidekicks, or fellow warriors to provide guidance or backup in *Hey Baby*. Furthermore, the game is exclusively single-player, meaning participants are unable to collaborate with friends or family against sexism. Instead, the player is positioned as the sole target of street harassment and the only one with the tools to fight back. It is difficult to determine whether the creators of *Hey Baby* purposeful chose the single-player format to comment on street harassment as an isolate experience, or if multiplayer was simply less technologically feasible. Regardless, by not offering opportunity for collective action in the digital space, the rhetoric of *Hey Baby* indicates that cooperative effort is not a useful strategy for resisting street harassment in the outside world.

Along with the gameplay, an individualist mentality was also characteristic of *Hey Baby*'s public reception. *Hey Baby* has garnered a considerable amount of attention and discussion. Nevertheless, the majority of the public discourse surveyed centered on *Hey Baby*'s use of simulated violence, rather than substantive dialogue on ending street harassment. For instance, the *New York Times* review of the game contained the headline: "A Woman with the Firepower to Silence Those Street Wolves" (Schiesel 2010). *Hey Baby*'s FPS format became a spectacle which detracted many writers and gamers from the primary political issue of street harassment. This distraction was reinforced by the fact that *Hey Baby*'s website does not supply visitors with a forum to develop solidarity or discuss the game's content. Transnational feminism is dependent on a deliberate commitment to participate in dialogue (Krolokee and Sorensen 2006, 20). *Hey Baby* focuses on the experience of playing the game to empower individual women, rather than using the game as a platform to facilitate connections between women once play concludes. As an FPS game, it is logical for *Hey Baby* to place additional emphasis on individualism. However, because the purpose behind *Hey Baby* was to create public dialogue and activism, its narrowed focus on individual intervention is quite limiting.

Conclusion

At the same time that computer games serve as popular enter-tainment, McAllister (2004) asserts "[c]omputer games do real work in the world. They change lives, not just those of game players, marketers, and developers, but increasingly those of everyone" (169). This analysis of *Hey Baby* illustrates how FPS games can function as a medium to articulate gender identities and address real-world social problems through digital performance. Unfortunately, through its polarization of agency, erasure of difference, and individualist orientation to social change, *Hey Baby* provides a feminized perfor-mance of hegemonic masculinity which destabilizes its political objectives.

Hey Baby also struggles to meet its goals by failing to promote collaboration between women and men. The game was exclusively designed and marketed to women with little consideration of the potential role of men in resolving street harassment. *Hey Baby's* decision not to directly incorporate men into the discussion of street harassment harms its effectiveness at facilitating significant social change. Interestingly, media coverage of *Hey Baby* did attract the attention of some men, who found the game's content to be rather enlightening. Columnist Seth Schiesel (2010) argues *Hey Baby* has a lot to offer men because it provides an "appreciation for what many women go through as part of their day-to-day lives" (par. 13). Rather than exclusively targeting women, *Hey Baby's* inclusion of men could have allowed the game to function as an educational tool for those who do not regularly experience street harassment.

Hey Baby's combination of feminist goals of empowerment and equality with traditional masculine approaches to conflict points to the paradoxical nature of gender performances in FPS games, which are simultaneously liberating and constraining. Although *Hey Baby* struggles to achieve its stated goal of creating public dialogue and advocacy against street harassment, the game does provide women players a potentially cathartic experience. Kenneth Burke (1966) explains that catharsis is best achieved through dramatic experience, which the game provides. According to Burke, for catharsis to occur it is essential for victims to move beyond the emotions of fear and pity and seek justice (298). *Hey Baby* fulfills this Burkean interpretation of catharsis because while the game could focus on the suffering of the victims of harassment, it instead goes beyond these emotions by allowing players to seek symbolic justice. Playing the game provides victims of street harassment a cathartic experience by allowing them to enact justice against those who harassed them. Although the justice in the game may literally be overkill, it still fulfills a cathartic function for those who play the game.

Hey Baby's cathartic power may also derive from its non-corporate origins. As previously mentioned, the gaming industry's marketing practices and stereotypical representations of gender are responsible for a considerable amount of inequality. Conversely, *Hey Baby* is a free FPS designed by women for women. It may be easy to dismiss the social and theoretical importance of *Hey Baby* and consider the game a non-platform gimmick due to its low production value and second-rate graphics. However, we contend that the creation of *Hey Baby* can be interpreted as a form of backlash against male-dominated production studios. The study of FPS games has been restricted to centralized sources of gaming which are less likely to risk potential profits for socially conscious objectives. Understanding the full significance of the FPS genre requires a scholarly focus on vernacular gaming—instances where gamers operate outside of the corporate orthodoxy to institute digital and material change.

As the digital age continues to mature, we are likely to see a growing number of socially aware incarnations in the FPS genre. Although we hold reservations over some of the creator's specific rhetorical choices, *Hey Baby* does exemplify an important democratization in the gaming universe. Whether women choose to play violent computer games is less significant than their ability to make such choices free of prejudice and ridicule. While violent computer games have been a bastion for patriarchal oppression, it may come to pass that such games contribute to its dismantling.

Notes

1 For this study we will use the term "computer games" over "videogames" in agreement with Simon Penny's (2004) argument that it is the presence of computers which defines the technological and aesthetic features of the medium (39). "Computer game" is also more applicable in this context because *Hey Baby* is not available for videogaming consoles and is only accessible via the internet.

2 Because *Hey Baby* is a rhetorical artifact of immense gender complexity, we believe it is important to position ourselves as two self-identified heterosexual white men of European decent. Analyzing multifarious meanings and interpretations of feminist resistance creates the threat of misrepresentation, and therefore, additional oppression. We attempted to address these challenges by engaging in research as if the communities being discussed were overlooking the development of the project (Royster 33).

3 Because this study views gender as performance, the majority of our theoretical support is third-wave and post-structuralist in nature. However, just as there are multiple forms of masculinity and femininity, feminism should not be seen as a singular or unified concept. Lisa Hogeland explains: "[w]e have in feminism radically different understandings of how change happens, of what constitutes change, and thus of the goals and purposes of feminism itself" (110). Hence, we do not mean to overgeneralize or imply that all feminist goals and theories are uniform. However, we believe it is fair to say that gender emancipation and empowerment have been historic goals of the feminist movement and are key in order to understand the rhetorical ambitions of *Hey Baby*.

References

Addis, Michael E. and James R. Mahalik. 2003. "Men, Masculinity, and the Contexts of Help Seeking." *American Psychologist* 58: 5–14.

Alloway, Nola and Pam Gilbert. 1998. "Video Game Culture: Playing with Masculinity, Violence, and Pleasure." In *Wired Up*, edited by Sue Howard, 95–115. London: University College London.

Anderson, Karrin Vasby and Jessie Stewart. 2005. "Politics and The Single Woman: The 'Sex and the City Voter' in Campaign 2004." *Rhetoric and Public Affairs* 8: 595–616.

Ashcraft, Karen Lee and Lisa A. Flores. 2000. "'Slaves With White Collars': Persistent Performances of Masculinity in Crisis." *Text and Performance Quarterly* 23: 1–29.

Beavis, Catherine and Claire Charles. 2007. "Would the 'Real' Girl Gamer Please Stand Up? Gender, LAN Cafés and the Reformulation of the 'Girl' Gamer." *Gender and Education* 6: 691–705.

Burke, Kenneth. 1966. *Language as Symbolic Action: Essays on Life, Literature, and Method*. Berkeley: University of California.

Butler, Judith. 2006. *Gender Trouble*. New York: Routledge.

Butterworth, Michael L. 2007. "Race in 'The Race': Mark McGwire, Sammy Sosa, and Heroic Constructions of Whiteness." *Critical Studies in Media Communication* 24: 228–44.

Cabreros-Sud, Veena. 1995. "Kicking Ass." In *Listen Up: Voices From the Next Feminist Generation,* edited by Barbara Findlen, 41–7. Emeryville, CA: Seal Press.

Cassell, Justine and Henry Jenkins. 1988. *From Barbie to Mortal Kombat: Gender and Computer Games*. Cambridge: Massachusetts Institute of Technology Press.

Connell, R. W. and James W. Messerschmidt. 2005. "Hegemonic Masculinity: Rethinking the Concept." *Gender and Society* 19: 829–59.

Crenshaw, Carrie. 1997. "Women in the Gulf War: Toward an Intersectional Rhetorical Criticism." *Howard Journal of Communication* 8: 219–35.

Davis, Deirdre E. 1997. "The Harm That Has No Name: Street Harassment, Embodiment, and African American Women." In *Critical Race Feminism*: *A Reader*, edited by Adrien Wing, 192–202. New York: New York University Press.

Flanagan, Mary. 2003. "'Next Level': Women's Digital Activism through Gaming." In *Digital Media Revisited*, edited by Gunnar Liestol, Andrew Morrison, and Terje Rasmussen, 359–88. Cambridge: Massachusetts Institute of Technology Press.

Gee, James P. 2003. *What Video Games Have to Teach Us About Learning and Literacy*. New York: Palgrave Macmillan.

Gibson, Megan. 2010. "*Hey Baby*: A Violent Game Geared to Women." *Time Magazine,* October 8.

Halberstam, Judith. 1998. *Female Masculinity*. Durham: Duke University Press.

Hess, Amanda. 2010. "'Hey Baby': The First-Person Shooter." *The Sexist,* June 2. http://www.washingtoncitypaper.com/blogs/sexist/2010/06/02/hey-baby-the-first-person-shooter/

Hogeland, Lisa Maria. 2001. "Against Generational Thinking, or, Some Things That 'Third Wave' Feminism Isn't." *Women's Studies in Communication* 24: 107–21.

Inness, Sherrie A. 1999. *Tough Girls: Women Warriors and Wonder Women in Popular Culture*. Philadelphia: University of Pennsylvania Press.

Kafia, Yesmin B., Carrie Heeter, Jill Deener, and Jennifer Y. Sun. 2008. *Beyond Barbie and Mortal Kombat: New Perspectives on Gender and Gaming*. The MIT Press.

Kearly, Holly. 2010. *Stop Street Harassment: Making Public Places Safe and Welcoming for Women*. Santa Barbara, CA: Praeger.

Kennedy, Helen W. 2006. "Illegitimate, Monstrous and Out There: Female *Quake* Players and Inappropriate Pleasures." In *Feminism in Popular Culture,* edited by Joanne Hollows and Rachel Moseley, 183–201. New York: Berg.

Kissling, Elizabeth Arveda. 1991. "Street Harassment: The Language of Sexual Terrorism." *Discourse and Society* 2: 451–60.

Labre, Magdala Peixoto and Lisa Duke. 2004. "'Nothing Like a Brisk Walk and a Spot of Demon Slaughter to Make a Girl's Night': The Construction of the Female Hero in the Buffy Video Game." *Journal of Communication Inquiry* 28: 138–56.

Lorde, Audre. 1984. "Age, Race, Class, Sex: Women Redefining Difference," in *Sister Outsider*, edited by Audre Lorde, 114–23. Freedom, CA: Crossing Press.

MacCallum-Stewart, Esther. 2009. "'The Street Smarts of a Cartoon Princess.' New Roles for Women in Games." *Digital Creativity* 20: 225–37.

McAllister, Ken S. 2004. *Game Work: Language, Power, and Computer Game Culture.* Tuscaloosa: University of Alabama Press.

NPR. "Video Game Lets Women Fight Back" *NPR*, June 8. www.npr.org/templates/story/story.php?storyId=127559029

Penny, Simon. 2004. "Representation, Enaction, and the Ethics of Simulation." In *First Person: New Media as Story, Performance, and Game*, edited by Noah Wardrip-Fruin and Pat Harrigan, 73–84. Cambridge, MA: Massachusetts Institute of Technology Press.

Ramos, Jeff. 2011. "Interview With *Hey Baby* Creator, Suyin Looui." *Games for Change: Real World Games, Real World Impact,* February 16. http://www.gamesforchange.org/main/newentry/interview_with_hey_baby_creator_suyin_looui/ (24 Mar. 2011).

Resser, Todd W. 2010. *Masculinities in Theory: An Introduction.* Oxford: Blackwell.

Rotundo, E. Anthony. 1994. *American Manhood: Transformations in Masculinity from the Revolution to the Modern Era.* New York: Basic Books.

Royse, Pam, Joon Lee, Baasanjav Undrahbuyan, Mark Hopson, and Mia Consalvo. 2007. "Women and Games: Technologies of the Gendered Self." *New Media & Society* 9: 351–72.

Royster, Jacqueline Jones. 1996. "When the First Voice You Hear is Not Your Own." *College Composition and Communication* 47: 29–40.

Scharrer, Erica. 2004. "Virtual Violence: Gender and Aggression in Video Game Advertisements." *Mass Communication & Society* 7: 393–412.

Schiesel, Seth. 2010. "A Woman with the Firepower to Silence Those Street Wolves." *The New York Times*, June 7.

Sloop, John M. 2004. *Disciplining Gender: Rhetorics of Sex Identity in*

Contemporary U.S. Culture. Amherst: University of Massachusetts Press.

Sullivan, Harmony B., Tracy L. Lord, and Maureen C. McHugh. 2010. "Creeps and Casanovas: Experiences, Explanations, and Effects of Street Harassment." In *Victims of Sexual Assault and Abuse,* edited by Michele A. Paludi and Florence L. Denmark, 237–59. Santa Barbara, CA: Praeger.

Taylor, Nicholas, Jen Jenson, and Suzanne de Castell. 2009. "Cheerleaders/booth babes/Halo hoes: Pro-Gaming, Gender and Jobs for the Boys." *Digital Creativity* 20: 239–52.

Trujillo, Nick. 1991. "Hegemonic Masculinity on the Mound: Media Representations of Nolan Ryan and American Sports Culture." *Critical Studies in Mass Communication* 8: 290–308.

Whittle, Kate. 2010. "Is Videogame 'Hey Baby' A Positive Response to Street Harassment?" *Ms. Magazine,* June 10. http://msmagazine. com/blog/blog/2010/06/10/is-videogame-hey-baby-a-positive-response-to-street-harassment/ (24 Mar 2011).

Games

Activision. 2003. *Call of Duty* [PlayStation 2, Xbox]. Activision Blizzard.

Bungie. 2001. *Halo: Combat Evolved* [Xbox]. Microsoft Game Studios.

Gearbox Software. 2009. *Borderlands* [Microsoft Windows, PlayStation 3, Xbox 360] 2K Games.

LadyKillas. 2010. "*Hey Baby*" [Unity]. LadyKillas Inc.: New York.

Rare. 2000. *Perfect Dark* [Nintendo 64]. Rare Ltd.

15

Invigorating Play: The Role of Affect in Online Multiplayer FPS Games

Christopher Moore

The first-person shooter (FPS) genre has its origins in the cinematic visual technique known as the first-person subjective camera angle (Galloway 2006, 40). The first-person view is framed by merging camera lens with the character's eye to create a "recti-linear plane of Albertian perspective" (O'Riley 1998, 18). The visual impression of this "Renaissance pictorial tactic" (Shinkle 2005, 24) produces a subjective view that is remediated through the technol-ogies of photography, cinema, and FPS games as an entirely modern sense of experiencing the world (O'Riley 1998).

Cinema incorporates the first-person subjective perspective through sound and vision to psychologically and cognitively "effect a sense of alienation, detachment, fear or violence" for the spectator (Galloway 2006, 40). The FPS further expands this experience through the cybernetic feedback systems of the PC or videogame console to include the participant's body, movement, and senses in its operation. The player is directly engaged in the production of both the symbolic and non-representational elements of the game, and while the elongated three-dimensional first-person perspective is still central to the experiences of play, it is less concerned with the identification of a character and more focused on the player's embodiment of the character's "point of view" (Golumbia 2009, 184).

Games studies often privilege the importance of representation, focusing on visual perception and semiotic activity (with the occasional regard to sound), but FPS players not only move and target, they direct movement, monitor sounds, manage inputs, and they experience rapid changes between conditions of excitement, panic, elation, or disappointment. The ideological operation involved in the production of meaning, from the content of the game to its role in the player's larger world beyond the game, is extensive, but it does not exhaustively account for the full spectrum of the player's experience. This is especially true of multiplayer FPS games as online spaces of male-dominated social interaction and competition. (See Taylor in this volume for further examination of the performativity of masculinity through competitive FPS play.)

In order for games studies to provide an exhaustive account of the full spectrum of the significance and experiences of games, it requires attention to detail that encompasses more than their representative content and ideological capacity; it must also closely examine the context of their production, play, and wider circulation within popular culture. The range of theoretical lenses available to the study of games has broadened dramatically in the short history of the field, and yet news media and other entertainment media continue to frame games in terms of the highly contested "effects." Games critics can respond by expanding their own critical dialogue and understanding of games and play, to consider play as kinetic and embodied actions taking place in real time across simultaneously material and digital spaces with strong affective dimensions that challenge established understanding of meaning and representation (Galloway, 2004).

This chapter examines just a few of the numerous affects involved in the play of FPS games, specifically the online multiplayer component of the dominant military-themed genre, with the aim of contributing to a broader perception of these games and what it means to play them. It proposes that a study of the degrees of affect involved in play of these games is a useful analytical tool for expanding the critical frame of games and their production, play, and players.

Just as feelings have an important but oppositional role to "thinking," affects have a complex relationship with cognition, but affects are not limited to emotional responses. Shouse (2005) considers the non-conscious experience of potential that the human body generates and infolds as it responds to the thousands of stimuli occurring at any one time, as an intensity or affect. In this view, emotions are the subjective translation of affect and effect, registering in the interplay between senses, consciousness, and autonomic functions of the body, which are manifested in games through the execution of intended actions and unintentional reactions. Affects modulate emotions, perceptions, and reactions, and are the "body's way of preparing itself for action in a given circumstance by adding a quantitative dimension of intensity to the quality of an experience" (Shouse 2005). Online multiplayer games offer a means for re-examining the conventional understanding of the representational strategies of military FPS games, expanding the comprehension of them as simultaneously modulating, trans-forming, and transmitting the capacities of the player (Shinkle 2005; Massumi 2002).

The military FPS genre makes a considerable case study in terms of the strength of the ideological power operations at work in the content of the games and the organizations involved in their production. (See Miller, Voorhees, and Welsh in this collection for alternative takes on the effects of militarism in FPS games.) This chapter seeks to contribute to the critique of military shooters, by expanding the consideration of the role of affect in FPS play and suggesting how this approach can inform the established discussion of military-themed multiplayer FPS games. To contribute to our understanding of why and how we play these games, this chapter highlights some of the many affective dimensions of play involved in the current generation of online multiplayer military-themed FPS games, including the *America's Army*, *Call of Duty*, *Battlefield*, and *Medal of Honor* series. Connecting to this debate, the chapter complicates notions of "immersion," "interactivity," and "realism" in FPS games founded in representational thinking, proposing instead a focus on the role of "invigoration" produced in the affective capacities of the FPS games and their play.

Representation and the Military FPS

A military FPS game typically includes physics and damage systems, a weapon or item in the foreground of the screen, and the accompaniment of non-diegetic (non-narrative) elements, such as the heads-up display (HUD), overlaying two-dimensional information on a three-dimensional simulation. Manovich (200) describes how this structure involves the player in a complex cyclical visual experience, a "temporal oscillation" between two distinct states: the illusionary and the interactive (120). The player moves between the competing concerns of perception and action, space and information. The simulation elements of FPS games are produced in the audible and visual information available to players control via keyboard and mouse, or wireless controller, as they remediate the doubled mode of perception of the modern soldier: video cameras, head-mounted displays, GPS, radar, microphones, earpieces, telescopic sights, and other weapons, vehicles, and technologies.

The result is a highly mediated perspective structuring the parameters of time, place, and space of the soldier's experience in a permanent state of preparation and anticipating of combat (Virilio 2002, 39). Virilio (1989) considers the systems of simulation that operate as the visible technologies of warfare (weapons, vehicles, troops, flying drones) to be entangled in the organizing structures of logistics, software, and interfaces, the same "invisible" structures that organize traffic and taxes (77). Stahl (2010) further suggests videogames are an active participant in the "interactive war," in which war-themed games constitute the player as a subject in the military discourse.

The release of new installments in the *Call of Duty* franchise is a massively popular cultural event, dominating the console and PC games charts. The debut of *Call of Duty: Black Ops* (Treyarch 2010) exceeded the worldwide sales record of $550 million set by the previous incarnation of the series, *Call of Duty: Modern Warfare 2* (Infinity Ward 2009), and reports from publisher Activision indicated sales exceeded US$1 billion soon after the game's release (Raman 2010). The *Call of Duty* series began on the PC in 2003, with multiple titles later developed for console and mobile markets. These games are not military simulations in the same sense as flight or tank simulators, but they market their own sense of "realism," advertising the fidelity of weapon and physics models, photorealistic patterns of light and particle rendering, dynamic weather effects, and other environmental details. (See Welsh's further discussion of this series later in this collection.)

The blurring of historical and mimetic realism is central to the advertised experience of the multiplayer setting. In *Medal of Honor* (2010) two human teams compete to eliminate each other and carry out various military-themed objectives. The games unfold across multiplayer "maps," sections of modeled terrains and buildings simulating the locations of battles in the 2001 US invasion of Afghanistan. The Cold War fantasy setting of *Call of Duty: Black Ops* (2010) samples a diverse range of historically and politically significant locations, such as the Berlin Wall and the Hanoi Hilton, to stage competitive battles, in game modes such as Capture the Flag (CTF) and Team Deathmatch (TDM).

The complex overlay of mimetic authenticity and historical realism rendered by the software, shaped to fit the generic conventions of the FPS game, result in what Galloway (2006) calls "realisticness" or that which is held up to representation as a "yardstick" to determine its authenticity:

> Realisticness is important, to be sure, but the more realisticness takes hold in gaming, the more removed from gaming it actually becomes, relegated instead to simulation or modelling. (73)

These regions of difference are collapsed in the connections made between military training and ideology, recruitment and propaganda, simulation and entertainment in what J. C. Herz (1997) refers to as the "military entertainment complex."

Games have long been used as simulations of military conflict and strategy (Deterding 2010), but military FPS games, suggest Hunteman and Payne (2009), are key elements in a post-Cold War phenomenon that further blurs the line between entertainment and militarism (4–5). Through the process of remediation (Bolter and Grusin 1999), videogames have appropriated multiple sources of mediated military ideology and propaganda, combining them with multiple levels of discursive reinforcement via the operation of the simulation. Deterding (2009) regards the videogame simulation as "blackboxing" its ideological and mechanical operations, obfuscating and naturalizing the embedded relations between militarization and videogames as part of what Der Derian (2009) calls the "military-industrial-media-entertainment network."

The nexus of entertainment and ideology in FPS games is an extension of the connections between warfare and media industries made by Virilio (1989), and FPS games mark an important stage in the development of these connections. Everything in the videogame industry may have at some point been financed by US military research (Wahrman, in Herz 1997, 205), but innovations like *Marine DOOM*, the US Army's modification of the FPS game *DOOM II* (id Software, 1994), and the FPS multiplayer game *America's Army*, reveal multiple directions in which remediation occurs; *Marine DOOM* was a transformation of the "high octane violence" of the original game to fulfill the role as training simulator (Richard 1998, 341), while *America's Army* mediates the basics of US military training in the first-person perspective in order to promote its agenda.

Halter's (2006) analysis of the links between videogames and the US Army argues such games are created explicitly to further nationalist propaganda and considers *America's Army* to be directly aligned with recruitment by encouraging the player to "try on the army for size" (Wardyinksi, in Delwiche 2007, 92). *America's Army* is described by Nieborg (2010) as a "strategic communication tool" functioning as an "immersive advertisement in the form of enter-tainment," combining educational, ludic, marketing, and propaganda elements in an FPS shape to promote "a highly politicised recruiting and public relations agenda" more dynamically than traditional forms of mediated and branded edutainment (54).

It is through the tandem operation of propaganda and ideologically aligned experiences in *America's Army* that Stahl (2010) argues videogames are increasingly both the medium and the metaphor by which we understand war "taking up quarters in our hearts and minds" (112):

> The two-way traffic between computer gaming and military simulations in the military-entertainment complex signposts a significant moment in the pure war tendency, one in which a further stage of the merger between the sphere of military and domestic activity and concerns is reached. (Crogan 2003, 280)

The concern is not only the militarization of entertainment as propaganda, but also the virtualization and digitalization of military ideology, as an extension of the conduct of war, by pure simulation and a sanitized geopolitical rendering of war (Der Derian 2009).

The "realisticness" of the simulation of *America's Army* minimizes mimetic and historical realism and lacks the more extensive photo-realism and graphic violence of *Medal of Honor* and *Call of Duty*. Players in the multiplayer matches of *America's Army* are only ever able to see themselves as US Army soldiers; both sides see themselves as American soldiers, while the opposing team are always rendered on-screen as the opposing force. A variety of races and uniforms is available in *Call of Duty: Black Ops*, and players in multiplayer version of *Medal of Honor* are split into the Coalition and the Opposing Forces, in a stylized and "realistic"—if not accurate—reproduction of Taliban uniforms and clothing.

Bogost (2008) considers all simulations as subjective representations that communicate ideology, but argues the "interpretation of a game relies as much or more on what the simulation excludes or leaves ambiguous than on what it includes" (105). As Stahl (2010) suggests:

> Presenting war in the guise of a game alone is not sufficient to play at war, the presentation must also be absent the horrors a high-tech military machine can effect. (111)

It is not only the full horror of weaponized violence that *America's Army* and other military games omit, as *The Onion* (2009) parody of the "next generation" *Call of Duty* game teases, it is also the "realism" (or naturalism) of hauling equipment, filling out paperwork, cleaning mess halls and "standing outside a photorealistic warehouse for hours" that are missing. The result of omission, argues Stahl (2010), is the extension of mainstream American news coverage, offering the player the opportunity to "fight a war largely without human consequence" (126).

Affects and Multiplayer FPS games

To paraphrase Grossberg (1992), videogames exist in an unpredictable, but productive, relation with those who play, operating in the domain of affects. Attention to this domain is crucial to a full understanding of the power of play and games which incorporate specific representations and realities (Grossberg 1997, 83). A simulation does not simply deploy its ideological content to the player in a predictable manner:

> … audiences are not made up of cultural dopes; people are often quite aware of their own implication in structures of power and domination, and of the ways in which cultural messages (can) manipulate them. (Grossberg, 1992, 53)

Affects are fleeting experiences and articulated in the practices which form relations between audiences and texts, economies, lives, and politics. They register in the participatory media cultures of FPS players producing online video, wikis, podcasts, mods, levels, maps, and weapons, running online servers and communities, and in the everyday play of gamers.

There are many types of "affect" and the term is often used as a synonym for emotions or feelings, but affects are different to purely cognitive functions and they transform our game experiences in unique ways. Emotions are produced in the articulation of signification and affect (Grossberg 1992, 1997) and the social and linguistic reordering of the quality of an experience (Massumi 1997,

2002); they are the displays of biographically constructed feeling that are broadcast, contrived or sincere, to communicate internal states (Shouse 2005). Affects are a modulation of investment; they register in the pitch of sensation that energizes emotion, meaning, identity, creativity, and relationships, and they provide tone to everyday life (Grossberg 1992, 56). Affects complement and complicate the semiotic and the social experience of an FPS game, "texturing" the processes of the experience:

> … texture refers to the qualitative experience of the social world, to embodied experience that has the capacity to transform as well as exceed social subjection (Hemmings 2005, 549).

Affects are also directly involved in the intensity of gameplay as an "incipience" of action and expression (Massumi 2001, 3) which challenges the way we typically approach concepts like "realism," "immersion," and "violence" in games.

In *Parables of the Virtual*, Massumi (2002), describes the "mystery of the missing half-second" (28), a recursive physiological ordering, a latency, or what FPS gamers would call a "lag" between "the beginning of a bodily event and its completion in an outwardly directed, active expression" (29). The half-second is not an empty moment, but an excess, just as cognitive functions are amplified and imbued with violation, performances of other reactions of the body occur in the brain, parallel to consciousness they are invigorated "between brain and finger but prior to action and expression" (ibid).

Massumi's half-second plays an important role in multiplayer FPS games, where it is referred to as the "twitch," the involuntary reaction of the body to events before the cognitive interpretation of action can occur. In the multiplayer environment the body's actions are antici- pated in the software code that attempts to compensate for the time it takes for signals to travel across networks. The twitch is part of the kinaesthetic pleasure of the cybernetic system operating with the body, between brain and finger, controls, hardware processors, game engines, rendering software and to the controls, fingers, and brains of other bodies involved in the game. It is a fleeting trace of affect, like the excitement, pitch, or tenor of a voice, or dramatic volley between players of opposing teams.

Affects leave a residue in the body, a lasting impression that accumulates over time and practice, like a muscle memory, producing particular kinds of bodily capacities to affect and to retain the potential to be affected; it shapes subjectivities, gathering in the materials of experience. Like the creativity of the dancer or professional athlete, games like sports leave traces of invigoration, or "innervation" as Swalwell (2008), following Hansen's use of Walter Benjamin's term, prefers: the creative conversion of somatic and motoric stimulation into new forms of action through the kinaesthetic involvement of affect required to "master" the game (86–7). As with the movements of a dancer or surgeon, the movements of an FPS gamer are not just the result of an accumulation of practice but the products of acts of invigorated creativity and spontaneous emissions from that range anywhere from elation to frustration, and through the processes of timing, repetition, and memory possessed by the body in combination with their affective and cognitive capacities, the player brings into being something new. Although more subtle, the movements of the gamer's body are just as crucial to the performance of the game.

Game scholars have only just begun to explore the potential for expanding the understanding of the play of games as events that involve visceral and bodily experiences (Carr 2006; Shaw and Warf 2009), but these accounts still tend to emphasize the degree to which "realism" and "immersion" have primacy in the understanding of FPS games. The games industry elevates "realism" and "immersion" by attracting attention to the visual and acoustic authenticity of its products, particularly in the FPS genre. This notion of "realism" contributes to the cycles of moral panic over videogame "violence" to a degree that often goes unrecognized by videogame critics, perpetuating the cause-and-effect view of the Columbine theory. The trap of the Columbine theory, argues Galloway (2006), is the proposition that games not only appear to be "realistic," but also generate "realistic" effects that are limited to the desensitizing of the player to acts of violence and the converse increase in aggression (78).

As part of the national debate on videogame violence and the lack of an R18 category for videogames in Australia, the Attorney-General's Department commissioned a review of the literature on the relationship between playing videogames, violence and aggression. The report concluded that the divided nature of the research reduced the literature's relevance to policy, as even the statistically "small to moderate range" for increased aggression in the short term after playing violent games did not indicate harmful effects in the long term, and that some studies demonstrated "cartoonish" violence was just as likely to have the same result as "realistic" violence (Attorney-General's Department 2010, 42). The debates over definitions and measures of "aggression," "violence," and "realism," and the failure to account for a fuller range of experiences when playing, belong to a regime governed by signification that attempts to organize understanding of the body's response to the play of FPS games confined within a narrow model of stimulus and response.

All military FPS games offer similar physics simulations, accurate weapon details and sounds, avatar models, and environmental textures, and they all feature standardized multiplayer game modes, yet each game plays and responds differently and each has its own "feel." The "weight" of the weapons as the player moves in the game, the depth of the menu and characterization interface, or the variation of the sounds, all produce very different player responses, even between games in the same series. This is also true of the way games play across different networks and platforms; not only the code differs but player styles and strategies also vary.

Battlefield: Bad Company 2 (2010) and the online multiplayer version of *Medal of Honor* (2010) were both developed by EA DICE Creative Entertainment (hereafter DICE), a Swedish games developer, with the Frostbite game engine. They each feature a range of playable classes for short, mid and long range combat that upgrade over time as the player earns experience points to expand their weapons, armor, and special abilities. The differences between the two games are apparent as soon as play begins and they make themselves known in the representational elements of the game, from the Kubal marketplace battles of *Medal of Honor* to the more anonymous military outfits and locations of the *Battlefield* games. Despite their common heritage in designers and code—or perhaps because of it—each game still takes time to adapt to; they each render terrain, lighting, accuracy, and weapon damage differently, forcing players to re-evaluate their tactical choices and playing styles. The games play and feel differently and result in individual, if similar, experiences, like two different codes of the same sport.

Promotional material for the 2010 "reboot" of the *Medal of Honor* series, published by Electronic Arts (hereafter EA), reveals the two-team structure of the multiplayer version was to split players into the "elite" US Special Forces and soldiers of the Taliban. This was not an unexpected set-up for those players who had been reinventing terrorist and counter-terrorist roles in *Counter-Strike* (Valve 2000) for a decade. Several weeks prior to launch, EA bowed to political and media pressure and withdrew the name "Taliban" from the team options, replacing it with the military designation for the "opposing forces" of enemy combatants, OPFOR, a move which Bogost (2010) considers to have undermined the legitimacy of the games indus- try's claim to freedom of speech in general and EA's specific claim to realism in the experience of play. Players on the OPFOR still have access to the Taliban-style uniforms, sound effects, and weapons, making the play experience of that side very distinct from the US "Special Forces." Removing the signification of the name, however, does not overly detract from the affective sensations that emerge through play of what remains.

Being an FPS gamer does not automatically align the player with the positive or negative ideological strategies embedded in the representational or simulated structural elements of the game to be naturalized without interrogation, but involves a complex set of competing concerns. The forms of engagement and investment a player has with a game can be considered in a mode of operation of what Grossberg (1992) calls a "sensibility" (54)—an investment within a particular cultural context, or "apparatus," that identifies how games and play practices are experienced. For example, to be a gamer—someone who seeks out games to play—indicates a special affective relationship with games, a sensibility involving an investment similar to that of a fan's relation to a sport, team, or cultural text. Investment in FPS games involves an active negotiation with meaning and subjectivity that produces a different sensibility to that of non-game texts. Despite the stereotype of the average gamer, this sensibility does not preclude interesting and informed public discourse in the digital and network spaces of the military

FPS genre. I have enjoyed *Call of Duty* games against self-described "Anarcho-Marxists" and read enthusiastic in-game text chat debates between pacifists and enlisted soldiers while playing *America's Army* matches. Snider et al. (in this collection) consider the shift involved in FPS "griefers" who deconstruct the representational and ludic functions of games, abstracting the metagame experience, as a form of creative user action that undermines the strategic elements of gameplay (rules, objectives, structures) through a tactical engagement that utilizes the affects of surprise, anger, humor in the construction of an alternative gamer persona. (See also Moore, 2011 for a discussion of the role of affect in creating online gamer persona.)

The console and PC versions of the current generation of military-themed FPS multiplayer games have access to digital distributions services, including Steam (Valve) on the PC and Xbox LIVE for the Xbox 360 (Microsoft). The player establishes an online identity, a "persona," very much connected to their "real" selves through commercial transactions of these services and based on their player name. The gamer persona is representational element of the affective investment in the game, a pool of collected scores, purchases, player histories, scores, and social interactions. It is an identity that is dominated by player statistics that are displayed in online forums like batting averages and in-game achievements are collected like trophies and displayed via online player profile pages (Moore 2011). Other social networking technologies connect gamers in networks of online "friends," groups and allegiances, supporting online communities often called "Clans" in the FPS genre (equivalent to "Guilds" in Massively Multiplayer Role Playing Games) developing further affective investment.

Online personas are collections of digital artifacts and complex traces of networks, relationships, activities, and histories of investment during play. In *Medal of Honor* and *Call of Duty: Black Ops* players can specialize the standard avatar equipment options available to all by "unlocking" further items in the game, inciting investment and new waves of excitement and interest. By participating, the player earns points to spend on in-game items, cosmetically and tactically personalizing the way their avatar and equipment function and appear to others. In the remit of impression management (Goffman 1959) the gamer persona gives information to others through the creative use of avatar and abilities, choice of in-game items, and management of the player profile. Information and affect is further exchanged, "given off" and transmitted by the other actions of the player in-game.

Immersion and Invigoration

The concept of "immersion," like the terms "realism" and "realistic," have become all-inclusive categories that collapse a range of cognitive and affective phenomena which occur when designing and playing videogames. It is typically assumed that the subjective perspective of FPS games increases the "immersion" of the player, meaning the player is "caught up" in the game (McMahan 2003, 86). Immersion is said to be evoked spatially and narratively as a "sense of presence in the virtual environment" expanded by the social forms of interaction that are part of the multiplayer experience (Thon 2006, 244). Murray (1997) considers the phenomenon of immersion to be involved in the sensation of being surrounded completely by another reality. Immersion follows the logic of Salen and Zimmerman's use of Huizinga's term the "magic circle" to describe how play unfolds within a specific time and space that suspends ordinary meanings, where the procedures of action and the communication of meaning are governed by modified rules and understandings (Salen and Zimmerman 2004, 95).

Refocusing attention to the affects of play, the sense of intensity and involvement of FPS games can instead be considered as "invigoration," and we can examine FPS games a product of affective alliances invested in the apparatus of the game that are part of the real world, and the everyday activities of gamers. In the multiplayer games like *Medal of Honor* and *Call of Duty: Black Ops*, where some game modes only last for minutes at a time, "invigoration" is the degree of modulation that aids the player's responses, enfolding the body and its reactions in the event. For many gamers FPS play is a casual activity, they come and go, it is part of a series of occasional activities, while for others it is an everyday event that heavily influences their sense of identity and ordering of social life. The "vlogging" YouTube practice, known as *Road to Commander*, is a live recorded commentary of the player's progress through a *Call of Duty* game to reach the rank of Commander at level 50 (see Whiteboy 7th St, 2011). The series provides a document of the types, ranges, and amplitude of the player's invigoration (and its opposite), a record of player's affects that may be observed in their exclamations, pitch, intensity, and their experiences over the duration of the challenge.

The invigoration of play has a quantity and a quality that matters according to sensibility and degree of investment in the individual game, the genre, and the act of playing. Unlike immersion, invigoration does not always result in the unnoticed passage of time; it survives interruption and does not require the surroundings to be all-encompassing. The "twitch" is one of many invigorated actions, but it is not a response that can be depended on as advantage in an FPS game as it is unpredictable and often passes without notice. Massumi (2002) considers consciousness and will to be subtractive, making the twitch unfaithful to intent; the body acts of its own accord, limited but rich with texture. The fast pace of *Call of Duty: Black Ops* online matches and short respawn times means that players are often dropped directly into an ongoing combat, where the twitch is just as likely to result in teamkills and other forms of "collateral damage" as it is to aid the player. Similarly, caught up in the affective sensations of game, the opposite of the twitch, the "freeze" also occurs where the player's affective capacities compete with the player's cognitive functions, resulting in a split-second pause. Where a gamer's competitive FPS strategy will focus on maximizing the representational elements (structures, rules, weapons, etc.) to impose an order on the competition, attempting to reduce the randomness of play, their tactics on the other hand are heavily influenced by the invigorated affective responses to the dynamic conditions of play, calling on heightened reactions, charged emotions and attenuated senses. (See Snider et al. in this volume, for a discussion of De Certeau's delineation between strategies and tactics in relation to the FPS practice of "griefing".)

Invigoration is one of the key dimensions of affect in multiplayer FPS games that complicate the role of ideology and signification. Play already exists in an altered state of engagement with meaning; it is a "meaningful" activity, according to Huizinga (1970/1949), but one that is spatially and temporally separate from the demands of meaning in everyday life. Game death, for example, does not "represent" death in the actual world (as Welsh describes later in the collection, the player does not in actuality "die" or "kill"), but rather game death is an invigoration and its occurrence preferences the affective reaction over its ideologically embedded representation. Game death occurs when the player's avatar is "damaged" enough to "kill" their avatar, forcing the player outside of the operational field into player limbo, where depending on the game mode they await their "respawn" into the action of game events where they can view the ongoing match from the perspective of their "live" teammates.

Game death, suggests Richard (1997), is a perpetual tabula rasa, allowing the player to pause and start over to rethink their previous moves and plan new paths, but each death matters as a ludic sensibility of movements, trajectories, and scores as well as being an abstraction of war and violence. Game death is an important part of FPS play, but the representation of death is not experienced or intended in the same way as death in other media, or in "actuality"; while perhaps initially frustrating, together with the respawn function game death becomes a transitive affect halting the state of frenetic activity of the battle, to enable reflection and clear the way for further invigoration.

The "occurrent" narrative of multiplayer FPS games as an event that is stimulated and subdued by the affects that occur during play, which shares a linear but unscripted experience with other sports and public performances. Game death is an embodied perception of the capacity to act and the result of the cybernetic interactions between players and the software and hardware of the networks involved. A highly cathartic event, game death is part of the full-bodied synaesthetic experience of embodied perception involved in play that Shinkle (2005) describes as "incorporating emotions but not reducible to them." Game death is undesirable, but also pleasurable; cognitive functions recompose the events, while the body deals with the experience of tension and its release. Feelings backfill, allowing the shock of the event to register in its completeness, frustration or elation emerges as cognition is required to take in the proceedings of the event. Game death emphasizes the drama of the occurrent narrative of the multiplayer FPS game and the more invigorated the player, the more potential they have to invest in the situation. Similarly, unlike warfare strategy, the multiplayer environment of any military FPS is at its most exciting when the two teams are well matched, even in ability and experience; when one team completely dominates another, the dampening of affect in the losing team is usually highly apparent.

Competitive matches are very different and highly regulated experiences when compared to casual public play. The coverage of the largest competitive *Call of Duty* gaming league in the US, *Major League Gaming*, remediates US sports and entertainment media to produce their own narrative from a successful broadcast model. Professional gamers, like competitive athletes, train and practice, learn strategy and communication skills. Galloway (2006) considers that to know the system is to win, but gamers also need to develop their own tactical responses, to produce what Massumi (2002) describes as player "style," small but crucial and embodied ways of directing the flow of events (77). A style, particularly a new style, is "a germinal individuation of the sport" (78) and a highly contagious provocation of the system and the established modes of play.

Many of the innovations in FPS games evolve this way: the classic *Counter-Strike* (Valve 2000) "bunny-hop" was discovered to exploit the way the system assigned targets making the jumping player hard to hit, the *Quake* (id Software 1996) rocket launcher was used by innovative players to create the "rocketjump" inverting the weapon to aid propulsion, flying the player across the map rapidly. In online *Call of Duty: Black Ops* communities, fans debate uses of particular weapon and ability combinations. Some of the game servers ban individual abilities and players harass others for using technically legitimate but socially unacceptable options, shaping the direction of the matches.

Gibbs (2001, 2008) writes of Gabriel de Tarde's account of the social life of the crowd as a site of affect contagion, producing mimetic communication between bodies. Gibbs also gives account of Tomkins' (1962) taxonomy of affect, which acknowledges the way affect is spread, such as the baby's smile or cry that triggers the affect of distress or enjoyment. Gibbs considers how facial expressions transmits affect televisually, illustrating how politicians use distress, anger, excitement to communicate mimetically to different social groups, facilitating amplification of the affect in progress. Media become amplifiers of affects, a process which Gibbs (2007) explains as an affect intensified in the degree of its arousal. Tomkins considered the face a primary site of affect transmission but it is not the only site—the voice and movement are also capable of mimetic communication. (See Taylor's account of the role of verbal communications in competitive *Halo* matches in this volume.) Many PC gamers use third-party software (Knap 2002) to host their multiplayer game voice chat; for games like *Medal of Honor* and *Call of Duty* on the PC it makes the public matches sound quieter and feel more isolated than when playing the console versions and other games enabled with in-game voice chat.

Games function as sites of affect amplification, magnification, and contagion, but not in the same fashion as television or cinema, and with unpredictable and surprising results. Wendig (2010) gives example of the importance of affect contagion in the events of a game of *Call of Duty: Modern Warfare 2*, when he writes that in other mediums saturated with adults a twelve-year-old male might be dismissed out of hand as a prepubescent not yet versed with the necessary experience to lead a team to victory, but he found that age, race, or gender matter less when confidence spreads like wildfire. Wendig describes a game in which the boy he nicknames Pip took control of the game not through rage or excitement, but in self-assurance, daring and style.

The affective relationship between gamers and their games accompanies the transition to online services as physical properties give way to digital distribution. The games industry has developed a range of marketing practices in order to capture the player's investment as affective capital. One of the most effective strategies has been the microtransaction adopted in the FPS genre by Valve in *Team Fortress 2* (2007). (See Manning in this volume and Moore [2011] for the analysis of the affective dimensions of the aesthetics and play of TF2.) Along with the next installment of *Call of Duty*, Activision will offer a subscription service for players to join the "*Call of Duty* Elite" to encourage player investment by gaining access to further degrees of connectivity to other players through social networking and player statistic tracking features, mobile apps and monthly downloadable content (DLC), all designed to expand the players' access to new customizations, maps, and game modes and maintain their investment in the game.

Conclusion

Affect is one of many non-representational ways of expanding the critical frame for thinking and talking about the transformative aspects of FPS games. This chapter has not rejected the critique of the ideological power of military FPS games, but has sought to expand its frame of reference. Affects are not neutral; if the invigoration of the player is also a politicization of the potential of the player, then its methods of control are equally politicised. Grossberg (1997) reminds us that "affective relations can be disempowering ... rendering ideological and material realities behind a screen of passion" (87). Crogan (2003) also sees a further danger, suggesting that games of war refigure time with anticipatory impulse that encourages action without reflection, leaving out ethical consideration. Galloway (2006) takes this refiguring perspective to the extreme, describing the FPS game as a realization of André Breton's "pure surrealist act" (103).

Massumi (2002) argues that affect holds the key to rethinking power after ideology, which is no longer encompassing or defining power, but still present and virulent (42). Grossberg (1992) acknowledges affect as the necessary condition of optimism, invigoration, and passion, "necessary for any struggle to change the world," and considers popular culture as providing a range of resources from which forms of struggle and resistance may be sourced and tested (86). Anderson (2010) suggests the points of "excess" of affect, like those in FPS games, can further the examination of systems of signification to provide "... ontological foundation for the promise of a new way to attend to the social or cultural in perpetual and unruly movement" (162), but acknowledges it is the transitive excess of affect, its intensification and modulation that is precisely the target of new forms of power.

References

Anderson, Ben. 2010. "Modulating the Excess of Artifact: Morale in a State of Total War." In *The Affect Theory Reader*, edited by Melissa Gregg and Gregory Seigworth, 161–85. Durham: Duke University Press.

Attorney-General's Department. 2010. *Literature Review on the Impact of Playing Violent Video Games on Aggression.* Commonwealth of Australia. http://www.ag.gov.au/gamesclassification#review.

Bogost, Ian. 2008. *Unit Operations: An Approach to Videogame Criticism.* Cambridge, Mass: MIT Press.

—2010. "Persuasive Games: Free Speech is Not a Marketing Plan." *Gamasutra.* http://www.gamasutra.com/view/feature/6158/persuasive_games_free_speech_is_.php?page=1

Bolter, Jay David and Richard Grusin. 1999. *Remediation.* Cambridge, Mass: MIT Press.

Carr, Diane. 2006. "Space, Navigation and Affect." In *Computer Games Text, Narrative, Play*, edited by Diane Carr, David Buckingham, Andrew Burn, and Gareth Schott, 59–71. Cambridge: Polity Press.

Crogan, Patrick. 2003. "Gametime: History, Narrative, and Temporality in Combat Flight Simulator II." In *The Video Game Theory Reader*, edited by Mark J. P. Wolf and Bernard Perron, 275–302. New York: Routledge.

Deleuze, Gilles. 1992. "Postscript on the Societies of Control." *October* 59: 3–7.

Delwiche, Aaron. 2007. "From *The Green Berets* to *America's Army*: Videogames as a Vehicle for Political Propaganda." In *The Player's Realm: Studies on the Culture of Video-games and Gaming*, edited by J. Patrick Williams and Jonas Heide-Smith, 91–109. NC: McFarland.

Der Derian, James. 2009. *Virtuous War: Mapping the Military-Industrial-Media-Entertainment-Network.* New York: Routledge.

Deterding, Sebastian. 2009. "Living Room Wars: Remediation, Boardgames, and the Early History of Video Wargaming." In *Joystick Soldiers, The Politics of Play in Military Video Games*, edited by Nina Huntemann and Matthew Thomas Payne, 1–16. Routledge: New York.

Galloway, Alexander. 2004. "Social Realism in Gaming." *Game Studies* 4 (1). http://gamestudies.org/0401/galloway/

—2006. *Gaming, Essays on Algorithmic Culture.* Minneapolis, MN: University of Minnesota Press.

Gibbs, Anna. 2001. "Contagious Feelings: Pauline Hanson and the Epidemiology of Affect." *Australian Humanities Review* 24. http://

www.australianhumanitiesreview.org/archive/Issue-December-2001/
gibbs.html

—2007."Horrified: Embodied Vision, Media Affect and the Images from
Abu Ghraib." In *Interrogating the War on Terror*, edited by Deborah
Staines, 125–42. Newcastle: Cambridge Scholars Publishing.

—2008. "Panic! Affect Contagion, Mimesis and Suggestion in the
Social Field." *Cultural Studies Review* 14 (2): 130–45.

Goffman, Erving. 1959. *The Presentation of Self in Everyday Life*. New
York: Doubleday.

Golumbia, David. 2009. "Games Without Play." *New Literary History* 40
(1): 179–204.

Grossberg, Lawrence. 1992. "Is There a Fan in the House: The
Affective Sensibility of Fandom." In *The Adoring Audience:
Fan Culture and Popular Media*, edited by Lisa A Lewis, 50–67.
Routledge: New York.

—1997. *We Gotta Get Out of this Place: Popular Conservatism and
Postmodern Culture*. New York: Routledge.

Halter, Ed. 2006. *From Sun Tzu to Xbox: War and Video Games*. New
York: Thunder's Mouth Press.

Hemmings, Clare. 2005. "Invoking Affect: Cultural Theory and the
Ontological Turn." *Cultural Studies* 19 (5): 548–67.

Herz, J. C. 1997. *Joystick Nation: How Videogames Ate Our Quarters,
Won Our Hearts, and Rewired Our Minds*. Boston: Little, Brown and
Company.

Huizinga, Johan. 1970 /1949. *Homo Ludens: A Study of the Play
Element in Culture*. London: Temple Smith.

Hunteman, Nina and Matthew Thomas Payne. 2009. "Introduction." In
Joystick Soldiers: The Politics of Play in Military Video Games, edited
by Nina Huntemann and Matthew Thomas Payne, 1–16. Routledge:
New York.

Knapp, Brian. 2002. *Ventrillo*. [Microsoft Windows] Freeware. *http://
www.ventrilo.com/*

Manovich, Lev. 2001. *The Language of New Media*. Cambridge, Mass:
The MIT Press.

Massumi, Brian. 1997. "The Autonomy of Affect." In *Deleuze: A Critical
Reader*, edited by Paul Patton, 217–39. Oxford: Blackwell.

—2002. *Parables For the Virtual: Movement, Affect, Sensation*. Durham:
Duke University Press.

McMahan, Alison. 2003. "Immersion, Engagement and Presence: A
Method for Analyzing 3-D Video Games." In *The Video Game Theory
Reader*, edited by Mark J. P. Wolf and Bernard Perron, 67–86. New
York: Routledge, New York.

Moore, Christopher. 2011. "Hats of Affect: A Study of Affect,
Achievements and Hats in *Team Fortress 2*." *Game Studies* 11(1).
http://gamestudies.org/1101/articles/moore

Murray, Janet. 1997. *Hamlet on the Holodeck*, New York: The MIT Press.

Nieborg, David. 2010. "Training Recruits and Conditioning Youth: The Soft Power of Military Games." In *Joystick Soldiers: The Politics of Play in Military Video Games*, edited by Nina Huntemann and Matthew Thomas Payne, 53–66. New York: Routledge.

Onion, The. 2009. "Ultra-Realistic Modern Warfare Game Features Awaiting Orders, Repairing Trucks." *The Onion*. Accessed 10 April 2011. *http://www.theonion.com/video/ultrarealistic-modern-warfare-game-features-awaiti,14382/*

O'Riley, Tim. 1998. *Representing Illusions: Space, Narrative and the Spectator in Fine Art Practice*. Chelsea College of Art and Design, London, The London Institute Fine Art. Accessed April 4, 2011. http://www.timoriley.net/

Raman, Manikandan. 2010. "Call of Duty: Black Ops Sales Top $1 Bln." International Business Times. Accessed 25 April 2011. http://au.ibtimes.com/articles/94558/20101222/activision-video-game-shooting-game-call-of-duty-black-ops-call-of-duty-modern-warfare-2-xbox-360-pl.htm.

Richard, Birgit. 1998. "Norn Attacks and Marine DOOM." In *Ars Electronica: Facing the Future*, edited by Timothy Duckrey, 153–63. Massachusetts: The MIT Press.

Salen, Katie and Zimmerman, Eric. 2004. *Rules of Play: Game Design Fundamentals*. Cambridge: The MIT Press.

Seigworth, Gregory. 2005. "From Affection to Soul." In *Gilles Deleuze, Key Concepts*, edited by Charles Stivale, 159–69. Chesham: Acumen.

Shaw, Ian and Warf, Barney. 2009. "Worlds of Affect: Virtual Geographies of Video Games." *Environment and Planning A* 41 (6): 1332–43.

Shinkle Eugénie. 2005. "Corporealis Ergo Sum: Affective Responses in Digital Games." In *Digital Gameplay: Essays on the Nexus of Game and Gamers*, edited by Nate Garrelts, 21–35. Jefferson: McFarland & Company.

Shouse, Eric. 2005. "Feeling, Emotion, Affect." *M/C Journal* 8 (6). http://journal.media-culture.org.au/0512/03-shouse.php.

Stahl, Roger. 2010. *Miltainment, Inc. War Media and Popular Culture*. London: Routledge.

Swalwell, Melanie. 2008. "Movement and Kinaesthetic Responsiveness: A Neglected Pleasure." In *The Pleasures of Computer Gaming*, edited by Melanie Swalwell and Jason Wilson. 72–93. Jefferson: McFarland & Company.

Thon, Jan-Noel. 2006. "Communication and Interaction in Multiplayer First-Person Shooter Games." In *Communication to Presence,* edited by Giuseppe Riva, M. Teresa Anguera, Brenda Wiederhold, and Mantovani Fabrizia, 239–61. Amsterdam: IOS Press.

Tomkins, Silvan. 1962. *Affect, Imagery, Consciousness, Volume 1.* New York: Springer.

Virilio, Paul. 1989. *War and Cinema: The Logistics of Perception.* Translated by Patrick Camiller. London: Verso.

—2002. *Desert Screen: War at the Speed of Light.* London: Continuum.

Watkins, Megan. 2010. "Desiring Recognition, Accumulating Affect." In *The Affect Theory Reader,* edited by Melissa Gregg and Gregory Seigworth, 269–86. Durham: Duke University Press.

Wendig, Chuck. 2010. "The 12-Year-Old English Kid Who Carried Us to Victory." *The Escapist.* December 28. http://www.escapistmagazine. com/articles/view/issues/issue_286/8463-The-12-Year-Old-English-Kid-Who-Carried-Us-to-Victory.

Games

Danger Close and DICE. 2010. *Medal of Honor* [Microsoft Windows, PlayStation 3, Xbox 360]. Electronic Arts.

DICE, 2010. *Battlefield: Bad Company 2* [Microsoft Windows, Xbox 360, PlayStation 3, iOS] Electronic Arts.

id Software, 1994. *DOOM II* [DOS, Microsoft Windows]. GT Interactive.

—1996. *Quake* [Microsoft Windows]. GT Interactive.

Infinity Ward. 2009. *Call of Duty: Modern Warfare 2* [Microsoft Windows, PlayStation 3, Xbox 360]. Activision.

Treyarch. 2010. *Call of Duty: Black Ops.* [Xbox 360, PlayStation 3, Microsoft Windows, Wii]. Activision.

US Army. 2009. *America's Army* (v.3) [Microsoft Windows, Xbox]. US Army.

Valve. 2000. *Counter-Strike* [Microsoft Windows]. Valve.

—2007. *Team Fortress 2* [Microsoft Windows, PlayStation 3, Xbox 360]. Valve.

16

Repelling the Invasion of the "Other": Post-Apocalyptic Alien Shooter Videogames Addressing Contemporary Cultural Attitudes[1]

Ryan Lizardi

The current videogame cultural landscape contains many popular genres and formats. Frequently, certain types of games that deal with the same subject matter are released within a relatively short time period. Much like dynamics present in other forms of media, this can be explained partially by the economics of the culture industry, which will latch onto a profitable popular idea. However, it can also be explained by examining cultural preoccupations with certain themes and ideas. One such subject matter that has recently become prevalent within the videogaming world is the post-apocalyptic game that depicts an invasion and defense from an outside and most times alien force. From the enormously popular *Halo* series (Bungie 2001 to present) to the *Gears of War* series (Epic Games 2006 to present), there are countless versions of the same basic story of an alien force that must be repelled by the human race to secure its freedom and future existence.

The US videogame industry in particular has recently been flooded with these alien invasion videogames. That is not to say that other areas of the world do not delve into this subgenre, but when viewed in terms of popularity and volume of titles the appearance of a cultural preoccupation is evident in the US. Over the past seven or eight years this type of game, with its generic and stylistic similarities, has consistently finished in the top ten of US game sales, with certain series like *Halo* (Bungie 2001) and *Gears of War* (Epic Games 2006) dominating sales when they were released (NPD Group 2009). For instance, "*Halo 3*, the best-selling title of 2007, took in more revenue in its first day of sales than the biggest opening weekend ever for a movie" (Guzder 2008). If one compares sales of these kinds of games in Japan, one of the most important global videogame markets, other than the first *Gears of War* they never finish close to the top ten and many times do not make the top one hundred (Famitsu 2011). There are many series, such as *Crysis* (Crytek Frankfurt 2007 to present) and *Killzone* (Guerrilla Games 2004 to present) that are published in Europe and that deal with many of these issues, but they typically sell better in the US market so remain important for this analysis.

What are the cultural implications of the US preoccupation with these dynamics and themes occurring so often in the videogame medium? With the frequency and potency of these games on the rise, there is no doubt that American gamers are preoccupied with this form of story, immersing themselves in the post-apocalyptic world with increasing frequency. If one wants to make sense of this attraction, it is important to understand the historically contingent issues that have surrounded the rise of this subgenre's popularity. Ismail Xavier has posed a useful theory for these purposes, known as historical allegories, which looks at the way media texts address historically grounded issues through symbolism (2004). Along these lines, scholarly works have dealt with videogames addressing issues like post-9/11 culture, but little attention has been paid to the alien invasion games that, while trading in the same fear of destruction, have transcended these political and cultural concerns. Instead, they address deeper-held Western ideas, such as a Eurocentric view of the world, which features a sharp distinction between Insiders and Outsider "Others," and the related theme of US reputation overseas.

Videogames are viewed many times as the province of children's toys, and to some they appear to constitute mere "entertainment," but one could also argue that because of the level of interactivity, their cultural impact is significant. Game designers may feel as if they are simply telling multidimensional stories, but when interactive texts are imbued with latent political significations and disseminate ideological positions, then nothing could be more important to study. Structuralist Louis Althusser (1971) advised that "a work of art can become an *element* of the *ideological*" (244), and Roland Barthes, in dealing with cultural myths, discussed how anything from laundry detergent to wrestling can carry great ideological significance (1972). For this analysis, it is most significant that these games speak to contemporary US politics and ideological beliefs that may be damaging to society and US reputations.

In studying this cultural phenomenon, it will be important to look at the videogame texts themselves to see how they deal with important historically contingent issues. This textual analysis will employ a semiotic framework and will look at both the in-game narrative content, such as story, characters, and environments, as well as the equally important gameplay elements, such as player controls, perspectives, and interfaces. Both areas of the texts are to be explored, aligning this analysis with Jesper Juul, who discusses the "'war' between ludology and narratology" and says that there should be a "balanced" approach to this debate (Egenfeldt-Nielsen et al. 2008, 195). In fact, Juul's work in this area of videogame research is invaluable when trying to consider both these areas. Juul (2005) states that "fiction *matters* in games and it is important to remember the duality of the formal and the experiential perspectives" (199). Narrative elements speak allegorically to contemporary issues and ludic elements can be seen as a way for players to "work through" and reify difficult cultural ideologies that arise in important historical contexts.

There are quite a few examples of these games to examine, with the "shooter" subgenre being no stranger to the videogame world. Games like *Duke Nukem* (3D Realms 1996), and close relatives *Half-Life* (Valve 1998) and *DOOM* (id Software 1993), were released long before the current trend this analysis is addressing, but videogames are currently inundated with post-apocalyptic alien shooters. This analysis will perform a close examination of the *Resistance* (Insomniac Games 2006 to present), *Gears of War*, and *Killzone* series, while touching briefly on other examples from the subgenre, such as *Halo*, *BioShock* (2K Games 2007 to present), and *Dead Space* (Visceral Games 2008 to present). These specific series are emblematic of the larger subgenre of games that deal with an alien force that must be destroyed or repelled for the sake of mankind. There will be a specific focus on videogames of this subject matter that are part of a series, both because of the large amount of content and gameplay to be viewed, and also to show the remarkable consistency of symbolic allegorical content over time.

Allegories, 9/11, and Ethnocentrism

Though Xavier's theory for understanding historical allegory has mostly been used to study films, it is also helpful for unpacking the abstract subject matter and narrative structure of videogames. Historical allegory theory is especially adept at making sense of rashes of a specific subject matter, in that they can adapt at different key historical junctures to symbolize "an encompassing view of history presented in a condensed way" and "can intervene in cultural and political debates" (Xavier 2004, 361). This subgenre of games deals with subject matter that cannot be said to literally deal with issues of today's culture and society, because they are set in a post-apocalyptic world and the enemies are not other people but aliens. In this same volume, Gerald Voorhees discusses the normalization of the FPS genre once there was a shift from fantastical alien settings to a more grounded, realistic, and human antagonist. Though on the surface this seems to be in opposition to this chapter's ascertainment of this genre's increasing reliance on these fantastical alien settings as allegory, when examined deeper both chapters argue for legitimization through engaging with America's strategic overseas endeavors, even if it is symbolic in the case of alien "invasion" games. Another author in this volume, Timothy Welsh, offers a different take on the realism scale by arguing that when presented with detached and indifferent digital violence, such as using an unmanned and remote-controlled Predator plane to attack adversaries in *Call of Duty 4: Modern Warfare* (Infinity Ward 2007), players are led to potentially questioning their position in the military-industrial complex. For this chapter, as well as Voorhees' and Welsh's, a main issue is realism's connection to the FPS, and historical allegory theory works well in this case as it examines content on a symbolic level within specific historical contexts.

While prior theoretical examinations of the contemporary culture of videogames have not used historical allegory as a framework, many do look at the way videogames address societal issues. Much has been written about recent games speaking to the issues of a post-9/11 society, and they make some important claims, but the subgenre dealt with in this analysis has moved past these issues and onto more long-term cultural preoccupations of broader US relationships with the outside world. An example of the standard post-9/11-centric analysis is the idea that "game publishers shelved or delayed projects with images, plotlines or game-actions reminiscent of the events" and that the games released since then "have become a medium for responding to an environment of threat and uncertainty" (Lowood 2008, 78). Toby Miller also addresses, in this volume, the increasingly close ties videogames have with military attitudes, recruitment, and interestingly with labor concerns. These theorists deal mostly with games like *America's Army* (US Army 2002) and the *SOCOM* series (2002 to present), with contemporary settings and events as their subject matter. These insights are important, but do not completely address the issues and themes that are prevalent in the alien invasion games analyzed here.

Though not dealing with the same subgenre, Nowell Marshall is helpful for this analysis because he develops a framework in the discussion of how videogames symbolically and allegorically deal with broader US attitudes towards the outside world. Marshall (2004) analyzes the game *City of Heroes*, and says that this game contains "rigid xenophobic borders against a variety of aberrant bodies" (141). Marc Ouellette (2008) is even more direct in saying "I want to analyze videogames which function allegorically (at the very least metaphorically) and pedagogically through their imbrication with the web of so-called 'post-9/11' narratives" (par. 2). Building off of and expanding on this notion, this analysis will move past the issues society dealt with during and after the events of 9/11. It will look at how these particular videogames speak to the more long-lasting, broader issues of US attitudes toward outsiders and the ways in which Western notions and ideals are the paramount lens with which the nation sees itself in relation to those culturally different.

It is one thing to simply state that the United States has a tenuous contemporary relationship and attitude towards other countries and regions around the world, but it is necessary to explain how these dynamics have originated and how they factor into the experience provided by these videogames. Significant historical events must be discussed and cultural theories, like Shohat and Stam's examination of Eurocentrism, must be explained to ground this videogame subgenre.

The set of games that deal with a post-apocalyptic world, and the resistance against an opposing force that threatens humanity, became prevalent and popular at a time when the US was in a negotiation with how it was perceived by the rest of the world. This is not to say that this time period, loosely defined as 2002 until the present, was the first time that videogames dealt with this subject matter. In fact, one could even make the argument that the under-lying stories of early games like *Space Invaders* (Taito Corporation 1978) and *Missile Command* (Atari Inc. 1980) were very similar. But the addition of historically contingent details, like the wars in Iraq and Afghanistan not universally popular around the globe, created and enhanced some tenuous relationships with outside countries.

Possibly the most widely discussed tense relationship due to these events came about because France openly did not support the US decision to invade Iraq. The ensuing fallout from this tension resulted in the temporary push to change things like french fries to "freedom" fries (Loughlin 2003). This is an example of a culture shifting to adapt to historical issues. Inevitably, pop culture begins to address these issues as well. An episode of *The Simpsons* from 2005 has Lisa traveling abroad and donning a Canadian patch on her backpack because "some people in Europe think that America has made some stupid choices for the past, oh, five years" (Groening 2005). This analysis will show how a similar kind of cultural referencing happens in post-apocalyptic videogames, only on a more symbolic allegorical level. This is not to say that these events and videogames are not intertwined with the post-9/11 dynamics discussed by other theorists, it is just that the kind of referencing going on is symptomatic of long-term attitudinal change in the way the US views itself in relation to other countries. Like an overcompensation of sorts, these videogames address the idea that the United States is pushing other countries away because it feels unaccepted. In pop culture, the United States is going to take its metaphoric ball and go home, because it did not want to play with the other countries anyway.

Shohat and Stam posed some helpful ideas about this type of attitude in their influential book entitled *Unthinking Eurocentrism* (1994). Obviously many of the tensions in these recent historical events involve US relationships with not only cultural "Others" like Iraq, but also some countries in Europe itself, evident with the "freedom fries" example. So a more proper term for the purposes of this analysis might be the more widely known ethnocentrism. Shohat and Stam (1994) view ethnocentrism as seeing "the world through the lenses provided by its own culture" (22), and specifically for these theorists this attitude can lead to an "idealized notion" of one's own viewpoint (14). This refers to the static assumption that everything is how it has always been, and that things like "science and technology" as well as "all theory" come from one's own culture (14). Another related term that is helpful in this explanation of ethnocentrism is Said's "orientalism." Said (1978) discusses a devaluing of cultures different from one's own and says that comparing cultures "always get involved either in self-congratulation (when one discusses one's own) or hostility and aggression (when one discusses the 'other')" (325). For the purposes of this analysis of the post-apocalyptic videogames, the terms ethnocentrism and orientalism will be used to explain the two related phenomena of believing that one's own culture is inherently ideal, and that other cultures are inherently inferior and need to be violently subdued in these games.

Repelling the "Other"

The actual videogame texts themselves are rich in details to study and there is no shortage of evidence to affirm their allegorical preoccupation with the concepts of ethnocentrism, orientalism, and the related US reputation overseas. This analysis will focus on the in-game story, characters, and environments, as well as the interactive gameplay perspectives, how the player controls the game, and the interfaces that the player encounters. These elements will be viewed through a semiotic lens to see how these different traits and characteristics of the narrative and ludic elements signify the dynamics of national identity discussed here. The signifiers in these videogames point to the struggles over land, freedom, survival, and the all-important "imulsion" (read oil) of the *Gears of War* series.

Beginning with the ways in which these games allegorically represent an ethnocentric viewpoint and the way they embody Said's orientalism, it is important to look at both the in-game traits of the "human" characters as opposed to the "aliens," as well as the perspective in which these games place their players. There is a blurry distinction between the characteristics that make up each "species" and this leads to the idea that both are derived from the same foundational base. Understanding the allegorical symbolism of the human within the alien is key to this chapter's argument, and is addressed in this volume's chapter by Dan Pinchbeck, who describes an adaptation process where supernatural elements in a novel are rendered predictable and knowable in the videogame. This is especially important when understanding the coding of the alien characters as cultural "Other" and the identification players feel with the protagonists of the game.

In the *Gears of War* series, for example, human beings have been attacked by creatures that have risen up out of the ground and destroyed most inhabited areas. These creatures walk on two legs, have the basic facial structure of human beings (eyes, mouth, nose), and speak in a form of garbled "English." These physical traits signify that they share a foundational genetic similarity with the humans themselves, and this opens up the possibility of reading them as signifying a different race than the protagonists. The skin color of the creatures, called Locust by the humans, as well as their uneven skin texture mark them as different and "Other." The protagonist characters in the *Gears of War* series would not all be considered White, with the main group including a man coded as Black and another coded as Latino, but with their English and their mannerisms they all signify American. The Locusts' speech, which can be understood to contain words like "Die Ground-Walker" as if it was spoken with a severe rasp, connotes that the language spoken by them is related to English but foreign at the same time. All of this points to the aliens being coded as human-like enough to understand, but as being racial and culturally different enough to repel. It is in their similarities that the connection can be made that these creatures do not simply denote a completely alien race attacking the humans, but instead they connote a race of humans that is strange and foreign to the protagonists. It should be noted that anthropomorphized alien creatures are not only common within the science fiction genre, but also make sense in shooter games for movement and aiming purposes. However, the addition of "garbled" English and features so closely resembling humans pushes this feature towards "Othering."

These same signifying dynamics are present in other videogames of the same subject matter. The *Resistance* series also depicts humanity under siege from an alien force that is threatening to take over all areas of the world. The creatures in this game, known as the Chimera, also walk on two legs and have the basic movements and characteristics of human beings. The connection between alien and human in this series is even more direct because the Chimera are "created" by incubating human beings in pods to "convert" them. They emerge from these pods with eight eyes and different-colored skin, signifying their connection with humanity alongside their "Otherness." In *Resistance 2* (Insomniac Games 2008), the protagonist Nathan Hale gets up close and personal with these pods as he encounters an infested small town where they hang from the very walls of idyllic small-town homes. Not only does the presence of the pods containing half-formed Chimera in the homes of the humans signify the connection between the two species, but also when Hale breaks open the pods there is an unmistakable splash of blood that sprays. Blood is an important theme throughout these games because, as Michel Foucault (1979) states, blood signifies and is "*a reality with a symbolic function*" (147). In this case, the red blood that breaks loose from the pod, along with the half-formed Chimera that falls out, signify the connection these creatures have to human beings. Some games are even more blatant about the connection between humans and the invading "alien" forces. The *Killzone* series depicts a post-apocalyptic world where a group of humans was forced to leave and live on the planet Helghast. These former humans, now known as Helghans, attack the remaining humans. The Helghans must wear respirator masks due to the Helghast atmosphere, but they are direct descendants of the human race.

Figure 16.1 The European box cover art for *Resistance 2* (Insomniac Games 2008) further highlights the connection between humanity and the invading alien "Other."

All of these examples of narrative elements speak to the connection of the alien forces to humanity and yet "Others" them so as to make them easily killable. This distinction between "Other" and normal, as a feature of media texts, is a process reminiscent of the canonical social psychological work of Henri Tafjel that discussed in-group and out-group dynamics. Tafjel (1974) states: "in order for the members of an in-group to be able to hate or dislike an out-group, or to discriminate against it, they must first have acquired a sense of belonging to a group which is clearly distinct from the one they hate, dislike or discriminate against" (66). In these alien invasion videogames, the in-group is established as the normal Western human beings and the out-group established as the "Other" aliens, which stand in for the broader cultural "Other." This coding and the added element of symbolic violence serve to attack cultural "Others" without complicating gamers' identification with game protagonists. Blurring the lines between human and alien helps to reify cultural fears of those that are different through serial violence done to the alien "Others."

With this dynamic present, the focus turns to which side of the fight the player identifies with the most. In the interactive videogame medium, this identification is tied up with a game's specific interface perspective. Videogames in general have seen an influx of games designed with the label "shooter" attached. Shooters are defined as "three dimensional navigation in virtual environments in which the player interacts in single or multiplayer combat sequences by using a range of weaponry in order to complete a mission or objective" (Nieborg 2003, 1). The three-dimensional aspect of the shooter is especially important for understanding how player identification is fostered through these games. Audiences identify with these games because they have "enormous persuasive potential" by creating "immersion, intense engagement, identification, and interactivity" (Delwiche 2007, 92). Nacke and Lindley (2008) discuss the immersive aspects of shooters and describe how playing this type of game increases "imaginative immersion and that this feeling is related to spatial presence" (86).

In the post-apocalyptic games examined here, identification is fostered directly by the three-dimensional nature of the genre and the perspective from which the player takes control. Most of these games are considered FPS, which means that the player sees the game environment as if they were looking through the eyes of the protagonist. This gameplay element gives the player a literal viewpoint from which to see the events of the game unfold. Doris Rusch (2008) states, "the visceral joy of first-hand experiences is strongly related to the experience of agency" (29), but this agency is also focused through the constraints of the game itself and so any meaning garnered from this environment will come through the protagonist's field of vision. When a player is controlling Nathan Hale, the main protagonist for the first two *Resistance* titles, they are seeing only what he sees and understanding the world through him. *Killzone*, *BioShock* and *Halo* are just a few of the examples of series that follow this perspective.

The *Gears of War* series is an exception to this FPS tendency, using a perspective called "third-person shooter." This is an important distinction, as *Gears of War* places its players over the shoulder of the protagonist Marcus Fenix. The third-person perspective does not give players the exact view of Marcus but does, however, not allow you to turn and see his face for most of the game. Because this third-person perspective is restrictive, it still has elements of identification with the main character and for the most part the player is still seeing what Marcus sees. Taking into account this variation on the tendency to use first-person perspective in these games, letting players only see through the eyes of the humans, the subject whom they are given to identify with, is still a prevalent technique used to foster identification with the protagonists in the post-apocalyptic subgenre, thereby de-emphasizing any kind of identification possibilities with the "Other" characters.

The physical distinctions between humans and aliens, and the perspective that players control the game through, are not the only dynamics that foster a sense of ethnocentrism within these games. The gaming environments and architecture also play a big role in making the fight over survival and freedom in these games one that is fought over the "important" areas of the world. The settings of the post-apocalyptic alien shooter games and even the buildings themselves are a constant reminder to the player of what is important to save in the fight to rid humanity of the invading forces. This spatial element can be seen as a hybrid of a narrative and ludic concern of the videogame texts, because though the settings and buildings play a part in how the story is constructed, they also are part of the physical environment of the game itself. Juul (2005) echoes this sentiment when he states "space in games can work as a combination of rules and fiction" (163). So not only is the player getting to experience a spectacle from the perspective of the shooter, but is also entering into a pact with the game by following the rules.

In many of the post-apocalyptic videogames being studied here, the tendency is to depict the world worth saving as one very familiar to Western or American areas. There are not many videogames that come to mind set in sub-Saharan Africa, with the somewhat related game *Resident Evil 5* (Capcom 2009) as a major exception. Instead, the contested spaces of these apocalypses are depicted as areas that are either exact depictions of Western landmarks or areas that bear an iconic resemblance to familiar places. This element is important to look at in games due to its signifying practices, as well as the idea that videogames can be seen "as a spatial art with its roots in architecture" where "everything was put on the screen for a purpose" (Jenkins & Squire 2002, 64).

In *Resistance 2*, when the battle for humanity's survival is fought in the looming shadow of the Golden Gate Bridge and on the iconic streets of Chicago, there is a powerful signified message about the importance of these areas to be saved. The *Resistance* series discusses the worldwide nature of the fight against the Chimera, shown through animated maps that depict a black spread over large sections of the globe, but significantly the player does not fight these creatures in Third World countries or the Middle East. This fight takes place in Britain and in the US. This geographically specific element even came under some scrutiny in the first game of the series, *Resistance: Fall of Man* (Insomniac Games 2006), as the Manchester Church of England publicized their disapproval of the game's combat scene that took place in a digitized version of the church (Edidin 2009). When digital representations of these areas and structures signify that the war over the freedom of humanity is to be fought in the West, they allegorically stand in as ethnocentric.

Even when the structures themselves are not digital representations of actual areas and buildings, these games still use architectural elements and historical tropes to index the Western world. These familiar environments help to reify the cultural Western values discussed here by creating a space that has a feel of value and verisimilitude. In the *Gears of War* series, it is important to note that the humans do not live on Earth, but instead have moved to the fictional planet Sera. The buildings and areas that exist in this gamespace cannot depict real-world counterparts, but what they do is index Western architectural history and First-World, upper-class structures. As players roam the streets of Sera in *Gears of War*, they encounter Gothic-style churches with flying buttresses and buildings that resemble an early American Colonial style. The human beings of Sera did not have to follow along this progression of architectural styles that were present on Earth. Instead, it would have been fully logical to skip past these historically iconic styles, to whatever style was prevalent on Earth when human beings left to colonize Sera. These architectural choices signify that the battle between the Locusts and humans is being fought in the West, even if it is on a different planet.

This dynamic is common in these post-apocalyptic games, with the planet Helghast in *Killzone 2* (Guerrilla Games 2009) looking like any First-World industrial planet at war and *BioShock* (2K Boston 2007) looking like Chicago, even though the game takes place under water. Even *Resistance 2*, which takes place among many recognizable places in the US, uses some of these more abstract iconic architectural signifiers. In the aforementioned level in which the player enters homes filled with pods of Chimera, the very ordinary nature of these homes and their white picket fences stands in for the Middle America ideal home. Peter Berger (2008) discusses how videogames create powerful signifiers when something within the games "mimic a believable element of the physical world" (51). All of the contested spaces in these videogames create powerful signifiers and, whether they are indexing real places or standing in as iconic, point allegorically to the ethnocentric viewpoint of what is worth saving in the apocalypse.

Another prevalent theme within this set of games related to the notion of an ethnocentric viewpoint is the sharp distinction between Insiders and Outsiders, one that is made all the more powerful by virtue of the interactive mode of identification with the protagonist hero. It is not surprising that this distinction would be made in a set of games that deal with war and with alien "invaders," but coupling this theme with the more insidious ethnocentrism makes the Insider/Outsider dynamic important to study. The distinction pushes into the realm of orientalism and manifests itself through three inter-related techniques in these games: the language used to describe the aliens, the attitude towards their presence, and the origins of the creatures themselves. All of these elements reflect not only the borders between the Insider group and the Outsider group, but also how this symbolically serves as a historical allegory for societal attitudes towards cultural "Others."

The language used to describe the "invading" forces in these post-apocalyptic videogames is abrasive and vitriolic, even in the derogatory nicknames that are used. The language always reflects the explicit distinction between Insiders and Outsiders in these worlds. In the *Gears of War* series, the Locusts are nicknamed Grubs and the descriptive terms that accompany this name, like "disgusting" and "dirty," reflect the distance the humans want to put between themselves and a Locust. When players kill a Locust the main character, Marcus, will say one of a few different lines, such as "Get back in your hole!" and "Scratch one Grub" or the

Figure 16.2 The appearance of the Locust in this *Gears of War* (Epic Games 2006) promotional screenshot emphasizes the similarities between them and the humans, making the language used to describe the Locust that much more problematic.

particularly abrasive "Eat shit and die!" This language sharply marks the Insider/Outsider distinction and what the humans really think of the creatures. These lexical "taglines" are reminiscent of 1980s masculine action films in which hyper-male characters "reacted" to masculinity challenges with "an especially vigorous re-assertion of heroic potency and virility" (Sparks 1996, 355). It is not only what the *Gears* protagonists say about these creatures—though calling them "abhorrent foes" is quite rough—it is also the vigor and contempt signified in their tone of voice that is significant.

In *Killzone 2*, there is equal disdain and hatred for the opposing Helghans, but instead of derogatory nicknames this game resorts to using a vast amount of expletives, unrepeatable in most situations, to describe these foes. This linguistic feature is not only present in the way the humans and aliens are described, but also in the attitude taken towards their mere presence. The irony of the lexical choices in this dynamic will be more evident in the discussion about the creatures' origins in these games, but for the moment it is important to note how the presence of the invading forces is discussed with disdain. Examples include the aforementioned *Gears* quote about sending the Locust "back in your hole" and a human reaction to a speech made by the opposing Helghans in *Killzone 2* to which the human replies "Listening to this shit makes me want to break something." Whether in the *Killzone* series, where the Helghans are considered "less than human," or in the *Halo* series, where the smaller creatures of "The Covenant" invaders are called "Grunts," the language used to describe the forces that must be repelled by the humans is reminiscent of cultural "Othering." It specifically marks them as Outsiders in comparison to the human Insiders. The leader of the humans in *Killzone 2* states "We have beaten back our foes, sent them running." In these games, this is language common in the Insider/Outsider distinction.

Perhaps most important in this Insider/Outsider discussion are the origins of the creatures themselves. Throughout this examination of the post-apocalyptic videogames, it has been necessary at times to make qualifications about the nature of terms like "aliens" or "invaders." This is because the origins of the various creatures in these games are not as clear-cut as they seem on the outset. A somewhat unexpected trend in these games is to place the origin of the force that the humans are fighting as already having been present in the areas of conflict. The story of an invading force coming down to Earth that humans must fight is not the story told in these games. Instead, it is that these creatures were already present where the fighting occurs and in some cases it is the humans that would actually be considered the "invaders." This is an important distinction to make, especially when considering the broader claim that these games are allegorizing contemporary US attitudes and issues.

Finding an example in these post-apocalyptic videogames that signifies the origin of the "alien" forces as already present is not hard. In fact, it is finding one that does not have this dynamic that is difficult. *Gears of War*, for example, follows the colonization of a planet named Sera by humans. Though these humans had time to build up Gothic churches and massive mansions, the Locusts inhabited Sera before the humans. The Locusts had been below "gathered under every major city" and "emerged" from the ground to attack the humans. This points both to the distinction between who is an Insider in this society and who is an Outsider, and makes the language used to describe disdain for the presence of the Locusts all the more ironic and significant. The ignorance in one of the human soldier's statements, "Were they down here, like, forever?", speaks also to the ways in which these colonial-like relationships ignore the history and heritage of the colonized. So when the leader of the humans states that the Locusts are "inhuman, genocidal monsters," these creatures are really just defending their own homes and resources.

The Insider/Outsider distinction is even more of an issue in the *Resistance* series. The "invading" creatures, known as Chimera, share nearly the exact same relationship with the humans that the Locusts do in *Gears*. The Chimera were also "already present" here on Earth, an issue made clear when it is revealed that the giant "spire" structures that act as bases for the Chimera were not built but excavated, and that the original "Pure Chimera" were on Earth 60 million years ago. Again, this makes the fact that such a sharp distinction is made between the humans and "aliens" in this game all the more significant. There is also the added element, discussed in the comparison of human and alien signifying traits, that the Chimera are created by converting human beings. How is it possible to make a clear distinction between who is a human Insider and who is a Chimera Outsider? Even Nathan Hale is infected with the Chimera virus, which makes him more powerful, signifying a continuing Insider/Outsider issue. In *Resistance 3* (Insomniac Games 2011), Nathan Hale is displaced by Joseph Capelli as the series protagonist, as Capelli needed to kill Hale at the end of the second game because his Chimera infection was out of hand, signifying that once Hale had truly become Chimera, therefore an Outsider, he needed to be eliminated.

Even when the "aliens" are not already present on Earth, or whatever area the humans occupy, there is still many times a tenuous relationship between "invaded"/"invader" and Insider/Outsider. In *Resistance 3* and *Gears of War 3* (Epic Games 2011), infighting amongst different factions of aliens is highlighted as just one of the ways these distinctions are clouded, but there is one narrative trend in this subgenre that is more problematic when considering ethnocentrism. Both the *Killzone* and the *Halo* series are about forces that "invade" the planet occupied by humans, but then as the series narrative progresses these humans take the fight to the planets of the original invaders. In *BioShock* (2K Boston 2007) and *BioShock 2* (2K Marin 2010), the plot takes place in an underwater city that never bothered any inhabited area above water. In fact, in the first game of the series a plaque adorning the entrance to this city states: "In what country is there a place for people like me?" In these games, who is signified as allowed to occupy the space of the Insider and who is relegated to the status of Outsider is important for contemporary historical allegories.

Stemming directly from these videogames' ethnocentric viewpoints and distinctions between Insiders and Outsiders is the third allegorical theme: the reputation and issues the US has with other countries. These games symbolically address attitudes and prevalent discourses that surround current historically contingent foreign relations, such as the justifications for war and contemporary versions of Said's orientalism. In these games, no matter how much the evidence is stacked against the humans that they should at the very least consider the possibility that they are not completely in the right, the humans continue to feel justified in their fight.

The opening cinematic when one turns on the game *Killzone 2* is emblematic of this theme's presence in the post-apocalyptic shooter games. The cinematic consists of a speech given by the leader of the "alien" Helghast forces, who are being invaded by humans and not the other way around. The Helghan leader states that the humans are attempting to "seize by force, what they cannot have by right" and that when this is all over "they will know, Helghan belongs to the Helghast." It is not a stretch to understand the logic of this speech, as it makes sense that the planet Helghan does indeed belong to the Helghast, but the human soldiers shown watching this speech still feeling justified in their fight. At least these soldiers might consider the hypocritical stance they occupy, but instead their actions signify their continued ethnocentrism. In fact, by the end of *Killzone 3* (Guerilla Games 2011) Helghan is irradiated by an element known as Petrusite, when human forces blown up a cruiser that contains nuclear warheads. Helghan might belong to the Helghast, but the humans have left it mostly inhabitable, even if they did so inadvertently.

The *Gears of War* series depicts an even more blatant version of allegorically speaking to contemporary reputations of the US overseas in their justifications of war. In this game, "imulsion" is a key resource on the human-occupied planet of Sera. It is described as a highly potent and powerful fuel source that runs underground and is very valuable. The humans had been occupying Sera for quite some time and using this "imulsion" when the Locusts decided to fight back, in part, against this use of their resources. It is quite easy to make the connection of "imulsion" as standing in for oil and the entire narrative of *Gears* as speaking to the larger attitudes and reputations about the US overseas. When the leader of the humans, Richard Prescott, states in *Gears of War 2* (Epic Games 2008) that they will take the fight to the Locusts and attack "where they live and where they breed, we will destroy them," this is said in the face of mounting evidence that it is the Locusts who are justified in this fight, not the humans. These elements in the *Gears of War* series signify a lack of consideration of Other cultures' rights and justifications, as well as a whitewashing of the historical factors that led society to this point. In the latest game in the series *Gears of War 3* (Epic Games 2011), the Locusts and humans learn they should work together to eradicate the "imulsion" as it is posed to destroy Sera, but peace is too hard to come by when there is so much animosity.

In contemporary US reputation and relations with other countries, tenuous discourses about the justifiability of war and the attitude taken to those who do not share their opinions has been common. Adding the theme of justified war to the other themes of an ethnocentric viewpoint and a preoccupation with who gets to be an Insider or Outsider, these videogame texts symbolize a set of long-lasting ideological issues and attitudes prevalent in contemporary US history. By appearing again and again in this contemporary game subgenre, these elements become allegorical for contemporary cultural preoccupations with battling threatening Otherness.

Conclusion

It signifies a great deal about a society when its cultural texts continually address the same subject matters and issues over a certain time frame. Ismail Xavier (2004) poses that in historically contingent situations, texts can speak to the concerns of a culture on an allegorical level and "can intervene in cultural and political debates" (361). One such cultural preoccupation that allegorizes US contemporary culture is the set of videogames that depict a post-apocalyptic world overrun by "invaders," who are most times shown as an alien force. Jesper Juul (2005) states that "players undoubtedly also want to be able to identify with the fictional protagonist and the goal of the game in the fictional world" (161). So what does it say about culture when players are identifying with a set of games that have an ethnocentric, Othering point of view?

These games, taking the form of the shooter genre, are widely popular and are able to allegorically address concerns because of their symbolic nature. Theirs is a story of war, but not of a conventional war between humans. They instead deal with a war of human beings fighting for their survival against "invading" hordes. When viewing these games through a semiotic/textual analysis lens, there are significant themes that emerge time after time. Through their narrative and ludic elements these texts exhibit an ethnocentric viewpoint, made clear through comparisons of humans and aliens as well as the perspective the players take. They are also preoccupied with signifying who is an Insider in these worlds and who is an Outsider and what this means for areas of the world that "deserve" to be fought over. As Ouellette (2008) describes, this is a "save everyone like you; kill everyone else" mentality (par. 15). Finally and related, these games possess the theme of justified war in the face of contrary evidence, manifesting itself because of the unexpected origins of the "invading" creatures. All of these themes are interrelated and intertwined, signifying, through historical allegory, that this set of post-apocalyptic shooters is addressing some of the long-term contemporary issues and attitudes that the US is dealing with, especially when it comes to foreign relations and reputation. Call it "imulsion" or call it oil, the allegorical significations for contemporary cultural attitudes remain the same.

Note

1 A previous version of this work originally appeared in 2009 in *Eludamos: Journal for Computer Games Culture* 3 (2): 295–308.

References

Althusser, Louis. 1971. *Lenin and Philosophies and Other Essays*. University of Michigan: New Left Books.

Barthes, Roland. 1972. *Mythologies*. New York: Hill and Wang.

Berger, P. 2008. "There and Back Again: Reuse, Signifiers and Consistency in Created Game Spaces." In *Computer Games as a Sociocultural Phenomenon: Games Without Frontiers, War Without Tears*, edited by Andreas Jahn-Sudmann, 47–55. New York: Palgrave Macmillan.

Delwiche, Aaron. 2007. "From *The Green Berets* to *America's Army*: Video Games as a Vehicle for Political Propaganda." In *The Player's Realm: Studies on the culture of video games and gaming*, edited by J. Patrick Williams and Jonas H. Smith, 91–109. Jefferson, NC: McFarland and Company, Inc.

Edidin, Peter. 2007. "Arts, Briefly: Sony says 'sorry.'" *The New York Times*, June 16. http://query.nytimes.com/gst/fullpage.html?res=9A0 2E6D6153FF935A25755C0A9619C8B63&scpt.

Egenfeldt-Nielsen, Simon, Smith, Jonas H., and Tosca, Susana P. 2008. *Understanding Video Games*. New York: Routledge.

Famitsu. 2011. http://www.famitsu.com

Foucault, Michel. 1979. *The History of Sexuality, vol. 1: An Introduction*. London: Allen Lane.

Groening, Matt. "The Italian Bob." *The Simpsons*. Television. Directed by James L. Brooks. Los Angeles, CA: 20th Century Fox Television, 2005.

Guzder, Deena. 2008. "Video Games: Still Booming in a Bad Economy." *Time.com*, December 24. http://www.time.com/time/business/article/0,8599,1868630,00.html.

Jenkins, Henry and Kurt Squire. 2002. "The Art of Contested Spaces." In *Game On: The history and culture of videogames*, edited by Lucien King, 63–74. London: Laurence King Publishing.

Juul, Jesper. 2005. *Half-Real: Video Games Between Real Rules and Fictional Worlds*. Cambridge, MA: MIT Press.

Loughlin, Sean. 2003. "House Cafeterias Change Names for 'French' Fries and 'French' Toast." *CNN.com*, March 12. http://www.cnn.com/2003/ALLPOLITICS/03/11/sprj.irq.fries.

Lowood, Henry. 2008. "Impotence and Agency: Computer Games as a Post-9/11 Battlefield." In *Computer Games as a Sociocultural Phenomenon: Games Without Frontiers, War Without Tears*, edited by Andreas Jahn-Sudmann, 78–86. New York: Palgrave Macmillan.

Marshall, Nowell. 2008. "Borders and Bodies in City of Heroes: (Re) Imaging American Identity Post-9/11." In *Computer Games as a Sociocultural Phenomenon: Games Without Frontiers, War Without Tears*, edited by Andreas Jahn-Sudmann, 140–9. New York: Palgrave Macmillan.

Nacke, Lennart and Craig A. Lindley. 2008. "Flow and Immersion in First-Person Shooters: Measuring the player's gameplay experience." Paper presented at *Future Play '08*, Toronto, Ontario, Canada, November 3–5: 81–8.

Nieborg, David B. 2003. "*America's Army*: More than a Game?" *Gamespace*. December 23. http://www.gamespace.nl/content/ISAGA_Nieborg.PDF.

NPD Group. 2009. "NPD sales figures." *Wikia Gaming*. http://vgsales.wikia.com/wiki/NPD_sales_figures.

Ouellette, M. A. 2008. "'I Hope You Never See Another Day Like This': Pedagogy & Allegory in 'Post 9/11' Video Games." *Game Studies* 8 (1). http://gamestudies.org/0801/articles/ouellette_m.

Rusch, Doris. 2008. "Emotional Design of Computer Games and Fiction Films." In *Computer Games as a Sociocultural Phenomenon: Games Without Frontiers, War Without Tears*, edited by Andreas Jahn-Sudmann, 22–31. New York: Palgrave Macmillan.

Said, Edward. 1978. *Orientalism*. New York: Routledge & Kegan Paul.

Sparks, Richard. 1996. "Masculinity and Heroism in the Hollywood 'Blockbuster'." *British Journal of Criminology* 36 (3): 348–60.

Shohat, Ella and Robert Stam. 1994. *Unthinking Eurocentrism: Multiculturalism and the Media.* New York: Routledge.

Tafjel, Henri. 1974. "Social Identity and Intergroup Behavior." *Social Science Information* 13 (2): 65–93.

Xavier, Ismail. 2004. "Historical Allegory." In *A Companion to Film Theory*, edited by Toby Miller and Robert Stam, 333–62. Malden, MA: Blackwell Publishing.

Games

2K Boston. 2007. *BioShock* [Mac OS X, Microsoft Windows, PlayStation 3, Xbox 360] 2K Games.

2K Marin. 2010. *BioShock 2* [Microsoft Windows, Xbox 360, PlayStation 3]. 2K Games.

3D Realms. 1996. *Duke Nukem 3D* [DOS]. GT Interactive Software.

Atari Inc. 1980. *Missile Command* [arcade]. Atari.

Bungie. 2001. *Halo: Combat Evolved* [Xbox]. Microsoft Game Studios.

Capcom. 2009. *Resident Evil 5* [Microsoft Windows, Xbox 360, PlayStation 3]. Capcom.

Crytek Frankfurt. 2007. *Crysis* [Microsoft Windows]. Electronic Arts.

Epic Games. 2006. *Gears of War* [Xbox 360]. Microsoft Game Studios.

—2008. *Gears of War 2* [Xbox 360]. Microsoft Game Studios.

—2011. *Gears of War 3* [Xbox 360]. Microsoft Game Studios.

Guerrilla Games. 2009. *Killzone 2* [PlayStation 3]. Sony Computer Entertainment.

—2011. *Killzone 3* [PlayStation 3]. Sony Computer Entertainment.

id Software. 1993. *DOOM* [DOS]. id Software.

Infinity Ward. 2007. *Call of Duty 4: Modern Warfare* [Microsoft Windows, PlayStation 3, Xbox 360]. Activision.

Insomniac Games. 2006. *Resistance: Fall of Man* [PlayStation 3]. Sony Computer Entertainment.

—2008. *Resistance 2* [PlayStation 3]. Sony Computer Entertainment.

—2011. *Resistance 3* [PlayStation 3]. Sony Computer Entertainment.

Taito Corporation. 1978. *Space Invaders* [arcade]. Midway.

Valve. 1998. *Half-Life* [multiplatform]. Sierra Studios.

Visceral Games. 2008. *Dead Space* [multiplatform]. Electronic Arts.

17

Face to Face: Humanizing the Digital Display in *Call of Duty: Modern Warfare 2*

Timothy Welsh

Within the first twenty-four hours of its release on 10 November 2009, Infinity Ward's *Call of Duty: Modern Warfare 2* (hereafter *MW2*) sold 4.7 million copies in the US and UK alone. A month prior, the game was already being discussed as a "terrorism simulator" (EDIDDY99 2009, Kietzmann 2009). Footage of the game's controversial "No Russian" level, in which the playable character participates in a terrorist attack on a fictional Moscow airport, leaked on the internet that October. *MW2* immediately reopened debates about violent videogames, a month before the game was even available to the general public to be played.

Ever since it was discovered that the Columbine shooters, Eric

Harris and Dylan Klebold, were fans of *DOOM* (id Software 1993), the FPS genre has been iconically linked to what Alexander Galloway (2006) calls the "'Columbine theory' of realism in gaming: games plus gore equals psychotic behavior, and round and round" (71). As discussed by Gerald Voorhees in this same volume, the mainstream has largely embraced videogaming along with its participation in Western militarism. Still, public reaction to *MW2* demonstrates that anxiety over the threat of real-world violence posed by virtual violence remains strong enough to supersede the experience of playing the game itself. For example, despite the fact that "No Russian" depicts an armed assault on civilians, when a suicide bomber detonated explosives in the real Domodedovo Airport in Moscow over a year after the game's release, members of the media in both Russia and the US claimed that the real-life attack "mirrored" the game (Thorsen 2011).

While the Columbine theory is still under debate (Kutner and Olsen 2008; Carnagey, Anderson, Bushman 2007), the oral arguments of the recent Supreme Court case *Schwarzenegger v. Entertainment Merchants Assn.* (2010) confirmed that the dominant conversation about videogame violence continues to presume a degree of compatibility between off-screen violence and its on-screen depiction. Justice Roberts, for example, explained the difference between games and books or movies as follows: "In these video games the child is not sitting there passively watching something; the child is doing the killing. The child is doing the maiming" (page 27, line 2). As Galloway points out, however, the Columbine theory assumes in-game violence has unidirectional influence. Because videogames "exert 'realistic' effects on the player," it does not matter how players access or interact with the content, only whether or not we want players, especially young players, participating in what we see on-screen (Galloway 2006, 78). From this perspective, it is sufficient to show "video clips of game play" as California Deputy Attorney General Zackery Morazzini did to support the claim that the "interactive nature of violent [games]," in which the player is "acting out this – this obscene level of violence," makes gaming "especially harmful to minors" (*Schwarzenegger v. Entertainment Merchants Assn.* 2010, page 5, line 25).

Arguments like Morazzini's take interactivity for granted, ignoring the fact that what the player can *do* in a videogame is always constituted by layers of mediation that determine the affordances by which the player can engage the virtual world. The player has a controller with a set of buttons mapped to in-game behaviors that trigger responses from the console to render the on-screen environment prompting the player for another button press and so on. The player's actual interaction with digital media is considerably mundane compared to the "obscene levels of violence" on-screen. Furthermore, gaming is necessarily metacommunicative, the player's actions in-game are framed by the context of play (Salen and Zimmerman 2003, 449). What happens on-screen is only ever "half-real" because the virtual environment never fully covers the rules of the game or the digital media itself (Juul 2005). Jesper Juul explains that as a result he can enjoy slamming a car into a busy intersection in *Burnout 2* (Criterion Games 2002), not because he wants to get into car accidents in real life, but precisely because it is a media-created event and the difference between the depicted crash and what it represents is never in question (193). No matter how compelling a gameworld may be, the videogame player is not doing the killing, the maiming, or anything equivalent to what happens on screen. He is playing a videogame and his in-game activities do not have the value or consequence of actual violence. The hapless airline patrons who fall victim to the player's assault in "No Russian" are only the visual representations of an algorithmic process. Players can shoot them again and again and they feel no pain and they always return when the level restarts. It is, therefore, remarkable that we show these inconsequential digital objects any sympathy at all.

This chapter discusses how the first-person perspective of the *Call of Duty: Modern Warfare* series (Infinity Ward 2007, 2009) organizes the player's affective response to non-playable characters (hereafter NPCs). A military shooter like *MW2* typically consists of eliminating wave after wave of interchangeable, insignificant NPCs. Though the prospect may outrage onlookers concerned about the apparent disregard for human life, players understand that these are infinitely respawning digital objects and therefore dispensable. The challenge for game-makers is less often to convince players to overcome an aversion to on-screen violence as it is to get them to attribute worth, value, and significance to an arrangement of pixels. Responding to this challenge, the *Modern Warfare* series uses its first-person viewport to personalize select NPCs by bringing them face-to-face with the player. Compared to "real" military encounters, however, such face-to-face confrontations fail to represent "authentic war experience" (Žižek 2001, 77). When the US military increasingly conducts its operations via real-time video feeds, networked surveillance data, and remote-controlled unmanned aerial vehicles (hereafter UAV), playing *MW2* most closely resembles *actual* modern warfare when it puts players behind the digital targeting interfaces of an AC-130 or the laptop controlling a Predator drone. Indeed, many of the same concerns about desensitized digitally mediated violence extend to contemporary military policy (Alston 2010). As I will argue, the coincidence of affects toward the digital within the military-entertainment complex (Sterling 1993; Lenoir 2000; Der Derian 2001; Wark 2007) situates players of the *Modern Warfare* series relation to the practice of actual war-at-a-distance. In this context, through their efforts to convince players to care about the NPCs they encounter face-to-face, these ultra-violent "terrorism simulators" become occasions for the articulation of new relationships to the virtualities of digital media.

This is not the first time a videogame has presented the opportunity for players to reflect on the relationship between gaming and militarized digital technology. The *Metal Gear* franchise in particular has distinguished itself by confronting players with their position in the military-entertainment complex through innovative use of the medium and intelligent self-reference (Higgin 2010). For example, the playable character Raiden from *Metal Gear Solid 2: Sons of Liberty* (KCEJ 2001) is "a virtual grunt of the digital age" who trained to be an elite counterterrorist exclusively in VR simulations, which are represented by gameplay footage from *Metal Gear Solid: VR Missions* (KCEJ 1999), the standalone release of "VR Mode" from *Metal Gear Solid* (KCEJ 1998).

The player's position as a gamer is central to the franchise's "critical rather than celebratory perspective on the military-entertainment complex" (Higgin 2010). As James Paul Gee explains, *Metal Gear* games consistently point out that "you are playing a video game, even a violent one, and even [suggest] that maybe such games are training for real violence and, hey, maybe you shouldn't be doing this." It achieves this complex positioning in a fundamental way through its "stealth action" gameplay, which rewards players for being "sneaky non-lethal" agents and avoiding confrontation (Gee 2009). The noteworthy boss battle against Sorrow in *Metal Gear Solid 3: Snake-Eater* (KCEJ 2004), for example, requires the player to move upstream as the spirits of all the NPCs he has killed to that point in the game impede his progress. The sequence turns a player's willingness to kill NPCs into an obstacle, hindering their ability to pass through the level. In doing so, the game inverts a foundational premise of the action genre, insisting on stealth rather than kill-count, and thereby complicates the player's position as a gamer in the context of digitally mediated warfare.

The *Modern Warfare* series, by contrast, situates gameplay in relation to modern military technologies through a full embrace of the conventions of the FPS genre. Ever since players squared off with cyborg Hitler in *Wolfenstein 3D* (id Software 1992), face-to-face confrontation with one's enemy has been a core element of the FPS experience. The *Modern Warfare* games are no different. Yet, in comparison to digitally mediated modern warfare, which is the subject material and context of the game, the spectacle of the face-to-face killing of another person has a quite different effect. As I will demonstrate, the *Modern Warfare* games in fact reconfigure virtual violence in and through the gruesomeness of confrontation itself. As Juul (2005) explains, "games – like stories – are things we use to relate to death and disaster" (193). Thus, crashing one's virtual car does not reduce one's aversion to being in an accident, but rather gives one a mechanism through which to think about car crashes. In this way, videogames can be an "extension of one's own social life," granting in-game virtualities significance well beyond their often violent content (Galloway 2006, 78). The first-person violence of games like *MW2*, even in the "No Russian" level, can therefore be a way for players to engage their position relative to actual modern warfare and the real violence mediated by digital technologies.

Modern Warfare

Infinity Ward's *Modern Warfare* series at time of writing consists of two games, *Call of Duty 4: Modern Warfare* (2007, hereafter *CoD4*) and *MW2* (2009), the first games in the *Call of Duty* franchise set in the contemporary period. More than just updating the scenery and weaponry, the *Modern Warfare* series shows politico-military conflict to be in a state of transition to what Galloway and Eugene Thacker (2007) call the "fearful new symmetry of networks fighting networks" (15). During the opening credits of *MW2*, images and audio clips from key moments in *CoD4* are projected on a huge map as network nodes illuminate and streams of green light establish connections across the globe, indicating that the events of the first game expanded the network of influence for the second game (Figure 17.1).

Indeed, the events of the series narrative precipitate from the US failing to recognize the limitations of opposing a networked enemy with a hierarchical force. In order to distract the world community while his Ultranationalists initiate the Second Civil War in Russia, Imran Zakaev provides support for a coup led by Khaled Al-Asad in an unnamed Middle Eastern country. When the US responds to the coup with 30,000 soldiers, Al-Asad's insurgents detonate a nuclear warhead, wiping out the US forces. The remainder of *CoD4* follows the members of counter-terrorism unit Task Force 141 as they uncover Al-Asad's connection to Zahkaev and eliminate the Russian revolutionary. *MW2* picks up five years later as Zahkaev's successor, Vladimir Makarov, frames the CIA for the terrorist attack

Figure 17.1 Opening credits sequence for *MW2* (Infinity Ward 2009) represents the series plot as a global network.

on Moscow airport depicted in "No Russian," instigating a full-scale war between Russia and the US. Seeing this as an opportunity to get revenge for the 30,000 troops he lost to the nuclear blast in the first game, Lieutenant General Shepherd attempts to destroy any evidence that would prove Makarov, and not the CIA, led the airport assault. Again, the remaining members of the 141 are the only ones who can prevent Shepherd from escalating the US-Russian war and reveal the truth about what happened at Moscow airport. Thus, even as Al-Asad's actions in the first game lead to open conflict of global superpowers, the outcome still depends on engagements between small, distributed, guerrilla forces such as the multinational 141, Russian, Middle Eastern, and South American insurgency groups, and contracted mercenaries. At the macro-level the series narrative certainly shows "nostalgia for the good old days of the Cold War," setting pro-Western US and British forces against the rise of anti-Western, communist ultra-nationalism in Russia (Galloway and Thacker 2007, 6). This showdown of global superpowers, however, is animated by an underlying network-vs.-network conflict.

Videogaming's participation in this "topological shift" has been well documented (Lenoir 2000; Halter 2006; Der Derian 2001; Wark 2007; Huntemann and Payne 2010). Exactly where commercial FPSs fit in today's military-entertainment complex, however, requires more discussion. In this volume, Toby Miller addresses how game development has brought about an imbrication of educational, industrial, and military contexts. Significantly, though, the military applications of those technologies common to the gaming industry aim largely at reducing or eliminating the kind of face-to-face altercation that is the hallmark and defining feature of the cinematic FPS. Galloway and Thacker explain that new technologies play a central role in "emerging 'new symmetry'" of network-vs-network conflict. They remark that the variety of new formations like "information-based military conflict ('cyber-war') and nonmilitary activity ('hacktivism'), criminal and terrorist networks (one 'face' of the so-called netwar), civil society protest and demonstration movements (the other 'face' of netwar), and the military formations made possible by new information technologies (C4I operations [command, control, communications, computers, and intelligence])" are united by their common use of "new technologies at various levels." This shift to network-vs-network topologies, buoyed by digital media, has the effect of *defacing* the opposition. Enmity typically takes an oppositional structure, allies facing enemies. Thus, as Ryan Lizardi discusses in this volume, FPS games are frequently set up as us-vs-them. When the opposition is a *network*, however, enmity is distributed and therefore has a "shapeless, amorphous, and faceless quality." A network is "a faceless foe, or a foe stripped of 'faciality' as such," and therefore the face-to-face confrontation of first-person perspective would seem ill fit to represent the structure of enmity of contemporary conflict (Galloway and Thacker 2007, 66).

Furthermore, the rise of this new topology is concurrent with the US military imperative toward what James Der Derian (2001) calls "virtuous war." Similarly facilitated by the "technical capability" of today's military, the virtuous war attempts to minimize casualties to "actualize violence from a distance" by "using networked information and virtual technologies to bring 'there' here in near-real time and with near-verisimilitude" (xv). Unmanned surveillance vehicles, satellite and real-time surveillance, and global positioning technologies support three-dimensional computer models, ballistics simulations, and long-distance precision-guided weaponry so that US soldiers never have to come face-to-face with the enemy. The prominence of UAV such as the Predator drone in current US military strategy exemplifies today's digitally enabled war-at-a-distance. Predator pilots never need to see the battlefield with their own eyes, instead conducting their missions from a safe distance via live-feed of a camera mounted on the UAV. Using a network connection and control console to guide their drones, the Predator pilot engages enemy combatants only as the pixelated silhouettes of his digital display. For this reason, the virtuous war is described frequently as "[reducing] war to a video game" (xvi). On some occasions, drone pilots even conduct their remote, on-screen assaults using videogame-style controllers (Hambling 2008).

Thus, an FPS like *MW2* more closely resembles actual modern warfare simply by presenting players with digitally mediated violence than by representing first-person, face-to-face encounters with the enemy. In fact, "because [drone] operators are based thousands of miles away from the battlefield, and undertake operations entirely through computer screens and remote audiofeed," the UN warns

Figure 17.2 AC-130 targeting interface in the "Death from Above" level from *CoD4* (Infinity Ward 2007).

against the potential for operators to develop a "'Playstation' mentality to killing" (Alston 2010, 25). Indeed, the concern about the co-articulation of gaming and war typically circulates around the disinterestedness of the digital. Both contexts share the same fear that repeated exposure to digital violence will train players and pilots to think killing is fun, war is a game, and the lives of enemy combatants are as dispensable as the thousands of digital representations gunned-down on-screen, merely "a blip of logistics" (Wark 2007, 010).

The *Modern Warfare* series presents players with this experience as well, giving them access to simulations of laptop-guided UAV and Predator drones and the targeting screens of attack choppers and AC-130s bombers. When players interact with these digital weapons systems, the vantage leaves the standard FPS perspective, which is always embodied in avatar's hands gripping a trigger, and fills the screen with the accurate representation of the real targeting display (Figure 17.2). Rather than showing the avatar's fingers pushing buttons on a console or the interior of the aircraft that would be in the gunner's peripheral view, the player's monitor itself simply becomes the targeting interface and his controller, the trigger. Where the player's mediated position undermines the first-person experience of ground combat, it reinforces his role as a remote combat specialist

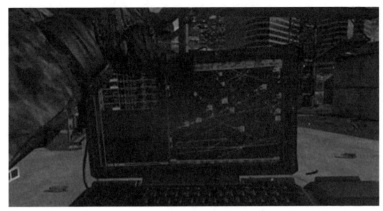

Figure 17.3 When a player deploys a Predator drone in *MW2* (Infinity Ward 2009), the playable character opens a laptop in order to target the missile (See Figure 17.4).

because both gamer and pilot are digital media users. Both sit in front of a monitor, miles from any actual fighting, use a computerized control interface to fire on a distant battlefield they will never physically inhabit, and are therefore susceptible to a "Playstation mentality." Of course, when the player pulls his trigger, no actual bomb is deployed.

In addition to the replication of realistic interfaces, Modern Warfare series also simulates radio chatter on the AC-130 ship.

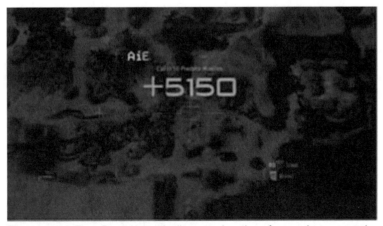

Figure 17.4 The Predator missile-targeting interface takes over the player's full display (Infinity Ward 2009).

Chatter is most prominent in *CoD4*'s "Death from Above" level, in which players act as the ship's gunner throughout the entire mission. The structure of the mission is relatively simple: the AC-130 has been called in to provide air support for a team on the ground that is attempting to move a VIP to a landing zone to be extracted by a helicopter. The player's goal is to protect the team, marked with flashing beacons, from having to engage hostile personnel face-to-face. As the player proceeds to clear the map of un-blinkered silhouettes, the voices of several team members give tactical information and instruction regarding the status of the ground team, the movements of friendly vehicles, the readiness of various weapons, and the location of enemy personnel and ambush points. In addition to this mission data, these disembodied voices provide feedback regarding the success of the player's shots. Hits are footnoted with comments such as "Hot damn!" or "Woah!"—suggesting awe at the explosive spectacle—or, more chillingly, understated confirmations such as "Yup, that was right on target," "Roger, you got that guy. Might have been within two feet of him," "Yeah, good kill. I see lots of little pieces down there," or, just simply, "Ka-boom." The majority of the game is fought as a soldier on the ground and is thus characterized by a chaotic barrage of escalating gunfire and explosions. High above the battlefield, by contrast, combat is eerily serene. The AC-130 gunner hears only the radio chatter, the sound of the plane engine, and the deployment of weapons, but not their collision with the earth. The detachment from the line of fire is reflected in the radio chatter's detached attitude toward the loss of human life on the ground below.

Chris Moore's essay in this volume discusses the degrees of affect involved in playing an FPS. Here, the ambivalence of the simulated radio chatter in the "Death from Above" mission situates the gamer in relation to military technologies as well as the political and ethical implications of their use. The mission makes explicit the connection between videogaming and remote combat through a fundamental problematic applicable to both media—the possibility that ephemerality of on-screen displays desensitizes users to violence done to real human beings. Of course, representations of digital mediation never draw the protests of parent groups and politicians. *CoD4* certainly has a sufficient level of gore to warrant its "Mature" rating; yet, the haunting indifference of the radio chatter in "Death from Above" is infinitely more disquieting than the stylized and innumerably repeated death animations that litter the screen through the majority of the game. The reason, I argue, is this articulation of simulated and real digitally mediated warfare. For all the high-definition graphics and advanced interactive technology, videogaming's "obscene" depictions of violence never quite comes off as realistic, for they are always belied by the player's embodied position, holding a plastic controller while sitting in front of a monitor. In the "Death from Above" sequence, that disassociation breaks down as players confront their position in a military-entertainment complex. Unlike the fantastic first-person gunfights on the ground, the actual playing of which is nothing remotely close to the experience of what it represents, when players fire bombs from behind the simulated targeting system, they engage the very technology, logics, and affect of the virtuous war.

Contrary to a long literary tradition describing "authentic war experience" as the brutality of killing another person face-to-face, Slavoj Žižek points out that in contemporary conflicts technology typically mediates engagement with opposing forces. "The truly traumatic feature [of combat]," therefore, "is *not* the awareness that I am killing another human being (to be obliterated through the 'dehumanization' and 'objectivization' of war into a technical procedure) but, on the contrary, this very 'objectivization,' which then generates the need to supplement it by fantasies of authentic personal encounters with the enemy." It is precisely this inversion that players experience in "Death from Above," removed from the graphic and deadly first-person gun battle to drop bombs on digital silhouettes to the dispassionate applause of radio chatter. Disquiet comes with the recognition that "it is thus not the fantasy of a purely aseptic war run as a videogame behind computer screens that protects us from the reality of the face to face killing of another person; on the contrary it is this fantasy of face to face encounter with an enemy killed bloodily that we construct in order to escape the Real of the depersonalized war turned into an anonymous technological operation" (Žižek 2001, 77). From this perspective, the "obscene" level of high-definition gore in contemporary games in fact obscures the reality of technologically efficient modern warfare. At the same time, however, the unease that accompanies our confrontation with that reality in the ambivalence of the radio chatter suggests the potential for a different relationship to the objectivized digital silhouettes. The radio chatter validating and encouraging the elimination of the remediated soldiers paradoxically confers on those insignificant virtualities a degree of humanity when the player recognizes in them the real-life victims of digitally mediated war to which they are iconically linked. Even though these NPCs bear no connection to any specific real person and are merely the graphic display of an algorithmic process, they invoke the problematics of modern warfare in a way that opens the possibility for players to respond to the digital in new ways.

Facing the Interface

Žižek's point is on display throughout the *Modern Warfare* series, but explicitly as the game repeatedly recasts the "technical operation" of button-pushing as the "authentic war experience" of face-to-face

Figure 17.5 When Khaled Al-Asad executes President Yasir Al-Fulani in *CoD4* (Infinity Ward 2007), the player is given Al-Fulani's first-person perspective.

confrontation. In the most dramatic examples of this technique, the playable character is shot or maimed straight on from close range with the first-person camera positioned to look the enemy eye-to-eye. During the opening credits of *CoD4*, for example, the player takes limited control of Al-Fulani, an abducted Middle Eastern president, as Al-Asad executes him with gunshot to the face.

The cinematic structure of this scene is repeated multiple times in the second game, notably in betrayals by Makarov and Shepherd. Both games also conclude with similar face-to-face confrontations, but with the player's character issuing the final blow. In both games, but particularly in *MW2*, the final "boss battle" is in stark contrast to the spectacular pyrotechnics leading up to that moment. After a fantastic high-speed boat chase during which Captain Price shoots down Shepherd's getaway helicopter before going over a waterfall, *MW2* concludes with a bloody fist-fight. The playable character, Soap McTavish, is disarmed of his knife by Shepherd, who plunges his own blade into Soap's chest. Shepherd draws his revolver and aims it into the viewport for another face-to-face execution. Just before he pulls the trigger, Price returns and knocks the gun away. The player and the mortally wounded Soap can only watch as Price exchanges punches with Shepherd just beyond the hilt of the protruding knife. Shepherd eventually gets the better of Price and begins pounding him repeatedly. The player then directs Soap, through furious button-mashing, to pull the knife from his own chest and finally pulls the trigger to lodge it between Shepherd's eyes. *MW2*, a game played largely through the remediated interfaces of radars, heartbeat sensors, and remote targeting systems, thus concludes with gruesomely analog combat.

By using first-person perspective to place players in face-to-face confrontations with enemy NPCs, the *Modern Warfare* series adds a visceral brutality to these virtual, immaterial altercations. The drawn-out, cinematic viciousness of these close-range conflicts also marks them off from the numberless NPCs encountered over the course of the game. The first-person standoffs with major enemies—Al-Asad, Makarov, Zakhaev, and General Shepherd—grant these characters individuality and importance over the hundreds of their nameless soldiers the player dispatches to get to them. Moreover, putting the player face-to-face with their executioner or betrayer reconstitutes the game's underlying network-vs-network conflict as a one-on-one showdown. Set aside global, multilateral antagonisms, when Al-Asad looks the player straight in the eye before pulling the trigger, his becomes the face of enmity and the fight is made personal. The face-to-face confrontation, therefore, plays a key role in organizing the plot, justifying the player's actions against countless NPC baddies, and establishing the emotional structure of the game experience.

In addition to personalizing enmity, face-to-face interactions personalize friendly NPCs as well. Take for example the opening sequence of the first non-tutorial mission of *CoD4*, "Crew Expendable," shot opposite Captain Price, professional badass, calmly smoking a cigar before boarding an enemy boat from a helicopter (Figure 17.6). This scene is echoed in *MW2* as the player watches Soap, the main playable character from the first game, finish his own cigar (Figure 17.7). This shot establishes Soap as Price's replacement and the player's commanding officer, demonstrates Soap's admiration for his predecessor, and sets the stage for their reunion later in the game.

Figure 17.6 Face-to-face introduction of cigar-smoking Captain Price in *CoD4* (Infinity Ward 2007).

Figure 17.7 Having replaced Price, Soap MacTavish gets his own cigar and face-to-face introduction in *MW2* (Infinity Ward 2009).

Aside from the lengthy between-level monologues by Shepherd and Price, there is little conversation to define personalities or relationships. Moreover, the player is constantly shifting between avatars and locations. With few characters speaking more than a couple lines or phrases and the frequent shifts in narrative context, these face-to-face presentations can quickly clarify who is who and how they relate to the playable character. Whereas face-to-face betrayals characterize the few significant enemies, teammates and

Figure 17.8 The previously unknown Private Wade hands the player a gun before being shot (Infinity Ward 2009).

friends rescue the player's character or pull him up from the ground. Saving the player from a brutal first-person death builds a sense of comradery and trust, presenting the NPC to the player as someone to care about. This method can work almost instantaneously, as in *MW2* when a previously unknown NPC hands the player a gun and is immediately shot in the head (Figure 17.8).

Even Shepherd first appears on-screen to pick up the playable character Joseph Allen (Figure 17.9). The game thus introduces him as a trustworthy compatriot, setting up his betrayal later on. Shepherd's face-to-face betrayal, in fact, comes just after a face-to-face rescue by 141-squadmate Ghost. At the conclusion of the "Loose Ends" mission, the player's character, Roach, falls while trying to escape Makarov's compound. Ghost drags and then supports him the rest of the way to the extraction point. Just as it seems they are in the clear with their commanding officer, Shepherd, coming to congratulate them, Shepherd immediately shoots both Roach and Ghost at point-blank range. The impact of Shepherd's betrayal in this scene is amplified because it follows after Ghost's rescue moments earlier had reinforced his importance to the playable character right before both are killed.

While this technique typically serves a narrative purpose— establishing relationships, heightening suspense, etc.—it can also introduce the possibility for players to respond to digital characters with greater deference. The first-person perspective in the *Modern*

Figure 17.9 The player meets Colonel Shepherd for the first time when he helps playable character Allen to his feet (Infinity Ward 2009).

Warfare series attaches emotional significance to the non-playable characters through the visceral quality of the face-to-face encounter, setting up players to have an affective reaction to the fate of an arrangement of pixels. A striking example occurs in a seemingly meaningless sequence of events during the final mission of the game. On the trail of Shepherd, Price and Soap must get past his private army of mercenaries to infiltrate his secret hideout. Much of the assault is typical of the rest of the game, involving stealthy movements and silenced takedowns. One interaction, however, has a unique animation that sets it apart from the rest of gameplay. Price and Soap use cables to descend a cliff face and come down directly on top of two unsuspecting guards. Playing as Soap, hanging above his prey, the player presses a button that initiates a cutscene in which Soap drops down on one of the guards, stabs him the chest, and muffles his mouth so he cannot alert other mercenaries. The camera's first-person perspective on this silent takedown puts the player face-to-face with his victim, looking into the eyes of the dying guard as they roll back in his head and his body goes limp (Figure 17.10).

This sequence appears to be an almost literal example of Žižek's comment. The player's banal pull of a trigger, one of thousands performed in the game, initiates a series of mathematical processes, with ties to the depersonalizing technologies that enable war-at-a-distance, depicted visually as the vicious "face to face killing of

Figure 17.10 Knifed in the chest, this NPC looks the player in the eye as he dies (Infinity Ward 2009).

another person." Yet, despite the verisimilitude of next-generation, HD graphics, the player knows very well that this is not another person. For Žižek, the "fantasy of face to face encounter" is constructed to retain some sense of humanity for the fallen soldier who, as Wark (2007) puts it, "has his death, like his life, managed by a computer in a blip of logistics" (10). Here, however, we have just the computer blip, just the mathematical process, to be executed without remorse or consequence. No life, only code. This scene, therefore, cannot be read, as Žižek would have it, as "constructed to escape the Real depersonalized war," because it asks players to conduct the humanizingly brutal kill by means of what is *already* an "anonymous technological operation." Making eye contact with this algorithm, in effect, counteracts this technological anonymity by challenging the player to see a human face in the digital display.

The player is presented with this problematic again in the very next sequence. Immediately after the gruesome face-to-face cutscene, Price and Soap move into the cave serving as Shepherd's base. Just inside they come upon a single soldier with his back to the cave entrance, smoking and watching a monitor. Price instructs the player not to engage the target as the two slip into the shadows to avoid a passing patrol, which leaves the lone mercenary with his television. Price then gives the player the option to kill this hapless

Figure 17.11 After the face-to-face knifing of a guard in the previous sequence (Figure 17.10), the player's next opportunity to eliminate an enemy is presented as a choice, kill or let pass (Infinity Ward 2009).

guard or leave him to exit the room on his own (Figure 17.11). This scenario has the basic same set-up as the player's previous encounter: an unsuspecting guard standing between the player and his objective. The difference is that in the previous encounter, the player had no choice how to proceed. Dangling from a rope over two guards, the player had no other option but to pull the trigger, initiating a gruesome cutscene. Here, we remain in-engine and are given the choice, just after initiating the face-to-face killing of another person, to kill again or not.

One would expect, given the popularity of morality mechanics in contemporary major-release videogames with FPS elements such as *BioShock* (2K Boston 2007), *Fallout 3* (Bethesda 2008), and the *Mass Effect* series (BioWare 2007, 2010) that this choice would have some narrative or gamic consequence. On the level of gameplay, however, the player's decision here makes no difference and consideration for the life or death of the NPC never enters the equation. Under the logic of the player's mission objectives, the determination to kill or wait is decided by efficiency; this is a low-level objective standing between the player and the high-level objective. Regardless of how he plays it, the player's approach affects only the number of guard-obstacles that engage him directly before he exits the room. The decision to kill or wait therefore has the same significance as selecting a weapon. The introduction of choice, however, intervenes in the overriding logic of efficiency. Following the harrowing face-to-face encounter of the previous sequence, the option to kill or wait presents an opportunity to enact the game mechanics through a more humanizing perspective. Thus, even players who shoot the TV-watching guard might recognize in the arraignment of pixels a life worth sparing. Even if this inconsequential, infinitely respawning NPC is not.

Sympathy for NPCs

Offering players the opportunity to re-evaluate their relationship with the digital in the context of modern warfare is ultimately the achievement of the controversial "No Russian" level as well. In this volume Evan Snider, Tim Lockridge, and Dan Lawson discuss tactics players use to subvert the win-focus and, by extension, militaristic ideologies of FPS gaming. For "No Russian," the game's narrative explicitly frames the player's participation within the objectivized logic of war. In order to keep tabs on Makarov, Shepherd handpicks playable character Joseph Allen to infiltrate the inner circle of Makarov's terror cell. During the between-mission briefing, Shepherd explains to Allen the cost-benefit analysis of maintaining his cover no matter what: "You don't want to know what it's cost to put you next to him. It will cost you a piece of yourself. It will cost nothing compared to everything you'll save." From the outset, then, the mission is justified through a utilitarian calculation; whatever unspeakable things Allen must do to gain Makarov's trust will be warranted by the lives saved in the end. The scene opens with Allen in an elevator with several heavily armed men in suits. One of the men, Makarov, seen by the player for the first time face-to-face, turns back to the camera as he says calmly, "Remember, no Russian." The doors of the elevator open, the armed men walk slowly out into the terminal, and open fire on the civilians standing on queue for their flights. The shooting begins without warning or explanation. Running and sprinting are disabled, forcing the player to walk slowly through the slaughter. The player may shoot the unarmed civilians or not; the level still creeps slowly forward regardless. Firing on Makarov's

Figure 17.12 As Makarov's crew takes aim, their victims turn to face the camera (Infinity Ward 2009).

team restarts the mission. NPCs run ahead trying to escape, some are injured dragging themselves to safety, a few attempt to help their downed compatriots. The corridor is full of bodies, blood, and baggage as the automated departures board flips all flights to "cancelled."

There is nothing fun about this level. It is shocking and uncomfortable, and it is hard to know what to do or how to feel the first time through. Part of that is the fault of the game. The narrative of *MW2* can be obtuse, hard to follow, and often illogical. Tom Bissell calls the "No Russian" scene in particular "morally confused and dramatically lazy." Despite its flaws, the scene is not, as Bissell concludes, "a kind of pointless test," precisely because of how the game positions players as digital media users within a military-entertainment complex (Bissell 2009). The "test" of "No Russian" is not how one would react if one were in Allen's shoes. That decision has already been scripted into the narrative; Allen chooses to let the massacre happen, sacrificing the few for the many Shepherd told him were at stake. The test for the player, rather, is whether he can recognize in these arrangements of pixels enough humanity to care about what happens to virtual victims. Putting players face-to-face with helpless targets, "No Russian" is structured to evoke an affective response to utterly inconsequential NPCs that are no more and no less than digital objects. Not only are these digital victims literally numerical values, Shepherd's voiceover framing the missions values them numerically. These are acceptable losses in a global conflict. Even so, players will likely feel some degree of sympathy for these virtual victims and have concerns about their own involvement in what happens to them.

While this may not seem like much on its own, in the context in which the game was released it is extremely significant. As the media debated *MW2*, "the terrorism simulator," the CIA escalated its use of Predator drone strikes in Pakistan (Shane 2009). The same month footage of "No Russian" was leaked, it was reported that three years of bombing had caused an estimated 320 civilian casualties (Shachtman 2009). Over the next year, the number of strikes more than doubled, confirming that remote, digitally mediated attacks had become a central strategy in the war on terror (New America Foundation 2011). When viewed in this context, instead of through concern about the potential effects of violent videogames, the "No Russian" sequence looks quite different. Rather than training players to be unaffected by (digital representations of) violence, the level is purposefully staged to affect and *re-sensitize* players and their interaction with the virtual. With run and sprint disabled, players must linger in the carnage of "No Russian" and watch it unfold. Even though the virtual airport patrons are utterly dispensable, just a visual display of a string of numbers that return immediately when one reboots the game, seeing them die is uncomfortable and disconcerting and it is supposed to be. "No Russian" succeeds by raisings questions about how one is to "play" such a gruesome level, as well as about the justified costs of war now frequently conducted through "a blip of logistics." By responding with sympathy for defenseless human beings represented by digital graphics, players demonstrate a capacity to look through objectivizing, few-for-many logics that Žižek claims are the Real of modern warfare.

The Playstation Mentality

I will be the first to acknowledge that this is probably not how most will play the *Modern Warfare* series. Many skip the story mode all together in favor of the multiplayer offerings. Those who do play the story are unlikely to think twice about dispensing the monitor-watching guard even after the face-to-face knifing of his colleague in the previous scene. Those who feel uncomfortable participating in "No Russian" are still unlikely to draw connections between the fate of some NPCs and visual feedback from cameras mounted on Predator drones. Even so, the ability to make those connections is what is at stake in recognizing the place of the videogamer within today's military-entertainment complex. While it may be easy to shrug off the *Modern Warfare* series as "just games," justifying whatever on-screen atrocities are visited on inconsequential, infinitely respawning NPCs, the ability to do so relies on the informatic, objectivized logic that is also at play in contemporary digitally mediated warfare, "the very pillars that prop those systems up" (Galloway and Thacker 2007, 115). Playing a *Modern Warfare* game thus bears more than a metaphorical relationship to actual modern warfare technologies and practices it represents on-screen. This is not to say that the enemy silhouettes scurrying across our (simulated) AC-130 targeting display correspond to real human lives; however, in the remediated YouTube videos or newsreel footage of actual AC-130 attacks, they do. As we increasingly live our lives in online environments and interact with one another through screens of various sizes, it is of utmost importance that we are able to recognize in the digital display the weight and value of human life, even if all we ever know is the outline of a pixelated silhouette.

References

Alston, Philip. 2010. "Addendum: Study on Targeted Killings." In *Report of the Special Rapporteur on Extrajudicial, Summary or Arbitrary Executions*, edited by the United Nations Human Rights Council. Geneva: United Nations.

Bissell, Tom. 2009. "It's a Massacre!: The Appalling Failure of *Modern Warfare 2*'s 'No Russian' Mission." *Crispy Gamer.* November 13. http://www.crispygamer.com/features/2009-11-13/its-a-massacre-the-appalling-failure-of-modern-warfare-2s-no-russian-mission.asp.

Der Derian, James. 2001. *Virtuous War: Mapping the Military-Industrial-Media-Entertainment Network.* Boulder, CO: Westview Press.

EDIDDY99. 2009. "Are We Ready for Modern Warfare? Terrorism Simulator *Spoilers*." *The Playstation Show Podcast.* October 28. http://theplaystationshow.com/news/are-we-ready-for-modern-warefare-spoilers/.

Galloway, Alexander R. 2006. *Gaming: Essays on Algorithmic Culture.* Minneapolis: University of Minnesota Press.

Galloway, Alexander R. and Eugene Thacker. 2007. *The Exploit: A Theory of Networks.* Minneapolis: University of Minnesota Press.

Halter, Ed. 2006. *From Sun Tzu to Xbox: War and Video Games.* New York: Thunder's Mouth Press.

Hambling, David. 2008. "Game Controllers Driving Drones, Nukes." *Danger Room* at *Wired.com.* April 19. http://www.wired.com/dangerroom/2008/07/wargames/.

Higgin, Tanner. 2010. "'Turn the Game Console off Right Now!' War, Subjectivity, and Control in *Metal Gear Solid 2*." In *Joystick Soldiers: The Politics of Play in Military Video Games*, edited by Nina Huntemann and Matthew Thomas Payne, 252–71. New York: Routledge.

Huntemann, Nina and Matthew Thomas Payne, eds. 2010. *Joystick*

Soldiers: The Politics of Play in Military Video Games. New York: Routledge.

Juul, Jesper. 2005. *Half-Real: Video Games between Real Rules and Fictional Worlds*. Cambridge, MA: The MIT Press.

Kietzmann, Ludwig. 2009. "New Modern Warfare: Airport Murder Simulator 2 Video Game Glorifies Terrorism." *Joystiq*. October 28. http://www.joystiq.com/2009/10/28/new-modern-warfare-airport-murder-simulator-2-video-game-glorif/.

Kutner, Lawrence and Cheryl Olson. 2008. *Grand Theft Childhood: The Surprising Truth About Violent Video Games and What Parents Can Do*. New York: Simon & Schuster.

Lenoir, Tim. 2000. "All But War Is Simulation: The Military-Entertainment Complex." *Configurations* 8 (3): 289–335.

New America Foundation. 2011. "The Year of the Drone: An Analysis of U.S. Drone Strikes in Pakistan, 2004–11." *Counterterrorism Strategy Initiative*. Accessed 21 April 2011. http://counterterrorism.newamerica.net/drones.

Salen, Katie and Eric Zimmerman. 2003. *Rules of Play: Game Design Fundamentals*. Cambridge, MA: The MIT Press.

Schwarzenegger v. Entertainment Merchants Association. 2010. Transcript of Oral Argument. 564 U. S. ____ (No. 08–1448). http://www.supremecourt.gov/oral_arguments/argument_transcripts/08-1448.pdf.

Shachtman, Noah. 2009. "Up to 320 Civilians Killed in Pakistan Drone War: Report." *Danger Room* at *Wired.com*. October 19. http://www.wired.com/dangerroom/2009/10/up-to-320-civilians-killed-in-pakistan-drone-war-report/.

Shane, Scott. 2009. "C.I.A. to Expand Use of Drones in Pakistan." *New York Times*, December 4. http://www.nytimes.com/2009/12/04/world/asia/04drones.html.

Sterling, Bruce. 1993. "War Is Virtual Hell." *Wired*, Issue 1.01, April. http://www.wired.com/wired/archive/1.01/virthell_pr.html.

Wark, McKenzie. 2007. *Gamer Theory*. Cambridge, MA: Harvard University Press.

Žižek, Slavoj. 2001. *The Fragile Absolute: or, Why is the Christian Legacy Worth Fighting For?* New York: Verso.

Games

2K Boston. 2007. *BioShock* [Mac OS X, Microsoft Windows, PlayStation 3, Xbox 360]. 2K Games.

Bethesda Game Studios. 2008. *Fallout 3* [Microsoft Windows, PlayStation3, Xbox 360]. Bethesda Softworks and Zenimax Media.

BioWare. 2007. *Mass Effect* [Xbox 360, Microsoft Windows]. Electronic
    Arts.
—2010. *Mass Effect 2* [Microsoft Windows, PlayStation3, Xbox 360].
    Microsoft Game Studios.
Criterion Games. 2002. *Burnout 2: Point of Impact* [Nintendo
    GameCube, PlayStation, Xbox]. Acclaim Entertainment.
Infinity Ward. 2007. *Call of Duty 4: Modern Warfare* [Microsoft
    Windows, PlayStation 3, Xbox 360]. Activision.
—2009. *Call of Duty: Modern Warfare 2* [Microsoft Windows,
    PlayStation 3, Xbox 360]. Activision.
KCEJ. 1998. *Metal Gear Solid* [PlayStation]. Konami.
—1999. *Metal Gear Solid: VR Missions* [PlayStation]. Konami.
—2001. *Metal Gear Solid 2: Sons of Liberty* [PlayStation2]. Konami.
—2004. *Metal Gear Solid 3: Snake-Eater* [PlayStation2]. Konami.
id Software. 1992. *Wolfenstein 3D* [MS-DOS]. id Software
—1993. *DOOM* [DOS]. id Software.

About the contributors

Daniel Ashton (PhD, Lancaster University) is Senior Lecturer in Media Communications at Bath Spa University. His research on digital gaming has examined archiving and walkthroughs (*M/C Journal*; *Fibreculture*; *Transformations*), and "gameswork" in relation to industry, identity, and education (*Convergence*; *Information Technology and People*).

Josh Call (PhD, The University of Nebraska-Lincoln) is an Assistant Professor of English at Grand View University in Des Moines, IA. He teaches courses in composition, literacy, rhetoric and visual culture, and humanities. He is currently researching the connections between games and pedagogy, focusing on reclaiming play in the classroom for better learning. He lives in Iowa with his wife Nichole, daughter Kairie, and son Colin.

Aaron Duncan (PhD, The University of Nebraska-Lincoln) is the Director of Speech & Debate at the University of Nebraska-Lincoln. He received his MA in Communication from Kansas State University in 2005. Dr Duncan's research focuses on the intersection between the rhetoric of popular culture and political culture.

Stephanie Fisher (MEd, York University) is a doctoral student in the Faculty of Education at York University in Toronto, Canada. In her Master's thesis, she examined how players of WWII FPS games appropriated these games to learn about the event, arguing that these games can aid in constructing educational spaces where players can perform and develop historical inquiry skills that are not always taught in school history classrooms.

Daniel Lawson (PhD, Virginia Tech) is Assistant Professor of English and Director of the Writing Center at Central College, Iowa. His research focuses on writing pedagogy, visual rhetoric, and the rhetorical character of ideology. He is particularly interested in the ways pop culture media rearticulate or subvert dominant discourses.

Ryan Lizardi (PhD, Penn State University) recently completed his dissertation on contemporary nostalgic media. Among others, Ryan has published works on slasher horror film remakes and videogame console downloadable content, and places a research emphasis on the connection between ideology and representations of the past in media.

Tim Lockridge (MFA, Virginia Tech) is a PhD candidate in Rhetoric and Writing at Virginia Tech. His scholarship has appeared in *Reconstruction: Studies in Contemporary Culture* and *The Journal of College Writing*, and he is an Assistant Editor at *Kairos: A Journal of Rhetoric, Technology, and Pedagogy*. He teaches and writes about the intersections of texts and technologies.

James Manning (MA, University of the West of England) is Senior Lecturer in Animation and Games Design at University of Wales, Newport.

Alan Meades (MA Electronic Arts, Middlesex University) is Senior Lecturer in the Department of Media, Art and Design at Canterbury Christ Church University. He is Programme Director of the Digital Design Suite of degree programmes at the University's Broadstairs Campus. Alan is currently studying for a PhD in Rhetorics of Transgressive Play at Brunel University UK, under the supervision of Professor Tanya Krzywinska, where he is exploring glitching, game modding and hardware hacking on console platforms.

Toby Miller (PhD, Murdoch University) is a British-Australian-US interdisciplinary social scientist. He is the author and editor of over 30 books, has published essays in more than 100 journals, and edited collections, and is a frequent guest commentator on television and radio programs. His teaching and research cover the media, sports, labor, gender, race, citizenship, politics, and cultural policy, as well as the success of Hollywood overseas and the adverse effects of electronic waste. Miller's work has been translated into Chinese, Japanese, Swedish, German, Spanish, and Portuguese. He taught at Murdoch, Griffith University, and the University of New South Wales and was a professor at New York University from 1993 to 2004, when he joined the University of California, Riverside. Miller is now chair of a new Department of Media & Cultural Studies and lives near the ocean in Los Angeles.

Christopher Moore (PhD, University of Wollongong) is a Lecturer in Media and Communication in the School of Communication and Creative Arts, Faculty of Arts and Education at Deakin University, Melbourne, Australia.

Víctor Navarro (MA, University Rovira i Virgili) is a PhD student in the Department of Communication at the University Rovira i Virgili.

James Newman (PhD, Lancaster University) is Professor of Digital Media, Course Leader in Creative Media Practice and Director of the Media Futures Research Centre at Bath Spa University. He researches, writes, and teaches on digital media, videogames, and the cultures of play and has written five books on videogames and gaming cultures for publishers including Routledge and the BFI. James is a producer of the GameCity international festival www.gamecity.org and a co-founder of the National Videogame Archive <www.nationalvideogamearchive.org> which is the UK's official collection of videogames and the ephemera of games culture. James is currently writing books on gaming history and digital preservation for BFI Publishing and Routledge.

Jessy Ohl (MA, The University of Alabama) is a PhD student in Rhetoric and Public Culture at the University of Nebraska-Lincoln. His research focuses on political communication and the rhetoric of war in a digital age.

Gwyneth Peaty (BA, with honors, University of Western Australia) is in the final stages of her PhD in English and Cultural Studies at the University of Western Australia. Her doctoral research focuses on the representation of grotesque bodies in a wide spectrum of visual media, including film, television, magazines, comics, and videogames. Peaty's wider interests include science fiction, Gothic, gender, and whiteness studies. Recently, her chapter "Infected with Life: Neo-supernaturalism and the Gothic Zombie" was published in *Gothic Science Fiction: 1980–2010,* and she has presented her work at a variety of national and international conferences.

Dan Pinchbeck (PhD, University of Portsmouth) is Reader in Computer Games at the University of Portsmouth. He specializes in first-person gaming, particularly the relationship between content and gameplay; and experimental game development. He is Creative Director of thechineseroom, whose games include the award-winning, internationally acclaimed *Dear Esther* and the cult horror *Korsakovia*. He is author of the forthcoming book *DOOM: Scarydarkfast* (University of Michigan Press, Landmarks of Videogames Series).

Evan Snider (MA, University of Maine) is a Doctoral Fellow in Rhetoric and Writing at Virginia Tech and an Instructor at Ball State University. He teaches document design and professional writing, and his research interests include digital communities, visual rhetoric, and ePortfolios.

Nick Taylor (PhD, York University) is currently serving as a Post-doctoral Researcher and Project Manager on the Virtual Environment Real User Study, a collaboration between Simon Fraser University, York University, and SRI International.

Gerald Voorhees (PhD, The University of Iowa) is an Assistant Professor at Oregon State University jointly appointed in Speech Communication and Digital Communication. He teaches classes in media studies, rhetorical studies, and game studies. His research focuses on games and new media sites for the construction and contestation of identity and culture. He is also interested in public discourse pertaining to games and new media, as well as rhetorics of race and ethnicity in mediated public discourse.

Timothy Welsh (PhD, University of Washington) is an Assistant Professor in the Film + Digital Media division of the English Department at Loyola University, New Orleans. His research and teaching combine literary and media studies approaches to address twentieth-century fiction, digital technologies, and videogames. He is a founding member of the Critical Gaming Project at the University of Washington.

Mark J. P. Wolf (PhD, University of Southern California) is a Professor in the Communication Department at Concordia University Wisconsin. His books include *Abstracting Reality: Art, Communication, and Cognition in the Digital Age* (2000), *The Medium of the Video Game* (2001), *Virtual Morality: Morals, Ethics, and New Media* (2003), *The Video Game Theory Reader* (2003), *The Video Game Explosion: A History from PONG to PlayStation and Beyond* (2007), *The Video Game Theory Reader 2* (2008), *Myst and Riven: The World of the D'ni* (2011), and *Before the Crash: An Anthology of Early Video Game History* (2012). He lives in Wisconsin with his wife Diane and his sons Michael, Christian, and Francis.

Index of Authors

Index of Games

General Index